THE MOZART COMPANION

THE
MOZART
COMPANION

BY

GERALD ABRAHAM
FRIEDRICH BLUME
OTTO ERICH DEUTSCH
HANS ENGEL
KARL GEIRINGER
PAUL HAMBURGER
ARTHUR HUTCHINGS
HANS KELLER
H. C. ROBBINS LANDON
JENS PETER LARSEN
DONALD MITCHELL

Edited by

H. C. ROBBINS LANDON
& DONALD MITCHELL

The Norton Library
W · W · NORTON & COMPANY · INC ·
NEW YORK

Books That Live
The Norton imprint on a book means that in the publisher's
estimation it is a book not for a single season but for the years.
W. W. Norton & Company, Inc.

PRINTED IN THE UNITED STATES OF AMERICA

1 2 3 4 5 6 7 8 9 0

182712

THIS BOOK IS DEDICATED
TO THE MEMORY OF
ALFRED EINSTEIN

PREFATORY NOTE

WE gratefully acknowledge permission to use throughout this book Emily Anderson's translations of *The Letters of Mozart and his Family* (3 vols., Macmillan, London, 1938).

The opportunity has been taken to make a number of minor corrections to the text of the book, which was originally planned and published as a contribution to the Mozart bicentenary celebrations of 1956.

H.C.R.L.
D.M.

Buggiano Castello,
Italy, 1964

EDITORS' NOTES

Throughout this book, where applicable, the numbers of Köchel's thematic catalogue of Mozart's works precede those of the third edition prepared by Alfred Einstein in 1937 and further revised in 1947.

The following abbreviations have been used in our music examples:

Flute	. .	Fl.	Cembalo (harp-	
Oboe	. .	Ob.	sichord) .	Cemb.
Clarinet .	.	Cl.	Violin . .	Vl.
Basset horn	.	Basset hn. & Cor.	Viola . .	Va.
		di bassetto.	Violoncello .	Vc.
Bassoon .	.	Fag.	Double-bass .	D.B. or B.
Woodwind	.	Ww.	Strings . .	Str.
Horn	.	Hn.	Orchestra .	Orch.
Trumpet	.	Trpt.	Soprano . .	Sop.
Winds	.	W.	Alto . .	Alt.
Timpani	.	Timp.	Tenor . .	Ten.
Pianoforte	.	Pfte.	Bass . .	Bass.
			Concertante .	Conc.

CONTENTS

ILLUSTRATIONS IN THE TEXT

"Together with the puzzle he gives you the solution."
BUSONI ON MOZART

FOREWORD

An obvious defect of a symposium is its lack of unity. Yet with some composers the very variety of a symposial approach may prove both appropriate and beneficial. Such a composer is surely Mozart, who, of all the great composers, offers not only a very wide range of expression, a range which includes the strongest contrasts of styles and feelings (often within the confines of a single work), but expressed himself in an almost bewildering number of forms, all of which (church music excepted), whether the piano concerto, opera – *seria* or *buffa* – the quartet (or, more especially, the quintet), the symphony, the serenade – he developed to a quite exceptional degree of perfection. Mozart's extraordinary versatility, the ease with which he worked in the various media (though we must not underestimate how hard he worked at crucial junctures to make things sound 'easy'), makes it almost impossible for one commentator satisfyingly to treat of his work as a whole. The picture of the whole Mozart is too complex in extent and content – too enigmatic, one might say – for one mind to comprehend the total unity which exists behind the dazzling variety. The late Dr. Alfred Einstein, to whom this book is gratefully dedicated, came wonderfully near catching Mozart's essential spirit in a very compressed space; yet much detail was inevitably lacking, particularly in his discussion of the music, and perhaps not every facet of Mozart's personality was revealed. One really needs the possibility of three life-spans, the opportunity to adopt half-a-dozen personalities, before arriving at a complete understanding of Mozart's legacy. One needs something of Mozart's own facility for assuming the characters of his *dramatis personae*. Mozart himself presents a complex ensemble of styles, moods, characterizations and media; no sooner does he penetrate the depths of one role than he moves on to explore the features of another. Here the tragical, there the comic; the humorous or satirical; farce or wit; serenity or terror; the magical or mundane; the mystical or rational; the chaste or passionate: the list is endless, and more often than not the 'opposites' are inextricably combined (as in the operas) or immediately juxtaposed (as in the instrumental music). It is simple enough to pin down one mood, or to distinguish between two successively presented; what amazes, and sometimes confuses, is Mozart's mercurial synthesizing, his fleet passing from one mood to another: what one might term his essential ambiguity. How often do we find ourselves confronted with a movement whose character defies verbal analysis, whose content challenges our sensibility, the quality of our responses, at their very deepest level, where emotions are not distinct or defined, but partake one of another – which are, as it were, nameless ? Mozart sounds, in its double sense, what cannot be named, those deep recesses of the human spirit where opposites are identical, where joy is grief, comedy is tragedy, and laughter another way of weeping – or *vice versa*, if you so wish it. Paradox is a prime constituent of the human personality and of the world we live in; it is one of the mainsprings of Mozart's art.

This ambiguity illumines many vital aspects of Mozart's music and the many varying interpretations of it, which are as various as the composer's shifts in mood, in dramatic and artistic standpoint. No century has seen him alike; each age has found in Mozart what it needed of him, because he can fulfil the most contrasted, the most opposite of requirements. His artistic personality allows of many different stresses and emphases, some doubtless of greater significance than others, but all of them true. Perhaps our own time, with its realization that one truth does not exclude its opposite, or, perhaps more accurately, that one truth implies its opposite, has the best chance of seeing him in the round. Everything points in the direction of this central ambivalence; not only the music's content, which we have touched upon, but also its very character and shape. Hence Mozart's formality, yet his astonishing formal freedom (the piano concertos, for instance); his order and regularity, yet his perpetual variation; his conventionality, yet his quite unprecedented unorthodoxy. (*In toto*, what an unorthodox phenomenon he is altogether.) It is not, we suggest, fanciful even to hear in Mozart's love of the clarinet not only his typical interest in exploiting a new instrument, but his response to an instrument whose timbre is as sweet as it is sour, whose line can soothe or pungently stimulate. It is no accident that both his late clarinet masterpieces inhabit an atmosphere to which it is impossible to apply a comprehensive label. If we admit bubbling good spirits, we must admit the profoundest melancholy – and so on. Such works are outside the rough grasp of language and open only to factual analysis or to the deepest of our feelings, feelings which are beyond the reach of dictionaries and must, so to speak, remain anonymous.

Perhaps, then, the diversity of opinion represented by a symposium reflects something of the diversity of Mozart's art. Each contributor selects the works he discusses within his own field – this book does not attempt to mention Mozart's every composition – and reveals his own attitude to the composer; in each case, part of the essential Mozart is revealed, and he emerges triumphant and undiminished from the most various of approaches – from the historical, the musicological, the textual and rigorously analytical. Our views, doubtless, are as symposial as those of history itself. One only needs to note a few of the composers who have lavished praise upon Mozart – Haydn, Brahms, Chopin, for example – to realize how wide a scope of musical opinion their collected judgments would disclose. Even here, paradox raises its head. Tchaikovsky was an unexpected yet devoted Mozartean, unexpected, that is, but for the strict logic of the laws of opposites; though one should remember that while Tchaikovsky probably thought Mozart his unattainable ideal of symmetry and equipoise, Mozart's sometimes unleashed and even violent passion – the daily currency of Tchaikovsky's language, and thus neglected by him – provides a common factor between seemingly diametrically opposed artistic personalities. But every age, as we have remarked above, has found in Mozart what it needed of him, and if *Mozartiana* by the highly emotional Tchaikovsky pays tribute to Mozart the elegant and refined, we should recall that it was Mozart's own elegant age which was discomfited by his full-blooded passion. It all depends where the stress is laid. Tchaikovsky chose to emphasize divergences, but he as well might have emphasized common ground. That Mr. Britten, of a later generation, favours both Mozart *and* Tchaikovsky seals the apparently paradoxical bond.

Irony is an offshoot of paradox, and Mozart is often an ironical composer. (He was also a very ironical man, as his letters show.) Professor Abraham rightly points to examples of irony from the operas, thereby usefully discounting the popular impression that music and irony are inimical; Mozart's irony, moreover, functions in his instrumental music, not only in the dramatic context of his operas. Of all his operas, however, it is *Così fan tutte* in which he gives his irony – that derivative of his characteristic ambiguity – its freest rein; and while we thoroughly endorse our contributor's opinion of the beauty of *Così*'s music, we cannot share his view that the work fails through its lack of characterization – or, rather, through the lack of the possibility of characterization. On the contrary, the text of *Così* must have made as special an appeal to Mozart's musical personality as the texts of *Die Zauberflöte* or *Figaro*. Characterization in *Così* is not really attempted, because characterization (in the manner of *Figaro* or *Giovanni*) is not the point at issue. In *Così* the characters are stripped of their skins, and we are invited to enjoy the subtlest of interplay not between Mozart's habitually memorable characterizations but between disembodied, though pronouncedly human, motives. Mozart, as it were, omits the top level of characterization and plunges us into the tangle of motives which precipitate human action; and there is a further refinement, which corresponds most precisely to psychic truth, in that the motives revealed prove to be strictly two-faced. *Così*, in short, while pretending to test virtue, offers a commentary on the duplicity of human motives, not in any moralizing sense, but as established fact. One thought, that is, may often be accompanied by another, its contrary; one feeling, as genuine as we may wish, may be supplanted or given rise to by another, no less sincere, but its strict opposite. The simulated feelings of the two pairs of lovers could be no less real than their 'real' feelings. Through the opera's central dramatic device, Guglielmo and Ferrando are able to act out – safely to expose – the deeper, contradictory motives which lie at the back of their seemingly harmless deception. The lovers put fidelity on trial, and it proves to be a neat way of exhibiting without risk the incontinent aspirations that accompany their protestations of virtue, aspirations that would have had to remain hidden but for the possibility of their being expressed as a joke.

Così, of course, could only be expressed as comedy: it would otherwise strike us as too painfully true; and it is *Così*'s two-sided truth which is, perhaps, the very quintessence of Mozart's ambiguity, his ambivalence, his love of paradox. Doubtless it was the sheer difficulty of coming to terms with its complexity of content that was responsible for the misunderstanding of *Così* in particular and of Mozart's music in general. There is nothing easier than to be baffled by the ambiguity of Mozart's art, and nothing easier than to interpret one's lack of contact with its singular feeling as emotional inadequacy on the part of the composer, while at the same time guiltily over-praising his exquisite taste. In such terms was cast many a nineteenth century criticism (or appreciation), and *Così*, it will be remembered, was the last of the operas to gain recognition, though its first act is probably the most miraculous of Mozart's dramatic structures. *Così* offers a whole truth – not the half truth offered by much art and most of life – and the maximum of beauty; doubtless there is a relationship between the opera's singular truthfulness and the degree of beauty which Mozart felt compelled to lavish upon it, to make it palatable perhaps. It is not surprising, but fitting merely, that his most 'artificial' opera discloses simultaneously an acute realism and a peculiarly modern turn of mind, that he built a whole opera out of a world of ambiguity, dramatized that world and gave it unity. The very virtuosity of Mozart's genius is a paradox in itself.

DONALD MITCHELL

Cottingham,
East Yorkshire
October, 1955

OTTO ERICH DEUTSCH

MOZART PORTRAITS

Iconography, in the sense of the study of portraiture, is no
science, but a matter of experience, grounded in knowledge of
physiognomy and psychology, of history in general and art history in particular, of acquaintance with the 'art' of forgery, the
vanity of collectors, the 'tricks of the trade', and fallacious family
traditions. There are several works of reference, German and
English, concerned with the portraits of famous people; but not
one of them can justly make any claim to scientific value. And
the catalogues of the large portrait collections present a jumble
of data – accurate, dubious, and false. The only official institu-
tion which is deserving of confidence is the National Portrait
Gallery, London, and its staff.

Unfortunately, it is not often that an historian knows enough
about art to provide his books with illustrations which are historically genuine. The Editor of the Italian National Encylo-
paedia is a rare exception. Literary historians and musicologists
with an artistic education are met with even less frequently, yet
it is they, in particular, who need such an equipment when il-
lustrating the biography of a poet or composer. The popular
ambition to embellish this sort of book with a hitherto unknown portrait almost always exposes the author to ridicule.

Naturally, the number of authentic pictures of a great man,
especially of one who died young, is bound to be limited, a circumstance intensified by the fact that genius, often for a long
time, goes unrecognized; nor, as a rule, does the outward appearance of genius exert any special fascination for great pain-
ters or sculptors. Since minor artists, and especially dilettantes,
often portray such a genius, it is difficult for posterity to get a
true picture of the subject even from authentic likenesses. And if
a Beethoven does happen to fall in with a truly great artist such
as Ferdinand Georg Waldmüller, then it may happen that the
result is worse than that of a bungler.

To all these difficulties must be added the fact that formerly
biographers were quite content to use graphic reproductions,
while today they base their judgments on photographs or auto-

types without having seen more than one or two of the originals. It is true that certain museums devoted to great masters, such as the house where Mozart was born in Salzburg, have assembled a number of important likenesses, apart from some that are dubious or spurious. But again and again students and journalists fall victim to the spurious, just because they share, or pander to, the tastes of the crowd.

As an illustration of scholarly naivety, we may mention the case of a notorious Austrian silhouette forger, a man named Josef Kuderna, who produced hundreds of clumsy silhouettes from a handful of prototypes, and attached fantastic inscriptions to his handiwork. His subjects included both the nobility and artists, and among his most frequent creations were Mozart and his father. Fritz Wagner reproduced one of these silhouettes in the *Mozart-Jahrbuch* for 1929, with the caption: "Leopold Mozart, in the house of [Karl von] Dalberg at Erfurt, reads the text of his son's opera, *Idomeneo*." It is true that the editor of the *Jahrbuch*, the well-known Mozart biographer, Hermann Abert, was puzzled by this hitherto unknown visit paid by Mozart's father to Erfurt (in about 1781); yet he made the comment: "On the other hand, it is hardly likely that this picture represents any attempt to mystify. The silhouette, in any case, is old." In fact, it was only twenty years old at the most. At about the same time, the town of Raab (Györ), in Hungary, bought a series of silhouettes which had previously belonged in turn to two well-known collectors. These silhouettes, two of which were supposed to represent Leopold and Wolfgang, suggested that both father and son had visited Raab and there enjoyed noble patronage. This led a Hungarian historian, Dr. Rudolf Galos, to publish an illustrated article in the periodical *Györi Szemle*, November–December 1930, in which he ascribed this previously unknown visit to the year 1768. If Dr. Galos had seen the *Mozart-Jahrbuch* for 1929 he could hardly have helped noticing that Leopold Mozart looked exactly the same at Erfurt in 1781 as at Raab in 1768, where he was said to have been seen "at a concert". Then, in 1938, Frau Adele Egger fell victim to Herr Kuderna; on the strength of two silhouettes of Leopold and Wolfgang Mozart, she wrote an article entitled 'Ein Aufenthalt Mozarts in Graz' for the Graz *Blätter für Heimatkunde*. In 1940, Georg Schünemann reproduced a silhouette of Mozart in the *Jahrbuch der Musikbibliothek Peters*; the original, said to have

Haydn

Gluck

Mozart

Salieri

Fig. 1. Four silhouettes engraved by H. Löschenkohl for the *Österreichischer Nationalkalender auf das Jahr 1786*, showing Haydn, Gluck, Mozart and Salieri.

been done by Mozart's sister, was in the possession of the Preussische Staatsbibliothek, and this, too, was unmistakably Kuderna's work. (The silhouettes representing groups, one of their members allegedly being Mozart, are all spurious, and by another hand.)

Literary sources do not tell us much about Mozart's outward appearance. In 1799 his sister Nannerl wrote to Breitkopf & Son:

"My brother was a rather pretty child. Only after he had smallpox [in 1767] was he so much disfigured, and still worse, when he came back from Italy [the journey of 1771] he got the Italian yellow hue which made him quite unrecognizable."

In a letter to Josef Sonnleithner she wrote in 1819 of the three portraits then in her possession:

"The one made on his return from the journey to Italy is the oldest, for then he was only sixteen years of age; but as he had just recovered from a very bad illness, the picture makes him look sickly and yellow; the portrait in the family group, done when he was twenty-two [twenty-four?] years old, is very good, and the miniature done when he was twenty-six is the latest I possess."

Unfortunately the third of these, perhaps a copy of Josef Lange's portrait sent to Leopold in 1783, has been lost. Other contemporaries, such as Michael Kelly, Josef Frank, Ludwig Tieck, and Franz Niemtschek, testify that Mozart was of small and slight build, with a big head, a pale complexion, thick, fair hair, blue, short-sighted eyes, a large nose, and small, plump hands. He was more like his mother than his father.

During the past forty years a number of investigators has studied the problem of Mozart portraits. The picture books which Engel, Schiedermair, and Bory produced as illustrations of Mozart's life and works are not very discriminating in their juxtaposition of genuine, spurious, and posthumous portraits. Schurig, who twice revised the opinions he had expressed in the first edition of his Mozart biography, finally came to the correct conclusion that –

"Mozart has been the subject of more portraits having no connection with his actual appearance than any other famous man; and there is no famous man of whom a worshipful posterity has had a more incorrect physical picture than is generally the case with Mozart."

The art historian Julius Leisching's condemnation of false pictures is even more sweeping than Schurig's. A Munich collector of Mozartiana, Dr. Max Zenger, has done us the service of listing the spurious portraits as a form of negative iconography. The nineteenth century gave Mozart's likeness a rococo sweetness, but it was reserved for the twentieth to imagine the visage of Mozart in every painting of a young man with jabot and a powdered periwig (just as they have recognized a Schubert in every young man with spectacles, sidepieces, and 'cut-throat' collars).

The following notes attempt to provide a chronological survey of the genuine portraits of Mozart:

(1) The anonymous oil-painting, showing Mozart as a six-year-old, wearing a court suit originally intended for the little Archduke Maximilian. It was painted at Salzburg about 1762, perhaps by Pietro Antonio Lorenzoni (Mozart Museum, Salzburg). The value of this picture has been somewhat diminished since Franz Martin established that its counterpart, the portrait of Marianne in court dress, was used as a dummy by a Salzburg painter; in other words, the same picture served to portray other girls, only the head being changed (*Mozart-Jahrbuch*, 1950, pp. 49–61). This recalls the fact that Maria Theresa's court painter, Martin von Meytens, frequently painted only the heads of his many portraits, leaving his pupils to fill in the rest. Unfortunately, the portrait of the boy Mozart does not derive from the Meytens studio, though this has sometimes been stated to be the case.

(2) Leopold Mozart with his two children, making music. A watercolour by Louis Carrogis, called Carmontelle, Paris, November 1763; it was engraved by Jean-Baptiste Delafosse in 1764. Of the four or five versions of that picture, the one in the Condé Museum, Chantilly, is most to be preferred. In this picture Wolfgang's portrait is even less characteristic than that of 1762.

(3) A tea party at Prince Louis François de Conti's residence in the 'Temple', with Mozart at the harpsichord. This is an oil-painting by Michel Barthélemy Ollivier, Paris, summer of 1766 (?) (Louvre, Paris). Wolfgang's figure is so small that the picture is worthless iconographically.

(4) Mozart at the pianoforte. An oil-painting by Saverio dalla Rosa, Verona, 6–7 January 1770. Commissioned by Pietro Lugiati, Wolfgang's Veronese patron. On the original frame is a Latin inscription (Alfred Cortot, Switzerland). The diamond ring on Wolfgang's right hand may have been the one given to him by Maria Theresa, which was lost in Salzburg in 1945. Undoubtedly the best picture of the young Mozart, it has hitherto been attributed to Fra Felice Cignaroli, an uncle of dalla Rosa. (Cf. L. von Sonnleithner: 'Ein neu aufgefundenes Original-Portrait von Mozart', *Blätter für Musik, Theater, und Kunst*, Vienna, 13 March 1857, and R. Brenzoni: *Verona nella vita di W. A. Mozart*, Verona, 1954.)

(4a) Mozart at the pianoforte. An oil-painting by Thaddäus Helbling, Rome (?), about 1770 (?) (Mozart Museum, Salzburg). Only Vogel has so far doubted the authenticity of this picture, which has a good 'pedigree': it belonged to the landlord of the Mozarts' Salzburg lodging, Lorenz Hagenauer. But it cannot be accepted entirely without reservation.

(4b) A miniature on ivory, by Martin Knoller (?), Milan (?), spring of 1773 (?) (Mozart Museum, Salzburg). This picture, perhaps identical with that of the sixteen-year-old Mozart which his sister mentioned in 1819, remains doubtful.

(5) Mozart as a Chevalier of the Golden Spur. An anonymous oil-painting, Salzburg, 1777. The original has disappeared. A copy made for Padre Giambattista Martini is now in the Liceo Musicale, Bologna. (A copy of the copy is in the Mozart Museum, Salzburg.) The dubious group portrait which represents Mozart as a member of the Philharmonic Academy in Bologna, in the company of the Academy's President and patron, is even worse (private possession, Sweden).

(6) The family picture. An oil-painting by Johann Nepomuk della Croce, Salzburg, late autumn of 1780 to the beginning of 1781 (Mozart Museum, Salzburg). It represents Leopold with his two children, making music; the portrait of the dead mother is on the wall. Wolfgang's portrait was the first to be completed. Together with a lost picture (probably a reduced copy of the

Lange painting, No. 7, sent to Leopold in 1783), it was used by the distinguished artist, Barbara Krafft, at Salzburg in 1819 when she was commissioned to paint Mozart's portrait for Josef Sonnleithner's Gallery of Composers (now in the Gesell-schaft der Musikfreunde, Vienna). This posthumous picture was painted under his sister's supervision, and appears to be the best and most faithful likeness of all. (Cf. O. E. Deutsch: 'Ein Mozartbildnis von Barbara Krafft,' *Bergland*, Innsbruck, August 1936, pp. 2–5.)

(7) A sketch in oils by Josef Lange, Mozart's brother-in-law, Vienna, winter of 1782–3 (Mozart Museum, Salzburg). This picture, unfortunately never completed, represents Mozart in the attitude of a pianist, without wig. The copy, probably reduced, which Mozart sent to his father at Salzburg on 3 April 1783 has not survived (cf. No. 6, above). The picture of Constanze Mozart, painted at the same time, a copy of which was also sent to Salzburg in 1783, is probably identical with the picture now in the possession of the University of Glasgow.

(8) A silhouette, engraved by Hieronymus Löschenkohl, Vienna, the end of 1785. It first appeared in the *Österreichischer Nationalkalender* for the year 1786. Copies of this silhouette are in the Vienna Nationalbibliothek and Stadtbibliothek. (Cf. O. E. Deutsch: *Mozart und die Wiener Logen*, Vienna, 1932, p. 35.) (See Fig. 1.)

(9) A wax relief by Leonhard Posch, Vienna, 1788. The original was destroyed or disappeared at Salzburg in 1945. A modern bronze cast of the shattered plaster model of another version is in the Coins and Medals Collection, Vienna. A replica of this version in boxwood, done in 1789, is in the Mozart Museum, Salzburg. A third replica, made of meerschaum and fitted into a belt-buckle for Constanze Mozart, was destroyed, or lost, again at Salzburg in 1945.

(10) A silver-crayon drawing by Dora Stock, Dresden, 16 or 17 April 1789 (Musikbibliothek Peters, Leipzig). All the last three pictures mentioned (Nos. 8–10) appear to flatter Mozart.

The very last likeness of Mozart was the death-mask, which Count Josef Deym had taken on 5 December 1791. Deym, who was living in Vienna at the time under the name of Müller, owned the 'Müller Art Gallery', for the clockwork machines of which Mozart wrote several pieces. The mask was probably made by Posch, who worked for Deym's 'Panoptikum'. Constanze, clumsily, broke it.

To conclude, we give a brief survey of the spurious portraits, the most important of those done anonymously and all those which bear artists' names:

Anonymous: Mozart with Salomon Gessner in Zürich, 1766; Mozart with the diamond ring, Salzburg, *c*. 1775; Miniature formerly in the possession of Mozart's cousin, 'Bäsle', Mannheim, November 1777; and Mozart attending a performance of *Die Entführung*, Berlin, 1789.

With artists' names: Pompeo Batoni, G. B. Bosio, Breitkopf, Joseph S. Duplessis, Josef Grassi, Jean-Baptiste Greuze, Karl Christian Klass, J. J. Langenhöffel, J. F. Rigaud, Augustin de Saint-Aubin, E. Schütz, Dominicus van Smissen, E. Gottlieb Thelott, Anton Wilhelm Tischbein and John Zoffany.

BOOK LIST

R. Bory, *La Vie et l'œuvre de Wolfgang Amadeus Mozart par l'image* (*The Life and Works of W. A. M. in Pictures*), Geneva, 1948, with 62 portraits.

E. W. Engel, *Wolfgang Amade Mozart* (calendar), Vienna, 1914, with 28 portraits.

J. E. Engl: *W. A. Mozart in den Schilderungen seiner Biographen, in seiner körperlichen Erscheinung im Leben und im Bilde*, Salzburg, 1887.

J. Leisching: 'Wolfgang A. Mozarts Bildnisse', *Salzburger Museumsblätter*, Jahrgang 5, Nos. 5/6, pp. 1–6, Salzburg, December 1926.

G. N. von Nissen: 'Mozarts Bildnisse, in Kupfer gestochen und in Holz geschnitten, Silhouetten, Gemälde, Büsten', *Biographie W. A. Mozarts*, Leipzig, 1828, Appendix, pp. 179–81.

L. Schiedermair: 'Mozart-Ikonographie', *Briefe W. A. Mozarts und seiner Familie*, Vol. V, Munich, 1914, with 35 portraits.

A. Schurig: 'Mozart-Ikonographie', *Leopold Mozarts Reise-Aufzeichnungen 1763–1771*, Dresden, 1920, pp. 81–102.

—— 'Die Bildnisse W. A. Mozarts, 1762 bis 1791', *Wolfgang Amade Mozart*, Leipzig, 1923, Vol. II, pp. 441–52. (Second edition of the biography published in 1913.)

E. Vogel, 'Mozart-Portraits', *Jahrbuch der Musikbibliothek Peters für 1899*, Leipzig.

M. Zenger: 'Falsche Mozartbildnisse' (engravings), *Neues Mozart-Jahrbuch*, Regensburg, 1941, Vol. I, pp. 218–24.

—— *Noch einmal: falsche Mozartbildnisse* (paintings), ibid., Vol. II, pp. 176–80, 1942.

MOZART'S STYLE AND INFLUENCE

WHILE Leopold Mozart was staying with his son and daughter-in-law at Vienna in 1785, one Saturday evening in February "three new" string quartets were played. Today we know them as Nos. 4–6 of the series dedicated to Joseph Haydn (K.458, 464, 465, composed between November 1784 and January 1785). At that time they had not yet been dedicated to Haydn: as printed in Artaria's first edition of the six string quartets, the dedication was dated 1 September 1785. Among the others present in the Mozart home that Saturday evening was Haydn himself. But he had already heard the quartets before, for Leopold wrote from Salzburg to his daughter at St. Gilgen on 22 January 1785, mentioning that Wolfgang had informed him that "last Saturday he performed his six quartets for his dear friend Haydn and other good friends, and that he has sold them to Artaria for a hundred ducats". It is probably that evening early in January 1785 to which Mozart alluded in the text of his dedication: "You yourself, my very dear friend, during your last sojourn in this capital, expressed your pleasure to me. Your support encourages me. . . ." On the same day, 12 February 1785, when Leopold Mozart and Joseph Haydn were Wolfgang's guests and heard the three quartets (they were "somewhat easier" than the first three, Leopold considered, "but at the same time excellent compositions") Haydn turned to the elder Mozart and expressed the opinion which later became famous: "Before God and as an honest man, I tell you that your son is the greatest composer known to me either in person or by name. He has taste and, what is more, the most profound knowledge of composition." Leopold wrote to his daughter in a letter of 14/16 February 1785, and told her of Haydn's remark in his own simple though self-confident manner, without fuss, but with obvious pride. By then Haydn was already the most distinguished musician in Europe. His word carried great weight; his judgment was the highest recognition that Wolfgang could have received at that period. And when the dedication referred to Haydn as "a very celebrated man" it was not simply

a polite euphemism. Haydn's judgment of 12 February was
echoed in Mozart's dedication, where he says "my six children
are indeed the fruit of long and arduous toil", but adds that
Haydn's recognition had encouraged him to place the six quartets under his protection.

Far from being an adulatory compliment such as was common among musicians of the time, Haydn's remark put the position in a nutshell. As is well known, he expressed his high esteem
of Mozart again and again on later occasions – for instance,
during the Vienna wrangle over *Don Giovanni*, and perhaps
best of all in his letter to the Prague theatre official, Roth, in
1787:

"For if I could convince every music lover – and especially
those in high positions – of the inimitable works of Mozart; if
they would judge them, as I do, seriously and with musical understanding; if they would let his music touch their souls as it
does my own – why, then the nations would compete with one
another for possession of such a jewel within their borders. . . . I
am furious that this unique Mozart has not yet been taken into
the service of an imperial or royal court. Forgive me if I lose my
temper; I hold the man too dear."

Neither Leopold Mozart nor Haydn tended to indulge in exaggeration. They were both men of sense and sound judgment,
who were conscious of their responsibility. Haydn's judgments
are all the more valuable to posterity, since, as is well known,
Mozart's worth was far from being generally recognized during
his ten years in Vienna. The immediate recognition he received after his concerts and performances of his operas was
counter-balanced not only by the mass of critical views which
have come down to us, but, above all, by the unequivocal testimony supplied by the comparative failure of his works with the
publishers. And at that time, failure to please music publishers
implied a previous failure with the public; for if there was a
public demand for a work, a publisher printed it. In 1800
Beethoven was able to boast:

"My compositions bring me in a great deal, and I can say
that I have more commissions than I can execute, and that I
can rejoice. Also, for every work I write I could have six or seven

publishers and even more; I am no longer bargained with; I demand, and they pay" (to Wegeler, 29 June 1800).

Haydn could have said the same of himself. In those years success in terms of publication was a reliable criterion of artistic influence. Haydn's words, "For if I could . . ." and "I am furious . . .", also clearly indicate his desire to do something to offset the prejudice or lack of public recognition.

There is, it is true, evidence that indicates an extraordinarily high appreciation of Mozart at an amazingly early date; for instance, the notice that Neefe wrote for Cramer's *Magazin für Musik* in March 1783, on the occasion of the publication of Beethoven's Nine Variations on a March by E. Chr. Dressler: "This young genius [Beethoven] would certainly be a second Wolfgang Amadeus Mozart if he continues thus to progress. . . ." Remembering that at that date Neefe could not have been acquainted with many of Mozart's works, that he could hardly have ever met Mozart in person, and that he himself came from the somewhat old-fashioned Saxonian school of Doles and J. A. Hiller, one cannot but wonder how he recognized the, so to speak, still unappreciated genius of humanity in music not as Haydn but as Mozart. It would seem as if there were in Bonn a special understanding of Mozart's music; this is attested at a later date by the entry which Count Ferdinand Waldstein made in Beethoven's album, on 29 October 1792:

"Mozart's genius still mourns and bewails the death of its pupil. It has found refuge with the inexhaustible Haydn, but not employment; through him it desires once again to be united with another. Through constant industry you shall receive Mozart's spirit from Haydn's hands."

That dictum, made by a musically inspired dilettante barely a year after Mozart's death, is a remarkable appreciation of the relationships between the three composers, Haydn, Mozart, and Beethoven.

The influence which Mozart exerted on his contemporaries has never yet been satisfactorily studied. Certainly it cannot be compared with Haydn's universal success. The enthusiastic opinions of Mozart's immediate circle of family and friends prove little; to set against them we have too many unfavourable judgments on the part of the wider circles of 'connoisseurs' and 'amateurs'. Musicians like Nägeli and Koželuch, amateurs like the Count Grassalkowics or even Emperor Joseph II, expressed themselves sceptically, reservedly, or quite negatively. When Thomas Attwood, who was, according to Kelly, Mozart's "favourite pupil", and his friend, sent the six string quartets dedicated to Haydn to G. G. Ferrari in Naples, he found it necessary to warn him against too precipitate a rejection. In his *Leben des K.K. Kapellmeisters Wolfgang Gottlieb Mozart* of 1798, Niemtschek related that the objection was often made, "But Mozart's works are so difficult, so critical, so full of art and containing little for the ear". He attempted to refute the objection: "The difficult in his works is not deliberate; it is only the consequence of the greatness and originality of his genius." In Florence, after nine abortive attempts, the first act of *Don Giovanni* was laid aside as 'unperformable'. "Write in a more popular style, otherwise I cannot publish and pay for anything more of yours," the publisher Hoffmeister is said to have told Mozart. To which Mozart is supposed to have answered: "Well, then I shall earn no more and I shall starve and go to the devil." The picture of Mozart in his own day is by no means clear. The child-prodigy's mercurial rise to the position of an applauded *maestro* of the Milan opera was followed by the 'Storm and Stress' of the Mannheim–Paris episode; here Mozart is revealed in conflict with himself and his milieu – certainly anything but successful. Soon after his return home he broke with the society of the *ancien régime*, broke with the traditional manner of life of the musician, to achieve artistic and social emancipation. But the last ten years, which Mozart spent in Vienna in the self-chosen solitude of the 'artist' (in the romantic sense of the word) devoted to his creation, also brought with them an ever-increasing isolation. The only Mozart opera which was widely performed and had a decisive success in his lifetime was *Die Entführung*. After his death *Die Zauberflöte* conquered the European stage very swiftly; *Don Giovanni* and *Figaro* were slower, and *Così fan tutte* followed suit only after a considerable interval.[1] The great mass of Mozart's instrumental music was first made generally known through André's editions – broadly speaking, about 1800; only comparatively few works were published in

---

[1] *La Clemenza di Tito* was much more of a favourite with the public. Goethe had the famous Lauchstedt theatre opened (in 1802) with a performance of the opera.

his lifetime. Some were circulated in manuscript, but this applied only to a few, chiefly orchestral works. It can be said without exaggeration that, compared with Joseph Haydn, with Dittersdorf, Koželuch, Vanhal (Wanhal), Clementi, and dozens of lesser masters, Mozart was not generally accepted as a composer during his lifetime. Great success did not arrive until the generation of the young romantics, who found in Mozart what they believed to be a kindred spirit. The incomprehensible, twilight aspect of Mozart, which, however, was really only one side to his character, found powerful expression; and this explains his belated, but enduring and increasing success. The aesthetes and poets of the romantic era, such as Wackenroder and Tieck, A. W. Schlegel and E. T. A. Hoffmann, idolized Mozart. *Die Zauberflöte* moved not only Goethe to write its sequel (*Die Zauberflöte, Zweiter Teil*, a fragment); it also influenced Schlegel's *Ehrenpforte*, Tieck's *Gestiefelter Kater*, and Grillparzer's *Der Traum ein Leben*, not to mention the many operatic imitations which it fathered. *Don Giovanni* was echoed in Hoffmann's famous novels, his *Serapionsbrüder*, his *Kater Murr*, in the person of Kapellmeister Kreisler; everywhere in his work one catches echoes of Mozart, which were then bequeathed to Robert Schumann. Wagner's cult of Mozart was nourished by the same source. Fundamentally, even here Mozart was the victim of artistic misunderstanding; his art succumbed to romantic speculation. The romantic artist felt a great love for Mozart, a passionate enthusiasm for Beethoven; but for Haydn he had only an indulgent smile. It must not be overlooked, however, that men like the poet Jean Paul, who was seven years younger than Mozart, and the musician C. F. Zelter, two years younger, saw their ideal realized far more in Haydn than in Mozart; and it is highly significant that in a letter to Goethe, Zelter attempted to sum up Mozart by comparing him with Bach:

"Mozart to Bach is as the Netherland masters are to the Italian and Greek artists, and only since I steadily perceive this fact more and more clearly do I hold both in the highest esteem, not demanding from one what is accomplished by the other."

As early as the Viennese classical age, the prime ground for estimating the value of a composer consisted wholly in the immediate impression he made on widespread musical circles.

The days when music had been esteemed more as a 'science' than as an 'art', when musicians were valued more for their 'learning' than for the influence they exerted on their contemporaries, were past. The power to pass judgment had been transferred more and more from the 'connoisseurs' to the 'amateurs', and from them to the great audiences of the public concerts. Simultaneously, instrumental music had displaced vocal music (with the sole exception of opera) from its leading position. The composer who wished to be appreciated was now confronted with the task of influencing the mass of music lovers through instrumental language, or from the operatic stage, and these friends were no longer differentiated according to position or rank, denomination or education – nor even according to nation or speech. Haydn's oft-quoted words, "My language is understood all over the world", are to be understood quite literally; this language speaks to men of all nations, conditions, and denominations. Thousands made pilgrimages to Haydn's *Schöpfung*, and the First Consul honoured its first Paris performance with his presence. Of Mozart's *Die Zauberflöte* Goethe's mother wrote: "No man will admit that he has not seen it. All the craftsmen, gardeners, and even the Sachsenhausers,[1] whose children act the parts of apes and lions, are going to see it. There has never been such a spectacle[2] here before."

This was perhaps the most far-reaching revolution that has ever been known in the history of music. For a thousand years the musician had always remained in his appointed place in the social hierarchy and intellectual order; he had certain prescribed tasks to perform, and his compositions had to satisfy demands, strictly regulated by convention, made by firmly defined strata of society or by patrons. Court celebrations, ecclesiastical ceremonies, the city's representative functions, and the numerous other occasions of burgher and public life were his sphere. Each composition had its own appointed occasion and an appointed circle of recipients. To compose 'music for all', music that would suit the prince and his valet, the lady and the burgher's daughter, the Englishman and the Italian; to compose music that had to be both highly refined and highly popular, was a new and unprecedented task. It is perhaps the

---

[1] At that time Sachsenhausen was a rural suburb of Frankfurt.

[2] The German word for 'spectacle' has the double meaning of a 'show' and 'uproar'.

greatest achievement of the mature Viennese classical style that
it could master this task. The composer could create the new
'language of the heart', which was simultaneously to be a 'language
of humanity', only out of his own inner being. All earlier
music had been firmly bound to strict traditions, both in form
and content. But in language, form, and content Haydn's string
quartets and symphonies were an entirely new world. The composer
no longer wrote for the church, the council chamber, the
princely salon (though he still quite frequently obtained his
commissions from these sources); not for the liturgy, not for
ceremonial, for the ball or the table, but for the public concert,
for the consumers of music; and that meant for the publisher
also. The 'permanent revolution' which began in the second half
of the eighteenth century, has not ended even in the twentieth;
for with the modern development of radio and the mechanical
dissemination of music, it has only entered a new phase; it has
not been freed from the old one. This revolution, in releasing the
musician from his previously close ties to society and its tasks,
also forced him to walk alone. It brought him the Greek gift of
'artistic freedom'. But at the same time, the ancient tradition
which allowed the composer to pursue his calling within customary
forms and with customary methods came to an end; the
musician's altered social function peremptorily required that his
work should be 'original'. Haydn understood the change with
his customary and dispassionate insight – "so I had to become
original". He approached music's new tasks firmly and logically
and thus won the love and highest esteem of his contemporaries.
Mozart broke sharply with tradition, and was ruined: artistic
misunderstandings and material want accompanied him
throughout the ten years of his greatest maturity. In this respect,
Beethoven was heir to his predecessors. He lorded over
and tyrannized his milieu: "They no longer bargain with me;
I demand. . . ."

These historical circumstances provided the basis for the
widely differing contemporary estimation of the three masters,
for the great variety in their styles. It was a variety far greater
than had ever existed among the masters of earlier ages. And it
is not simply a question of the others being at a greater distance
in time, for to us the style of the Germans in the days of Bach or
Schütz, the style of the Italians in the days of Pergolesi or Monteverdi,
seem much more uniform than the style of the Viennese

classical masters. It is, however, extremely difficult to express in concrete terms the stylistic differences between Haydn, Mozart, and Beethoven, or exactly to define how Mozart's style differs from that of the others. It is obvious that the theme of the Largo of Beethoven's piano Sonata, Op. 10, No. 3 (*c.* 1797), could never have been written by Haydn or Mozart; the theme of the Andante from Haydn's last symphony (No. 104, 1795) could never have been written by Mozart or Beethoven; the theme of the Adagio of Mozart's clarinet Concerto (K.622, 1791) could never have been written by Haydn or Beethoven; to say this is to say the obvious. Wherein do the differences lie? Of course there are border-line cases; there is much that is very close to Mozart in Beethoven's early wind compositions (the Octet, Op. 103; the Trio, Op. 87; the Sextet, Op. 71; the Quintet, Op. 16; the Serenade, Op. 25; the Septet, Op. 20, all dating from 1792–1800); and Haydn's string quartets, Op. 50 (1787), make it very clear that the older man knew the string quartets dedicated to him by his young contemporary. None the less, thematic similarity hardly ever goes so far that one could confuse the authors.

One difficulty in formulating these differences arises from the fact that the composers of that age made use of similar external forms, both large and small. 'Sonata form' was never in fact taken as an absolute standard, though musical literature mistakenly insists that it was; it has always been flexible, and its application to individual cases has been subjected to the greatest variations. In Beethoven's piano sonatas, Opp. 2–10, it was uniformly submitted to a strict standardization, but Beethoven himself broke away from it more and more from Op. 14 onwards. In Mozart's and Haydn's piano sonatas the scheme of the 'sonata form' was never a fixed one. For his symphonies, Haydn constructed his own 'sonata form' scheme, which, as a rule, did not even have a second subject. And he applied this scheme generally to all his last twenty to twenty-five symphonies. Beethoven's first two symphonies take over Haydn's form, but Mozart's last three deviate from it quite extensively. What is true of 'sonata form' applies still more to the form of the 'lyrical' movement (the slow movement), the minuet or scherzo, and the rondo (finale). A very general scheme is common to all three masters, but within that scheme they move freely. This attitude applies to other strict forms; one general scheme of the first movements of Mozart's concertos and of Beethoven's early concertos (in this *genre* Haydn can scarcely be considered), can be reduced to the simple formula: four tuttis and three solos, with a big middle solo and a cadenza after the third. But in every detail, in tonal and thematic organization, etc., the scheme was subjected to infinite variation, especially by Mozart. In formal respects, it is, perhaps, in the string quartet that the three masters reveal the greatest similarities: here Haydn's Opp. 20 (1772) and 33 (1781) set the pattern which, from Mozart's D minor Quartet, K.173 (1773), down to Beethoven's series, Op. 18 (1798–1800), became a kind of canon. It is true that here, too, the variation in detail is very considerable. The individual work derives its individuality from the individual character and expression with which it is packed. It is the same in the sphere of vocal music; certain schemes for the operatic aria or for the various sections of the mass are common property; but the individual differences are great, and no composer observes any single blueprint.

It would be a fruitless task to attempt to deduce Mozart's personal style from the forms of his movements; forms which are extremely elastic and inconstant. They are always determined by the particular instance, and elude any attempt at a schematic reduction. Moreover, we run up against another difficulty in trying to determine Mozart's style. His early works, such as the three symphonies K.81, 97, 95(73l–n), written in Rome, or the string quartet, K.80(73f), and perhaps the church music dating from his residence at Salzburg in 1769 and 1771 – all these works are based strictly on other composers' models, and so we have no unequivocal means of recognizing a personal style. In that case the question automatically arises: What in fact *can* be described as Mozart's style? Is there anything in his music that can be regarded as a uniform 'Mozart style'? Which of his works may be considered as the final expression of his personality in musical terms?

*   *   *

Mozart's extensive reliance on contemporary models suggests the possibility of drawing a line at which the 'youthful' or 'developmental' phase of his compositional activity ends and the mature period of his own personal style begins. But where is the line to be drawn? In the winter of 1773–4, perhaps? In that case, one might be justified in regarding the string Quartet, K.173, the

Quintet, K.174, and the first piano Concerto, K.175, as the first indications of a definite independence; and one would include such a characteristic work as the G minor Symphony, K.183, the piano sonatas K.279–83(189d–h) and *La finta giardiniera* (K.196) in his 'mature phase'. But one would be quite unjustified in rejecting such works as the divertimenti, K.136–8(125a–c), the Sonata for piano (four-hands), K.381(123a), the operas *Mitridate*, K.87(74a), *Ascanio in Alba*, K.111, *Il sogno di Scipione*, K.126, and *Lucio Silla*, K.135, as 'uncharacteristic'. Obviously that line is not good enough. If it is drawn at such a point it certainly excludes much that is dependent on models and is not specially characteristic of Mozart, but much, too, that is stylistically significant. Even in the *Singspiel*, *Bastien und Bastienne*, K.50(46b), written by the twelve-year-old Mozart in 1768, are there not pieces that recommend themselves as 'highly Mozartean'?

The line of demarcation in Mozart between the 'youthful' and the 'mature' is easily reduced to absurdity. Formerly it was thought that the winter of 1777–8 (the Mannheim–Paris journey) could be regarded as marking the beginning of Mozart's artistic maturity; but those who thought so did not stop to reflect that this demarcation line degraded as 'immature' a large number of works which in fact did not deserve such a fate; and that, on the other hand, by no means everything he wrote after his Paris sojourn can be regarded as mature. Mozart is in reality a Proteus. Anyone who attempts to formulate the style of that Proteus in words would do well to consider the works of his late period, which express indubitable and distinctive Mozartean features at their purest. If by artistic development one means an ever-growing capacity to express increasingly profound concepts in more and more distinctive forms, and if we accept Joseph Haydn as the standard example in musical history of such a development, then we must certainly fail to find any 'artistic development' in Mozart. Mozart the youth displays an incomparable ability to assimilate, coupled with a stupendous early maturity in the mastery of his craft; and at the end of his life there is a phase (the years in Vienna) in which craftsmanship becomes the 'sovereign handmaiden' of the intellect, and the "*Fülle der Gesichte*", the "fulness of visions", in Goethe's phrase, is, in one or the other work, compressed into the pithiest formal patterns. The music that lies between these two periods cannot be described as 'development', as continuous progression; rather does that Protean nature undergo a continual self-transformation.

Anyone attempting to describe Mozart's style would be well advised to ponder on the works of the late period; but he must always be conscious of the fact that to consider Mozart's personal style as fully expressed in the late works exclusively is to show a complete misunderstanding of the composer's character.

This train of thought brings us back yet again to the Haydn–Mozart–Beethoven comparison, and demonstrates the fundamental difference between the three masters. Haydn followed a consistent development, which in its last phase led to the formulation of a style simultaneously universal and highly personal. Looking back from Haydn's late symphonies to his earlier symphonies and quartets, one sees no false roads, no sudden interruptions, and no change. Beethoven also experienced an artistic development, but it was not a consistent one. It led by way of many false turns and many interruptions to the supremely personal and by no means universally applicable late style of a solitary individual. Looking back from Beethoven's last string quartets and piano sonatas, one sees the earlier works in these *genres* as sporadic outbreaks, as occasional meteorites, from which hardly a road appears to lead to the later works. Even in this sense Mozart did not experience a personal 'development'. Each of his last symphonies, string quartets, and string quintets testifies to a pure and consummate expression of his innermost self. The youthful assimilation of innumerable other models resulted in an amalgam from which everything disproportionate and characterless was little by little eliminated. Looking back from this point to the earlier works, one gets a general impression of a constant simplification, clarification, and refinement. At the end of the way, we come to works highly individual and personal, works which are at once supremely simple and profoundly subtle, supremely straightforward and profoundly unfathomable. In his last years Haydn could be and necessarily had to be truly popular. The Beethoven of the last years could not be popular, nor did he want to be. The late Mozart also was not popular, but the reasons were very different. The only exception is *Die Zauberflöte*, in which supreme refinement and condensation are blended with the popular. So when Arnold Schering described Mozart's late works as the consummate expression of that cosmopolitan age, his remark was inept: that was much more true of the last works of Haydn.

The fact that many of Mozart's works began to be widely disseminated and even to achieve popularity so soon after his death was due to many complex causes. One was the belief of the romantic poets and writers of that period that they had found in his late works the unreal, the other-worldly and daemonic which they themselves made their own spheres. In his novel, *Don Juan* (1814), E. T. A. Hoffmann speaks of the "deeper significance of the opera of all operas"; "this conflict of the divine and the daemonic powers gives birth to the concept of the terrestrial, just as the victory won gives birth to the concept of the celestial". Hoffmann was also one of the first to realize that for his classical operas Mozart "chose only the story really suited to his music, paradoxical as that may seem to many"; to Hoffmann, Mozart's music is "the mysterious language of a distant spiritual kingdom, whose marvellous accents echo in our inner being and arouse a higher, intensive life" (*Der Dichter und der Komponist*, 1813). The turn to Mozart was founded on a deeper understanding of the *ideas* which it was thought were to be found in his art. But it would not have been possible without a deep understanding of Mozart's late musical *style*, which now suddenly touched the hearts of the romantic generation. Above all else, undoubtedly, it was Mozart's melody that opened the way. Melodies such as 'Ein Mädchen oder Weibchen', 'Bei Männern, welche Liebe fühlen', 'La ci darem la mano', and 'Se vuol ballare', were soon proved to be popular by Beethoven's early variations (1792–1801). Many others were also circulated quite early. From *Don Giovanni* were published the serenade 'Deh, vieni alla finestra', Zerlina's 'Vedrai carino', and, strange to say, Elvira's E flat aria 'Mi tradì' (to completely different German words), all in separate editions and all in 1788–9. In 1789–90 were published Cherubino's 'Voi che sapete' and the Count–Susanna duet, 'Crudel, perchè finora' from *Figaro*. Many items from *Die Zauberflöte* were in popular demand as early as 1791. Melody was the most accessible factor in Mozart's music, and especially in these instances, where a relatively 'simple' lyric melody was not framed in a highly developed harmonic scheme. Historical experience shows that highly artistic elaboration of a song-like melody does not hinder its popularization, but favours it; parallel instances are Haydn's 'Gott erhalte' (which is still today the

German national hymn); Haydn's 'Ein Mädchen, das auf Ehre hielt', Schubert's 'Heidenröslein' and 'Lindenbaum'. In fact, quite a number of tunes which have become common property were derived from Mozart's most consummate melodies. An outstanding example is the song 'Komm, lieber Mai' (K.596, written in 1791), which every German schoolchild still sings to-day. That its melody, like many in *Die Zauberflöte*, has a folk-tune as its basis makes no difference, for it was in Mozart's version that it became common property. The great majority of musical people fails to notice that the apparent simplicity is really the result of the greatest refinement, and that in fact such a melody is really the fruit of great artistic labour. The musical public gathers the fruit, which then enters the common consciousness as a spontaneous invention, in the sense Goethe had in mind when speaking of the songs in *Des Knaben Wunderhorn*: "They have fulfilled their destiny and may now be lost again, even though written and printed, since they have passed into the life and culture of the nation."

In truth the melodies of the late Mozart are supreme art, and their apparent simplicity only shows how the amazing maturity of his artistic faculty eliminated all suggestion of difficulty or ineptitude. Richard Strauss, himself a great melodist, had something to say on this question to the critic Max Marschalk, in 1918:[1]

"I spend a great deal of time on my melodies; from the first idea to its final melodic shape is a long way. . . . The motive is a matter of inspiration; it is the idea, and most of us are satisfied with the idea, whereas true art first arises with the development of the idea. Art is not a matter of the beginning of a melody, but of its continuation, its development to a complete melodic shape. . . . The most perfect melodic shapes are found in Mozart; he has the lightness of touch which is the true objective. With Beethoven the melodies are heavier; one is clearly conscious of the labour. Listen to the remarkable expansion of a Mozart melody, to Cherubino's 'Voi che sapete', for instance. You think it is coming to an end, but it goes farther, ever farther."

Strauss told how Brahms had advised him as a young man to study Schubert's dances for their melodic structure, and went on:

[1] See F. Trenner: *R. Strauss, Dokumente*, Munich, 1954.

"Of course to construct the melodic shape is a question of talent; but here we are also concerned with one of the most difficult of technical problems. . . . A melody which seems to have been born in a moment is almost always the result of intense labour."

This is an admirable description. If Mozart's melodies appear so 'light' of touch, that of course is a tribute to his talent; but it was possible only because of his consummate mastery of technique. The description which his sister-in-law, Sophie Haibl, has left of how Mozart strode about the room, in deep meditation, when at work, seems to prove that a profound co-ordinating effort preceded the elaboration of the melody. The elaboration is an affair of the writing-desk; invention requires premeditation.

The features that strike the present-day student of Mozart's melodies are conveyed in such terms as 'lucidity', 'facility', 'lightness', 'perfection of proportions', 'tranquil urgency'. The themes of the Adagio in the clarinet Concerto, K.622, the Larghetto of the piano Concerto, K.595, the Andante of the Symphony, K.543, the Andante of the string Trio, K.563, the variations of the string Quartet, K.464, the Andante of the string Quintet, K.614, the Larghetto of the clarinet Quintet, K.581, and innumerable others, are the instrumental counterparts to the popular melodies from the operas. They failed to achieve a similar popularity because of their instrumental character: popular currency requires a word form. What is specifically Mozartean about them?

They all make use of the simple basic scheme of an eight-bar period (though with many variants). Normally the eight-bar period is divided into two four-bar groups, each of which is, as a rule, subdivided into two groups of two bars. There could not be a simpler scheme. In this *Diastematik* (ebb and flow) the two-bar subdivisions form small contrasts; the basic scheme *a–b–a–b* comes into being (e.g., the Andante of K.614, the Andante of K.543, the Larghetto of K.595). Or to the first *a* is linked a varied or enhanced *a*, perhaps even a third *a*, and only the fourth two-bar subdivision contains the antithetical *a–b* (e.g., the Adagio of K.622). There are many other combinations; they can easily violate the eight-bar scheme without the hearer being aware of the fact; only someone with a keen sense of proportion notices the slight extension to nine bars which occurs in the

'statement' of the theme of the Andante in K.581, or the extension of the 'response' to eleven bars. In the Adagio of the piano
Concerto K.488, the melodic scheme $a–b–a–a'–a''–a$ extends
across twelve bars. There is no limit to the variability of the
scheme. No matter what the melodic-metrical relationships may
be, one always has the impression of consummate equipoise and
proportion. The later the work, the simpler the theme, and the
more symmetrical, restful, reflective, and clear it is. Of the slow
movements, perhaps the Adagio of the clarinet Concerto, K.622,
is one of the most perfect examples; among the piano concertos
the last, K.595, has the 'simplest' thematic material in all three
movements.

In Mozart's late works this melodic quality is always associated with the simplest of harmony in the first announcement
of the melody. The tonic, the two dominants, and the nearest related keys suffice. As a rule, the two-bar group shifts from one
basic function to another; after two bars the dominant is
reached; after two more the tonic again; after six bars, perhaps
the subdominant, or a parallel; after eight bars the dominant.
This very rough schematic outline is only meant to show that
harmonically, too, the relationships are of the simplest kind.
The rhythm emphasizes the slight inner contrasts within the
theme by means of slightly contrary motion. Yet in late Mozart
these rhythmic shadings often remain no more than hardly perceptible gradations, simple intimations (e.g., the Andante of the
Quintet, K.614), or fade away completely (the Andante of the
string Trio, K.563). In the Adagio of the clarinet Concerto,
K.622, the flow of the accompaniment continues quite un-
changed, while the melody extends itself above it in very delicate and supple rhythms.

This kind of description might apply to the themes of most
slow movements in Mozart's late works. But they also apply to
very many of Haydn's slow movement themes: for instance, to
the Adagio of Op. 76, No. 1, the Andante of Op. 76, No. 2, the
Largo of Op. 76, No. 5, and the Fantasia of Op. 76, No. 6. These
themes show that Haydn not only loved Mozart, but studied
him too. The Andante of the string Quartet Op. 42 (1785) reveals a similar attitude. Yet only a short time before, in 1781,
the slow movements of Op. 33, Nos. 1, 2, 4, 5, and 6, still retained a more ornamental, *galant* quality, in melodic, rhythmic,
and harmonic respects moving more restlessly and intricately;

only Op. 33, No. 3, in the theme of its Andante, very closely approaches Mozart. Similar observations can be made when comparing the themes of Mozart's late slow movements to themes from early Beethoven. In a number of works, especially in his early chamber pieces, Beethoven clearly uses Mozart as his model; but soon, particularly in the piano sonatas, a new type of broad, cantabile theme, saturated with emotion, comes into existence. We meet with a heroic pathos which is not to be found in either Mozart or Haydn; one gets a strong impression of direct, personal speech, of a direct appeal to the listener, whereas Mozart's thematic material had confined itself to the floating realm of an expressively powerful musical absolute. Putting it very roughly: Mozart's themes are timeless, those of Beethoven were written expressly for his time. In his last years, Mozart's characteristic 'floating' between extremes – between the popular and the esoteric, between passion and refinement, between voluptuousness and formal restraint, in brief, between 'nature' and 'art' in Goethe's sense – achieved its most perfect consummation and purest fulfilment.

> "Natur und Kunst, sie scheinen sich zu fliehen
> Und haben sich, eh' man es denkt, gefunden."[1]

> ["Nature and art, they seem to flee each other,
> And yet, ere one has thought, they find each other."]

Unless we are completely deceived, it is this supreme consummation which has made it possible for Mozart's works to pass into the consciousness of the nations – and into the consciousness of humanity.

*   *   *

For the late Mozart, the manner in which he built up his slow themes into movements is just as significant as the style of those themes themselves. We have already said that with all their variability in detail the external forms of the movements as a whole proceed more or less according to a scheme. But no easy method of determining Mozart's style can be obtained from the forms. In details their execution is certainly of an overwhelming richness in melody, harmony, rhythm, structural metamorphoses and variations, in shading and figuration, which

[1] Goethe: *Gedenkausgabe der Werke*, Zürich, 1949, Artemis, Vol. II, p. 141.

has no parallel in either Haydn or the early Beethoven, or even in Schubert. For not only do the melodies unfold "farther, ever farther", as Strauss said, but out of themselves they produce an abundance of related and contrasting musical phenomena, which are soon woven into a compact entity. Technically, this can be accomplished by new structures emerging as antitheses after the close of the theme; or the theme grows its own antithesis in the shape of a counterpoint. In the Andante of the G minor Symphony, K.550, the theme, even at its first appearance during the movement's first nineteen bars, develops three contrapuntal motives, and thereafter the whole movement is extended contrapuntally, tonally, and colouristically in a glittering *exposé* of this material (e.g., the E flat minor phrase of the first section, or the chromatic shifts to the beginning of the second section). No further new material is introduced; the flowing transformations which take place in the course of this pulsing, vibrant movement consist, technically speaking, only of contrapuntal combinations, of modulations, and of the colourful richness of the instrumentation. In the Andante of the E flat Symphony (K.543), the shadows of the impending A flat minor are to be found even in the homely, song-like theme. Fresh thematic material is introduced as antithesis after the close of the opening theme; and, finally, intricacies of harmony and shading lead to the dreamy happiness of the woodwind theme (bars 54 et seq., bars 125 et seq.), which, in the cadential phrase given to the strings, brings forth the unfolding of a blossom of the purest beauty. In this movement, too, the richness of the shading is achieved by means of a manifold contrapuntal superimposition (e.g., bars 76 et seq., bars 87 et seq.). How thoroughly the instrumental and harmonic colours interpenetrate, and are, indeed, fundamentally identical, is shown by the modulation from A flat minor to B major (bars 91 et seq.), where the silky sheen of the orchestration and the delicate flexibility of the enharmonic transformation (A flat = G sharp) are fused in a matchless unity. This same passage demonstrates the movement's organic unity; the strong enharmonic-*cum*-thematic extension is based on the troubled section in A flat minor which was already hinted at in the theme. Thus when, before the last return of the theme (bar 144), the clarinets prepare, with magical arabesques above the horn pedal point, the movement's calm resolution, this turn of events is heard as an outcome, perfectly consistent in both its thematicism and its colours, of the movement's structural growth.

The stylistic devices with which Mozart develops his slow movements are extraordinarily diversified. In the piano concertos the accent is often placed more strongly on shading than on counterpoint. The woodwind enter with their own episodes, as in K.491, with its interludes in C minor and A flat, or with the A major interlude in K.488. In the last piano Concerto, K.595, the 'simplest' of all, the Larghetto is given a beautiful and delicate enhancement by the phrase in G flat, without resort to obvious colouristic or contrapuntal means. On the other hand, in the Andante of the C major Symphony, K.551, the contrasts are set firmly one against another; the song-like thematic material is immediately broken up into little motives (bars 11 et seq.), then interrupted by two episodes which clash together in the strongest of dissonances (bars 19 et seq. and bars 47 et seq.); and above these dramatic, wildly passionate outbursts, the song-like flow of the melody joins with its self-produced counterpoint to close in beatific fulness. It is all 'simple'. Even the famous dissonant episodes consist of simple suspensions and passing notes. In this respect, they remind one strongly of the equally famous, controversial and oft-criticized Adagio introduction to the C major string Quartet, K.465. But with those 'simple' means, effects are achieved which the entire nineteenth century, with all its over-exploitation of means and all the subtlety of its shading, never again achieved, just as all the nineteenth century never produced verse like Goethe's 'Mondlied' or 'Mailied'. Where rich tonal colour cannot be used, as in the sonatas or string quartets, there is much more resort to motivic dissection, to contrapuntal treatment and harmonic modulation, as a means of development.

In the G major string Quartet, K.387, the individual motives for the contrapuntal continuation of the movement are drawn directly from the theme of the Andante; but already in bars 8 et seq., we find the germ of the harmonic broadening out to D flat, which later (bars 63 et seq.) becomes the main basis of the movement. In the Adagio of the violin Sonata K.481, the emphasis is laid clearly on richness of harmonic development; it runs from A flat through F minor to the broad cantabile of the D flat theme, then through C sharp minor and A major to G sharp minor, after which (though not simultaneously in piano and violin) it undergoes enharmonic transformation to A flat, in which key there is a very daring passage shortly before the close. The violin and piano sonatas do not offer much opportunity for counterpoint and tonal shading, thus their harmonic aspect is developed all the more exuberantly. The Andante of the A major violin Sonata, K.526, presents a similar effect, very delicately yet impressively, though in a much more discreet but not less striking manner. The A flat Adagio of the string Trio, K.563, also employs the richest of harmonic resources, and the subtlest rhythmic delicacy partly compensates for the lack of instrumental shading.

In general, what is true of the slow movements' themes is true of their structure: the later the work, the simpler, the more restrained and unobtrusive it is. The slow movements of the string quartets K.575 and 590 are hardly to be surpassed for their 'simplicity', whereas the andante movements of the quartets K.465 and 499 are rich in complex contrapuntal devices, and the Adagio of the G minor Quintet, K.516, contains the most daring enharmonic superimposition (bars 63–4) to be found in all Mozart. The structure of each movement is individual to the highest degree. There is no repetition between movements. Within the frame of a more or less conventional external form exists a satisfying abundance of ideas. But this abundance is always saved from exuberance by strict economy and consequently an exclusion of all superfluity, so that the unity of its form is preserved. Mozart never goes so far as the aphoristic style of the late Beethoven, nor does he ever drop into a stereotyped formal treatment, such as is common with Schubert. While in Beethoven's late string quartets the abundance of ideas makes mock of every rule and shatters the form, and while in Schubert's symphonies and sonatas the form becomes the rattling skeleton housing an unlimited flow of ideas, Mozart's late slow movements always achieve a consummate unity of their thematic content, of their development and their external form; they are tense and elastic from the first to the last note, unobtrusive in their restrained concision, and overflowing in the wealth of their invention and thematic combinations; the listener never gets a feeling of an inflexible mechanism operating for the rigid fulfilment of a scheme. This kind of development of a movement is clearly different from that of the late Haydn. Of course, Haydn, too, was not lacking in richness of invention and thematic combinations, in sensuous sound and variety of form; but in his case one is *conscious* of the form, while in Mozart's it simply unravels as a vapour-thin web of musical content. To put it another way: Mozart had so consummate an ability to fuse form and content that his movements are apprehended only as miracles of concise formulation, whereas in Haydn it is often possible to foresee, or to think one foresees, the course of a movement as soon as it has begun. It is the miracle of consummate form without constraint, rich abundance without extravagance, the seemingly lucid which does not rely on convention, that distinguishes Mozart's slow movements from those of all other masters.

Of course, no description can convey that ultimate content which remains the secret of the creative spirit. The man who has come to a genuine understanding of Mozart will recognize and wonder again and again at the fulness within the symmetry, the symmetry of the fulness. Goethe's formula of the *"geprägten Form, die lebend sich entwickelt"* [the "moulded form which has living development"] (which he meant in quite a different sense) applies to Mozart as if it had been written for him; his 'Daimon' realizes the *"Gesetz, nach dem er angetreten"* [the "law according to which he began"],[1] in the ever newly-moulded forms of living development. In that respect he was unique – unique, too, in the balance between the purely musical and the emotional. The simplest of comparisons with Beethoven reveals that in a number of early movements (especially the chamber music of the years 1792–1802) Beethoven perfectly achieves Mozart's fluent formal elegance, though the emotional content is not equal to Mozart's; but very soon in Beethoven's music (possibly as early as the piano Sonata, Op. 2) the emotional content assumes the foreground and the musical absolute is thrust into the background. Complete symmetry even the early Beethoven did not possess, the later Beethoven less so. His effects derive more from the immediacy with which he violently attacks his listener. In all his works, the relation between the absolute quality of the musical shape and its emotional content (in other words, the relation which is often tabulated as 'form' and 'content') is quite different from that of Mozart's. And it is different again in Haydn's case. In Haydn the emotional content is never weaker than Mozart's (though it is often thought to be): it is only

---

[1] Goethe: *Urworte Orphisch, Gedenkausgabe*, Zürich, 1949, Artemis, Vol. I, p. 523.

communicated differently; perhaps one may say – with circum-
spection and every reservation – that it is simpler and more
rational, whereas Mozart's spiritual content betrays the manifold, incomprehensible, and changeable features of his Protean
character. Each of the three masters has his own way of expressing
humanity in the form of the musical absolute. But again, each
had a different way. It is the way in which Mozart utters the
absolute that contains the secret of the ultimate content which
defies definition.

The example of the slow movements can be taken as *pars pro
toto*. Similar deductions can be made in regard to all Mozart's
movements and works, vocal as well as instrumental, sonata
movements and rondos as well as minuets and overtures. Today
we have accurate knowledge, down to the minutest detail, of
Mozart's life and milieu, and our sources for his works have been
subjected innumerable times to musicological criticism and
textual scrutiny (which does not necessarily mean, of course,
that all the problems have been solved). But even today Mozart's
style has not yet been subjected to more precise and comprehensive definition. The extremely valuable results which we
have derived from Wyzewa and St.-Foix's great book on Mozart
are still confined more to a comparison of his external style with
that of other masters than to an attempt to interpret the essence
of the style itself. At the end of his two-volume work on Mozart,
Abert said: "Now really a third book should follow: on Mozart's
style." Anyone who seeks to determine the extent and nature of
the influence of Mozart's works on his own time and on posterity can do so only in so far as he tries to establish the specific
qualities of style which distinguish Mozart from other masters,
and in so far as he attempts to deduce the special nature of
Mozart's influence from those qualities. The present essay
should be regarded as an attempt towards achieving this aim.

Our description of the specific qualities of Mozart's style by
reference to the slow movements of his instrumental music could
be enriched by many other general characteristics and details.
But the qualities we have mentioned possess universal validity
for *all* the compositions of the late Mozart, and thus can, with
prudence, be used to measure the 'specific' element in the early
works. If we accept these specific qualities as criteria for Mozart's
personal style, we can elucidate some part of Mozart's influence.
The delicate lucidity of his melodic invention made him famous

among the widest circles of listeners. The supreme artistry of his contrapuntal combinations, the structure of his movements, his use of counterpoint, harmonic modulations and tonal colour won him the admiration of experts and professional musicians like Haydn and Neefe. The irrational and incomprehensible element, the 'dark' emotional content of his works, irritated many of his contemporaries, and their technical difficulty frightened many others away. But it was the complex nature of his style, the consummate unity of the musical absolute and spiritual content, the almost mysterious versatility, the interplay of the serene with the sinister, the "living development of the moulded form" that struck related chords in the souls of the romantics and made them adopt Mozart as the unattainable idol of their yearning. But it was the romantic age, too, that founded Mozart's world fame.

[*Translated by H. C. Stevens*]

ARTHUR HUTCHINGS

THE KEYBOARD MUSIC

Very few home pianists know the best of Mozart's piano music outside the concertos – such pieces as the Adagio in B minor (K.540), the Rondo in A minor (K.511) or the four-hand Sonata in F (K.497). The sonatas are widely known because they are used for teaching; when the intelligent pupil's mind and fingers are more advanced, he naturally explores the volume for deeper musical thought than he encountered in the first pages he was set to learn, but he secures supreme satisfaction only from two or three whole sonatas and occasional fine movements in others. Still more disappointed is the player who expects consistent advance of musical thought with the advance in dates of composition, and therefore unfairly compares Mozart with Beethoven or even with C. P. E. Bach.

It seems necessary, if naive, to remember that Mozart did not compose a book of eighteen sonatas as Bach composed two books of twenty-four preludes and fugues; nor, for that matter, did Beethoven, but Beethoven's sonatas completely chart his gradually widening adventure. Mozart's sonatas do no such thing. What Mozart sonata stands with one of the famous works in C Minor or D minor? What solo piece brilliantly fuses the elements of fugue and sonata design? What set of variations has the quality of certain movements in the concertos or quartets? Mozart was the first great composer to have a piano in his workroom and – let there be no mistake – his, apart from certain of Haydn's sonatas,[1] is the first great piano music; but there is no evidence that the instrument which ousted others to become the companion of his solitude also became, as Beethoven's without doubt became, his chief confidant.

It would be difficult to make plausible a theory that Mozart's music in general was greatly affected by the piano; Beethoven's music, on the other hand, owes as much to his love of the piano as to his love of the string quartet; this is not just because the confidant of his study gave him all shades of piano and forte, all gradings of crescendo and diminuendo, a staccato as sharp as a

[1] e.g., Sonata No. 20 in C minor (1771), Sonata No. 46 in A flat (c. 1768). – Eds.

harpsichord's and a cantabile smoother than a clavichord's, but because he could imagine himself to be controlling an orchestra or even a chorus with orchestra. The one instrument suggested many. It is important to know that this instrument was not Mozart's piano. Even in the year of his death, Mozart is un-likely to have played an instrument like Beethoven's Broad-wood, though anybody who is familiar with the rich harmony of his fantasias may wonder what music he might have com-posed for the later type of piano had he lived to know it well. Whatever our speculations, it is wrong to Beethovenize even the fantasias; Mozart was distinctly Mozart to the end, and his keyboard style had its proper instrument.

The mere appearance of the three pianos photographed on Plate 53 of the fifth edition of Grove (the same picture is to be found in earlier editions) shows far more difference between the first and second instruments, respectively Mozart's and Beethoven's, than between the second and the third, a Broad-wood used by Chopin. Mozart's piano by Anton Walther of Vienna is as small as a single-manual harpsichord of five octaves, has the shallow fall of key which facilitates smooth and rapid playing, and appears to be without contrivances having the effect of the pedals which Broadwood patented in 1783, though we know from Mozart's letters of a "mechanism worked by one's knee". (The 'pedal' referred to in Leopold Mozart's letter to Nannerl, 12 March 1785,[1] is a pedalier or set of pedal-keys simi-lar to those of an organ.[2]) Reminiscences by those who heard Mozart assure us that he used the sustaining pedal very spar-ingly, and that the singing tone for which he was so much ad-mired did not depend upon pedalling but had been cultivated in his early days. The phrase "should flow like oil" recurs often in his letters, and he advises his sister not to spend much time in practising Clementi's chains of sixths and octaves lest her play-ing become 'choppy'.[3]

[1] See E. Anderson: *Letters of Mozart*, London, 1938, Vol. III, p. 1325.
[2] cf. also A. Hyatt King: *Mozart in Retrospect*, London, 1955, pp. 245-7.
[3] cf. Anderson, op. cit., Vol. III, p. 1267.
Beethoven, curiously, said just the opposite about Mozart's piano playing. Karl Czerny told Otto Jahn, when the latter was in Vienna on 15 September 1852, that "Beethoven said to Czerny that he had heard Mozart play; [Mozart] had a delicate but choppy touch, with no legato, which Beethoven at first found very strange, since he was accustomed to treat the pianoforte like an organ" (Jahn's MS. notes, Berlin State Library). L. Nohl (*Beethoven. Nach den Schilderungen seiner Zeitgenossen*, Stuttgart, 1877, p. 9) quotes Czerny in a similar report: "Beethoven,

This favourite simile of oil, his ridicule of awkward posture at the keyboard, his alertness to angularity and rhythmic roughness, and the testimony of musicians who knew his style – all suggest his regarding the piano as encompassing the combined capabilities of other keyboard instruments, which it surpassed in its ready response to the demands which he would have made from them and perhaps did make from them when they could not fully meet them. However turgid the emotions of some of his last works for keyboard, however much he needed a loud and clear instrument in his later concertos, his style underwent no radical change of performing technique.

A few years ago, Hugh Gough brought several instruments to illustrate his paper on 'The Classical Grand Pianoforte' at a meeting of the Royal Musical Association.[1] His first exhibit, a German piano with the nameboard missing, had the action and measurements of one by Stein of Augsburg, whom Mr. Gough felt certain to be the maker. So brilliant and colourful did a Mozart sonata sound when played on this instrument that the unaided ear, though alert to the difference between what it heard and what it normally hears, could not easily suppose that this was a 'museum' piano. Mozart's rapturous praise of Stein's pianos has so often been quoted that only a few of its sentences need be given here for emphasis of important points. The relevant letter of 17–18 October 1777[2] says: ". . . Späth's claviers had always been my favourites. But now I much prefer Stein's, for they damp ever so much better than the Regensburg instruments. . . . In whatever way I touch the keys, the tone is always even. . . . His instruments have this special advantage over others, that they are made with escape action." Mr. Gough's praise of a similar piano put Mozart's own praise in a modern

---

who had heard Mozart play, later said that his touch was neat and clean, but rather empty, flat, and antiquated." That Beethoven really felt this way about Mozart's pianoforte playing is clearly indicated in his *Conversations-Heft* for the last part of the year 1825. The passage dealing with Mozart begins at p. 26a; Beethoven is talking with Karl Holz, and though we only have Holz's written questions and answers, we can easily imagine the gist of the conversation.

(Holz:) "Haydn considered Don Juan Mozart's greatest work." . . .

(Holz:) "Was Mozart a good piano player?"

(Holz:) "Well [the piano] was still in its cradle then." – EDS.

[1] *Proceedings*: Vol. LXXVII, London, 1951, p. 41.
[2] Anderson: op. cit., Vol. II, pp. 478f.

way. He said that the instrument was free from blocking – the deficiency known even in modern pianos when a damper or a hammer lodges against its string and makes its key mute; he also said that the action was perfect of its kind, allowing the player to rely on uniformity of weight throughout the keyboard, so that only his own deficiency could prevent the realization of his will from contact with a key to its release. To the declaration that the action was perfect of its kind, one has only to add that the sound was, and still is, ideal for Mozart's music.

I do not intend to lay down rules for the performance of Mozart on a modern piano. Only the more foolish organ-lovers show violent certainty as to the way in which Bach should be played on an instrument he neither heard nor conceived, and the speculation that he would have liked this or that modern performance is quite unhelpful. We can be sure that we obey or disobey the composer's orders in one or two matters only – for instance, we know sometimes that Bach intends both hands to be on one keyboard, and we know that Mozart insisted upon strict rhythm in the left hand when the right hand used tempo rubato;[1] but pianos differ greatly, even when they are from the same maker. I must be content to point out a few of the many passages that I cannot make fully Mozartean on my home instrument – a small Bechstein of about 1920 – and to express my conviction that Mozart is ill served if one does not make the best of such passages and others on the instrument provided. (For instance, it seems silly to play a whole sonata una corda, or to withhold the greater range of crescendo or diminuendo allowed by the modern instrument.)

Very early in the collected sonatas we meet passages that remind us of the clavichord and of Mozart's affection for that instrument before he bought his piano, on which, with its shallow keys and 'flutey' tone, Ex. 1 could be controlled as I cannot control it on my Bechstein. Unless I am careful, I find that all modern pianos make too violent the contrasts of Mozart's alternate *f* and *p*. Quotation is unnecessary; bars 30–5 of the popular early G major Sonata (K.283(189h)) or bars 8–12 of the finale of the E flat Sonata just before it (K.282(189g)) will serve for illustration. The range of tone in a crescendo seems welcome,

---

[1] Letter from Mozart to his father, 23 October 1777. Cf. Anderson: op. cit., Vol. II, p. 497.

but the sudden demonstration of that range is not, and a toning down of the contrast seems merely decent, not falsely historical. Quotation is also unnecessary to show the innumerable places in which Mozart's sensitive ear did not expect close notes in the bass to sound thick; a shake in the lower registers of the instrument can be controlled, but it is very difficult to make pleasant the sound of broken chords when they are to be played fast. Sometimes, as in bars 32ff. of the slow movement of the A minor Sonata (K.310(300d)), the omission of notes may be desired, but is ineffective.

Ex.1

It is in the very works which at first sight suggest the glories of later pianism that one most longs for Mozart's instrument. One wishes that a left-hand sostenuto would sing, not boom, against repeated chords in the right hand that would sound brilliant rather than noisy. The sensitive player wants to give direct rein to the expression without the complication of extempore editing – by which I do not mean omission or addition of notes and rests. The point may be made a little clearer if one remembers that, almost unconsciously, one adopts a near-staccato in playing rapid passages, as one does in the G major Prelude and Fugue in Book II of the 'Forty-eight'. Players who have no knowledge of the clavichord or of the early pianoforte will do this from apparently instinctive response to music which seems the worse for heavy resonance. In four-handed pieces, or in solo pieces which use double thirds or other 'octave-coupler' effects, this resonance is very apparent. So it is whenever chords are in close position. The wonderful A minor sonata just mentioned must have been the despair of many a fine piano recitalist. How crude its very opening can sound!

All Mozart's mature keyboard works, with one or two exceptions, were played on the piano and intended for it, and to the reflection that some of his contemporaries must have played his piano pieces on harpsichord or clavichord one should add: 'but not in public'. During the last decade of Mozart's life nearly all professional musicians owned pianos, for there was quite a boom in their manufacture during the 1770s and 1780s. The ascendance of the *galant* concerto as *the* fashionable choice among concert-goers brought the piano into concert-rooms and halls. There, as in the theatre, it took over from the harpsichord the role of continuo instrument – a role fast becoming moribund; but it will be remembered that Haydn sat at the piano[1] to 'direct' his London symphonies. Mozart uses the generic terms 'Clavier' and 'Cembalo', the latter always in concertos, but there need no longer be controversy as to the instrument he had in mind. Nathan Broder has sifted every scrap of available evidence and published a convincing summary.[2]

Just before the ascendance of the new piano – that is to say, in Mozart's boyhood – the clavichord enjoyed a brief climax of special favour, chiefly in Germany. Its champion was C. P. E. Bach, who commended it for the instruction of the young because it was intimate, soulful, and expressive, the best vehicle of *Empfindsamkeit*, or style of tender sentiment, which seemed then to be the antithesis of the *galant* style. The harpsichord was still needed as a concert and continuo instrument, for only its public brilliance could oppose the orchestra in the fashionable concerto until it was ousted by the piano. In Mozart the once-rival styles were fused. When people ceased to regard him as the wonder-child, his playing was admired chiefly for its tender and often disturbing sentiment and for its singing tone. It is therefore significant that in his early twenties, when he was making even more brilliant the style of his friend J. C. Bach in the public concerto, his father mentioned his choice of the clavichord for more intimate playing in a letter of 20 April 1778: "If you could find in Paris a good clavichord, such as we have, you would no doubt prefer it and it would suit you better than a harpsichord."[3] The clavichord which Wolfgang owned after his marriage can be seen in the Salzburg Mozarteum.

The general reader cannot easily examine the fifty or so pieces for harpsichord or clavichord that remain to show Mozart's work for solo keyboard before the writing down of his first set of six sonatas.[4] At present one is tantalized when a scholar who

---

[1] Also at the harpsichord. – EDS.

[2] N. Broder: 'Mozart and the "Clavier",' *Musical Quarterly*, New York, XXVII/4/1941, pp. 422–32.

[3] cf. Anderson: op. cit., Vol. II, p. 781.

[4] A useful miscellany is published by the Associated Board, edited by York Bowen.

has had access to originals quotes some striking or prophetic
passage like Ex. 2. This comes from an Andante in B flat
(K.9b(5b)) composed when the child was seven and printed in
L'Enfant Prodige, the first monumental volume of Mozart biography and criticism undertaken by Wyzewa and St.-Foix.[1] If
Hyatt King had not quoted Ex. 2 in one of his own articles,[2] it
would probably be missing from this one:

There seems to be no reason why, in the age of C. P. E. Bach,
Jomelli, Gluck, and Traetta – the age just after that in which
Rameau had been arraigned as a "distiller of baroque harmonies" – even a convention-loving boy like Mozart should
promise a remarkable future by writing down an occasional
passage of diminished sevenths or other pathetic harmonies.
One does not wish to regard Mozart as any less a prodigy by declaring that, in composition and therefore extemporization, his
claim to the description lies in his doing at seven or eight what
even remarkably musical boys rarely achieve until they are at
least in their fourteenth year. Facility in composition should not
be taken as a promise of significant musical expression. The
great artist is sometimes a boy prodigy and sometimes a slow
and labouring imitator.

The first of Mozart's surviving keyboard pieces were written
down in a note-book to occupy his time in London while his
father was unwell, first with a cold, then a quinsy, during the
winter months of 1764–5. There are over forty, and few of them
foretell that personal style which shows the great impress of
J. C. Bach upon the young man. The few in minor keys would
not attract special attention but for our predisposition to examine them carefully. Scholars assure us that many passages in
these pieces reflect, as we should expect, his acquaintance with
music by his father, by numerous forgotten musicians whose
galant trifles came into the Mozart household at Salzburg, by
the fashionable German musicians who had settled in Paris, especially Schobert, Eckard, and Honauer, by Wagenseil and

[1] cf. Book List, p. 65.   [2] cf. Book List, p. 65.

Vanhal of Vienna, and by Rutini. The chapter on 'Mozart and His Contemporaries' in Einstein's *Mozart*[1] may interest the reader who does not wish to trace 'influences' through the detailed analyses of St.-Foix.

It is from no desire to minimize the achievement of a boy still of our primary school age that one expresses curiosity at the late appearance of that sensitiveness and elegance with which one associates Mozart. Some of the keyboard music of this period, by Mozart and by others, seems a little crude when one of two parts sounds like a continuo bass without figures. Were the chords sometimes filled in? Did Mozart really play Ex. 3(a)? The answer seems to be 'yes', because in the second variation on the theme from which the passage is taken, a third strand of harmony is written out, as at Ex. 3(b). In the first variation the passage remains crude (Ex. 3(c)). A much later set of variations,

sufficiently interesting to be worth playing, includes blemishes like Ex. 4. The consecutive octaves and fifths are not surprising, for there are plenty of these in young Mozart's work. They do not 'stick' or offend the convention-loving ear if one of them occurs in a chord of the seventh. What one does not expect in Mozart is the progression over the bar line in Ex. 4.

[1] A. Einstein: *Mozart*, London, 1946, pp. 108–34.

From a sonata composed as late as 1778 comes Ex. 5(a) with the ungainly similar motion to the octave; in later years he would have altered this to something like Ex. 5(b).

It would be mistaken to say that one could determine the musical value of a piece by Mozart, or its degree of originality, by its elegance or technical perfection; but it is not mistaken to assert that Mozart's stylistic congruity developed along with his originality. It is worth noting that a mature musician of mere general ability can often compose with more invention than the immature genius. 'Invention' describes the *conscious* search for attractive rhythms, the *conscious* avoidance of trite harmony or melody which is the mark of the good professional musician – the Kapellmeister or film composer who knows he is no genius, but has been well trained in self-criticism and is qualified to guide a budding artist destined to be six times his size. Thus the minuets composed in his mid-twenties by Attwood for Mozart's correction seem more inventive than any of the minuets composed by Mozart himself in his early teens.

Apart from a number of very early and musically unimportant works (e.g., K.Anh.199–202(33d–g)), the first six sonatas which need to be discussed are K.279–284(189d–h and 205b). They belong to the years 1774–5, and it seems fairly obvious that they were written down so that a copy could be taken by the sort of admirer on whose recommendations a touring musician's success largely depended in the eighteenth century. One cannot but hold those critics mistaken who think them to have been written chiefly for teaching pupils. This purpose is advanced to explain their alleged weakness and complaisance, for even C. B. Oldman in the new Grove, scouting the 'teaching' idea, speaks of the first six sonatas as "the weakest". In all humility, one wishes the word had not been used. When one returns to them after long neglect, one marvels at their excellence at their own level.

Mozart's letters prove conclusively how, when planning concertos for the public concerts by which he first supported himself after breaking away from Salzburg and the Archbishop, he deliberately courted the taste of his audiences while gradually acclimatizing them to music that was personal and complicated, both structurally and emotionally. Köchel's catalogue gives clear proof that he followed similar considerations with his first sonatas, for K.312(189i) is the first movement of an unfinished sonata in G minor. Its mere opening, Ex. 6,[1] shows that here is the first of the famous succession of works in G minor of which an example is notably missing from the complete sonatas,

yet this might have been one of the first set of six! Can there be any doubt as to why it was not?

There are one or two decidedly arresting movements in the first set of sonatas, notably the slow movement in F minor, significantly marked adagio, in K.280(189e), the second sonata, and pointing to the great Rondo in A minor; then the opening Adagio of the fourth (K.282(189g)), in E flat, and the theme of the variations in the last (K.284(205b)), with the so-called 'irregular' barring that is rare in Mozart's themes. Moreover, this D major Sonata, the last of the group, which was composed for Baron Dürnitz, is the most forceful, ambitious, and unusual in its sequence of movements – Allegro, 'Rondeau en Polonaise' (Andante), theme and variations. But it is not these remarkable pieces which need defence; rather does one feel impelled to call for recognition of the merits of the sonatas as a whole and the enjoyment of them for what they are, not for what we wish that they were. "Art is not entertainment", a critic recently and sincerely proclaimed, but he could as truthfully have said, "Food is not cake". The quality of its entertainment, its light music and dance music, tells us if an age or a race is civilized, and the fact that much modern music, when not associated with an ambitious design or elevated purpose, sounds machine-made, dull, silly, or downright moronic, shows that democracy has a poor taste in pleasures. The poetic vein of Mozart's

[1] The left hand doubles at the lower octave, as at the opening of the great C minor Fantasia, which this opening foretells.

great music is obvious; what needs recognition is the growth of seemingly conventional details into exquisite paragraphs and movements in music which we are foolish to depreciate from a supposition that what is perfect for the drawing-room would be better if it smelt of the schoolroom, church, theatre, or study. When we hear a first-rate player manage Ex. 7 perfectly we can regard Mozart's early sonatas as unambitious:

The writing of the first set of six sonatas began when Mozart was nearly nineteen, and if all facts were known we should probably find that references in letters to "my sonata in . . ." (this or that key) were sometimes to works that had *not* been written but were known to his family. Mozart had not only a phenomenal memory, but also the ability of the mathematician and the fine chess or billiards player to imagine the state of a problem or game 'several moves ahead'; such ability is precious to a composer whose life is full of distractions from the solitude of a study, and it enables us to understand how a man who confesses to giving "enormous time and labour" to composition had a reputation for extreme speed in the process. He is observed to be silent at the end of a meal, and to be folding and unfolding his napkin; he withdraws and returns in an incredibly short time and in good spirits, having fully scored a complete movement. The speed is in the writing; as to how long and how arduous was the previous process – the real composition – nobody could tell unless Mozart himself remembered. It is ridiculous to suppose, therefore, that the composer himself thought less than highly of sonatas which he had long in mind, and could have revised before writing[1] after noting their effect at the various houses in which he stayed on his tours.

[1] Mozart made many more drafts and sketches than is often realized. Probably most of these were destroyed immediately after they had served their purpose, and it is only sheer accident that some have survived. The autograph of the 'Dürnitz' Sonata in D, K.284(205b), includes seventy-one bars of a draft to the Allegro which is significantly different from the final version. Facsimile in Robert Haas, *Mozart*, Potsdam, 2/1950, pp. 53f. – Eds.

Undoubtedly, however, Mozart disappoints us, in the keyboard works as in symphonies, when the next work in a series seems to show artistic retrogression rather than advance. The G minor Sonata was not finished. Nothing like it follows, just as nothing comparable follows the wonderful A minor Sonata composed in Paris. The next two solo sonatas, after the first six, were composed to extend his repertory on his visit to Mannheim in 1777, after his meeting with Stein and his glowing tribute to the new pianos. The first, K.309(284b) in C, had already been played at Augsburg before it was written down at Mannheim, for in a letter of 23 October 1777 he says that at his last concert in Augsburg he played "all of a sudden a magnificent sonata in C major, out of my head, and a Rondo to finish up with".[1] When it was written down it must have been given a new middle movement, for he declared that this piece was a portrait of Rosa Cannabich, daughter of the brilliant Mannheim Kapellmeister.[2]

It is not fanciful to see these two sonatas as influenced by the composer's enthusiasm for the Stein instrument. They are richer than the earlier ones, and the last two movements of K.311(284c) in D are expansive and assured, almost as if their materials could be used in concertos; the finale, we note, is the first to have the six-eight rondo of a type used in concertos. There is a lame passage in the first movement which shows that even a Mozart did not at once master an unusual procedure. He begins his middle section by what became a favourite device – developing a little coda to the first section. He proceeds admirably till bar 54. Three bars later, for the first time in the sonatas, he departs from convention by introducing one of his former second-group themes in the key of G, instead of going to a formal reprise of

Ex.8

his opening idea in D (Ex. 8); but surely his artifice is not well enough concealed to be called *summa ars*. Had he revised the

[1] Anderson: op. cit., Vol. II, p. 498.
[2] See, however, Einstein's remarks in his revision of Köchel, p. 353. – EDS.

sonata in later years he might have used his 'extension' technique, for one recalls the sort of thing parodied by Ex. 8(a):

Ex. 8(a)

The unconventional procedure is one of several which could be quoted to oppose the ridiculous untruth that composers before Beethoven were "content to recapitulate their expositions with the necessary adjustment of key". The passage quoted at Ex. 1 occurs only in the so-called recapitulatory section; Ex. 7 should be compared with its original form in the exposition, and by the time we reach the few sonatas written in the years of the best concertos, quartets, quintets, and symphonies we may often find the most exquisite work precisely at the "necessary adjustment of key". Sometimes, as in the C minor Sonata, K.457, at bars 120ff., completely new and pathetic ideas are introduced; sometimes, as in the Sonata in F, K.533, at bar 154ff., the texture reveals contrapuntal possibilities that were formerly withheld.

We need no finer example of the art just mentioned than bars 88ff. of the next work to be discussed, the Sonata in A minor, K.310(300d), one of the greatest of the piano sonatas. The extreme difficulty of a work like this – slow movement and finale as well as first movement – is not that of, say, the 'Hammerklavier' Sonata, which needs a virtuoso if all notes are to be played and all directions obeyed; most holders of piano-playing diplomas can depress the right keys in this Mozart sonata, but rarely with the right relative force or in the required rhythm. Few can let the music breathe its own life, for the tares grow with simultaneous vitality. What recitalist plays this first movement maestoso, as directed, and finishes at the opening speed? The intense developments over pedal points in the middle section are difficult to control, and so is much of the left-hand part. Few players can make the runs of semiquavers on the lower stave "flow like oil" or prevent ♩♩ from becoming ♩♩♩. Only one previous work by Mozart, the violin Sonata in E minor (K.304(300c)) composed a month or so earlier, contains music at all like this.

The four sonatas, K.330–333(300h–k and 315c), written in Paris during the summer and autumn of 1778, seem to show the composer's reaction to a cold reception of the work in A minor. The texture of the first, in C major, is almost as finely wrought as that of its predecessor, but only the deservedly popular slow movement, with its haunting strophes in a minor key, reaches a comparable emotional level. The next sonata, in Mozart's sunniest key, A major, was surely designed to please Paris by its exceptional sequence of movements – variations, minuet, rondo 'Alla Turca'. Einstein calls the variations' theme "utterly French", and notices that the sonata contains "instead of a polonaise[1] the most French of all dance forms", and "ends with a true *scène de ballet*".[2] Perhaps these facts explain one's feeling that the sonata, being more of its own time than of all time, is less attractive than its neighbours.

Its successor in F, K.332, is better known than any other except the fine 'Trumpet' Sonata in D, K.576. The student could hardly undertake a finer lesson in composition than the comparison of their first movements. The F major spreads; seven isolable, lengthy ideas, most of them lyrical, are used before we reach the middle section, which is begun with yet another new minuet-like melody. The D major is compact, and could be used to illustrate the prevalent conception of 'sonata form' as based on two 'subjects' – the first a 'motive', capable of contrapuntal and imitative development, the second for 'lyrical contrast'. If, within a general design, mastery of form is shown by organic growth of ideas (and not the pre-fabrication and forcing of ideas into a mould) then 'economy' is no term of praise unless it takes its original connotation and is not a synonym of 'parsimony'. Despite much modern teaching, there is no great achievement in composing a monothematic movement unless it has as much interest as a polythematic one.

Undoubtedly, however, Mozart sometimes used the type of thematic economy we associate with Beethoven, and did so without anticipating Beethovenian effects. The last piano Concerto (K.595, in B flat) and the last complete piano sonata are outstanding examples, and this F major sonata in the middle of the 'Paris' group is their antithesis both in design and effect. Its three splendid movements, without often suggesting orchestral technique (except when there are 'horn fifths' or ''cello

[1] cf. the sequence of movements of K.284, p. 41.   [2] op. cit., p. 245.

tunes'), show the futility of considering only the influence of keyboard music upon Mozart's finest piano works. Yet the slow
movement, which must surely have been enjoyed by Chopin,
could well represent the summit of expression that Mozart
reached without departing from the formality and reticence of
his epoch. Here is the art of J. C. Bach made ethereal, the very
opening paragraph having the general and subsidiary antitheses of the most polished Popian couplets. The B flat Sonata
(K.333(315c)), which completes the 'Paris' set, is also polished
and *galant*, and there can be little doubt that J. C. Bach, who
visited Paris in the late summer of 1778, had given Mozart a
preview of the sonatas he was soon to publish (Op. 17). We
should probably hold Mozart's last Paris sonata in greater
esteem but for the great popularity of its predecessor in F, to
which it is no rival in spaciousness of effect; but the rhythm and
chromatic harmony just after the double bar in the slow movement is audacious beyond anything in the other Paris sonatas.

Mozart needed no new sonatas when he left Paris for a return
visit to Mannheim, which he loved, and in which he saw several
new operas and hoped for an operatic commission: nor did he
need new sonatas when he returned to conservative Salzburg.
In his home town during the next two years he composed
masses and other church music, including organ sonatas, some
divertimenti, the Concerto for two pianos (K.365(316a)), and
the lovely Sinfonia Concertante for violin and viola, K.364
(320d). Then came news from Munich, which he had visited
on the way home from Mannheim: he was to compose the
opera for the carnival of 1781, and so *Idomeneo* (K.366) fully
occupied his attention. His relations with the Archbishop were
reaching a climax, and when he had broken free from that de-
tested service he set out to conquer Vienna by his 'academies' –
the subscription concerts for which the great series of piano
concertos was inaugurated. No doubt sonatas, as also sets of
variations and extempore playing, were served to his new audiences, but with his settlement in Vienna his next compositions
for chamber groups began. It is therefore easy to understand
why we lack a new piano sonata composed during the six years
after Mozart's return from Paris. He wrote most of a very fine
first movement in B flat (K.400(372a)) which is included in Ser.
XXIV of the *Collected Works*, with the recapitulatory section
ably finished by the Abbé Stadler.

Mozart himself published the C minor Sonata of October 1784 together with the wonderful fantasia in the same key. They rightly appear together in our collections as 'Fantasia and Sonata in C minor', K.475 and 457, the fantasia having been written down later, May 1785. This fantasia is unique because no other piece by Mozart contains such strongly contrasted ideas in so short a space. It is also the only one of Mozart's solo fantasias that is quite satisfactory when played as a single work, for the others sound like preludes, and need either a following movement or a final section to fulfil the promise of a stormy beginning. The noble C minor Sonata opens with such drive and energy that the fantasia can precede it without spoiling it, and the slow movement, though less nervous and arresting than the slow section of the fantasia, reminds us of it. Its phrases are less powerful than those of the fantasia only because we know that they will not explode; instead of being charged in a way that leads to storm, they are charged with pathos and lyrical yearning. The storm is over, but the clouds are still of a kind that are seen only when there has been storm. In technical terms, this Adagio is full of an intricate play of expression and dynamic marks – there are six within the first three bars. No wonder that this music seems linked with the fantasia; if it were charged heavily enough to bring storm again, it could not have its present wonderful expansiveness and symphonic effect.

This C minor Sonata, still more the fantasia, is called Beethovenian by more than one musician who should pass the remark with more caution. Only the opening ideas of the fantasia and of the two outside movements of the sonata could have been penned by Beethoven – the affinity could be explained by common ancestry in the expression of C. P. E. Bach and Haydn – but the very first treatment of those ideas is utterly un-Beethovenian, and if anyone supposes the pathetic modulations in any of these movements to be Beethovenian, he has far to go before he knows Mozart well. Strange though the fact may seem to the average reader, Mozart's harmonic vocabulary is wider than Beethoven's – a statement not to be taken as implying that his expressive use of that vocabulary exceeded Beethoven's, but that in two comparable works, such as this fantasia-cum-sonata and Beethoven's 'Sonata pathétique' in the same key, Mozart's expression needs a larger number of technical descriptions if we have nothing better to do than draw up a list of the chords used.

If the harmonic technique is not Beethovenian, neither is the performing technique. The basic style of playing does not change with Mozart's increasing demands upon a pianist's hands, and no doubt Mozart played this fiery music with as few shifts of the body and hand as were needed in one of his urbane concerto movements. An illustration from the work under discussion may show the point. The downward arpeggio in Ex. 9 from the Adagio of this sonata forms a diminished seventh chord; the passage and the content would be quite satisfying to the ear if it were a dominant seventh chord, but in that case the B naturals would become B flats, and if the reader cares to try the passage with this alteration he will see that technical as well as expressive reasons account for Mozart's choice, even if he was quite unconscious of alternatives at this point:

The work happens to be dedicated to one of Mozart's pupils, Therese von Trattner, whose husband was a printer and publisher. Mozart calls it Opus XI,[1] and, as Einstein says, the lost instruction for its performance must have been "one of the most important documents of Mozart's aesthetic practice".[2]

From this time (1785–6), the magnificent quality of the C minor sonata is maintained in future sonatas except the 'beginners'' Sonata in C, K.545, which, alone among the collected sonatas, was avowedly composed for teaching and is not important enough for discussion here.[3]

Some readers may think the Sonata in F major of 1788, K.533, to be even finer than K.457 in C minor, not just because of its

[1] It was published with the fantasia by Artaria in 1785. – EDS.

[2] op. cit., p. 247.

[3] Nevertheless, the sonata's irregular recapitulation of its first subject (in F major!) is of interest, particularly so in view of the pedagogic context. K.Anh.135 and 138a(547a, formerly 54), in F major, composed in 1788, includes not only Mozart's own transcription of the 'Andante con variazioni' from K.547 (a 'beginners'' Sonata in F for violin and piano) but the finale of K.545 (used as second movement). That Mozart turned again to K.545 when putting together K.547a suggests that he did not think ill of the earlier sonata. – EDS.

clever counterpoint (Mozart had written several fugues in the previous few months), but because in it he achieves the feat of expressing intense feelings with a major key. In the first movement the main themes themselves do not seem emotional, and the emotions aroused by their treatment with biting harmony and unexpected counterpoint cannot be named, for they belong entirely to music, not literature. The way in which Mozart fashions the wonderful ending of this movement is not described, lest any reader who has not yet explored it should lose the pleasure of discovery; let one clue suffice – no new theme is introduced. The sonata was not finished. For a finale Mozart tacked on the Rondo in F, K.494, composed previously for a pupil, as were other rondos. Einstein declares that Mozart "paid no attention to . . . unity of style". There were special circumstances; "he owed his friend and publisher Hoffmeister money . . . and . . . partly acquitted the debt with this sonata". He also observes that the first two movements are "for an entirely different and more powerful instrument than is the innocent rondo, which is written mostly for the middle register".[1] Nevertheless, only one who knew the facts would notice the incongruity after hearing the beautiful three-part polyphony of the section in F minor, and the masterly *trompe-l'oreille* of the 'false stretto' that begins the cadenza.

The 'little piano Sonata in C for Beginners' has been mentioned. There follows another, K.570 in B flat, that is almost as little in length, but decidedly not for beginners. On the contrary, it may serve as a test of connoisseurs. Like the D major Sonata, K.576, the last in our volumes, it has the perfect workmanship of those fine and happy movements in quartets and quintets which are less memorable than the pathetic ones because we tend to be more impressed by art that is emotionally disturbing than by art that is simply sunny or athletic – adjectives which could describe these last two sonatas respectively. Both date from 1789, two years before the end, and though the vigour and virtuosity of composition in the D major is so obvious that the sonata takes precedence in general favour, the B flat is scarcely

---

[1] op. cit., p. 248. The rondo is by no means as innocent as Einstein believes. Moreover, Mozart thoroughly revised the movement when publishing it as the sonata's finale. In the original version of K.494, the cadenza of twenty-seven bars is missing entirely. Indeed, it is by no means impossible that the first two movements were written especially to precede K.494. – EDS.

less masterly. It is therefore one of the sonatas concerning which one often hears a pianist speak with enthusiasm after 'rediscovering' it.

Fifteen sets of variations for solo keyboard are printed in Ser. XXI of the *Collected Works*. None touches the heights of the variation movements in the piano concertos and chamber works nor of the set in G for piano duet. Like most of the sonatas, they belong to the earlier stages of Mozart's career. Each set is at present being reprinted by Augener, and therefore the reader may like to know the complete list in chronological order, with the source of the 'airs'. An asterisk is placed against those sets the 'rediscovery' of which is most likely to please the home pianist.

Written in Holland (The Hague) in January 1766, when the boy was aged ten. Published in March 1766.	K.Anh.208 (24)	8 vns. in G. Theme 'Laat ons Juichen', a patriotic song by C. E. Graaf, born in 1723, composer and director 'de la musique princière' at The Hague.
Written in Amsterdam in February 1766 and published in the same year.	K.25	7 vns. in D on the national song 'Willem van Nassau',[1] probably dating from early seventeenth cent., composer not known.
Written during the short visit to Vienna in the autumn of 1773. Published *c.* 1780 (1778?).	*K.180(173c)	6 vns. in G on 'Mio caro Adone', air from Salieri's opera, *La fiera di Venezia*.
Written at Salzburg in the summer of 1774. Published *c.* 1780 (1778?).	K.179(189a)	12 vns. in G on a minuet by Johann Christian Fischer (1733–1800), a North German oboist who settled in London, was a friend of J. C. Bach's, and took a prominent part in the Bach-Abel and Vauxhall concerts.
Written in Paris during the late summer of 1778. Published in 1786.	K.264(315d)	9 vns. in C on 'Lison dormait', air from an immensely popular opera, *Julie*. The origins and life of its composer, N. Dezède, are wrapped in mystery, but he held the French lyric stage until after the Revolution.
Written in Paris during the early summer of 1778. Published *c.* 1785.	*K.265(300e)	9 vns. in C on 'Ah, vous dirai-je, Maman'. The tune is known in English nurseries to 'Baa, baa, black sheep'. Dezède is thought by some scholars to be its composer, but by the time of Mozart's visit, France had "adopted it as a folk-song" as these islands had adopted 'Lilliburlero'.
Written in Paris during the summer of 1778. Published in 1786.	K.353(300f)	12 vns. in E flat on the song 'La belle Françoise'. Source unknown.[2] Its character suggests a 'village opera'.
Written in Paris during the spring or summer of 1778. Published *c.* 1780 (1778?).	K.354(299a)	12 vns. in E flat on the song 'Je suis Lindor' from the music to Beaumarchais's *Le Barbier de Séville*. Composer unknown, perhaps Beaumarchais himself.
Written in Vienna in June 1781. Published in 1786.	K.352(374c)	8 vns. in F on a march from Grétry's opera, *Les Mariages samnites*.
Played (probably improvised) by Mozart at his Vienna concert of 23 March 1783. Like the previous set of vns., it was published in Vienna by Artaria in 1786.	*K.398(416e)	6 vns. in F on the male voice chorus 'Salve tu, Domine' from Paisiello's *I filosofi immaginarii*.

[1] Mozart wrote a fugue on 'Willem van Nassau' as No. 18 of his *Galimathias musicum* (K.Anh.100a(K.32)). See *The Smaller Orchestral Works*, pp. 152f. – EDS.

[2] See, however, Einstein's revision of Köchel, p. 1000. – EDS.

Composed June 1784; omitted from Mozart's own catalogue; published in 1806.	K.460(454a)	8 vns. in A on the aria 'Come un' agnello' from Sarti's opera, *Fra i due litiganti il terzo gode*. The same tune is played by the tiny wind-band of waits during Don Giovanni's supper, and is quoted in the second of the German Dances, K.509.[1]
Extemporized at Mozart's concert of 23 March 1783, at which Gluck was present. Written on 25 August 1784. No. 7 in Mozart's catalogue. Published in 1785.	**K.455	10 vns. in G on the comic song 'Unser dummer Pöbel meint' from Gluck's *Singspiel*, *Pilger von Mekka*. In the French version of this work, *La rencontre imprévue*, the song is called 'Les hommes pieusement'.
Written on 12 September 1786 in Vienna. No. 45 in Mozart's catalogue. Published by Hoffmeister, c. 1786.	K.500	12 vns. in B flat upon an 'Allegretto', whether by Mozart or another composer we do not know.
Written in Potsdam on 29 April 1789. No. 105 in Mozart's catalogue. Published in 1792.	K.573	9 vns. in D on a minuet by Jean Pierre Duport, leading 'cellist and later director of Frederick the Great's orchestra. Frederick William II, to whom Mozart was presented at this time, was Duport's pupil.
Written in Vienna in March 1791. No. 134 in Mozart's catalogue. Published in 1791.	*K.613	8 vns. in F on the song 'Ein Weib ist das herrlichste Ding', by B. Schack (or F. Gerl), used in Schikaneder's play, *Der dumme Gärtner*. The first sentence of the theme is the introduction to the song.

To say that sets of variations were acceptable to home players and therefore accepted by publishers, that young ladies and their parents liked them because they were easy to follow and sounded more difficult than they really were, and that Mozart used them for teaching pupils – all this is not apologist's fancy. The number of references in the correspondence between father and son to some of the least valuable sets of variations is disproportionate to their importance except as regards the composer's advance in popular favour. A letter of 10 December 1778[2] from Leopold suggests that the circulation of manuscript copies[3] impairs the sale of printed ones, and it is noticeable that sets of variations are among the rare keyboard works to be published at all before Mozart's death. For a long time the 'Fischer' (K.179(189a)) set was one of Mozart's show pieces, used, as were others, for 'encores' at his concerts. This is a set which sold well, and it is one of the most empty.

The sets given an asterisk in the above list are not merely those which contain a moving 'minor' variation or one marked 'adagio', nor those wherein Mozart makes widest departure from the theme or composes a grand finale. A set like K.265(300e) or 398(416e) is worth playing as one of Mozart's pupils would have been made to play it. We should practise

---

[1] See *The Smaller Orchestral Works*, pp. 147f. – EDS.

[2] Anderson: op. cit., Vol. II, pp. 950–1.

[3] Leopold Mozart does not actually mention manuscript copies, but the danger of too frequent performance.

each variation as a little study till the whole set "flows like oil" and at the right speed. The opinion seems universally held that the set on Gluck's chorus is the finest of these, and it certainly recalls the finale of the G major Concerto, K.453, of the same year. If he had chosen the Gluck theme for the finale of the concerto, the variations could have been of the same order as they are now, for the last of them is expanded with the same wit as the last one in the concerto and already has its cadenza.

The solo variations are eclipsed by the superb set in G for piano duet, K.501. The fact that the theme is not found in any other extant music by Mozart prevents our asserting that it is his own. Though it seems perfect for its purpose, it can also be imagined as occurring in a play or opera, either as a song or as

Ex.10 *Andante*

incidental music. The sheer arrangement of the enchanting theme and variations now being discussed is sensitive beyond anything else written for piano duet, and a passage from the

theme is quoted here along with one of its variations so that the
reader who does not know the work may know his or her loss
(Ex. 10 and Ex. 10(a)):

Because publishers expected no large sale, four-handed music
was rarely printed until Mozart's time. Several libraries contain
duet sonatas by J. C. and W. F. Bach, but Wotquenne mentions
none by C. P. E. Bach. Burney's sonatas for two instruments
were printed in 1777 and J. C. Bach's for four hands at one instrument two years previously. We may have lost many manuscripts of duets, including some either composed by the boy
Mozart or acquired for him. Part of the public exhibition of
Mozart and his sister included their playing together at one
keyboard, as shown in one of the family portraits.[1]

The Sonata in C, K.19d, is dated by Einstein in his edition
of Köchel "before 9 July 1765 in London", with the cautionary
note that the quotation Nissen makes from a letter of Leopold

[1] cf. Einstein: op. cit., plate facing p. 372. See also n.1, p. 83, of Anderson:
op. cit., Vol. I.

Mozart, supposedly authenticating the date, is suspect.[1] St.-
Foix discovered in Paris a printed copy of the work. If it does
belong to 1765, then Mozart at nine could distribute music
between four hands better than J. C. Bach, especially in the
splendid minuet and trio which forms the middle movement. So
well written is this sonata that the duets of seven years later
seem to show very little advance. Can it therefore be a much
later work?[2] Mozart's sister wrote to Breitkopf & Härtel in
1800, declaring that she could not trace the copies of the
duets which she played with her brother when they were on
tour.

Yet the first two four-hand sonatas usually found in our collections were undoubtedly composed for performance with his
sister. K.381(123a) in D (*c.* 1772) and K.358(186c) in B flat
(1774) were both written in Salzburg, and both are known to
have been played in Paris and Vienna. If they were reduced to
two staves and arranged for two hands, they would be markedly
inferior to the first set of solo sonatas, but the very comparison is
a little foolish. To their first audiences, four-hand sonatas were
still novelties whose chief interest lay in their textures and play
of sonorities – the doublings of melody, the scraps of dialogue
and concertante with which modern students are soon satiated
after playing a few duet arrangements of orchestral works. It is a
pity, therefore, that critics have led us to believe that the slow
movements alone are worth inspection. It was as easy for
Mozart to 'turn on' tender sentiment as to 'turn on' rattling brilliance, and we should be sure that we do not yield to our own
sentimental fallacy when we seek more than well-contrived display in work obviously intended for display. Several writers
commend the slow movements but regard the last movement of
K.358(186c) as the emptiest of the six finales. If one sets out
with the 'art is not entertainment' text, a huge amount of
Mozart's finest work, including the deservedly popular Sonata
in D for two pianos, K.448(375a), and some of the most enchanting and brilliant finales to his concertos, could illustrate
a sermon on vanity. If one does not, the finale of K.358 is
particularly enjoyable.

Many years after these Salzburg sonatas came the great four-

---

[1] cf. also Einstein: op. cit., p. 270.

[2] Mozart seems to recall the theme of the sonata's finale in the Serenade for
winds, K.361(370a). See *The Serenades for Wind Band*, p. 76. – EDS.

handed specimens in F, K.497[1] – the finest of all duet sonatas –
and in C, K.521.[2] We know the date of the C major from a letter
of 29 May 1787 asking Baron Gottfried von Jacquin to give it to
his sister and to tell her to practise it at once, "for it is rather
difficult".[3] This is still a display piece, but of a finer order than
the Salzburg works, for it contains on every page some of the
most felicitous examples of interplay between the duettists, and
reveals much of the technique Mozart had acquired during his
mastery of the piano concerto. Nevertheless, it sounds no more
than it is – an excellent concert piece for young ladies. Mozart
later dedicated it to the daughters of a rich merchant, Natorp,
and not to the Jacquins. The magnificent earlier Sonata, K.497,
is not entertainment for Jacquins and Natorps; its performers
should have been Mozart and Schubert. Like Schubert's 'Grand
Duo', it is on a symphonic scale with a magnificent and lengthy
slow introduction and three following movements which contain
the full wealth of Mozartean contrast – euphony and counterpoint, brilliance and tenderness, suggestion of the orchestra and
suggestion of chorus and solo work in opera. The first allegro
movement points to Schubert, especially the Schubert of the
Fifth Symphony in B flat, a work that is not the less Schubertian
because it notably reveals its composer's debt to Mozart. Several
people have attempted to score K.497, for one cannot help hearing a pair of oboes, a pair of horns, and, above all, Mozart's
important viola line. Yet the work remains pure piano concertante and baffles the clever orchestrator as much as does
Schubert's 'Grand Duo'.

The fine but, to me, emotionally unimpressive Sonata in D
for two pianos, K.448, was composed in November 1781 for
performance by Mozart and Fräulein von Aurnhammer, a lady
who is said to have been enamoured of him. She certainly pes-
tered him for lessons, and he certainly admired her playing,
for he often chose her as his partner in the E flat Concerto,
K.365(316c), to which he had added clarinets, trumpets, and
drums for its performances in Vienna. The D major Sonata is
one of Mozart's supreme essays in the *galant* style. Einstein has

[1] K.357(497a), the substantial fragments of the first two movements of a sonata
in G (four hands), belongs to the same period. – Eds.

[2] "It is not without significance that Mozart wrote on the autograph of the two
parts *Cembalo primo* and *Cembalo secondo*, for the work would only gain by being
performed on two instruments." Einstein: op. cit., p. 272. Cf. also K.501.

[3] Anderson: op. cit., Vol. III, p. 1352.

well written of it: "The art with which the two parts are made completely equal, the play of the dialogue, the delicacy and re-finement of the figuration, the feeling for sonority in the com-bination and exploitation of the registers of the two instruments – all these things exhibit such mastery that this apparently super-ficial and entertaining work is at the same time one of the most profound and most mature of all Mozart's compositions."[1] One cavils only at "profound", which one reserves for works one feels as well as admires at a certain depth. Of such a work Fate has deprived us, for Mozart began another sonata for piano duet in the key of B flat, written early in 1782, with an intro-ductory Grave followed by a Presto in triple measure and a beautiful Andante that seems like a theme for variations. These impressive fragments, K.Anh.42(375b), seem to belong to an-other and even finer sonata for Mozart to play with Josephine Aurnhammer. (The fragments are printed in the *Collected Edition*.)

'Fantasias' is given inverted commas, for it is quite a mis-nomer when applied to the two tremendous two-movement duets in F minor, K.594 and K.608, both written for a musical clock (the transcriptions are not Mozart's). The first is a brilliant, contrapuntal Allegro in F, in the style of an organ concerto by Handel, but an Adagio in F minor is prologue and epilogue to it. The second, a favourite with organ recitalists, is extremely difficult for four hands or for two hands and feet. A grand prelude in which a grupetto figure is punctuated by crashing chords, such as diminished sevenths, leads to one of the most convincing fugues Mozart ever wrote; a tender and digni-fied slow movement follows in the relative major, and then the fugue returns with a new countersubject and a more climactic build, as becomes the final section of a great work. These grand duets, which Bach might have called overtures, partitas, or even concertos, contain none of the wayward, quasi-impro-visando rhapsodizing of the solo fantasias, no doubt so named after C. P. E. Bach's example. On the contrary, their structure is monumentally dignified, the paragraphs symmetrical, the details precise. We are concerned with them only as duets, for only thus were they issued, the first during Mozart's life, and the second after his death by an admirer called Mederitsch.

The clockwork organ was in a museum of antique and Orien-

[1] op. cit., p. 273.

tal curiosities collected by Count Deym, who was soon to col-
lect Mozart's death mask. The important new addition of 1790
was a wax figure of Field-Marshal Laudon, who had died in the
summer. It was shown in a mausoleum, and perhaps the F
minor 'Fantasia' (K.594), in its archaic 'baroque' style, was
designed to heighten the *tombeau* effect. Mozart began what he
called "the Adagio" (not called 'Fantasia' until issued for piano
duet) while on his way to Frankfurt's coronation celebrations,
at which he hoped to have more part than the playing of his
'Coronation' Concerto in D, K.537. The composition of the
piece was distasteful to him, and in a letter to his wife of 3
October he wrote: "I have to break off now and then, as I get
bored. . . . If . . . the work would sound like an organ piece,
then I might get some fun out of it. But as it is, the works consist solely of little pipes, which sound too high-pitched and too
childish for my taste."[1] Very long ears would guess that this
Adagio bored its composer. Let it be granted that K.608 ("an
organ piece for a clock"), the fiery one of the two 'fantasias', is
rather the greater of the two, but both works are the most
powerful, sonorous, and original piano duets Mozart ever invented; each is unique music utterly unlike anything for a clockwork organ. Although we cannot see how the texture of the
'fantasias' transforms that of the pieces for the clockwork organ,
we can compare one of Mozart's blue-prints for Deym (or his
mechanic) with its translation for piano because the incipits are
shown in Köchel. The Andante "for a little clockwork organ",
K.616, is on two treble staves, as are the pieces for glass harmonica listed near it; the translation for piano, K.Anh.145a, is
called 'Rondo'.[2]

One more four-handed work has to be mentioned, the Fugue
in C minor for two pianos, K.426, composed in 1783. Mozart
began an impressive prelude to it[3] (the Allegro in C minor,
K.Anh.44(426a)), but did not finish it. He later scored the
Fugue for string quartet[4] or string orchestra and added the
beautiful introductory Adagio, K.546. An arrangement of the
Adagio is usually played when the Fugue is given in its original

[1] Anderson: op. cit., Vol. III, pp. 1403ff.
[2] A volume of Mozart's fantasias and rondos, edited by L. Köhler and R.
Schmidt, is published by Novello.
[3] Einstein: op. cit., p. 273.
[4] See *The Chamber Music*, pp. 130f. – EDS.

form by two pianists. For a clear interplay of the partners, the Fugue is too full of entries and, but for the crossing of its parts, might as well be played on one piano. It is probably better appreciated, therefore, on strings.

The Fugue in C minor is a noble work, but a strained one, strenuous in a way that the most complex of Bach's demonstrations of the art never are, and for reasons unknown to Bach.[1] A fugue by Haydn or Mozart is like a 'gothic' church of the Laud-Cosin period, where shapes that were once the natural outcome of a general design were set before the builder as an 'applied design'; the analogy breaks down because the composer is both builder and designer. Now, if cross-fertilization of styles were to be condemned outright as pastiche, then we should wish that St. Paul's and the Wren churches had all been destroyed. Renaissance architecture does not strike us as archaic, and we do not find it any less a manifestation of genius when it shows a touch of the curious or precious. What tells is something to which the copying was first necessary as a catalyst. Academic copying of classical models (in visual arts or in music) is a means to greater insight into the originals and the minds of their creators. This is a cultural study, like the learning of a classical language; it is not a creative study if by that we mean a highway to urgent modern expression. Imitation is creative in one sense of the word if delight in the process makes the imitator share the experience of the composer he imitates. Mozart and Beethoven, like van Swieten and even Mozart's musically intelligent wife, recognized something in the fugal art of an older generation that no contemporaries could show, and they thought, quite rightly, that it could invigorate urgent expression. Only that expression concerns us; we do not play Beethoven's fugues for Albrechtsberger at recitals, for they are now curiosities, not works of art. Nor do we need most of Mozart's fugues for solo piano, for the plain reason that they contain little Mozart and we can always play the 'Forty-eight'.

For all its over-strenuousness, the C minor Fugue for two pianos (or for strings) contains a great deal of fine Mozart. What he did not at first recognize, and what many teachers of an abstraction called 'fugue' still often fail to recognize in

---

[1] There is a fascinating chapter entitled 'Mozart and Counterpoint' in Einstein, op. cit., pp. 144–56. Cf. also A. Hutchings: *A Companion to Mozart's Piano Concertos*, London, 1948, pp. 123ff.

Bach's fugues is that one differs from another in structure and therefore in character as do other men's symphonies, sonatas, or quartets. Teaching is stultified if one kind of design is set up as absolutely ideal, so that any subject must be forced through all the devices of a ricercar and made to flatter the nonsensical declaration that "fugue is essentially cumulative". There is no living entity called 'fugue' or 'sonata'. Like modern students, Mozart attempted the more taut fugal designs with subjects that would have suited loose ones. A display of exercise is sometimes part and parcel of a display of creative intelligence, and it is so in the K.608 Fantasia for four hands at one piano; but in the C minor Fugue for two pianos, though we are aware of great and original Mozart, exercise is a little too obvious. The freedom of Bach's fugues is enjoyed in Mozart's works only when they do not bear the forbidding title 'Fugue'; it should not be forbidding, but in Mozart's day it certainly was, for Mozart finished only one of the six fugues he intended for van Swieten.

Therefore we need spend little time in discussing his fugues for piano solo. The best, that in C major, K.394(383a), shows little constructive originality, and yet it is not only unmistakably by Mozart, but has a distinct nobility of an austere order if played, as Mozart insisted, andante maestoso. The Fugue was composed before the Fantasia which precedes it; together, the two works form K.394(383a). From the same year, 1782, date Mozart's arrangement for string quartet of six fugues from the 'Forty-eight'. To see how much he had to learn of Bach's art we have only to compare the grim, determined 'counterpoint' of K.394 with the easy-going work in the 'Forty-eight' upon which Mozart's seems to be modelled – the A flat major fugue from Book II.

The Fugues in E flat, K.153(375b), and G minor, K.154 (385k), may have been some of the proposed six for van Swieten also composed in 1782. They are worthless except as documents. Not an entry in them is an event and the 'points', if phraseable at all, are the small change of instruction books. They were finished by Simon Sechter, the Viennese theorist, long after Mozart's death. These fugues merely 'go on', less crudely than the one in Mozart's 'Musical Joke' (K.522), but with the same problems unsolved.[1] No single reason can always

[1] It must be emphasized that these fugues were only sketches, some of them very brief. – EDS.

nced for the vitality or deadness of music; some of Han-
's most inspiring fugues seem to enliven formulae that were
the common stock of his own time and of generations before
him, and are now the contrapuntal tags found in treatises.

The only fantasia by Mozart for solo piano that is widely
known seems to be the fine one in C minor that goes with the
sonata in that key, but the album mentioned above gathers three
other magnificent pieces with the same title. The obvious example for any late eighteenth-century composer of single fantasias and rondos is C. P. E. Bach, but the first thing to learn
about Mozart, if we are not to misunderstand him or regard
him at his best when he reminds us of Beethoven, is that bold
imagination can breathe just as powerfully under the façade of
convention as in explosive and imprecise forms. In fact, it is possible that Mozart's best fantasias and rondos would have inspired C. P. E. Bach to make his own boldness of imagination
more effective by greater integration. He might have learnt
from Mozart what his own father demonstrated in his preludes
and fantasias for organ, and it is plain that J. S. Bach is more
under tribute from Mozart than is C. P. E. Bach. The fantasias
now under discussion all belong to 1782, and therefore to the
period of Mozart's fugal studies and his special interest in Bach
and Handel.

In the fantasias, Mozart suggests his great powers as an extempore player. Look, for instance, at K.394(383a), the fantasia already mentioned as introductory to the C major fugue.
It begins with improvisatory deliberation, but it covers long-
range thinking; it proceeds to agitated texture with cross-hands
technique and thence to digital fireworks; but they are not
mere spurts which go up like the rocket and come down like the
stick; they storm in grand paragraphs, and the tread of their
harmony is purposeful. So it is in the shortest of the fantasias,
that in D minor, K.397(385g). What a perfect short piece for a
recital! Here there seems to be a deliberate contrast between
the *Empfindsamkeit* of C. P. E. Bach and the *galant* style. The
piece begins (alone among the fantasias) with the broken chords
that suggest a long, rambling work, but it soon turns to tender
lyricism that alternates with two other textures, one sad and one
petulant. Already there is enough subject-matter for a sonata
movement, but the conclusion is a sunny Allegretto, the opening idea of which suggests one of Haydn's finales. Thus the con-

trast of styles is maintained throughout, and one cannot agree with those who wish that the fantasia had remained loose and moody. The Fantasia in C minor, K.396(385b), though accepted as a complete and magnificent work for solo piano, was intended for violin and piano. The introduction for piano alone takes up the first two pages of the printed copy (Novello edition, full close in E flat, last line but one of p. 7), and the autograph from this point is in Stadler's hand. The magnificent, stormy paragraphs which follow are unmistakably Mozartean, and the fact that they are too long for quotation is a tribute to their greatness. This fantasia also ends with a grandiose section in the major key.

The Suite, K.399(385i), in the style of Handel, also called 'Overture' (as Bach called the suite or partita known as the 'French Overture'), is interesting as a document rather than as music. It shows how Handel was regarded by Mozart's generation, and it is noteworthy that the French–German elements in Handel's style are also parodied in 'Ah fuggi il traditor' in *Don Giovanni*. Supposed imitations of Handel by more recent musicians all ape his Italianisms, or 'le grand simple', or both. (None known to the writer could possibly be mistaken for Handel, but neither could Mozart's essays. Handel is as inimitable as any genius, even though the musical formulae of his day are more obvious than those of other epochs.) The 'French Overture' that opens this work has a splendid first page. Its fugue, however, like the two binary pieces that follow, which seem to be modelled on the allemande and courante of a Bach suite, tries to exhibit too many points of style in too short a space. The nervous modulations and insistent cross-rhythms are not so much unlike Handel as unlike Mozart when sure of himself and able to use such means expressively.

I have mentioned two rondos in F. One of them, K.616, is the Andante for a clockwork organ which, translated for piano as Andante (Rondo), K.Anh.145a, enables us to imagine its original sound. The rapid passages in thirds, the repeated staccato notes with a melody above or below them, the disposition of rests and of ornaments – all contribute to a clockwork idiom. Despite the simple style and structure, the piece has chromatic passages and modulations in its middle section, a beautiful final section, and other proofs that it is late Mozart. Even including the great piece in A minor, the rondos have this feature in common: they begin innocently or complacently, but surprise us later – sometimes later than pleases people who are impatient of *galant* shallowness. The other rondo in F, K.494, is used as finale to the sonata, K.533; its unpromised delights are the F minor part and the final section.

The Rondo in D, K.485, seems the shallowest. The opening style persists, so that one is inclined to regard it as written for a wealthy pupil. (It is dedicated to a Charlotte von Würben.) It has no emotional surprise and might have been by J. C. Bach as far as structure is concerned. Its main theme is the second subject of J. C. Bach's Quintet in D, Op. 11, No. 6. Despite careful study of C. P. E. Bach's rondos, I perceive in Mozart's work no tribute comparable with that to the older composer's fantasias. The surprise in K.485 is our recognition of a satisfying feat of structure, for if we had to produce the last link between a sonata and a rondo design, this would be the work. If Mozart's humour had led him to call it 'First movement of an unfinished sonata', probably nobody to this day would have corrected the title, yet the piece is a perfect 'text-book' rondo.

Of the short, single pieces for piano, I consider the following to be of the finest quality:

> Rondo in A minor, K.511
> Minuet in D, K.355(594a)
> *Eine kleine Gigue* in G, K.574
> Adagio in B minor, K.540

The only premonition of a wonderful totality in the first page of the A minor rondo is its indication of a unique mood, lovely in musical expression like this, but morbid beyond pathos in a man's behaviour. Though it is dangerous to imagine connections between artistic expression and the artist's personal circumstances, and though Mozart may often have composed poignantly or in a minor key because he enjoyed discovering his powers as detachedly as when he composed thus for a character in an opera, it is hard not to regard the resignation of this rondo as personal – resignation to a despair beyond tears; and simply because this mood is unique it is not fancifully called subjective. The description does not, however, suggest that the piece reflects Mozart's circumstances or his mood on 11 March 1787, for it may not have been conceived on the day of its notation on paper. Measured by the clock, its length is unusual, yet the player finds himself lingering over it and wishing it were even longer.

The Minuet in D (*c.* 1790) has no trio and may at first seem strangely placed among music that is either emotionally deep or technically clever. But it clearly illustrates a Mozartean vein once disliked by people who could not use 'chromatics' without prefixing 'sugary'. It passed to Spohr, Mendelssohn, and that other admirable and underestimated musician, Gounod. Like their minor contemporaries, they occasionally used it weakly; as the sentiments it conveyed were then in high fashion, they would have been very great composers indeed had they avoided its weaker manifestations. Mozart, being not merely acknowledged by them as greater, but endowed more than the most fastidious of his contemporaries with certainty of taste, could use extreme chromatic sweetness without losing control or scrutiny. To this fact let Ex. 11(a) and Ex. 11(b) testify:

Ex.11(a)

Ex.11(b)

A short piece representing Mozart as the student of baroque counterpoint and the keen member of van Swieten's circle is the clever and difficult little Gigue in G[1] which, within one

[1] Paul Hamburger in *Music Review*, XIII/3/1952, pp. 217–18, points to a significant relation between the (eleven-note!) minor version of the theme in the Gigue's development and the (twelve-note) theme of the Gigue in Schoenberg's Suite, Op. 29. Mr. Hamburger comments that it is the "harmonic boldness" of the piece "that endears it to the expressionist". – EDS.

printed page, succeeds brilliantly in being utterly Mozartean in
the humorous, parodistic manner that was not quite successful
in the Suite, K.399(385i).

The Adagio in B minor has been kept till last for discussion
because I think it is Mozart's finest single work for piano solo.
The A minor rondo is quiet and pathetic, tempting one often
to use tempo rubato and respond to every implied or marked
nuance of shading, but this Adagio goes deeper. It is inade-
quately described by 'tragic', a word overused and belonging
strictly to music that is composed for a tragedy or suggests a
tragic programme. If we recall the last three symphonies, the
folly of naming a finest among movements that should be regarded as disparate, because they represent no more than a
fraction of Mozart's range, becomes obvious. The last movement of the last symphony is the most obviously brilliant, but
the slow movement of the same work is quite as virtuosic in a
different way. It also represents its kind, not its composer. If
we are more impressed by 'G minor Mozart', how shall a movement from the relevant symphony represent the man who took
galanterie to greatness? Now for all its magnificent integrity, the
B minor Adagio reflects during its course facets of expression and
details of technique found in works as diverse as variations,
rondos, fantasias, and sonatas. Passages that could occur in the
quintets and others that remind us of poignant wind-scoring lie
beside the embroidery and hand-crossing of pure Mozartean
pianism. Here is even the contrapuntist – not just the student of
traditional device, but master of yearning discord. Here is even
a trace of *galanterie*, for what other composer in this mood
would use dotted rhythm in the opening idea? What a noble
span has that idea and in what fine lengths are other sentences!
How much less moving would be the attempt at similar expression by one who sought freedom from the limits of style. The
rich diversity and perfect unity are the bases of my claim, for the
classical control, the timing of contrasts, the formalities within
the organic form are what give this music its secret power, and I
echo a quotation from Gerard Manley Hopkins used by J. A.
Westrup to express his admiration of Purcell's best music:
"It is the forgéd feature finds me."

BOOK LIST

H. Abert: *W. A. Mozart*, revised edition, Leipzig, 1923.

N. Broder: 'Mozart and the "Clavier"', *Musical Quarterly*, XXVII/4/1941, pp. 422ff.

A. Einstein: 'Mozart and His Contemporaries' and 'The Clavier', *Mozart*, London, 1946.

H. Gough: 'The Classical Grand Pianoforte', *Proceedings of the Royal Musical Association*, Vol. LXXVII, London, 1951.

R. Haas: *Mozart*, Potsdam, ²/1950.

P. Hamburger: ['Mozart's Gigue, K.574'], *Music Review*, XIII/3/1952, pp. 217ff.

A. Hutchings: 'Mozart and Modern Performance', *A Companion to Mozart's Piano Concerto*, London, 1948.

A. H. King: 'Mozart's Piano Music', *Music Review*, V/2/1944, pp. 163–91.

—— *Mozart in Retrospect*, London, 1955.

John F. Russell: 'Mozart and the Pianoforte', *Music Review*, I/3/1940, pp. 226–44.

Wyzewa and St.-Foix: *W. A. Mozart: sa vie musicale et son œuvre*, Paris, 1940.

DONALD MITCHELL

THE SERENADES FOR WIND BAND

I_T may seem quixotic to deal with only three of Mozart's serenades, divertimenti, notturni, and so forth. But faced with some half-hundred works, and only a few thousand words in which to deal with them, the problem of selection was acute. At one stage, I thought that I might have dealt briefly with the best pieces in each category. Often, however, the 'best' piece proves to have strayed right outside its strict classification as serenade or divertimento, and thus finds a place in another chapter altogether, for example the serenade which became the 'Haffner' Symphony (K.385)[1] and the string Trio (Divertimento), K.563.[2]

The three serenades for winds form a convenient group. They are singular in character, and the finest of them, K.388(384a), while undoubtedly transcending its own species, stands in a class by itself and does not trespass upon the preserves of other media (except in its later arrangement as a string Quintet, K.406(516b)). The three works offer an organic development in which Mozart gradually abandons the suite-like row of movements characterizing the serenade. K.361(370a), 375, and 388[3] progressively diminish the number of their movements, from the seven of K.361 through the five of K.375 to the four of K.388. The masterly growth of this small group of wind serenades, which finally results in the last serenade's formal economy and profundity of invention, is typical; the same trend may be discerned in the larger groups of serenades and divertimenti for diverse combinations. The two earlier works, moreover, retain, despite their progressive trend, many features which are typical of Mozart's serenades in general. These two facts together mean that a particularized description of the three pieces illuminates the whole field of Mozart's activity in the serenade sphere. The

---

[1] See *The Symphonies*, pp. 184ff.   [2] See *The Chamber Music*, pp. 134f.

[3] It would seem pedantic to continue to offer both old and new K. numbers in a short chapter dealing with only three works. Henceforth only the old K. numbers are used in identifying the three serenades which are the chapter's main topic.

kind of musical approach met with in these works is encountered again and again in other serenades and divertimenti. Another reason for the special consideration of these pieces is the quality of their instrumentation. Mozart's writing for winds was far in advance of his time,[1] and the sonorities these serenades divulge seem to be peculiarly relevant to the sound-ideals of our own time, when the winds and small wind-ensembles have undergone a far-reaching revival.

There follow on pp. 68–69 a few items of historical and musical information in chart-form. The B flat Serenade (K.361) is the longest of the three and the most loosely built. It also uses the largest group of winds. (It was in this work that Mozart, for the first time, used basset horns.) The thirteenth instrument Mozart quite definitely indicated as a double-bass; he did not offer a double-bassoon as alternative. The presence of one string instrument scarcely affects the instrumental character of the work – K.361 remains a serenade for winds – but it does, perhaps, underline the work's transitional features. K.361 does not completely align itself with the sound-ideals of the serenades K.375 and 388; and of the three it is the most serenade-like. Hence, no doubt, the richness of its instrumental resources – an extra pair of horns, and a pair of basset horns, in addition to the customary winds. The very nature of its themes, and moods of its movements, require a variety of instrumental treatment. In K.375 and 388, the cogency of the musical arguments, the altogether more serious content of the music, increasingly rule out dabbling with instrumental colour for its own sake. Thus, K.361 displays an almost luxuriant instrumental character which is missing in K.388 and very much refined in K.375; in its instrumentation, as in other formal and stylistic respects, K.375 occupies a midway position.

Of the three allegro first movements, the most loosely-built and light-weight in invention belongs to K.361. The Allegro is, in fact, rather overshadowed by the extensive introduction

---

[1] Its distinctive quality was recognized early; cf., for example, Thomas Busby's *A History of Music* (1819): "[Mozart's] felicity in the use of wind instruments is so well known, that it would be superfluous to insist upon the unrivalled art he uniformly displays in their management. His accompaniments derive from his peculiar skill, a charm that no other resource of his genius could have supplied. But with Mozart, it was a NATURAL resource. The breathing sweetness of the flute, pouring reediness of the hautboy, and mellow murmuring of the bassoon, accorded with the passive delicacy of his nerves, and lively tenderness of his sensations."

K.361 (37 1a)
('Gran partitta') 2 ob.,
2 clnt., 2 bst. hn., 4
hn., 2 bsn., d-b.

Composed in the first half of 1781 in Munich and Vienna. The first three movements and finale were later (?) arranged as a string Quintet (K.46), but not by Mozart. A more authentic arrangement, "which may very well have been Mozart's own idea", for 2 ob., 2 clnt., 2 bsn., 2 hn., also exists (K.Anh.182).

Mozart, Einstein writes (op. cit., p. 203), "had begun [K.361] in Munich at the beginning of 1781, at the time of the performance of *Idomeneo*, and completed it in Vienna, at the time of his most strenuous efforts to escape from the bonds of Salzburg. In composing it he probably had in mind the excellent wind-players of Munich, as well as the intention of once more trying to insinuate himself into the favour of [the Elector] Carl Theodor by means of an extraordinary piece. We have no evidence that the 13 players ever actually came together in Vienna. . . ."

Scheme:

1 Largo/Allegro — B flat

2 Minuet — B flat
[Trio I — E flat]
[Trio II — G minor]

3 Adagio — E flat

4 Minuet — B flat
[Trio I — B flat minor]
[Trio II — F major]

5 Adagio/Allegretto/Adagio (Romanze) — E flat

6 Theme and Variations (Andante) — B flat

7 Rondo (Allegro molto) — B flat

Min. score: Eulenburg, No. 100.

K.375
2 clnt., 2 hns, 2 bsn. In
July 1782 Mozart
added 2 ob. [See
footnote 1, p. 83.]

Composed in October 1781 in Vienna. The fragment of a March exists (K.384b) which Mozart may have composed when he added the pair of oboes. Einstein (in Köchel) thinks the March (in B flat) might have replaced the second minuet in order to relieve the serenade's continuous E flat (all five movements are in the tonic). If such were Mozart's intention (which I think improbable), and had it been realized, an unusual scheme would have evolved. K.375 would then have been his only serenade in which the last two movements did not confirm the tonic. All the serenades (with the exception of the four-movement K.522), and most of the divertimenti, conform to a

Einstein writes (op. cit., pp. 204–5): "Mozart himself has given us precise information concerning the origin of [K.375] and the identity of the person for whom it was written. . .

"*I wrote it for St. Theresa's day, for Frau von Hickel's sister, or rather the sister-in-law of Herr von Hickel, court painter, at whose house it was performed* [15 October 1781] *for the first time. The six gentlemen who executed it are poor beggars who, however, play quite well together, particularly the first clarinet and the two horns. But the chief reason why I composed it was in order to let Herr von Strack, who goes there every day, hear something of my composition; so I wrote it rather carefully. It has won great applause too and on St. Theresa's night it was performed in three different places; for as soon as they finished playing it in one place, they were taken off somewhere else and paid to play it. . . .*"

"The six poor devils had the decency to render their thanks to Mozart himself on his name-day, 31 October:

"*'At eleven o'clock at night I was treated to a serenade performed by two clarinets, two horns, and two bassoons – and that too of my own composition . . . these musicians asked that the street door might be opened and, placing themselves in the centre of the courtyard, surprised me, just as I was about to undress, in the most pleasant fashion imaginable with the first chord in E♭.'* [Letter to his father, 3 November 1781.]"

T–T sequence for their penultimate movements and finales. On the other hand, K.375 is the only serenade which remains faithful to the tonic in all its movements. Some of the divertimenti (e.g., K.Anh.227(196f), K.253, K.289(271g), and the two notturni, K.239 and 286(269a)) offer monotonal parallels, but none is on the scale of K.375. A maturer example is the continuous E flat of the Sinfonia Concertante, K.Anh.9/(297b).

	1	2	3	4	5
Scheme	Allegro E flat	Minuet E flat [Trio C minor]	Adagio E flat	Minuet E flat [Trio A flat]	Allegro E flat

Min. score: Eulenburg, No. 308.

K.388(384a) ('Nacht Musique'). 2 ob, 2 clnt, 2 hn, 2 bsn.

Composed end of July 1782 in Vienna. There is the fragment of a slow movement in E flat which Einstein (in Köchel) suggests may have been the start of a different Andante. In 1787 Mozart arranged the serenade as a string Quintet, K.406(516b), perhaps not only for 'business' reasons (as Einstein suggests, op. cit., p. 194), but also to stress his own evaluation of the work – even to leave it in a less 'occasional' guise?

Einstein writes (op. cit., p. 205): "The last and most important of these works [i.e., K.388] is shrouded in mystery. Mozart, in a letter to his father (27 July 1782), says only this about it: '. . . I have had to compose in a great hurry a serenade, but only for wind-instruments . . .', so that the work could not be used for a local Salzburg festivity in the home of the Haffners. But he is silent about the fact that its whole character is not at all suitable for a festivity. We know nothing about the occasion, nothing about the person who commissioned it, nothing about whether this client desired so explosive a serenade or whether that is simply what poured forth from Mozart's soul."

	1	2	3	4
Scheme	Allegro C minor	Andante E flat	Minuet C minor [Trio C major]	Allegro (Theme and Variations) C minor (→ major)

Min. Score: Eulenburg, No. 309.

1 A. Einstein: *Mozart*, London, 1946, p. 203.

(*Largo*) which precedes it. (Mozart drops the introduction in
K.388 and modifies the principle in K.375.) For the first movement of K.361, Mozart, as in other works, employs that earlier
type of sonata movement in which the customary thematic
dualism is absent. The pervasive head-motive (Ex. 1) of the first

subject plays an important role in the formation of the second.
Throughout, this first movement retains a festive, typically
serenade-like character. An expansive closing section to the exposition offers ample room for the introduction of appropriately
gay motives, all of which reappear in the recapitulation, together with a coda. The coda, however, contains a more serious
intervention in the shape of an extension of the head-motive
(Ex. 1). Mozart often reserves such thoughts for his codas.

The development begins with a new, genial tune in the clarinets and bassoons; new though it sounds, it is, of course, related
to the material of the closing section, which itself emerges from
characteristic features of the first subject. In view of the monothematic exposition, this new, eight-bar tune – the first new
melodic thought of substance since the first subject – serves as a
delayed, displaced second subject. The principle recurs in the
first, and similarly monothematic, movement of the piano Trio
in B flat (K.502), in the first movement of the string Quartet in
B flat (K.458), and in the first movement of the violin Sonata in
B flat (K.378(317d)), whose first and second subjects offer little
by way of thematic contrast. The introduction of the new tune
in the dominant stresses its function as compensation for the
preceding lack of a contrasting second theme.[1] The development continues (bar 103) with a section based on part of the
second subject, expands the head-motive (Ex. 1) in overlapping
entries (bar 116), and closes with an extension of the final bars
of the exposition's closing section, to which is appended the
graceful, three-bar lead-back to the recapitulation. I only men-

[1] See also *The Chamber Music*, pp. 120f.

tion the sequence of events in this development to show how consequent are all its topics. A very real unity underlies the whole movement, despite the free atmosphere, but it is the bridge passage between the first and second subjects, with its close imitation between oboes and clarinets, rapid modulations, and abrupt dive into, and departure from, a stormy G minor, which most nearly looks forward to the taut organization and packed textures of K.375 and 388. K.361 was not, as it were, composed under pressure, and its first movement – indeed, the entire piece – breathes spaciously. Mozart, however, never rambles, even when most relaxed.

In the first movement (*Allegro maestoso*) of K.375, the introduction is reduced to solemn, repeated E flat chords, whose weight is carefully regulated by the following dynamic scheme, successively *sf*, *fp*, *fp*, *f*, *p*. The chords at once yield seventeen bars' placid reiteration of Ex. 2. Gently-clashing suspensions

Ex.2 *(Allegro maestoso)*

characterize the harmonic texture. The clarinet always propels the descending phrase, and the bassoon echoes it, with an upward thrust which, eventually, is taken up by the clarinet, enlarged, and finally opened out into the athletic bridge passage leading to the second subject. The repetition of Ex. 2 constitutes an unusual first subject stage in which motion seems to be suspended. The first subject stage, in fact, retains the static quality of the introductory chords from which it naturally and thematically evolves. It is not until the bridge passage is reached that the Allegro proper begins. The movement's first twenty-four bars correspond perhaps to the maestoso part of the Allegro, and a performance should allow for the adjustment in tempo necessary at the onset of the bridge passage.

The solemn introductory chords open the development, which largely confines itself to a C minor repetition of the second subject's first half. (The development, altogether, is very brief – but twenty-one bars in length.) The minor character of the theme has already been disclosed in the exposition, where its first half – rather surprisingly and certainly contrastingly – enters on the dominant minor (Ex. 3). The major is not asserted

until we reach the theme's continuation, after a silent bar. This procedure is unusual. In the second (A major) subject of the 'Prague' Symphony (K.504), for example, Mozart repeats the theme in the minor and picks up the major again with the theme's continuation; but the theme does not first emerge in A minor. B flat minor, on this occasion, certainly intrudes a new mood, to which Mozart returns in the development. The new mood, however, would not suit the recapitulation of what is largely a cheerful movement. In any case, Ex. 3 has, so to speak, been pre-recapitulated in the development. Thus, at the very point in the recapitulation where a recurrence of Ex. 3 is expected, Mozart offers a surprise in the shape of a new second subject (Ex. 4), delivered by the horn and repeated by the oboe

and clarinet in octave partnership. The 'new' tune proves to have had fragmentary preparation in the exposition, hence the new note it strikes does not disturb the movement's unity. Compare, for instance, Ex. 5(a) with x in Ex. 4 above, and Ex. 5(b) with z. (Ex. 5(a), incidentally, is reminiscent in character of a

principal theme in the Concerto for two pianos, K.365(316a), in E flat.) The new tune over, it is succeeded by the 'lost' second subject's continuation, and the movement proceeds to its close. The recapitulation would not be complete without any reference to Ex. 4 at all, and the movement's coda, initiated by the solemn introductory chords, slyly introduces a broken-up outline of the missing second subject, six bars before the end. One

last little subtlety results as a consequence of the replacement of Ex. 3 by Ex. 4. Ex. 5(a), which, in the exposition, followed the B flat minor second subject proper but previewed its (tonic) replacement, in the recapitulation succeeds, as a matter of course, the full-blown theme of which it was originally a fertilizing motive, a sequence of events which now proclaims the motive's identity and peculiar significance.

As in K.361, a large closing section to the exposition easily accommodates a new group of motives (almost a third group), but in K.375 it seems expressly to have been designed to show off the paces of the instrumentalists, both solo and in pairs. In both K.361 and 375 it is instructive to compare the expositions of these first movements with their recapitulations (as, indeed, of the other movements, where their forms allow). Many instances will be found of Mozart's customary variations, of his instrumentation (especially in K.375), and of his themes. Mozart always succeeds in conveying an impression of formal exactitude while never once quite repeating himself.

The irregularity which marks the first movement of K.375 is also a feature of the finale – both movements tend to show that Mozart's attitude to his forms was far from passive, if not actively innovatory – but before moving on to the serenades' three last movements, the first of K.388 remains to be considered.

The Allegro of K.375, despite its deviation, is a much tighter piece, formally, than the corresponding Allegro of K.361. The invention, too, is more disciplined, the first and (both!) second subjects strongly contrasted, while the introductory chords sound their solemn note throughout. It may have been that those who first heard K.375 were a little surprised by the serious character of the first movement. What can the reaction have been to the Allegro of K.388? It is indeed significant that we know nothing of the occasion which prompted the composition of this remarkable serenade. It is, in fact, hard to imagine a function of a social nature at which this kind of unprecedented and disturbing serenade would have been acceptable. Of the three first movements under discussion, it is this Allegro which is the most economical in its instrumentation – the instrumentation of the recapitulation (cf. K.361 and 375) is almost regular – the most compact in form, and the most pungent in invention. It says what it has to say with exceptional brevity. It is noticeable that the closing section of the recapitulation concerns itself with only one striking, martial figure (Ex. 6). There is no place

Ex.6

here for the voluble, volatile closing sections which grace K.361 and 375. There is scarcely a coda; rather, the movement hurtles to its conclusion through a passionate, chromatic extension and intensification of the recapitulation's closing part. The recapitulation plus coda of K.388 accumulates only seven bars, as against twenty in K.361. The closing section to the recapitulation of K.361 is extended by nineteen bars – in K.388 by two.

By way of thematic material, the first movement of K.361 is by far the most occasional in character, though there are already signs of the approaching profundity of invention of K.388. The Allegro of K.375 anticipates more directly the conciseness of utterance which marks the later work. As I have suggested above, the three serenades together constitute an organic development. K.388 flourishes its singularity through its choice of key (C minor), its tempestuous, impassioned, gloomy mood, and, above all, through the complexity of its thematic invention. There is no introduction. We are immediately presented with a first subject (Ex. 7), less a theme than an extended thematic complex, comprising five distinct limbs, not all of them symmetrical. Each limb, after the first, offers a contrasting, though strictly logical, consequent to its predecessor. There is even room for development within the complex itself. The fourth limb, Ex. 7(d), is built up out of motive *x* – the drooping, mournful, diminished seventh – which terminates the first, Ex. 7(a). It is significant that it is this motive which is at once stressed. It is not only basic in mood (its shape is expressive of the work's content), but its appearance in all four movements of the serenade

reveals it as a basic motive. The bridge passage to the contrasted second subject is no simple transition. It introduces not only the urgent rhythm (i.e., [musical notation] *etc.*) which is to play a prominent role throughout the movement, especially in the development, but also one of the principal contours (i.e., [musical notation] *etc.*) of the advancing second subject (i.e., [musical notation] *etc.*). The thematic and unifying character of the passage is increased by the projection of its first five bars over the first limb (Ex. 7(a)) of the first subject. It is obvious that a thematic complex of the nature of Ex. 7 will break down, for developmental purposes, into its constituent limbs. Mozart does not use Ex. 7(a) as such in the movement's development, the calm opening of which is savagely disturbed by his selection of Exx. 7(c) and (d) as disruptive agents. The development then continues with an extended passage based on motive *x* (see Exx. 7(a) and (d)), in which the entries of the motive (oboes and bassoons) overlap. Emphatic statements of the fateful basic rhythm conclude the development and lead, after a pause, to the recapitulation. In the exposition the second subject, in the relative major, has offered momentary relaxation of the prevailing tension. In the recapitulation the second subject, now in the tonic minor and varied, registers the impact of the development. The important bridge passage between first and second subjects is substantially extended, in the main by an extension of Ex. 7(a) and its pervasive motive *x*. The graceful but disconsolate variation of the second subject[1] can scarcely be overlooked. No less exquisite, but perhaps rather more concealed, is the chromatic transformation of the second clarinet's accompaniment of the recapitulation's closing figure (Ex. 6 – compare bars 209–13 with bars 74–8).

This extraordinary Allegro alone places the C minor Serenade at the side of such works as the G minor Symphony (K.550), the C minor piano Concerto (K.491), the G minor Quintet (K.516), and the D minor Quartet K.421(417b), works with which it shares much in mood and achievement. The finale, a set of variations, "anticipating the spirit of the Finale of the C minor Concerto",[2] lives up to the challenge of the formidable Allegro and is the most serious and functional of the wind serenades' last movements. K.388 has a totality of conception and execution which is missing in K.361 and 375. K.361, for instance, might have ended sooner, with the sixth of its row of seven movements. The final, and rather crude, concluding Rondo (No. 7) seems to be no more than tacked on to the end of the line. No. 6, a theme and variations taken from the flute Quartet K.Anh.171(285b), would have served better as a finale. The Rondo merely rattles along, reviving, rather noisily (as Einstein remarks),[3] recollections of the last movement of the early piano-duet Sonata, K.19d. The variations, the first finale as it were, have much grace and charm (particularly in their instrumentation), and offer not a few inspirations. Variation 2 should be studied for its sound (basset horns coupled with bassoons, in the first section) and its structure (the clarinet contributes, meanwhile, a descant – a favourite variation procedure of Mozart's, cf. the finale of the clarinet Quintet (K.581), variation 1, and, more especially, variation 2); variation 3 presents contrasting instrumental textures and a comical little fugato (of four bars) interpolated between the two halves of the varied theme (in the bassoons and double-bass, before and after the interpolation); variation 4 (B flat minor) offers broken, halting phrasing (Ex. 8(a)), which is sealed up in the variation's second part by cunning overlapping (see Ex. 8(b)). Even the inbreak of

---

[1] The central (C minor) episode of the rondo finale of the Quintet for piano and winds in E flat (K.452) offers a theme which seems to recollect this varied second subject from the first movement of K.388.

[2] Einstein: op. cit., p. 206.   [3] op. cit., p. 204.

the oboe does not ruffle the smooth continuity of the chain of phrases.

In view of the Rondo and the arrangement of the movement from K.Anh.171(285b), Einstein comments: "very possibly, after the exertion and outpouring of invention of the first five movements, Mozart was willing to permit himself a little relaxation".[1] It is true, indeed, of K.361 that the last two movements – even the admirable variations – do not maintain the level of the first five; the work, that is, becomes increasingly occasional in the character of its movements and the quality of their invention. It is true, again, of K.375, of whose five movements the first three might, in achievement, be regarded as counterparts to like movements from K.388, despite, of course, the diametrically opposed characters of the two allegros. But in K.375, after three movements, one of which is a sublime Adagio, Mozart suddenly seems to have remembered that he was writing for an occasion, and there follow a rather commonplace minuet and a cheery finale, neither of which quite sustain the mood or invention of the preceding movements. Unlike K.388, K.375 does not end at the high level at which it began.

The finale, however, has its points. This breezy sonata rondo, with a gay principal theme of a popular character, discloses an unexpectedly thorough development, opening, in C minor, with a fluent fugato (see Ex. 9(e)). The learned style is very lightly worn and 'fits' despite the movement's vernacular spirit. Eventually, the development yields an appearance of the entire second subject, a premature (tonic!) recapitulation which absolves Mozart of the necessity of reintroducing the theme in his

[1] op. cit., p. 204.

recapitulation proper;[1] as replacement, after the return of the
principal theme, we have an extended closing section which
leads into the coda. The second subject itself (Ex. 9) is worth
attention, in particular its continuation with an immediate self-
variation (Ex. 9(a)). In the development's pre-recapitulation of
Ex. 9, Mozart subjects the theme to his habitual recapitulatory
variations; he varies (Ex. 9(b)) not only the theme (Ex. 9), but
also (Ex. 9(c)) the original variation (Ex. 9(a)). Especially
effective is the unexpected octave leap in the sixth bar of Ex.
9(b). Such melodic variations, though simpler than those met

with in more elaborate works (e.g., the superbly varied recapitulation of the second subject in the first movement of the clarinet
Quintet (K.581)), are typical of Mozart's unrepetitive repeti-

---

[1] In the Divertimento for string quartet and two horns, K.287(271b), the brief
development of the (sonata) first movement includes towards its close a restatement of the second subject (though not in the tonic), a total 'pre-recapitulation'
which, to my mind, is undoubtedly related to the surprising curtailment of the
first subject in the immediately succeeding recapitulation proper; i.e., the role of
the second subject in the development is part compensation for the ensuing de-
capitation of the first subject. This characteristic scheme works well, but unlike
the finale of K.375, the second subject undergoes official recapitulation, and its
third appearance strikes me as one too many.

tions. It is surprising how even modest variations of this kind can result in increased tension, to which, as in this case, the altered lie of the parts may contribute (cf. bars 33–6 with bars 122–5. The chromatic intensification of the clarinet accompaniment in the latter group has a parallel in K.388, see p. 76). One final subtlety should be remarked. The development's fugato (Ex. 9(e)) evolves from the horns' arpeggio (Ex. 9(d)), which acts as a link between the rondo's first and second subjects. Einstein writes of this finale that "there is as much depth and workmanship as the category and the festive occasion allow".[1] Certainly the workmanship of the movement is never in doubt, as some of the details discussed above suggest. It disappoints as a finale to K.375 simply because it takes account of the "festive occasion", whereas the earlier movements, particularly the first and third, transcend the social function for which the serenade was intended.

The magnificent finale to K.388 – a theme and variations – is quite the equal of the work's first movement. It is hardly possible here to devote sufficient space to these masterful variations of a compact theme (see Ex. 16(b)), stated initially, with the very minimum of adornment, by the oboes and bassoons (in pairs). The first four variations maintain the character of the first movement – they are, successively, forceful, poignant, urgently mysterious, and boldly passionate. As might be expected, there are few resemblances to the more genial variations of K.361, but the fourth variation of K.388 exploits the broken rhythmic scheme of the fourth (B flat minor) variation of the earlier serenade. The syncopated third variation, however, is plainly the model for the G minor variation in the finale of the G major piano Concerto, K.453. In this C minor variation, the coupling of oboes with bassoons recalls the sound of basset horns doubled with bassoons in K.361, variation 2, but here the effect is positively sepulchral. All the first four variations of K.388 constitute separate 'numbers' and relentlessly pursue the minor. "The Finale", writes Einstein, "begins with impassioned and sombre variations in minor, anticipating the spirit of the Finale of the C minor Concerto, and seems about to end in minor also, when the E-flat of the horns falls like a gentle beam of light. . . ."[2]

---

[1] op. cit., p. 205.

[2] op. cit., p. 206. The finale of K.388 does more than anticipate the spirit of the finale of K.491. Indeed, the relationship between the serenade and the piano

This is a crucial juncture in the finale, the first moment of relaxation after unrelieved tension. The E flat variation is the most far-reaching of the set, and introduces, almost in operatic fashion, as a new 'character', not only a new mood but also, of course, a new key. As Einstein points out, the four-bar motive (Ex. 10(a)) which introduces the variation occurs again in the sextet from Act II of *Don Giovanni*, though there (Ex. 10(b)) the motive, in fact, confirms the new key – here it initiates it. The real parallel to *Don Giovanni* is established when the motive, acting as a link between this variation and the next, confirms the return of the tonic, C minor (Ex. 10(c)). After the peaceful dis-

Ex. 10 (a)

Ex. 10 (b) *Don Giovanni* (Act II)

Ex. 10 (c)

ruption of E flat in a wholly C minor context, and a variation of the nature of an independent interlude, both theme and tonic must be reinforced. Thus the succeeding variation plunges into C minor, and the theme, over a brilliant, virtuoso bassoon accompaniment, is recapitulated in its original shape. However justified, the return of the theme is unusual. Normally, Mozart only recalls his theme – or, at least, its first half – in the variation which is designed to be the last, as, for example, in the

concerto is altogether more exact. The basic diminished seventh motive (see Ex. 7(a), *x*) which characterizes the serenade throughout, plays a fundamental role in the principal themes of the concerto's first and last movements (in both inverted and straight guise); while the first four-bar phrase of the main theme of the concerto's finale and the first limb of the serenade's first subject (Ex. 7(a)) share the same melodic structure – the C minor arpeggio plus motive *x*. It is significant that the same means of unification unite two works closely related in the character of their inspiration.

finales of K.581 or 421. Here, however, the theme does not grow a new continuation, but exactly repeats its second half. While this striking return of theme plus tonic is determined by the character and key of the preceding interlude, it also fulfils the finale's dramatic scheme. As Einstein puts it, "victory is achieved",[1] in the shape of the final variation in the tonic major. The E flat interlude is both a relaxation of tension and – retrospectively – a promise of a brighter horizon. C major, if it is not to sound trite, must conquer, not simply succeed, the prevailing tragic atmosphere, and it is the minor return of the theme – the reverse picture of the impending major version – and the following profoundly disturbed variation, where, as Abert remarks, "the theme at the close appears to fall to pieces",[2] which together prepare for the resolution in the major by intensifying the movement's gloomy passion; to such darkness, light is the only possible consequent. At the same time, these two tonic minor variations counter-balance the interruption of the E flat interlude. The demands of purely musical exigencies and dramatic structure are wonderfully managed in this finale.

In the concluding major variation, the second half of the theme, true to a recurring type among Mozart's last variations, comprises a new continuation, which seems to comment, half-sardonically, on the changed circumstances in which the theme finds itself. The masterfully conceived link between the fifth and sixth variations, and the superb transition effected between the penultimate variation and the last, make of this finale a particularly cohering and continuous structure.[3] Perhaps I may add that in its string Quintet version, K.406(516b), the serenade seems to me to lose much of its characteristically caustic, even rather acrid, timbre. It is only in the finale's C major variation that I feel the strings are to be preferred; at this juncture the wind band sounds merely cheery, while the strings are capable of a greater expressiveness, of revealing that ambiguity which always lies close to the heart of Mozart's gaiety.

No discussion of this finale would be complete without

[1] op. cit., p. 206.

[2] 'Mozart', in *Cobbett's Cyclopedic Survey of Chamber Music*, London, 1930, Vol. II, p. 180.

[3] I am indebted to Hans Keller for solving some of the puzzles with which I found myself confronted in this movement.

reference to the recurrence of the basic diminished seventh motive
(see Ex. 7(a), *x*), which has a role in all four movements of
K.388. Its appearances throughout the variations are too numerous, too pervasive (see *x* in Ex. 16(b)), to tabulate *in extenso*, and
two must suffice. Ex. 11(a), at most a thinly disguised quotation
(see *x*), occurs, significantly enough, in the penultimate variation. Ex. 11(b) is part of the second half of the theme, and here
the motive is not straight but, to use Reti's useful term, interverted[1] – the order of the motive's notes is changed:

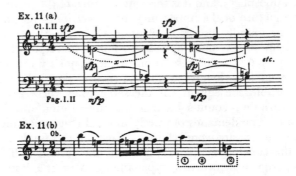

This pungent motive seems to express, in the narrowest space,
the very essence of the serenade's unique spirit, and that
Mozart 'remembers' it in the finale's penultimate variation, not
long before the onset of the work's C major exit, stresses its
prime, generative importance.

There remain to be discussed the three serenades' minuets
and slow movements. The seven-movement K.361 (in B flat)
offers two minuets, placed as Nos. 2 and 4. Both include two
trios, strongly contrasted in character. Both minor trios, the
second, in G minor, of No. 2 (N.B. the Schubertian (almost
Mahlerian!) major–minor contrasts, bars 103–7 and 136–40),
and the first, in B flat minor, of No. 4, are magical. The two
weighty minuets are surprisingly varied in content, invention,
and instrumentation; they are only consistent in their inspiration (e.g., the charming four-bar clarinet phrase tacked on to
the first minuet's first half, an afterthought, but thematic, and
typically varied in the second half). In the five-movement K.375
(in E flat), the two minuets occupy the same positions as in

[1] R. Reti: *The Thematic Process in Music*, London, 1961, p. 72.

K.361. Each has only one trio,[1] and neither minuet is as robust
as the minuets in K.361, where more rustic characteristics – and
two trios – were more easily accommodated. The minuets in
K.375 are more refined, more chamber-musical, and more
economical, though the second is the weakest of the four examples. The first, festive in atmosphere and terse in structure, is
remarkable for the extent of its trio, which allows, in its second
half, for the development of a pregnant motive (Ex. 12). The
trio, in length and invention, far outdistances the minuet.

Ex. 12
Fag.

Crowning the minuets of either K.361 or 375 is the C minor
'Menuetto in Canone' of K.388, which foreshadows in stormy
energy and sinewy counterpoint the minuet of the G minor
Symphony, K.550. The minuet's contrapuntal character is sustained from the onset and scarcely relaxed. The theme appears
in canon, the minuet's less tense middle part is not free of imitation (i.e., bars 17–21), and the return of the canon indulges, by
way of intensification, in a remarkable melodic extension. The
new extension makes plain reference (see Ex. 13(a), *x*) to the
diminished seventh – basic – motive (see Ex. 7(a), *x*) from the
first movement's thematic complex. The inspired outgrowth of
the theme may best be viewed by juxtaposing its original form
(Ex. 13) with its extension (Ex. 13(a)).

Einstein calls this minuet "a contrapuntal display-piece, with
all sorts of canonic effects",[2] and its strenuous counterpoint is

---

[1] The 'original' version of K.375, i.e., the wind sextet of 1781 (2 clnt., 2 bsn.,
2 hn.), has been published by Musica Rara (London, 1955) in an edition supervised
by Karl Haas. In his preface to the parts, Mr. Haas details the many differences
– some of them quite substantial – which exist between the sextet and octet
versions, one of which is a *second trio* (B flat) in the sextet's second minuet, whose
tune runs thus:

(Trio II)
Cl. I

It is interesting that in the coda to the finale, Mozart, in the octet version, adds
seven bars' recapitulation of the rondo's principal theme – in view of the missing
second subject, a significant extension.

[2] op. cit., p. 206.

reminiscent of another "display-piece", the C minor Fugue for
two pianos, K.426. At one point – the return of the minuet's
principal section – one of these canonic effects suggests that the

canon is to enlarge to three voices, but the first entry (clarinet)
proves to be a false one, and peters out in its third bar; the oboes
are left in the lead, as before, with the bassoons treading on
their heels at one bar's distance.

In the G minor Symphony, K.550, the minuet's trio is the
only point where Mozart uses G major. Likewise in K.388, the
tonic major – but for the finale's last variation – only emerges in
the minuet's trio. But while the trio of K.550 retains something
of its dance character and is not contrapuntal, the trio of K.388,
while offering a marked contrast in mood to the minuet, comprises another canon, 'al roviesco' ('in reverse'; see Ex. 14):

Out of this placid material, two oboes and two bassoons weave the smoothest and purest of textures, whose unruffled flow, coloured in its final section by the bassoons' chromatics, is ensured by the largely conjunct motion of the voices, by phrasing sealed up across the bar lines (as in the trio's second half), and by neat dovetailing, as in Ex. 14(a) below, where the theme

Ex. 14(a)

is resumed before the previous section has ended – a 'concealed entry', as the road sign would warn us.

When we come to survey the three wind serenades' slow movements – four in all, since K.361 has two – we find that the earliest serenade (K.361) is fully the equal of its successors. Indeed, its first slow movement (No. 3), an Adagio (E flat), is perhaps the profoundest of all four examples. It is a simple ternary shape, throughout which one basic rhythmic figure (Ex. 15) remains constant, but for five bars (one introductory in function, two transitional, and two conclusive):

Ex. 15

Ex. 15 is delivered over a bass moving, almost without a break, in quavers. Against the combined background of this ostinato and Ex. 15, the winds spin their long, ravishing melody, one instrument advancing into prominence as another recedes. The splitting-up of the melodic material among the instruments is characteristic (cf. the Adagio of K.375), but here it is extremely imaginative, diverse, and rich in effect. It is the monochrome, monorhythmic background supplied by Ex. 15 that throws the solo instruments' poignant phrases into relief and yet binds together their kaleidoscopic alternations of timbre. The first section maintains a mood of rapt, solemn lyricism; the middle part introduces us not to a contrast but, rather, to a continuation of the prevailing mood differently inflected. One bar of transition drops us into the darker region of the dominant minor, and the middle part maintains its minor character until the return of the first section and its regular recapitulation. The movement dies away in a coda of five bars, linked to the recapitulation by the bar (here varied) that led into the middle part.

The second slow movement (No. 5, E flat), a 'Romanze', follows the general scheme and character of Mozart's similarly titled movements. The extended, allegretto, C minor middle section of this movement (surely urgent and mysterious and not "oddly burlesque" as Einstein[1] would have it?) is surrounded by a rather conventional, ternary Adagio, to the return of which is added a long coda (nineteen bars to the Adagio's twenty-four). The theme of the Allegretto seems to look forward to the theme of the variations in K.388, and its first statement (Ex. 16(a)), especially in instrumental lay-out (N.B. bassoons), reminds one of the sixth variation (see Ex. 16(b)) from the C minor Serenade's finale:

The Adagio (E flat) of K.375 offers a long theme which is first shared out (see Ex. 17) between the clarinet and oboe, then taken up by the horn and given a new continuation, and finally subsides in echoing exchanges between the oboes and clarinets (in pairs – they echo themselves and each other), the bassoon and horn, which come to rest on the dominant. The variety

[1] op. cit., p. 204.

of the instrumentation, the disposition of theme and phrases among the solo winds, recall the kaleidoscopic principle of the B flat Adagio of K.361.

Ex. 17

The second theme is a tender, sublime lullaby, first rocked in partnership by the clarinet and bassoons. It does not reappear in the recapitulation,[1] but the haunting oboe phrases (Exx. 18(a) and (b)), which respectively mark the second theme's closing section and the lead-back to the recapitulation, both emerge at the movement's end. Ex. 18(a) now rounds off not the second theme (the missing lullaby), but the return of the main theme (see below, and Ex. 17), while Ex. 18(b), extended and varied (see clarinets and bassoons, bars 84–5), forms the

Ex. 18(a)

Ex. 18(b)

coda. The recapitulation is newly instrumented. The clarinet now plays Ex. 17 entire, and the oboe takes up what was previously the horn's continuation; the oboe's continuation varies the horn's and contracts it. The ensuing echo exchanges, originally initiated by the oboes, are now given to the clarinets, succeeded by the oboes, and followed up by the bassoon and clarinets. This section is extended (fifteen bars against the exposition's eleven), but it lands up again at the same bar (cf. bars 25 and 73), which, in the exposition, preceded the lullaby; now, however, it is greeted by the absent theme's closing figure

---

[1] The abridged sonata form of this movement seems to have a parallel in the slow movement of the D major string Quartet, K.575.

(Ex. 18(a)), cadencing in the tonic. A feature of this recapitulation is an increase in the complexity of the texture, largely achieved by the addition of a bubbling arpeggio figure, first contributed by the horn and then running through all the instruments.[1] The variations in instrumentation are typical of Mozart's recapitulatory methods, hence their rather detailed description.

The slow movement of the C minor Serenade, K.388, is a compact Andante (E flat). It is, perhaps, the most perfectly shaped of the four slow movements. The first statement of its once repeated, sweet, yet solemn, main theme (Ex. 19) contains the movement's only reference to the basic diminished seventh motive (see *x*; cf. *x* in Exx. 7, 11, and 13, preceding). The repetition of the theme avoids the first statement's 'basic motive' cadence, and closes on the tonic. It is, in fact, with this repetition of the main theme that the recapitulation opens; hence *x* in Ex. 19 appears only in the exposition.

Ex. 19

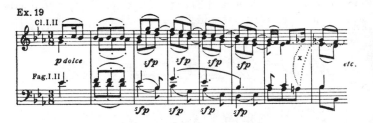

The second theme begins mildly, but gathers intensity in its repeat through variation and chromatic intensification (in the oboes), syncopated accompaniments (horns and clarinets), and the pronounced rhythmic and upward thrust of the bassoons (see Ex. 20 (horns and clarinets omitted)). The movement, indeed, derives a noticeable tension from this contrast between the solemnity of the first theme and the disconsolate bonhomie of the second. The hang-dog, wind-band character of the second theme's repetition is about the nearest Mozart approaches to a popular serenade atmosphere in the whole work. In its context, the theme assumes both a poignant and even ironic significance.

The short, highly functional, development concentrates on three attempted resumptions of the main theme, each of which

[1] The figure is, in fact, first introduced by the bassoon in the exposition, just before the entry of the 'lullaby' – a characteristic preview of later events.

is interrupted. Each resumption-plus-interruption is longer than its predecessor, and the recapitulation's return of the main theme (the exposition's second statement of it) is felt as a natural fulfilment of the caterpillar-like extensions of the theme's thrice-interrupted re-evolution in the development.

The recapitulation is regular;[1] but for the insignificant variants in the last four bars, there are no variations, either instrumental or thematic, and there are no extensions; allowing for the excision of the exposition's first statement of the first theme from the recapitulation, both exposition and recapitulation are symmetrical to the last quaver. In its economy, this movement is true to the generally economical character of K.388, a trend which distinguishes it from its predecessors (though they, too, shared an increasing discipline of invention) and anticipates the developing simplicity and economy of Mozart's late style, of which another, and more famous, serenade (*Eine kleine Nachtmusik*, K.525)[2] is a particularly brilliant example.

BOOK LIST

H. Abert: 'Mozart', in *Cobbett's Cyclopedic Survey of Chamber Music*, London, 1930, Vol. II, pp. 150–83.

A. Einstein: 'Divertimento, Cassation, Serenade', in *Mozart*, London, 1946, pp. 196–214.

G. Hausswald: *Mozarts Serenaden*, Leipzig, 1951.

[1] It should be noted, however, that so far as the second theme is concerned, it is its repetition which establishes the tonic. The first statement is still in the dominant. This delayed appearance of the tonic reminds me – not more, for it is not a true parallel – of the E flat Adagio of the Divertimento, K.287(271b), whose recapitulation begins in A flat. The tonic is not established for some bars.

[2] *The Times* of 6 May 1955 reported that the autograph of K.525, missing for nearly a century, had been recovered (source unspecified). It seems, however, that the lost first minuet remains lost. The autograph, I understand, shows unmistakable traces of the first minuet having been torn out. A facsimile edition has been published by Bärenreiter Verlag.

THE CHAMBER MUSIC

My approach to the task I have been given in this book is
not the usual one. For one thing, there will be no outlines of self-
evident forms, no discoveries of 'contrasting' second subjects or
middle sections: analysis will replace tautological description.
For another thing, I shall address myself not merely to the
listener on the one hand, or the public performer on the other,
but also to the chamber musician. It is he for whom Mozart's
chamber music was written; the listener is his more or less
excusable eavesdropper, the concert performer his usually in-
excusable usurper. If the chamber musician dies out – as, with
the help of the gramophone record and the concert hall, he may
well do – chamber music will die out too, both the great masterpieces of the past and the potential masterpieces of the future.
You can come to understand a symphony by listening to it, but
you cannot completely understand a string quartet without
playing it. The string quartet is the esoteric symphony, and the
more esoteric a truth, the more absolute the need for its immediate experience. You cannot either confess or be psycho-
analysed by proxy.

Analysis, then, will be linked with practical synthesis: the
points I hope to make about the unity of a work will be complemented, as far as possible, by advice about how to unify
and/or diversify it in interpretation.

I. Unity

What usually goes by the name of analysis is nothing of the
sort. Most critics have never grasped the essential difference between analysis and description. Description gives a verbal account of what you hear and is essentially unnecessary. Can anyone seriously suggest that a music-lover has to be told that a
contrasting theme is a contrasting theme?

Verbal or symbolic analysis shows, on the other hand, the
elements of what you hear. In a great piece, these are always
the elements of unity, not of diversity, because a great piece

grows from an all-embracing idea. Great music diversifies a unity; mere good music unites diverse elements. As soon as you have analysed the unity of a great work, its variety explains itself, whereas when you describe its, or indeed any work's, diversity, nothing is explained at all.

If you wish to explain the contrast between the notion of a prostitute and that of a saintly virgin, you will not get far beyond what your addressee knows anyway if you describe the respective lives and activities of the two figures. But if you know about the underlying unity, if you are aware that both notions spring from the same Oedipal phantasy and are in fact two extremely contrasting versions of the same basic idea of the mother, you will automatically arrive at a complete understanding of the contrast. The one essential point about a contrast is its unity, and if the unity is not stronger and deeper than that between a charwoman and a chairman, the contrast, however violent on the descriptive level, is not very interesting either.

I have talked too much about psychoanalysis to the backward musical intelligentsia not to know what I am in for with my psychological comparison which, however, I have chosen for the most relevant of reasons. The age of description is over. As far as philosophy has not had to give way to psychology, it has embarked upon analyses of terms which it had previously employed on the descriptive plane, while psychology itself has taken the plunge from the descriptive study of the conscious mind to the analytical study of the elemental and elementary unconscious. Freud's *Interpretation of Dreams*, which is the mother of the new psychology, demonstrated the unity of the most chaotically diverse dream by analysing the *latent* content of the *manifest* dream, and demonstrating that behind all the dreamy contrasts there was the single-minded, basic motive of wishfulfilment.

It will be the *latent* basic motifs, and generally the unitive forces behind the *manifest* music, on which my analytic observations will concentrate. The most uncomfortable questions, hardly ever as much as touched upon, will clamour for an answer: why or how does the contrasting second subject necessarily belong to the first? why is a particular movement an integral part of a particular work and of no other? and so forth.

With the space at my disposal, my analytic observations

cannot hope to be anything like complete. In the circumstances, I shall always try to answer (*a*) the thorniest questions and (*b*) certain central questions whose solution will enable the reader to conduct his own investigation into the rest of the analytic problems involved. I shall not refer to analytic facts which are obvious from the viewpoint of my method, even though they may be of the greatest importance for the construction of a work. To give an example: I shall not often mention development sections, because usually the working-out brings the latent background to the fore anyway. A development tends to contain its own analysis, expressed in musical terms – though the first work discussed will prove to contain an exception to this rule.

My aims then, it will be seen, are ambitious, and I shall probably fail on various occasions; but this chapter will have served its purpose if, in its weakest spots, the reader beats me with my own weapons.

My method itself is essentially naive, though I think I have worked out for myself a firm theoretical foundation; its formulation, however, would fill my entire space, and must therefore be reserved for a later occasion. By 'naive' I mean that I listen inwardly to contrasts until their unity emerges, and without any theoretical preconceptions. Usually, since I know all these works very well, my self-analytic reaction is immediate, and its formulation amounts to no more than a rationalization of spontaneous emotions, sifted, to be sure, by my technical knowledge. I shall not put anything into words or symbols that has not been felt on the one hand, and – alas, privately – substantiated in theory on the other. I must ask the reader for one favour – to keep the harmonic aspect of any passage or motif in mind throughout its discussion. Many of my observations on thematic unity will stand or fall with the harmony of the melodic entity analysed, but it would be cumbersome to add harmonic riders in every single instance, though where necessary or convenient I shall do so. There will also be occasions when I shall regard essential rhythmic relations as self-evident. I hope nobody will think that I am 'picking out any old notes' to suit my purposes before he has satisfied himself about the harmonic and rhythmic implications of my analysis. My fear is not paranoic, but simply a reaction to a foolish, though 'professional' criticism of Rudolph Reti's *The Thematic Process in Music*[1] made to me in private.

[1] New York, 1951; London, 1961.

Reti's effort brings me to the four men who would seem to have provided my method with stimulating incentives. I think that his own approach exaggerates the. melodic aspect, but it breaks new ground and helps others to do likewise. Schenker, on the other hand, may be guilty of harmonic exaggeration and of neglecting melodic and rhythmic forces, but his *Urlinien* and *Ursätze* ('basic lines' and 'basic structures' are perhaps preferable translations to the 'fundamental lines' and 'fundamental structures' which Victor Zuckerkandl[1] suggests in his brilliantly condensed article on the subject) open the analyst's and the player's ears alike to the latent driving forces of manifest form. Schoenberg's analyses, without which Reti's would be unthinkable, avoid either exaggeration and, few though they are, represent perhaps the most revolutionary event in the history of music criticism. The fact is not surprising, since Schoenberg was the first great composer who analysed in public. There is no really musical analyst whom Schoenberg has not helped to re-think in creative terms. Last but first, there is Oskar Adler, Schoenberg's first teacher and lifelong friend, who, generations later, became my teacher and most intimate musical friend. From my early childhood I lived in his chamber-musical world, first passively, later actively. He did not care two hoots about analysis, but his uniquely organic and motif-conscious way of playing taught me more about the essentials of chamber-musical forms and textures than any analytical teacher could possibly have done.

II. UNIFICATION AND DIVERSIFICATION

When we have to face problems of interpretation, we must eventually move back from the analytic to the descriptive level, from the latent motifs to the manifest music, from unity to diversity: the great creator diversifies a unity, and the good re-creator must first get at the unity from the manifest diversity, and then diversify it. A monotonous player has never understood the unity of a work, whence he is forced to substitute uniformity for it; an erratic player has never understood its diversity, whence he deems it a good idea to juxtapose a charwoman and a chairman for the sake of variety, and is proud of their underlying unity too.

[1] 'Urlinie, Ursatz', in W. Apel: *Harvard Dictionary of Music*, London, 1946, pp. 779f.

III. Principles of Selection and Procedure

It has been a terrifying problem how best to utilize my very strictly prescribed number of words. My choice of material has been determined by the fact that I am primarily addressing myself to the string quartet player, who hears the heart-beat of chamber music, and by two constant principles, practicality and musical value, which sometimes harmonize and sometimes conflict with each other. It would have been both musically juster and spatially easier to concentrate on the quintets rather than the quartets, but since two violas are rarer than one, it would have been less practical.

Like the teacher, the critic should make himself unnecessary. Incidental analyses apart, my analytic procedure will take the approximate course of an inverse geometrical progression. The farther we get, the less I say: the reader will, I hope, be gradually enabled to do my work for himself. The only quartet that will be analysed at all comprehensively will be Mozart's first great one – for no other reasons than that it is the first, and that I am proceeding chronologically within each *genre* in order to facilitate quick reference. For self-evident purposes, I shall, however, break the chronological order on two occasions (with K.458 and K.478 respectively).

Finally, with a few exceptions, *my music examples are not so much examples as references : it is not they that ought to be studied, but the passages amd sections and total contexts to which they direct the reader's attention.*

IV. Incidental Information

I shall not hesitate to give information that is incidental to my main purposes of analysis and synthesis as long as it is new and of musical import. The writer is not there for the self-loving form of his piece, but for the reader.

A. THE STRING QUARTETS
(1) The Early Works

On the whole, Mozart's early quartets are quite abominable; far from being suitable for concert performance, most of them are not even worth-while playing within the confines of a really musical chamber. The solemn faces in front of their radios listening to a Third Programme broadcast of, say, the Haydn imitations of K.168–73 (1773) are a product of our age's unmusical musicological snobbery; such people have no right to the musician's duty, which is unbounded humility in the face of the later masterpieces. Even the worst early works are, of course, of genuine musicological interest, but why play them at all and thus insult Mozart's genius? The fact is that as a genius (and as opposed to Mendelssohn), Mozart was no prodigy at all; on the contrary, the eruption of his original creative force was retarded by his astonishing if intermittent technical facility and his passive and eclectic character: Beethoven's more awkward genius exploded far earlier. I speak of "intermittent" facility because most of the early quartets show serious defects even on an elementary technical level, both in texture and in transitional and developmental procedure. In one word, they are not Mozart. Many of Boccherini's masterpieces are, of course, immeasurably superior, and are herewith recommended to the chamber-musician instead of most early Mozart.

There are, however, a few playable exceptions among these immature quartets, and on one or two occasions even Mozart himself puts in an appearance. Two of the earliest six quartets (if we disregard his very first effort and the 'orchestral' quartets, K.136–8 (125a–c)) are in fact the best – in thought as well as in formal technique and textural lay-out.

K.156(134b) in G, a perfect and inspired miniature (1772), is a fascinating preview of the great Mozart, and an excellent practice for the novice. (My pupils play quartets as soon as they can crawl on the instrument.) The opening movement is based on a waltz theme which Mozart invented and re-invented at the beginning and end of his career respectively – in neither case, however, as a waltz theme proper. In the present work he races it along in presto tempo,

while in the last days of his life he wellnigh completely divests it of its waltz character (even though retaining the waltz's characteristic 'two–three' in the accompaniment) and puts it in his most tragic key, which is not G minor:

When playing the quartet, it will be good to remember both the theme's latent waltz rhythm and its 'Requiem' version, in order to prevent too reckless a speed and to invest the gaiety of the melody with the kind of flowing gracefulness which, by its very insistence on pure joy, warns us that sadness is round the corner. The player will note that in both Exx. 1(a) and 1(b) Mozart tries his best to prevent heavy bar accents and produce a flowing development of the rhythmic structure and melodic line – in the gay version by way of the presto characterization, in the sad version through the 12/8 time, which rolls four of Ex. 1(a)'s bars into one where a 6/8 might have rolled them into two. Take the first two bars as an upbeat.

Of the development section, which anticipates the key of the second movement, Einstein[1] says that "it bears indeed no relation to the themes of the exposition; but can it be called *galant*? Nothing like this can be found in any other composer [Ex. 1(c): misprinted in Einstein; here reduced to one stave]":

The justification of my initial fuss about the difference between analysis and description here becomes immediately clear. On the descriptive level, Einstein's observation, which professes to be analytic, is true enough, though it merely describes what the listener hears anyway – if not less. On the analytic level, it is untrue, and leaves unanswered the one question in which the player and listener are interested: why does this particular development necessarily belong to this particular exposition? He feels it belongs, and all that Einstein does is give the lie to his feeling.

[1] A. Einstein: *Mozart*, London, 1946, p. 174.

The truth is that while there is no manifest relation between development and exposition, the latent relation is all the stricter. (I have come to the widely-tested conclusion that this is true of all good music: the looser the manifest integration, the stricter the demonstrable latent unification. I use this criterion as one of my critical tools for objective evaluation.) Ex. 1(a) consists of four notes: (1) dominant (stressed by sustainment), (2) mediant, (3) tonic (stressed by repetition and shake), and (4) leading note. In Ex. 1(c) we find precisely the same line: (1) dominant (stressed by repetition and shake-like figuration which, at the same time, introduces the key of the relative minor via the flat sixth, after the feminine dominant cadence with which the exposition ends), (2) mediant, (3) tonic (stressed by an overlapping 'repetition', i.e. by octave doubling), (4) leading note. It will be seen that while basic stresses are retained, including even, differently distributed, their particular formulations, the theme is rendered superficially unrecognizable (*a*) because its harmonico-rhythmic structure and articulation are drastically changed, to the extent of a complete relinquishment of Ex. 1(a)'s thematic unit, and (*b*) because of its octave-transpositions. In one word, these four notes are treated in the same manner as a Schoenbergian note-row. Here as elsewhere (cf. Ex.16(b) on p. 110), the chordal origin of serial octave-transpositions can be observed. We shall anon have occasion to point to more complex examples of Mozart's as yet unrecognized serial technique. Meanwhile, if the reader has any difficulty in hearing the relation between Exx. 1(c) and 1(a), he is advised to proceed acoustically via the 'Requiem' version (Ex. 1(b)), which, like Ex. 1(c), is in the minor. For the rest, it is no wonder that Einstein could find "nothing like this . . . in any other composer": extreme latent unity beneath extreme manifest variety is the mark of genius.

The quartet continues to show the real Mozart in the slow movement, one of his few in the minor and still fewer in adagio tempo. Again the integration of the theme (Ex. 2(a)) is impressive; I shall save quite a few technical words if I reshape it in the metre of Ex. 1(b) (see Ex. 2(b)),

whereupon its relation to the theme of the opening movement (Ex. 1(a)) will at once be clear: Exx. 1(b) and 2(b) might be complementary phrases in the same period. The unifying principle confronting us here is a forerunner of what I call the 'principle of reversed and postponed antecedents and consequents' which I have found to obtain quite often in later Mozart (see pp. 104ff., 112, 126).

The tyro playing one of the lower parts might be warned that this is one of those very slow movements where the two halves of the bar are so heavily articulated that they may sometimes be thoughtlessly mistaken for two bars. If he plays the second violin, a great task awaits him in the first bar of the second subject. Let him beware of 'shouting' here, overjoyed at his sudden solo function; especially in the exposition, a feeling and flexible restraint is indicated, with due regard for the first fiddle's figuration: the timbre of the E-string will do the rest. Though detached, the semiquavers on the second and fourth beats should be taken on the same bow as the ensuing quavers in order to avoid over-accentuation. It may be added that this bar came to be wellnigh literally quoted in the Quartet of the *Entführung*, where Mozart's notes explain its phrasing better than do my present words.

The opening movement of K.157 (late 1772 or early 1773) in C is another masterly miniature, eminently suitable for acquiring the feel of a genuine quartet texture on an elementary level: the lower parts can be played in the first position. The thematic integration is again exceptionally close and subtle; the cadential scalic phrase of the first subject (Ex. 3(a)), for instance, itself a derivative of the basic motif, goes to form, in diminution, the

Ex.3 *Allegro*

motif of its continuation (Ex. 3(b)); appears in a new rhythmic variation as thematic basis of the bridge passage (Ex. 3(c)); is broadly augmented to preside over the climax of the second sub-

ject (Ex. 3(d)); and returns to its diminutive rhythm for the
closing section (Ex. 3(e)), on which the development is based.
By the end of this chapter, we shall perhaps realize that all
great music is latently monothematic and, if in more than one
movement, cyclic.

When playing the quartet with a virginal second fiddler, care
should be taken to start it in a tempo which will accommodate
his semiquaver passages in the first subject's continuation and
in the lead-back. On a slightly more advanced level, the violin-
ists and viola player should exchange parts in order to obtain a
thorough experience of the medium. The contemporary tendency towards specialization and rigid separation between
fiddling and viola-playing is to be discouraged. There actually
are viola players who cannot play the violin – not to speak of
the many fiddlers who do not play the viola.

Though not a masterpiece, K.160(159a) in E flat (1773) is
a useful and often pleasant quartet for near-beginners, whose
opening, basic motif (Ex. 4) is among the well-wearable
eighteenth-century clichés (cf. Ex. 3(c)):

Ex.4 *Allegro*

Again the lower parts can, if they must, stick to the first position,
and an exchange of parts will relieve the occasional boredom of
the somewhat primitive work.

K.170 in C (1773) has little musical value and shows multiple
defects, but the opening Andante, a variation movement in da
capo form with four variations in the middle, gives the beginner-
leader a chance to develop the kind of imaginative, subtle, and
considerate concertante style without which a string quartet
never comes of age. In the first variation, in particular, he can
surrender to the virtuosic manner without having to fear that
the gods of technique will anon punish his *hubris*, for even in
this very uncertain quartet, the seventeen-year-old Mozart
knew instinctively how to make the fiddle brilliantly easy,
how to make child's play sound giant's play – something
which the composer of what is quite wrongly considered the
greatest violin concerto never learnt. For the rest, I must leave
it to the prospective quartet leader to realize and maybe even

complement Mozart's youthful art of variation through and by his own.

Like K.169 in A (1773), K.173 in D minor (1773) is again based on the scale motif descending from the dominant to the tonic (cf. Exx. 4 and 3(c)):

It is an unsuccessful Haydn imitation, packed with clichés and topped by a dreadful fugue on a chromatic seventeenth-century theme. Indeed, except for its D minor chromaticism, which in any case is an historical (Dorian) rather than an individual phenomenon, the quartet can in no way be considered a forerunner of the famous D minor. At the same time, its interest does lie in one or two prophecies it contains. For one thing, the chromatic lead-back motif (Ex. 6), a cliché well-known from

Haydn with which we shall have to concern ourselves more than once (see pp. 114f. and 121), is already used in an original way, leading to the dominant instead of the tonic. It is true that this employment is somewhat awkward, but in the music of a dormant genius, painful moments are often the birth-pangs of originality. For another thing, the rhythmic and melodic structure of the slow movement theme,

ultimately influenced, no doubt, by the gavotte's third beat, foreshadows a whole series of great Mozart themes, down to the slow movement of the master's last Haydn-imitation, the partly incomprehensible E flat Quintet which he wrote in the year of his death (see p. 132); the theme there (Ex. 7(b)) is in fact closely

modelled on Ex. 7(a), both straight and inverted, and including
of course the harmonico-rhythmic structure:

('I' means inversion, 'O' (original form) the straight version.)
The present movement's integration with the first movement is
achieved by complementation: Ex. 5 approaches the tonic from
the dominant above, Ex. 7(a) from the dominant below. The
triplets are unmotivated and therefore bad: cf. pp. 125f.

The minuet, (Ex. 8(a)) whose relation to the opening movement (Ex. 5) is obvious, derives thematically, tonally, and formally from the minuet of Haydn's Op. 9, No. 4 (Ex. 8(b)),

with which it is also connected by a rhythmic figure. Einstein[1]
does point out that Mozart imitated Haydn in K.168–73, but
fails to take Haydn's Op. 9 into consideration. More interesting
from the standpoint of his creative development, in any case, is
the fact that Mozart's primitive minuet is the obvious father of
the A major trio in *Don Giovanni*:

K.173 will best be played once and then discarded for good.

(ii) The 'Ten' and the 'Adagio and Fugue'

The editions of Haydn's 'Ten' or 'Fifteen Celebrated Quartets' do not in any way give a sufficient picture of the

[1] op. cit., pp. 175ff.

composer's lasting achievements in the *genre* in which his genius developed at its purest and deepest, and Beethoven never wrote any 'celebrated' quartets at all. On the other hand, characteristically enough, Mozart's popular ten are not only the 'Ten Celebrated', but at the same time his only great and mature masterpieces among the string quartets (apart from the *Kleine Nachtmusik* (K.525, 1787) – from the quartet player's standpoint the easiest introduction to great, perfect Mozart – and the 'Adagio and Fugue' (K.546)). Not all of them may be absolutely flawless, but where they are, they represent a consummation of artistic perfection the like of which has, perhaps, never again been achieved in chamber music, except in Schoenberg's string Trio. What is the price that Mozart pays for having it both ways, for his simultaneous depth and finished surface, his originality and appeal – for his public privacy? With Haydn (from Op. 9 onwards) and Beethoven, a new quartet is a new quartet, revolutionarily unlike its predecessors, employing hitherto untried means of diversifying a basic idea. Mozart's originality does not similarly renew itself; it is always there, but often it has been there before. He tends to adhere to his own, highly original, conventions, whereas Haydn and Beethoven do not only break other people's conventions, but also their own. Consequently, any two great Mozart quartets are more alike in form than any two great Haydn or Beethoven quartets, and if we are honest, we do not always find it easy to say, on purely musical grounds, which Mozart quartet is the earlier and which the later. Haydn and Beethoven obviously were more strongly developing characters, but at the same time we should beware of facile musical characterology: in the operas, the piano concertos and, above all, in the string quintets, Mozart shows an otherwise unsuspected developmental drive which does in fact create a new form in almost every instance.

On the whole, the six quartets dedicated to Haydn are even profounder and more accomplished masterpieces than the later three dedicated to the King of Prussia. The reason seems to be twofold, positive and negative. On the one hand, there is no doubt that Mozart made, if the phrase be permitted, a special effort in view of his expert dedicatee, to whom he would also be psychologically prepared to confide his deepest secrets. On the other hand, His 'Cello-playing Majesty created very particular and grave textural problems with which any other composer, including probably Haydn and Beethoven, would have been unable to cope on a high creative level. Mozart's solutions show an almost incredible capacity for adjustment, a mastery of the medium in circumstances that were nothing short of a textural emergency. Nevertheless the 'Prussian' Quartets are very special cases of string quartets rather than string quartets proper: they almost represent a different – and not so ideal – medium.

(α) The 'Haydn' Quartets

The melodic evolution of K.387 in G (1787) immediately shows both the master and the genius; every note is over-determined, and everything springs from the basic motif (x).

Ex.9 *Allegro vivace assai*

Original Edition

Autograph and Einstein

The basic fourth is at once reversed and filled up scale-wise (x^1), in which basic shape it serves as main thematic material. The first half of the second bar represents, in diminution, a retrograde version of the first bar, while the cadential motif of its second half is a straight (con)sequence of the first bar's second half, and just as a semitone is here replaced by a whole tone, a whole tone has been replaced by a semitone in the four-quaver motif. x^1 appears in straight form in the second half of the third bar, but in the first half it develops towards what is ultimately to become the second subject. The shake itself increases the oscillating motion that is to become the characteristic rhythmic feature of the subsidiary theme (see Ex. 11); whereas the semi-quaver diminution of x^1 establishes the actual rhythm of this feature, whose notes (mediant and sharpened supertonic) come from bar 4's cadential motif, itself a crab of x^1's cadential notes $(g''-f\sharp'')$, though from the standpoint of rhythmic structure, its immediate model is bar 2's cadential motif, to which it forms the formal and harmonic complement. The fundamental motif

of the consequent (bar 5) introduces a rhythmic variation of x
(minus upbeat) plus x^1, and further develops the forthcoming
second subject's semiquaver rhythm; in fact, for rhythmico-
thematic reasons, I disagree with the autograph and Einstein's
'Authentic Edition' and concur with the Original Edition (see
Ex. 9) which, it must not be forgotten, was corrected by Mozart,
especially in the first violin part, where the identical problem arises in bar 7.[1] By the time the cadence (Ex. 10(b)) of the
bridge passage is reached, not even the staccato dots of its motif
which is again encompassed by x's basic fourth, are new, for
they derive from the equally thematic portato motif (Ex. 10(a))
that introduces the principal theme's perfect cadence four bars
after Ex. 9's last bar:

It is from Ex. 10(b) that the second subject grows, after a
quaver's rest:

The unity between the first and second subjects – or, to look at
the matter in the order of creative events – the rich and intensive variegation of the basic idea, is one of the greatest miracles
of which genius is capable. We are confronted with one of the
most deep-reaching applications of what I submit is the creative
principle of reversed and postponed antecedents and consequents (see

---

[1] Mozart's notation never makes any difference between the two versions, and
Einstein's print follows his handwriting – with the result that of late, we sometimes hear a short appoggiatura.

p. 98). Ex. 12(a) has been distilled from the first subject (Ex. 9),
Ex. 12(b) from the second (Ex. 11).

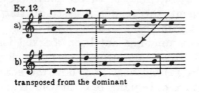

transposed from the dominant

We hear the complementary function of the two basic lines, as
well as their underlying unity. First, the line of the basic motif
(x^0; see x in Ex. 9) is complemented by the first three notes of
(b): where the tonic motif ascends triadically from tonic to
tonic, the dominant phrase (here transposed) ascends triadically
from its dominant to its dominant, one note of the triad being
omitted in either case – the mediant in the first subject, the
tonic in the dominant second. The octave outline as well as the
triadic nature of the basic motif is thus retained in the basic
phrase of the second subject and, indeed, re-emphasized by the
octave imitations in the 'cello and viola (Ex. 11, bars 2 and 4),
where we are reminded that great music's so-called 'free' devices are never free: where they free themselves of one commitment, they enter into another, all the stricter one. On the
descriptive level, that is to say, the 'cello indulges in rhythmic
imitations, melodically 'free', of the first violin's minor thirds, but
underneath, the 'free' octaves are over-determined by the wider
context and deeper content: x^4 in Ex. 11 imitates x^3, while
the viola's imitation, rhythmically freer, adheres to the (chor-
dally inverted) notes of the manifest imitational model (f$\sharp$'–a').

We immediately realize that the complementary relation of the
respective first 3 notes of (a) and (b) in Ex. 12 reverses the relation
of antecedent and consequent, (b) standing in an antecedental
relation to (a). But while this reversal continues to the end of the
two backgrounds, which, thus heard, smoothly merge, (b) running into (a) as if driven by the impulse of a tonal sequence, an
implication of a straight and sequential antecedent–consequent
relation between (a) and (b) is, at the same time, retained:

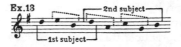

Note:—Both Ex. 13 and the lineal directive in Ex. 12 will be seen to indicate a unifying force that is active throughout the work: cf. Ex. 23 on p. 113. In the narrower context of the present movement, the reader is asked to start this series of notes (degrees) with the g″ (third note in Ex. 12(a)) which, owing to an erratum, has not been marked for the purpose. In this example (whose construction is made clear by the lineal directive in Ex. 12) we hear, too, how the basic motif's basic fourth (see x in Ex. 9) remains basic in what is manifestly a most dissimilar second subject.

An (a)–(b) relation and a (b)–(a) relation, then, run with each other against each other, the one securing postponed continuity, the other helping to produce second-subject tension on a unitary basis. I have come to regard this principle of reversal as highly important for polythematic integration in large-scale master-forms.

The rhythmic integration of the second subject parallels, intensifies, and complements the harmonico-thematic integration. The rhythmic disposition of the basic motif (x in Ex. 9: quaver upbeat with two ensuing crotchets) is precisely maintained in the first three notes of the second subject (Ex. 11), yet its rhythmic structure submits to extreme variation, owing to the repeated mediant crotchets (which pre-pone the repeated tonic crotchets of Ex. 9's bar 1!) and the static harmony of the tonic root position.

Both the unity and the diversity of the second subject must be brought out in performance; I must confess that I have never heard this theme logically played on any public occasion – and far be it from me to suggest that there is only one way of making its logic clear. On the one hand, an infinitesimal retardation, an indication that we are 'settling down' in the dominant is needed between the upbeat and the main beat (Ex. 11), introduced by a slightly more noticeable widening-out of tempo in the cadence of the bridge passage (Ex. 10(b)) and emphasized, perhaps, by a generous observance of the intervening quaver rest's articulation. On the other hand, we must not lose aural sight of 'the other end' of x^3 (Ex. 11), i.e., the upper octave (a'). The basic motif (x in Ex. 9) shoots up to the upper octave within half a bar and urges beyond it; the second subject is more leisurely in its journey to the upper octave, but it drives towards and beyond it nevertheless. In practice, this means that any fussing about in the first bar of the second subject is deadly. We have seen that, rhythmically, the semiquaver figure's immediate predecessor is the end of the bridge passage (Ex. 10(b)), its archetype the shake in bar 3 of the first subject (Ex. 9). Between the two, it forms a synthesis: metrically articulated like Ex. 10(b), it does not share its harmonic articulation, but, on the contrary, is as unimportant harmonically as a shake. The player must be absolutely conscious of its harmonic unimportance, of the fact that the two notes of the motif do not have the same rights and privileges. He will do well to remember that *khroma* means colour: the chromatic note merely colours the mediant in order to keep up the movement, and to over-articulate the figure would mean to brake, and thus to contradict its very purpose. Not even the main note, i.e. the first mediant, should receive any accent; the motif must float past as a simultaneous ornamental or figurational continuation of the second crotchet and an upbeat to the upbeat to the upper octave. A very unobtrusive and flexible spiccato will be indicated, femininely adjustable rather than masculinely brilliant and assertive. If the player cannot manage this without a self-conscious right hand – and our reminder goes for the highest professional circles as well as for amateurs – a light détaché will be preferable to a spiccato which may be faithful to the dots over the notes, but not to the meaning which the dots help to convey. The chief point is to have a clear idea of the phrase, rather than take a narcissistic joy in one's wrist. This auto-suggestive idea will perhaps also prompt the player to an imperceptible rubato which shortens the time prescribed for the semiquaver figure by *delaying it* slightly, not by anticipating the ensuing upbeat, which would result in amateurish hurrying and in an immediate destruction of rhythmic characterization, unity (the quaver value is thematic and a firm sequential and imitational model), and variety (bar 2's developmental variation of bar 1 depends on the upbeat's quaver value for the effect of its newly-emerging dotted crotchet).

A further difficulty inherent in the interpretation of the second subject is primarily textural: at the very point when unself-conscious playing is of vital importance, a self-conscious situation is created by the fact that the second fiddle is entrusted with the first, piano statement of the theme (like the *forte-piano* dualism, the principle of thematic distribution between the instruments pervades the entire work). The second violin's is by far the most difficult part in the string quartet, for both psychological and textural reasons (it plays the alto part without being an alto instrument), and its sudden emergences into the sunlight of solo playing are as precarious as its complex accompanimental tasks. The inexperienced player will tend to be too timid in the shaping of the subject, while the routineer will indulge in his well-formed habit of reacting against the occupational disease of second-fiddle timidity and will have destroyed both his own statement of the theme and the ensuing *primo* contrast by the time his first crotchet, unduly overstressed, is over. Only a crystal-clear awareness of the two contrasting statements will help here. The forte is but one aspect of the more masculine character of the varied restatement which goes so far as to increase the harmonic importance of the unimportant figuration (see, in the score, the first violin and viola in the bar after Ex. 11), a departure that has been prepared by the delayed imitation of the motif on the penultimate 'cello beat in Ex. 11: the unity with the original figure is preserved not only by its melodic identity but also by its falling on the same (third) beat of the bar, but it is a different third beat now, stressed by the cadential $^{6\,5}_{4\,3}$ in which the motif's harmonic note has become the all-important dominant bass, and the chromatic note its 'leading note', turning into the leading note proper in the viola figure of the bar after Ex. 11.

On the basis of our analysis of the first movement's latent unity, the integration of the minuet is well-nigh predictable, even though on the surface the structure is surprising. What happens is that the two halves of the triad (first three notes of Exx. 12(a) and (b) respectively), the two bases of the opening movement's contrasting subjects re-meet; the basic fourth, which opens the movement,

again carries the superficially contrasting continuation, this time single-, or rather double-handed, i.e. together with its chordal inversion, the fifth: Ex. 14(b) is distilled from Ex. 14(a)'s bars 3–8,

and will be seen to re-shuffle Ex. 13. The chromatic scales which fill in two of the quartal spaces derive from bar 4 of Ex. 9 – ultimately, that is to say, from bar 2 which, in its turn, we have seen to introduce a crab version of the first basic bar. Like other Mozart minuets which replace the more primitive dance by rhythmic complexity (cf. the D minor Quartet, p. 118), the present movement rolls a variety of rhythmic structures into one. (I have come to the conclusion that all good composition is compression, while bad composition at its best is – com-position.) It is, in fact, polyrhythmic not only between different parts, but also within one and the same part. The first two bars imply a latent 3/4, displaced by one crotchet and starting with an up-beat: see my first two dotted bar-lines. With the chromatic phrase, two backgrounds make themselves felt. The *forte-piano* dualism of the work is here compressed within the narrowest possible space and produces, for one thing, an implied change to 2/4: see my further dotted bar-lines. For another thing, however, as a background behind this background, the initial, displaced 3/4 background continues to operate:

This 3/4 time can be counted from my initial dotted bars (Ex. 14(a)) over Ex. 14(c) *and across the four intervening straighter bars* to the second violin's resumption of the chromatic phrase in bar 13 and beyond. When I rationalized my dark rhythmic feelings about the 'Sinfonia' from Strawinsky's wind Octet and discovered that you could count 3/16 across the ever-changing time signatures until you safely landed in 3/16 again, I thought that Strawinsky had done something new. It always pays to look for one's new finds in Mozart.

When the chromatic phrase appears in imitations, the poly-rhythmic structure expresses itself *poly-dynamically* –

– a unique example of uncompromising dynamic counter-point.

At what one might call the second-subject stage of the minuet, a thematic unit emerges which, on the descriptive level, one would regard as new (Ex. 16(a)). Analytically, however, it could not be older, for it simply retrogrades the previous varia-tion of the basic fourth (Ex. 16(b), R = retrograde version), availing itself of octave-transposition and lavish rhythmic varia-tion, and thus approaching serial transformation:

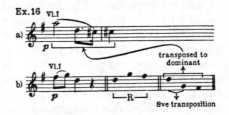

The ensuing diminution (Ex. 17) of the 'cello's crab version (see '!' in Ex. 14(a)) of the chromatic phrase, too, results in an extreme rhythmic variation and is, moreover, introduced by an octave-transposition of the basic fourth (first two notes in Ex. 17)

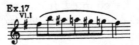

across the parts (first two notes of series marked '!' in Ex. 14(a)): altogether a concise summary of what were to become typically dodecaphonic devices. The diminution (Ex. 17) proceeds, of course, on the same harmonic degrees (in B minor) as the original retrograde form (in G major).

In the trio, whose initial integration we need no longer explain, the manifestly 'new' continuation

derives from the basic fourth via Ex. 16(a).

As for the tempo of the movement (see Ex. 14(a)), Einstein's 'Authentic Edition' reluctantly decides in favour of the Original Edition, although its first violin part does not contain any tempo indication at all; and it was precisely this part which Mozart corrected more carefully than the others. Einstein's sole reason seems to be that "*Allegro* tends to weaken the precision of the dynamic accentuation", and for the self-same reason I recommend this tempo: in view of our analysis, it will not do to push the latent rhythmic implications completely out of aural sight. Our knowledge of these backgrounds makes us respect Mozart's spontaneous tempo indication in the autograph; at a later stage, when the meaningful conflict between these rhythmic structures was no longer acute in his mind and had become, psychologically speaking, an established fact, he may no longer have been worried about expressing it all and may, instead, have started to worry about the tempo for other reasons, e.g. because the characterization might, in places, suffer at an exaggerated pace. Clearly, an allegretto-ish allegro rather than a allegroish allegretto is the consistent solution.

While the minuet's fundamental, triadic octave span is tonical like the first subject's in the opening movement (Ex. 9, x), the slow movement's triadic octave

spans the distance from dominant to dominant like the second subject of the first movement (Ex. 11, x³). Thus, while both middle movements reintegrate the two halves of the triad split by the two subjects of the first, they at the same time continue to represent one subject each: complete and final reintegration is reserved for the finale. The earlier movement is again the 'consequent', the later the 'antecedent':

transposed from subdominant

The 'new' dominant motif of this abridged sonata form stems, like the dominant motif of the minuet, from Ex. 16(b), which it reintroduces by way of *interversion* – an excellent new term of Reti's[1] denoting the re-grouping of notes within a motif or phrase:

In the context of the entire work, as well as of the finale's own wider structure, the tag that forms its first subject, though in itself meaningless, assumes pregnant significance:

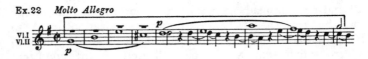

As distinct from an inspired idea as such, it is a conventional idea that has been inspired by Mozart. By means of the fugal exposition, the fundamental triad is now more fully mended: the first violin supplies the tonal answer to the question of the octave span. At the same time, the basic fourth creates a new tension within the triad, which, predetermined by the two subjects of the opening movement and their later consequences, immediately determines the outline of the conjunct counter-subject, just as the disjunct opening of the minuet had determined the ensuing conjunct motion (see Exx. 14(a) and (b)). In Ex. 23, I am juxtaposing my analytic combination of the first movement's first *cum* second subjects ((a), see Ex. 13) and the outlines of the minuet's continuation ((b), see Ex. 14(b)), of the

[1] op. cit., p. 72.

present fugue subject with its second entry (c), and of the counter-subject (d).

Ex.23

I have confined myself to marking the basic fourth and its inversions.

That the succeeding episode should derive from the counterpoint is nothing new, but that the one figure in it which does not should stand in consequential relation to the basic subject (see Ex. 22) shows the somnambulistic certainty with which, in an inspired master mind, every little chip of a thought has grown from the original idea. The proposition itself is commonplace, but when we try to demonstrate it we are invading holy music with our base intellect. The superstitious identification of knowlege and defilement is older than the Bible, in which the Hebrew word for 'know' expresses it. There may be a point to it, but if you do not want to know about music you should not read about it and, more important, should not write about it. You cannot have it no ways. In Ex. 24, I am (a) expressing the basic subject in the rhythm of the episode, and (b) quoting the latter's seemingly new figure.

Ex.24

The continuation of (b)

Ex.25

grows, by degrees,

Ex.26

into the accompanied tune of the second (sonata) subject,

in view of whose violent stylistic contrast – pure homophony against strict polyphony – there has been a great deal of literary commotion, although nobody has bothered to consider so much as the elements of its integration. The fact is that the basic motif's basic fourth (see first movement, Ex. 9) now reaches the final stages of the liquidation of the triad's split, and the attendant question of the octave span is not merely solved, but pointedly removed altogether: what used to be the dominant octave in the second subject of the first movement (Ex. 11) has become the dominant prime (the American term is preferable to the illogical English 'unison') in the second subject of the last.

On the same degrees as the basic fourth in Ex. 27, though modulating to the tonic, the chromatic transition and lead-back at the end of the exposition

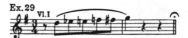

is another cliché inspired with the strictest structural significance; we remember its less masterly employment in early Mozart (K.173, see Ex. 6 on p. 100). In the present instance, it turns out to be not only a filled-in version of the basic fourth, but also a retrograde version of Ex. 17, identical, in augmentation, with the final cadential phrase of the minuet,

and deriving, at the same time, from the counter-subject of Ex. 22 via Ex. 30,

of which it forms, again, the crab version. For the rest, we need not analyse the importance of this conjunct version of the basic fourth, for Mozart does it for us in a development on which he worked very hard and which he revised repeatedly. The re-capitulation omits the fugal exposition of the first subject, whence arises an original interpretation of what would, in itself, be a primitive device – the subdominant-tonic key scheme which Schubert still uses in order to avoid a change in the modulatory conditions of the exposition. This is typical Mozart. Two structural devices, one formal and one harmonic, and each simple enough in itself, are combined towards a most complex effect: it rolls into one a telescoping of development and recapitulation and a stylistic contrast between the two, which a recapitulation of the fugato of the first subject could not have afforded, since it would have unhinged the balance and alter-nation between the different styles. In order to observe these devices in isolation, the reader is referred to K.218 on the one hand and K.545 on the other: I am choosing two instances where simplicity (as distinct from the present complexity) is realized with mastery. ('All mastery is simple' is one of those twaddling half-truths which put a convenient impression before thought. All mastery is as simple as possible. When it expresses something complex and new it is less simple than when it ex-presses something simple and old.)

In imitations, the transitional motif (Ex. 28) finally leads into, and builds up the coda which could not end so concisely if it were not so thematic,

Ex.31

for thematicism (in this instance the 'leading' minor second) is the soul of brevity. Thus, by way of a surprise sequence, does the *subsemitonium modi* reveal the fullest final significance, deriv-ing not only from the basic phrase of the movement but, farth-est beyond, from its retrograde form in the quartal basic shape (x^1 in Ex. 9) that evolves in the beginning of the entire work. One gradually begins to realize what Mozart meant when he recalled those beautiful moments of inner creation where the whole work sounded "like a picture", simultaneously; what Schoenberg meant when he talked of "the unity of musical space." The one-ness, the simultaneity is the inner reality, the Kantian thing-in-itself, the Schopenhauerian will, the Freudian unconscious (which is essentially timeless), while the temporal succession is its necessary appearance, the Schopenhauerian idea, the Freudian conscious. Thus experienced, *variety is the necessary means of expressing a unity* that would otherwise remain unexpressed, as indeed it remains silent in monotony, which cheats time of its purpose.

K.421(417b) in D minor (1783), the only master quartet in the minor and the first of the two great chamber works for strings in that mode, is in the same key as the first of the two piano Concertos in the minor. Technically, it is comparatively easy for the player, partly owing to the moderate speed of the outer movements: there is no fast movement, and the first violin's triplet passages in the first movement 'lie' as well as do the high ascents in the trio. Almost at the beginning of his chamber-musical development, then, the quartet leader has a chance to penetrate into one of the greatest tragedies in human creation – one, moreover, which stands above itself with an uncanny consistency and a smile, both confidential and confident, that was not to be renewed until Kafka. Usually the tragedy is behind the humour; here the humour is behind the tragedy.

The tonic minor movements represent three aspects of the basic, tragic idea:

The relations I have marked explain those I have not. The symbols are self-explanatory, except for the indexical '0' that appears in Ex. 32(a); 'b⁰' draws attention to the pre-manifest sixth upon the dominant which circumscribes this phrase and reappears in manifest shape in Ex. 32(b) ('ʀ' meaning retrograde version or chordal inversion), where it introduces the only note that is not part of the succession of notes marked 'a', 'a¹', and 'a²' respectively, i.e. the dominant (hence the dots over it). Exx. 32(b) and 32(c) are, intervertedly speaking, identical, and their dominant, which prevents their interverted identity with 'a', is part of the fourth that circumscribes 'd⁰' in Ex. 32(a). When examining these relations, the reader is asked to keep the rhythmic structures (including repetitions of notes and shakes) in mind. For the rest, as soon as a method of demonstration advances beyond the most primitive and essentially tautological descriptive devices, there are exclamations to the effect that you can prove anything. By the conscientious criteria here applied, however, you can prove nothing except the intensity of integration in a work of genius.

On the descriptive level, the most violent thematic contrasts emerge in the relative major region, i.e. in the opening movement's second subject and in the theme of the slow movement. Analytically, the two are not only related to the first subject, but related in their relation to it. By way of Ex. 33(a), the last phrase of Ex. 32(a) explains its development into Ex. 33(b) (the second subject), whose tonic, subdominant, repeated mediant, and supertonic Ex. 33(c) (the slow movement theme) interverts.

When, on the other hand, the second subject returns to the tonic minor,

its superficial contrast largely vanishes and its thematic build returns more immediately to the basic idea (first subject): Ex. 34 interverts the notes of 'a' in Ex. 32(a). We thus realize how closely the harmonic unity corresponds to the thematic, and how true is Schoenberg's concept of the "unity of musical space": descriptively, Ex. 34 is a variation of Ex. 33(b), but analytically, the exposition is a variation of the recapitulation, since the latter is the more primary configuration, the more immediate and manifest reproduction of the basic thought.

The linear polyrhythm (as I should like to call it) of the trio reminds us of the corresponding movement in the G major Quartet (see pp. 108ff.); it is analysed by way of Ex. 35, where the manifest line and its different rhythmic backgrounds are juxtaposed:

Ex.35

We here get a glimpse of the inspired scheme that underlies a great consequent: the ambiguity decreases, the three antecedent backgrounds corresponding to the three notes of the triad merge into two, respondent finality develops a substructure of increased rhythmic definition. This is genius, and nothing like it can be found in a good consequent that is merely masterly.

Polyrhythm returns on the largest scale in the second variation of the finale. Schoenberg[1] has analysed the texture, and I do not propose to chew any cud whatsoever, not even the most

[1] 'Brahms the Progressive', in *Style and Idea*, New York, 1950, and London, 1951, pp. 96f.

recent. But the performance of the variation needs comment.
Both as a public critic and as a private teacher, I regard the
section as a test piece for the second fiddle: both the unity and
the extreme variety of texture has to be realized, and it is not
enough for the player to keep in frictionless time (which, for the
inexperienced and nervous youngster, is difficult enough in all
conscience). He must be able to combine a strong feeling for the
rhythm of his own part with a flexible adjustment to the total
texture, a feat which is only possible if he is capable of really
listening to the first violin and viola instead of merely playing
'correctly' against them. As soon as he is able to listen to that extent and in fact habitually does so, he has become a genuine
chamber musician.

The only other passage whose performance must be discussed
as a matter of general principle is the quaver accompaniment of
the opening movement's principal subject. Rhythmically speaking, these repeated three quavers without a main beat are, of
course, a very common affair, whether in classical chamber
music or in opera where, with Mozart, they usually occur in a
faster tempo. The problem, however, is more glaring at the
moderato level, or at any rate in the slower type of allegro, e.g.
in Haydn's Op. 76, No. 2, which is in the same key as the present work and was no doubt influenced by it. If you play several
notes of equal pitch with, physically speaking, equal stresses, the
first will, for psychological reasons, sound the strongest. If,
therefore, it does not demand a rhythmic accent, you have to de-
accentuate it carefully, which means, in Schoenberg's self-
explanatory symbolology –

– and never mind the first dot: Mozart's slur counteracts
it, anyway. Otherwise, you irreparably inhibit the flow of
the melody. Perhaps this sounds elementary, but I continually hear the crime committed by the most illustrious executants.

K.458 in B♭, the 'Hunt' (1784), is the most popular and, save
for the Adagio, the weakest. The principal defects lie in the thematic inventions of the opening movement and the minuet, both
of whose main themes are obsessed with the tonic at cadential

junctures and thus brake the melodic motion. In addition, the first movement's later bridge passage and second subject are built upon an insignificant phrase whose only excuse would be the kind of treatment which the basic motif of Beethoven's Fifth receives; instead, however, we get repetitional and sequential methods, or rather mechanisms, which are somewhat primitive for Mozart and do not recur until his last quartet. It is only in the later part of the development that the phrase receives the treatment which a Mozart owes it.

However, 'weakness' in our present context still means genius and mastery. Beethoven has often been regarded as the father of the thematic shake, but his shakes are usually thematic entities, rhythmically more or less constant, rather than cells. The trill that seems but to enliven the inverted dominant pedal towards the end of the present principal subject, on the other hand, is a cell, and a daughter cell at that, springing from the opening basic motif by way of its semiquavering variation in bar 5 (the pun is strictly functional) and the semiquaver figure in the second fiddle's bar 8. Bar 29 thus consists, as it were, of a family gathering of cells – for musical cells are superior to all other cells in that they divide and yet remain whole. In fact, strictly speaking and taking the "unity of musical space" into account, the afore-mentioned figure in bar 8 is really a daughter of its own daughter, the shake. The reader will bear with me if I do not go into the exact familial position of what may crudely be called its grand-daughters in the bridge passage and its great-grand-daughters that make up the second subject; but the all-embracing unity will not escape him.

The second-subject tension is low, tonally because the dominant is reached very late after much insistence on the tonic (even the faults of the first subject are strictly functional and thus have a praiseworthy aspect in the wider context of the movement!), and thematically because there is not much of a subsidiary theme, at any rate so far as melodic development is concerned. Again in strict consequence, Mozart introduces the development with what assumes the role of a delayed second subject, a complete, lyrical tune in the dominant, new on the descriptive level. Mozart always seems to behave likewise in similar circumstances of low second-subject tension and, mysteriously enough, in the key of B flat. (Let us beware of having an explanation for everything.) In the B flat Trio, K.502, for instance (which, as a whole, is greater than the present quartet), the lay-out of the exposition is very manifestly monothematic, but the development 'repays' the second theme in the dominant, which shows precisely the same construction as the present instance: it is a lyrical, 'new' tune of 4 + 4 bars stated twice over, with the consequent (i.e. the respective latter four bars) resuming and resolving the antecedent. A slightly different case is the B flat violin Sonata, K.378(317d), whose somewhat higher second-subject tension in the first movement results in a tenser structure, a repayment of a singing tune in a more foreign currency at the beginning of the development: to be sure, the melody is in the dominant, but in the minor mode, and the rhythmic structure is not restated nor indeed symmetrical, but comprises six bars, the last being cut short by the overlapping working-out proper. For the rest, the reader is referred to the B flat Serenade, K.361(370a), which is examined in its appropriate place (p. 70).

The twice-discussed chromatic lead-back cliché (see pp. 100 and 114f.) reappears in the finale, again solo as in the G major, but this time as a lead-back proper. 1783 had probably been the year when it was at the height of its powers (though its use in the slow movement of that year's 'Linz' Symphony is not a patch on its integration in the G major Quartet's finale). Nevertheless, its thematicism is again inspired. Deriving from the finale's basic fourth on the dominant, it is preceded and succeeded by a complex variety of siblings (e.g., Vl. 1, bars 84–5, first note; or Vl. 1, bars 241–3). I think it was Mozart's revitalization of this conventional motif that secured its extraordinary longevity. Schubert actually seems to copy Mozart by way of a somewhat unsuccessful variation of the older master's method in the finale of his Fifth Symphony, writing in the key of the present work and using the cliché as a developmental motif like – or rather somewhat too unlike – Mozart in the G major finale: negatively, the degree of Mozart's integration can be gauged by the incomplete integration in Schubert's movement. But Mendelssohn, the nineteenth century's only supremely natural 'back-leader', reintroduces the cliché in the Mozartean spirit, i.e. with an utterly original and, at the same time, strictly functional approach to conventionality: hear the finale of the 'Scotch' Symphony, bars 38off.

Players: do not overdo the dots in the opening phrase of the

work, thus introducing illogical accents; do not let the second
fiddle shout in bars 188ff.; do not contribute voluntary sforzatos
in bars 16/3 etc. of the minuet; do not take the trio too fast (it
is slower rather than quicker than the principal section, whose
moderato character easily emerges by itself and should not be
over-emphasized); take your time in the Adagio's E flat arpeggio (bars 1–2); do not take the opening so fast that the natural
slowing up in C minor results in a break; do not forget that the
note on bar 17's second beat is a semiquaver and not a demisemiquaver; do not start to hurry into quieter waters when you
reach the imitations of bars 33ff.; do not jump on to the second
note of the finale theme at forte level; withdraw rather than
push the last two phrase-notes that form the first two quavers
of bar 36 (disregard the bar-line); and do not hold back bars
216, 218, etc.: the point is that the duologue is as continuous as a
monologue would be!

Despite its intermittently stunning greatness, the E flat Quartet, K.428 (1783) is not beyond criticism: the opening idea is
uninspired. Inspiration is held to be something mystical, beyond
proof or disproof. I have no doubt that inspiration is mystical,
but that does not make it mysterious in the sense that it cannot
be demonstrated. Life, the prototype of inspiration, is mystical
too; nevertheless, you can prove whether someone is alive or
dead. The basic inspiration of a great piece of music is what can
be shown to be its basic idea – that all-embracing thought which
the composer subsequently (or, creatively speaking, simultaneously) verifies. I submit that the E flat Quartet lacks such a basic
idea and that, instead, there appears a thought (x) which,
mutatis mutandis, would nowadays be called 'constructivist':

An anti-tonal motif, it would never have occurred to Mozart as
an inevitable thought, except at the highest degree of tension,
e.g. in a development section. As a basic idea, it is artificially
contrived: instead of being unavoidable, it avoids the dominant before it passes on to and over it, in a similar way as Dvořák

tries to get an immediate 'move on' at the beginning of his piano Quartet in the same key:

Ex.38   Dvořák, *Piano Quartet*, Op.87.
Allegro con fuoco

What distinguishes these evasive leaps compositorially is not so much their intervallic difference as their respective consequences, which are childish in the case of Dvořák's structure. But though he at once proceeds to functionalize it thematically, Mozart's expositive tritonal tension contradicts his harmonic terms of reference in general and his harmonic premises in particular. It must indeed be remembered that even at the stage of *Tristan* chromaticism, this tritonal motif is introduced *more conservatively* than in Mozart's Quartet, in that it *succeeds* its tonal model –

Ex.39   *Tristan, Act* III.
Engl. Hn.

– making, at the same time, a rhythmic virtue of an harmonic necessity such as is simply disregarded by Dvořák, who treats his B natural as if it were just colour, whereas it is, in fact, a major anti-harmonic event (of which his octave unison is perfectly aware!). If x in Ex. 37 were a genuine, inspired basic idea, a panchromatic composition would follow, something even more advanced historically than *Tristan*. Indeed, for another instance of an anti-tonal motif which does, at the same time, function as an all-embracing and all-producing basic motif, as an inspiration, we should have to search as far afield as *Pierrot lunaire*, the twenty-six bars of whose passacaglia avail themselves of the basic three-note motif for over a hundred times. Schoenberg's continuation,

Ex.40 Schoenberg, *Pierrot lunaire*, No.8: 'Nacht.'
B.Cl.in Bb (transposed)
♩ = ca.88
pp

is organized by means of semitones like Mozart's, and it is exposed in canon at the octave like Mozart's in the development, where, in fact, strict serial technique is applied. (The *Pierrot* passacaglia is serial, though of course pre-twelve-tonal.)

Schoenberg's continuation is a continued inspiration; whereas Mozart's is an inspired reparation. Walter Piston[1] has pointed to the "unusually satisfactory pitch balance of the theme", the "graceful quality of the curve". This is descriptive; the analytic interest lies in the chromatic integration, which, at the same time, prepares for a thorough serial utilization of the tritone in the development: a basic row or set (BS in Ex. 37) does already latently reappear, both straight and in retrograde inversion (A–Bb–E). The lack of initial inspiration does in fact draw Mozart into latent serial technique as early as the opening of the exposition (the minor second, too, immediately assumes the significance of a row); whereas his serial passages in works whose basic ideas are inspired never occur at the beginning and, in sonata movements, usually open the development. This is even true of the comparatively primitive and tonal serialism of K.156(134b) (see pp. 96f.), while the serial build-up of his anti-tonal development in K.550's finale closely parallels the present developmental opening in both organizing method and structure as well as in unharmonic texture: whenever a great tonal composer creates anti-tonal passages (which, if they extend beyond the length of a motif, are, in my submission, always serial, because the music must be organized somehow), he writes mono- or polyphonically, but never homophonically,[2] and *diabolus in musica* tends to shun celestial harmony, anyway.

The complex serial technique in bars 1–7 of the development avails itself of the two afore-mentioned rows, and is applied both horizontally and vertically.[3] To me it seems indeed quite obvious that the *Pierrot* passacaglia is strongly if unconsciously influenced by the present movement, even in the rhythmic structure of its theme (compare Ex. 40 with Ex. 37!) and, paradoxically enough, in its constructive atonality. I begin to understand why Schoenberg considered Mozart his teacher, though I am quite convinced that he himself did not know the

---

[1] *Counterpoint*, New York, 1947, and London, 1949, p. 19.

[2] See H. Keller: 'Strict Serial Technique in Classical Music', *Tempo*, London, Autumn, 1955.

[3] Vid. op. cit.

true reason, for he never consciously discovered Mozart's serial-ism – nor, consequently, did any other serial expert: everybody looks for the twelve notes in pre-Schoenbergian music (they are in fact exposed with downright dodecáphonic haste in the present passage too), but it must be realized that their significance is merely negative, i.e. atonal. Their re-integration is the creative thing to listen to, their constructive aspect, which is serial. In general, I would add that it is this kind of influence which the analyst ought to study, not the fact that Shaw sounds like Shakespeare because neither sounds like Chinese.

Players: the first violin should take great care to take the c″ in the slow movement's bar 88 below rather than above its true pitch and not to overdo the minuet's slurs *à la* Diabelli. Throughout this work, Einstein's 'Authentic Edition' ought to be closely adhered to.

K.464 in A (1785) is colloquially known as 'The Drum' amongst Austrian musicians in view of the ostinato rhythm in the variation movement's finale. The Quartet was Beethoven's favourite, no doubt because of the mono-motivic construction of the last movement. I do not understand the coda of the first movement, which seems to me abrupt; I can find no technical fault.

One corollary of my theory of unity against which I check my more intuitive observations is that every rhythm, too, however 'new' on the descriptive level, must be implicit in the basic idea. In early Haydn and Mozart as well as in bad Boccherini it will often be found that triplet continuations and transitions appear out of the blue, shocking you out of your structural wits (cf. Ex. 7(a) on p. 100). Perhaps the most baffling problem of inte-gration in the entire A major work is the highly natural emer-gence of central triplets as late as the second subject of the first movement. On the descriptive level, to be sure, they are easily dealt with: "We are then ready for the new theme, which is again graceful in character, but enlivened with bright running triplet groups."[1] Congratulations, but where do they come from? We notice that they are groups of nine notes in quaver triplets (Ex. 41(c)). The basic thought has nine quavers (Ex. 41(a)). If we displace their accents and re-hear them in triplet form (Ex. 41(b), transposed to V), they continue to make

[1] T. F. Dunhill, *Mozart's String Quartets*, London, 1927, ²/1948, Vol. II, p. 12.

implied harmonic and rhythmic sense and the latent unity becomes manifest:

Essentially, it is a case of diminution, though not of the textbook kind. I call the creative principle of variegation here in evidence that of *polyrhythmic diminution*. At the same time, the principle of reversed and postponed antecedents and consequents is in operation: hear x in Ex. 41(c) followed by y in Ex. 41(b).

In performance, the first subject's quavers must roll off in upbeat fashion, both at the beginning and in all later imitations; the oft-played involuntary accent on the second of the nine quavers is fatal. The first crotchet after the quavers is the accent to aim for and the aim to accent.

In the opening of the second subject in the Andante of K.465 (1785), the 'Dissonance', Einstein's 'Authentic Edition' adheres to the autograph and the Original Edition, neither of which shows the thematic upbeat in the first violin. It is impossible for me to accept this textual evidence, since it is musically absurd. I can only assume that Mozart omitted the self-evident phrase to begin with and later, when correcting the proofs, overlooked the omission. All editions I have seen insert the upbeat. In this musicological age, the *Urtext* is the thing, but the present instance is one of many where the naughty wrong editions are, after all, musically right. Our veneration for the letter is assuming irrational proportions. It is not so difficult to replace both one's ear and one's musical sense by an unshakable belief in authenticity, especially when one does not possess much of either, but even a bad arranger must needs be more musical than many a good textual critic.

The finale's extraordinary codetta amounts to a third subject (y in Ex. 42(f)) in the minor mediant (the flat sixth of the dominant) which is replaced by the flat sixth (the Neapolitan sixth of the dominant) and the Neapolitan sixth in the recapitulation. The surprising modulatory dive is undertaken from a springboard representing, to my knowledge, the most inspired and original use of cliché in history. For one thing, the cliché (x in Ex. 42(f)) is as firmly and indeed primarily integrated as the chromatic one in K.387 and 458 (see pp. 114f. and 121); in various interversions, always harmonically true, it is developed right from the outset. In bars 3–4 of the first movement's main

Ex. 42

subject, it appears in the permutation 2–1–3–4 as tonal sequence of the basic motif (Ex. 42(a), tranposed to V), and in the finale's main subject it already assumes its later rhythmic shape in the permutation 2–4–1–3 (Ex. 41(c)). In the ensuing second subject, it goes to form the fundamental motif (Ex. 42(d)) by way of the permutation 2–1–4–3, whose retrograde version ((d)^R in Ex. 42(e)) almost immediately precedes the emergence of the conventional turn of the phrase itself, overlapping, at the same time, with its diminution (x^1 in Ex. 42(e)). Introducing the cliché, x^1 thus assumes the significance of its model. In the wider context, then, the cliché evolves as a developmental variation; in its narrowest context, as a simple augmentation. Consequently, by the time it is due to appear in its habitual shape, it has already been invested with rich new meaning. Nor is this the end of the news.

For another thing, that is to say, the cliché's actual transitional function is something utterly unheard-of and could not, at the same time, have been achieved by way of a more original motif. The phrase is, in fact, perhaps the most-used eighteenth-century tag altogether;[1] and owing to its cadential energy on the one hand and its cantabile character on the other, it retained its power for a long time. For lesser-known, beautiful examples of its more conventional use in Mozart the reader is referred to the canzonet 'Ridente la calma' (conventional) or the G major flute Concerto K.313(285c) (not so conventional), while the opening ritornello of the *Entführung*'s 'Martern aller Arten' contains a specimen which he will be able to recall off-hand. Needless to add, the phrase never appears without its unambiguous harmony – except on the present occasion.

Its very conventionality makes the cliché the only possible springboard for the dangerous dive from the known into the unknown. It is both firm (familiar) and elastic, capable of giving an impetus. The elasticity is achieved through the exclusion of the harmony (see Ex. 42(f)). The ground is cut from under your feet which, instead, seesaw on the board. During the actual dive you are, of course, in the air, but the common element of support with which both the springboard and the water in which you land provide you is the bass G, which is tonal to both keys, in fact part of their respective tonic triads.

The surprise key, reached without proper modulation, without being established, must be confirmed by the strongest possible means – by a repeated statement of the E flat triad (y in Ex. 42(f)). Yet there is strict thematic unity in the very means of almost excessive tonal variety: y in Ex. 42(f) is but a developmental, interverting variation of the principal subject itself (Ex. 42(b), transposed to III♭), immediately clear to the ear as soon as one listens to it. It is my serious contention that given the design of the exposition, no other composer in the world would have been able to plunge into E flat at this juncture with such complete natural mastery.

Players: It is structurally impossible to take bar 30 in strict mechanical tempo: beware of your rubatophobia. The temptation of a strong accent on the first beat of bar 99 must be resisted if the ensuing continuation with its crescendo is not to be endangered. Bar 99 is still piano; the crescendo starts with the 'cello's upbeat, and an increased rather than a negligent piano is indicated before most crescendos. Bar 147: there is no excuse whatever for the 'cello's not playing a real piano; it is alone.

[1] cf. C. L. Cudworth: 'Cadence Galante: the story of a cliché', *Monthly Musical Record*, LXXIX, London, 1949.

Bar 195/3–4: the second violin's upbeat must be very strictly in the style of whatever the first fiddle has chosen to do four bars earlier on: the identity is a condition for the contrasting surprise of the first violin's imitation in bar 196; there, of course, the characterization must be altered. For the first fiddle to stress its second B♭ in the Andante's bar 10 is tautological; on the contrary, the figure should swiftly recede after the phrase's main accent on the first beat of the bar. The tempo of the minuet is usually taken quite wrongly – too heavily. In any event, the quavers must retain their upbeat significance; there is no stress whatsoever on the first main beat. Likewise, the forte quavers in octave unison must not lose the thematic sense of their fundamental line, which is B–C–D–E–F. In bars 24–5, the first fiddle should show enough imagination to play somewhat *senza misura*, entering late and softly shooting up to the a''. The leader must, of course, have the co-operation of the middle parts. Contrary to current professional opinion, such agogical modifications should not be practised; the first violin must be free to play the upbeat phrase with a slightly different articulation each time, and, accordingly, with different consequences. If the middle parts cannot change their minds alongside, or sleep elsewhere, they have no business in the musical chamber or on the concert platform. If the minuet is sufficiently lively, the subdued excitement of the trio can be expressed by way of a slightly slower pace. If it is impossible to slow down for the trio, the tempo of the principal section is suspect. In bars 41f. and 45f. of the finale, the middle parts should not blare out the syncopations. They will be heard, anyway, and it must not be forgotten that the first violin remains thematic. The more calmly the semiquaver passage of the second subject is taken, the faster and more brilliant it will sound. Rushing should be avoided at all costs. As usual with Mozart, the passage is as easy as it sounds virtuosic; do not spoil the impression of your concertante style by amateurish haste, even though, in the concert hall or on discs, you almost invariably hear a race developing in this passage as well as in the further course of the movement. A slight hesitation on the 'springboard' is only natural. The rests at the end of the exposition must be strictly adhered to. In the recapitulation, during the semiquavers in the middle parts, the thematic first violin should be heeded throughout, right to the end (i.e. the beginning of the second subject). In general, the first fiddler's imagination should be up to finely varying each return of the theme according to its context; this goes, particularly, for the opening motif, which is both yearning and gaily liberating, and where to glide *and* not to glide is the question (though, of course, not the only one).

(β) *The 'Hoffmeister' Quartet*

K.499 in D (1786) raises a ticklish question of integration at the relative minor beginning of the first movement's bridge passage. Where does the sudden diminished seventh (Ex. 43(b)) spring from? There is no diminished seventh, melodic or harmonic, in the basic idea or in any of its derivatives. However, if we transpose the first subject (bars 5f.) to vi (Ex. 43(a)), the unity presents itself in a flash:

Ex.43

In the interpretation, the first subject's first accent must definitely be postponed to the A. The overwhelming viola imitation in the recapitulation of the minuet's principal section should not be forced dynamically; it is for the other instruments, including the first violin, to throw it into relief.

(γ) *The C Minor Adagio and Fugue* [1]

K.546 (1788) consists of an arrangement of the two-piano fugue of 1783 (K.426) to which Mozart added an introduction, thus entering it in his musical diary: " – ditto. [26th June] *Ein kurzes Adagio. à 2 violini, viola, e basso, zu einer Fuge welche ich schon lange für 2 Klaviere geschrieben habe.*" (*A short Adagio . . . for a fugue which I had already written a long time ago for two pianos.*) In the words *zu einer Fuge* he seems to have slipped or changed his mind while writing. The passage is smudged and rubbed, and there is obviously something else underneath these words (do I detect a 'z' and a 'g'?), but it is impossible, for me at any rate, to decipher it. Did Mozart's unconscious draw attention to the difference between the Adagio and the fugue, feeling comparatively uneasy about the old piece

[1] See also *The Keyboard Music*, pp. 57ff.

in conjunction with the new? It is not so much that the o.
arranged for the medium and the other written for it (his a.
rangement is, needless to say, spotless), but that the introduction is Mozart at his very deepest and most esoteric, while the
fugue is a masterly contrapuntal show-piece which is more exclusively exoteric than most of his intentionally popular masterpieces. It follows that the rarely-played arrangement of the
work is preferable to the original. A string player who has never
interpreted it remains uneducated.

(δ) *The 'Solo' Quartets*

I choose this title, which is colloquially current in professional
German-speaking circles: while the 'Prussian' title of the quartets draws attention to their problem, 'Solo' indicates its solution. Mozart could hardly please the King to the extent of writing bottom-heavy 'cello quartets with the upper instruments
accompanying. If the 'cello was to take a leading part, so must,
in turns, the middle parts. The details of the resulting solo textures and structural adjustments deserve the closest scrutiny of
every composer, but for the less experienced player they make
things rather difficult, both in technique and in blend and
balance.

K.575 in D (1789) is called, for obvious reasons, 'The Violet'
in German-speaking countries. The theme of the first movement is taken up not only by the finale, but also by Schubert's
first B flat Symphony (No. 2, 1814–15). In the slow movement
it would be downright idiotic to talk of a bridge passage; instead, we get a lyrical melody which, step by step and solo by
solo, leads the structure with tender care through vi to V. In
both the minuet and the trio, the extended upbeat-phrases must
be heeded in interpretation.

K.589 in B flat (1790) is perhaps the intensest 'shocker' from
the players' point of view, especially in the minuet and trio, both
virtuosic in all directions. The middle section of the trio develops
the minuet! We might almost be in the twentieth century. I can
never understand why such things are so carefully noted in
modern music while they pass unnoticed in Mozart. Perhaps it
is because modern composers draw verbal attention to them
while Mozart's music draws the attention away from them.

K.590 in F has a minuet whose rhythmic structures are characterized by 7 (+7) and 5 + 5 in the respective outer sections,

are some almost primitively symmetrical build-
movement's duologues between 'cello and first
ls that here the 'Prussian' problem has not been
ved. In any case, this is not a last quartet in the
the 'Jupiter' is a last symphony. A similarly open
the series of

B. THE STRING QUINTETS.

K.174 in B flat (1773) is uninteresting. K.406(516b) in C
minor (1787) is discussed elsewhere;[1] over-sensitive ears may
prefer the quintet version from the point of view of intonation.
K.515 in C (1787), K.516 in G minor (1787), and K.593 in D
(1790) are the greatest and most original string quintets in existence and the greatest and most original symphonic structures
of Mozart, chamber-musical or otherwise. The tonic movements of K.614 in E flat (1791) are a stylistic mystery and a textural failure. It is incomprehensible to me why Eric Blom[2] considers this quintet "the most superb of all", and ascribes to it
"the highest sum-total of great invention plus great workmanship"

In the Andante of the C major Quintet you hear Mozart the
viola player. Profoundly imaginative freedom of delivery is absolutely essential. First violin and viola must give and take spontaneous inspiration. The finale theme has to be approached in
an even intenser spirit of interpretative variation than that of
the 'Haydn' quartet in the same key (see pp. 129f.); the question
of 'to glide and not to glide' is, incidentally, the same, as is, in
fact, the glissando itself.

The G minor Quintet is as great as the G minor Symphony,
whence it is greater: the same wealth of feeling must needs be
expressed yet more economically in the chamber work. Economy, moreover, is radiate. One ray is the instrumentation, another the tonal structure. In the opening exposition, tremendous
tension is created within the confines of the tonic. Abert[3]
rightly points to "the retention of G minor for the second subject", though it would be more analytic to say that the thematic

---

[1] See *The Serenades for Wind Band*, pp. 74ff.

[2] See *Mozart*, London, 1935, [6]/1946, pp. 246f.

[3] H. Abert: 'Mozart', in *Cobbett's Cyclopedic Survey of Chamber Music*, ed. W. W.
Cobbett, London, 1930, Vol. II, p. 162.

and the harmonic aspects of the second-subject stage are separated, each becoming simpler in itself. The resultant telescoping of the first- and second-subject stages, however, looks far into the complex future of sonata form, right down to the overlapping of statement and development in general, and of recapitulation and development section in particular (cf. also the G major Quartet's finale, p. 115). Genius's economy creates simplicity, and genius's simplicity creates complexity, which needs a new economy. As a result, the champions of 'masterly simplicity' and 'masterly complexity' respectively can at once have a marvellous time as long as they do not say what they are talking about, a condition which, on the whole, they seem ready to fulfil.

The Quintet teems with serial methods, thus showing its close relation to the G minor Symphony on the deepest technical level too.[1]

Players: the character of the initial accompaniment is all-important. A sprightly spiccato of staccato character finishes the movement from the start. The merest hint of spiccato is enough, and even that is not absolutely necessary. The fact that the accompaniment precedes the melody in the introduction to the finale does not mean that it should be less restrained than it would be if there were an immediate top line; on the contrary, the implied restraint is all the more intense. The quavers must be pregnant with suppressed emotion which is gradually released.

The D major Quintet is difficult and fragile, and should be approached with great care. The unity of the introduction and the body of the first movement may seem mysterious, but could not, in hidden fact, be closer. I am confining myself to analysing its most deeply concealed aspect, which is based on a principle we have already caught a glimpse of (p. 105), i.e. that of postponed tonal sequences – a brother principle, obviously, of the principle of postponed antecedents:

[1] See H. Keller, op. cit.

x in Ex. 44(a) is a latent sequential model of x[1] in Ex. 44(b),
rhythmic backgrounds included; the turn is compressed into a
shake in the quick tempo.

Most of the E flat Quintet sounds like a bad arrangement of a
wind piece in mock-Haydn style and is strictly unplayable in
that it cannot be rendered in tune – unless an imitation of the
awful sound of open-air wind serenades is intended; they usually seem composed out of tune too. Mozart entered it in his
diary on 12 April, and the writing looks somewhat shaky to me;
perhaps he was ill. The slow movement, however, is sublime.
The theme (Ex. 7(b) on p. 101) is the last of a series which includes Belmonte's B flat aria[1] and the slow movement of the
Kleine Nachtmusik. Its weighty 3–4 upbeat with its potential,
gavotte-like displacement of the bar-accent lends itself to a
characteristically Mozartean kind of imitation, a sample of which
has already been touched upon in my reminders to performers
on pp. 129f. ('Dissonance' Quartet, first movement, second subject). A more prominent example of the thematic type and its
imitational utilization will be found in the slow movement of
what is perhaps Mozart's greatest piano Trio, the E major one
(K.542, 1788), but the most shattering harmonic as well as
rhythmic results of these cross-accenting imitations Mozart reserved for the present piece:

Ex.45

The extremely personal nature of the movement, as well as its
original structure and immaculate texture, only increase the
musical mystery that surrounds this Quintet. I am unable to
find a solution.

C. THE STRING TRIO AND DUOS

The spotless and indeed profound Divertimento (a typically
Mozartean paradox!) in E flat, K.563 (1788) has only one equal
in the entire history of the *genre* – Schoenberg's string Trio. It

[1] cf. also E. Blom, loc. cit., for a sensitive description of the relation.

should be tackled as early as possible, not least as a practice for the players' imagination in the face of great music.

While the literature of string duos is not so poor musically as it may seem to the uninitiated – there are, for instance, master-pieces for two violins by Spohr, Mazas, and Rawsthorne – the two Mozart Duos of 1783 (K.423 in G and 424 in B flat) are, again, in a unique position, and not because they are for violin and viola, which is not a unique form. Curious as it may sound, they are in fact sovereign master-works – as far as I am aware, the only ones for the medium. Played in turns at either desk, they form an ideal introduction to the inner chamber of the string quartet and quintet.

D. FLUTE, OBOE, AND CLARINET

The flute Quartets show Mozart's hate for the instrument pretty clearly; it is no use pretending that they do not. The best is the D major (K.285, 1777), if only in view of the dominant minor and tonic minor stretches in the development section which, incidentally, is rich in thematic prophecies, including the basic phrase of the G minor Quintet. The oboe Quartet (K.370(368b) in F, 1781) is a much more substantial proposi-tion. The violin arrangements of these quartets make them ac-cessible to the ordinary house quartet; they should certainly be tried once or twice, though the violin part that replaces the concertante oboe is tricky in the rondo.

The clarinet works, both masterpieces of the greatest genius, clearly show Mozart's love for the instrument. The string ar-rangements are superb substitutes, and should regularly be

Ex.46 [*Andante*]

played. The Trio, K.498 in E flat (1786), develops a unique kind of monothematic integration in the opening movement: the first subject's concluding phrase (Ex. 46(a)) becomes, un-obtrusively, the opening phrase of the second (Ex. 46(b)). Both are, of course, (con)sequential variations of the basic motif,

and a renewed variation (Ex. 46(c)) establishes the basic
unity with the finale theme (Ex. 46(d)). As for the finale itself,
bars 67ff. (read on beyond double bar) reuse, in a similar
thematic context, the C minor section of the C minor Concerto's
slow movement, written a few months earlier. Three years later,
in the B flat piano Sonata, K.570, Mozart re-reuses the section,
again in a similar context though to a lesser extent.

K.581 in A (1789), the 'Stadler' Quintet, has been criticized
because of its development section. Those who think it mechanical are invited to close the score where, in their opinion, the
mechanical phrase-spinning starts, and to write out the rest of
the development for themselves. They will be surprised and en-
lightened. The finale's first variation superimposes a 'new'
melody on the theme, a device of which Mozart was fond in the
solo exposition of concertos: hear the A major violin Concerto
(K.219) for an earlier, the D minor piano Concerto (K.466)
(second subject) for a mature example. The melody (Ex. 47(a))
is not only resumed in the second (Ex. 47(b)) and fifth variations
but also retroacts on the preceding second trio (Ex. 47(c)),

which thus assumes the retrospective significance of a developing variation of a variation on the finale theme: compare the
unity of musical space in the D minor Quartet's opening movement (p. 118). All these tunes are of course derived, *inter alia* by
way of octave-transposition, from the basic motif of the work.

E. PIANO AND STRINGS

The two piano Quartets are, once again, the only absolutely
perfect, great, deep masterpieces of their problematic *genre*.
The miracle is not quite so incomprehensible with K.493 in
E flat (1786), which inclines towards a chamber concerto for
piano, but K.478 in G minor (1785) furnishes conclusive proof,
more than any other single masterpiece of his, that Mozart's
was the only truly omniscient ear of which we know.

His ear must be respected in the great and far too rarely-played series of violin sonatas and piano trios too. Piano and strings never mix naturally, and the problem is complicated by the fact that it is quite impossible to re-establish the physical conditions of sound to which Mozart was used, not only because we hear differently, not only because of the development of the piano, but also because violin and 'cello tone has irrevocably developed too, and inevitably in an entirely different direction. The usual conflict between pianist and strings misses the central point altogether, for it is not primarily a question of predominance at all; as a rule, you can hear both or all of them all too well. The problem is that of blend, and here it must be said that the pianists, who are not by nature, training, and their instrument's constitution, over-concerned with tone-modulation, sin more consistently than string players who, on the other hand, tend to develop persecution mania and consequently play accompanimental figures *sempre espressivo* and *molto vibrato* with an unvaryingly golden tone that conjures up the vision of a sausage without end and admittedly does not do much credit to their own feeling for tonal shading. We are together in this, as cinematic poetry has it, and together means for one another, perpetually, throughout a piece, and no matter who has the principal and who the subordinate part or accompaniment. Mozart's chamber music for piano and strings is exceptional in that it can be made to sound.

BOOK LIST

H. Abert: 'Mozart', *Cobbett's Cyclopedic Survey of Chamber Music*, London, 1930, Vol. II, p. 162.

E. Blom: *Mozart*, London, 1935, [6]/1946.

C. L. Cudworth: 'Cadence Galante: the story of a cliché', *Monthly Musical Record*, LXXIX, 1949.

T. F. Dunhill: *Mozart's String Quartets*, London, 1927, [2]/1948, Vol. II.

A. Einstein: *Mozart*, London, 1946.

H. Keller: 'Strict Serial Technique in Classical Music', *Tempo*, Autumn, 1955.

R. Reti: *The Thematic Process in Music*, London, 1961.

A. Schoenberg: 'Brahms the Progressive', *Style and Idea*, New York, 1950; London, 1951, pp. 96f.

THE SMALLER ORCHESTRAL WORKS

I. Dances

Music was originally bound up with dancing, as it still is for those who are in some ways a reflection of the childhood of the human race – primitive peoples and children. Modern man has been forced to suppress the urge to give outward bodily expression to his musicality. Dance music, rhythmically, is the most easily remembered, and its extreme antithesis is the kind of music that is free of clear-cut rhythmic periods – for example, the polyphonic music of the sixteenth century, whose indefinite accents ensure rhythmic obscurity. The adherents to the new style, of neo-Neapolitan, Mannheim origin, which arose *c.* 1750, loved regular, recurring periods, even to the point of repeating groups of four, eight, and sixteen bars (this was called 'squaring the thematic material'); they loved, in short, regular rhythms. In his maturity, Mozart avoided this kind of regularity by intertwining, diminishing, and augmenting his subjects. Nevertheless, the dance plays a very important part in his work, not only in the actual dances that he composed, but throughout all his music.[1] Many of his subjects, principal, 'second', and subsidiary, as well as the rondos, variations, serenades, divertimenti, and the finales of the symphonies and sonatas, derive, melodically and rhythmically, from the dance music, folk song and folk dance of his time. In Mozart's works we find allemandes, courantes, sicilianos, gigues, passepieds, chaconnes, passacaglias, polonaises, gavottes, fandangos, country dances, German Dances, marches, alla turcas, and other dances. Most numerous are the minuets, since – and this is another indication of the fondness for simple, dance-like periods, so typical of the new style, *c.* 1750 – the minuet, not without some opposition from the critics, had penetrated the symphony and sonata, though not the concerto.

A. Minuets

As a dance, the minuet had already passed its zenith by 1700. Nevertheless, it remained, until the end of the eighteenth cen-

[1] cf. H. Engel: 'Der Tanz in Mozarts Kompositionen', *Mozart-Jahrbuch*, Salzburg, 1953, pp. 29ff.

tury, not merely as a form of 'art music' (*Kunstmusik*) but the conventional dance of the courts and fashionable society. By then, however, its spirit and musical content were undergoing a long-drawn-out process of remoulding, which, due to the penetration of the minuet by melodic and rhythmic elements from the *Ländler* and the waltz, it is impossible to trace in detail. The waltz, originally called the *Weller* (*Wälzer*) or *Dreher*, is a German Dance which can be traced back to the sixteenth century at least. The delight aroused in Vienna in 1786 by the waltz in Martin y Soler's opera, *Cosa rara*, was probably caused more by the stage performance of the dance than by the actual music. About 1760, the *Dreher*, German Dance (*Ländler*), and waltz were slower than the waltz initiated by Lanner, but quicker than the minuet, to which Quantz assigns the tempo MM. 48. But there were various tempi in the minuet (for further details see below), and the minuet in *Don Giovanni* is decidedly slow, stiff, and ceremonial – so slow that one bar of the minuet in the ballroom scene corresponds to three bars of a German Dance and two bars of a contredanse.[1] The influence of the waltz on the minuet, including Mozart's, is best seen in the subdivision of the accompaniment. In the minuet every crotchet is accented by a continuous bass line, and a stressed accent is often concealed by a continuous quaver accompaniment in the middle parts; whilst in the later typical waltz accompaniment, the bass note is allotted the first crotchet beat and chords succeed on the second and third. This kind of accompaniment slowly invades the trio of the minuet, which very soon acquired the character of a *Ländler* or waltz, since its purpose is to provide a contrast to the minuet, and can be found in Mozart (e.g., in K.599, No. 4 (trio); K.601, No. 3 (trio). German Dances: K.536, No. 1; K.571, Nos. 2 (trio) and 4; K.586, No. 5 (trio); K.600, No. 6 (trio); K.602 (trios of Nos. 1 and 3). (See Ex. 1.)

Ex.1
K.571, No.2 (trio)

In the earlier period, the rhythm of the minuet's motives was based predominantly on crotchet movement in conjunct

[1] See *The Operas*, p. 320, Ex. 4.

motion or arpeggios, as may be seen from the examples quoted
below, or on melodic structures composed of minims and
crotchets. Quavers usually arose from ornamental figures, re-
solved thirds, and passing notes. Occasionally, the accent is intensified by march-like figures on the downbeats of the minuet
(but not of the trio), though this rarely occurs so obtrusively as
in K.176, No. 10, and K.461(488a), No. 1. (See Ex. 2.)

The trio, with its more easy-going, sauntering, rocking – in
fact, more waltz-like – motives, and correspondingly softer and
quieter instrumentation, offers a contrast to the minuet.

From a motivic point of view, the construction of these
minuets and trios is quite simple. In most cases (for example, in
sixteen cases out of nineteen in K.103(61d)) both comprise two
halves, each of eight bars and each repeated. Nevertheless, longer periods were evidently no hindrance to the dance.[1] The
structure is as follows:

$$\| : A \qquad\qquad : \| \quad : B \qquad\qquad : \|$$

$$4 \qquad 4 \qquad\qquad 4 \qquad 4$$

$$1. \qquad 2. \qquad\qquad 3. \qquad 4.$$

The four four-bar phrases are variously combined as, for ex-
ample, *ab* : || : *ab*, *ab* : || : *cb*, *aa* : || : *ba*, and many others. With
such motives, it is possible to indulge in playful permutation,
and a little book entitled *Musical Dice-Playing* (*Musikalisches
Würfelspiel*), wrongly attributed to Mozart, testifies to the
popularity of the game. A sheet of paper has survived on which
Mozart sketched a diagrammatic representation of possible
combinations (K.Anh.294d).[2] In addition to the binary form
AB there is the ternary, with repeat: || : A : || : B   A : || .

---

[1] There is a characteristic passage in a letter from Italy (Bologna) of 22 September 1770. Mozart wrote to his sister: "I like [Michael] Hayden's six minuets
better than the first twelve. . . . We should like to be able to introduce the German
taste in minuets into Italy, where they last nearly as long as a whole symphony."
Anderson: *Letters of Mozart*, London, 1938, Vol. I, p. 238.

[2] cf. Engel: op. cit., p. 35.

On rare occasions, the motivic construction can become more complex, as in the second half of the second of the minuets K.61h of 1769,[1] where Mozart lengthens the first group to six bars and shortens the second group, which resumes the first section of the first half, by two bars; or, to put it more accurately, he now states this first half in its normal form (a), whereas the beginning (a') has repeated the first two bars:

$$\| : a' \quad b : \| : c \quad a \quad b : \|$$
$$2 + 2 \quad 4 \quad \quad 6 \quad 2 \quad 4$$

In the later dances we find the most subtle thematic relationships, e.g., in the first minuet of K.568 (1788). In the third group of four bars of $\| : a\ b : \| : c\ b' : \|$ a motive from a (z) is three times repeated in inversion (Ex. 3):

Ex.3
K.568, No.1

The most frequent extension of the customary eight-bar period is obtained by an echo-like repeat of a second or fourth group of bars with changed dynamics (piano); by a changed position (to the lower octave); or by the older method of varying the instrumentation.[2]

Even in the period of his greatest maturity, Mozart wrote dances for dancing. From the middle of the nineteenth century serious composers no longer wrote dance music, but only stylized dances, as 'art music' (*Kunstmusik*) or ballets. Haydn, Mozart, and Beethoven all wrote dances for the Imperial and Royal masked balls held in Vienna's Redoutensaal: the court balls where, only a little later, Johann Strauss was to reign as king of the waltz. Schubert loved to play for dancing; Strauss and Reger only wrote 'art' and ballet dances, and Pfitzner would have regarded even those activities as degrading. The difference between 'dance' and 'art' music is not merely a matter of aesthetic or musical quality, but – and this is difficult

---

[1] cf. *Mozart-Jahrbuch*, I/ 1923, pp. 27ff., and especially pp. 28f.
[2] cf. Engel: op. cit., p. 36.

to explain – fundamentally sociological. Mozart's dances were written at a time when there was a much more vital relationship between art and everyday life. They are difficult to revive: unless it is a short sequence of dances from his final period that is performed, they are really out of place in the concert hall, and they can no longer be danced in the ballroom. The only possibility is a ballet performance in period costume, and that is bound to be rather self-consciously antiquarian.

Mozart's earliest dances for orchestra are the minuets which he wrote as a thirteen-year-old boy, in 1769, for the Salzburg Carnival. The six-year-old infant prodigy's first efforts had also been minuets. The first six series of minuets (from 1769?), of which four are still unpublished, look quite simple. The instrumentation is modest: in the seven minuets (K.65a(61b)) only the normal complement of strings is used: two violins and bass. The nineteen minuets (K.103(61d)) are also scored for woodwind, two oboes or flutes, and two horns or trumpets. In the trio movements of other minuets, flutes replace oboes, and horns replace trumpets: thus the same player was required to play two instruments, an impossibility today. But the winds are only used to strengthen the harmony or melody, like extra organ stops. In the trios, the volume of sound is reduced and softened. The thematic invention of these minuets, though stereotyped, is often charming, and the trios are well devised. The phrases are sometimes lengthened by echo repeats, as in one of the minuets of K.103(61d) (Ex. 4)

Ex.4
K.103 [Version Berlin MS.]

or by a repeat without any indication of dynamics, in which case it is an open question whether an echo effect should be introduced, e.g., in the ten bars of the seventh minuet. The key sequence of this series of minuets proceeds, alternately and group-fashion, first in a circle of fifths and then in a reverse direction, in unrelated keys: C, G, D→F; C→A; D→F; C, G→F; C, G→B flat; E flat→E; A, D, G. In the early period there are no minuets in the minor. In the six minuets (K.104(61e)) the second phrase in the third minuet is lengthened by adding to the repeated first section a repeat a third above: *a a'*: ‖ : *a'' a a'''* (third higher). In the fourth minuet we hear for the first time a *Ländler*-like, yodelling turn of melody (Ex. 5):

Ex.5
K.104, No.4

The six minuets of 1772 (K.164(130a)) are scored for two oboes and two trumpets in Nos. 1–3, and two horns in Nos. 4–6, in addition to two violins and bass; but in the trios a flute is added to the strings. Apart from the softer sound of the flute, the trios also differ from the minuets thematically and in stylistic requirements: they always need legato playing in contrast to the staccato character of the minuets. Here, too, the phrases are lengthened by an echo: it seems the dancers did not mind whether they danced thirty-two or thirty-six bars.

Sixteen further minuets (K.176) have survived from the year 1773, but have not been published. Oboes and flutes, horns and trumpets are used in alternation, and the bassoon is added to the string bass. The subjects have now become much livelier and more varied: the march-like accent of the first crotchet in No. 10 has already been mentioned (cf. Ex. 2, above) and the opening (N.B., imitation!) of No. 13 also deserves notice. The three minuets K.363 (probably from the year 1780) open with trumpets and drums, but it is only in the first minuet that these instruments are used. K.461(448a) already approaches the great series of the final period. These six minuets (not unified by their keys, C, E flat, G, B flat, F, D) have subjects of the utmost variety. No. 1 is intensely march-like; No. 2 almost solemn and symphonic (Ex. 6):

Ex.6
K.461, No.2

K.363 and K.461 represent the transition to the important series of minuets composed in Mozart's last years, in the period between the last great symphonies and *Die Zauberflöte*. The twelve minuets, K.568 (1788), which were written for an Imperial and Royal masked ball in Vienna, are scored for a large orchestra, including two flutes and piccolo, two oboes (clarinets take their place in Nos. 3, 4, and 7), bassoons, horns, trumpets, and kettledrums. As was the tradition, no violas were used, though the string parts were certainly executed by several players at each part.

The large orchestra is employed in a rich variety of ways. The thematic invention itself is as varied as possible, not only between minuet and trio (most of the dances, especially Nos. 4, 10, and 12, are ceremonious and brilliant in their principal sections), but also, quite frequently, between contrasting four-bar groups, as in Nos. 1, 3, and 12. As already explained, when sections are repeated, the repetition is not identical, note for note, with the original statement, but is intensified and differently instrumented, as, for example, in No. 4 (Ex. 7):

In the second group of two bars strings and wind are interchanged. But of even greater significance is the treatment of the winds in general. Neither in the piano concertos, where they are used in a very novel way, nor in the operas, are the woodwinds used so extensively as solo instruments as they are here – almost, it might be said, in chamber-musical style. In the trio of the fourth minuet mentioned above, the sauntering, legato theme is announced first by the violin, then, in the second group of four bars, repeated by the clarinet (in the higher octave) in partnership with the violin. The second clarinet then adds its voice, as accompaniment, in triplets, in its lowest (chalumeau) register (Ex. 8).

In the trios, Mozart is fond of coupling the violin subject with the bassoon two octaves lower (at times with the flute an octave above), which produces a rather comic effect. The fifth trio contains a simple melody which is played first by the violin with the

flute, then in combination with the bassoon. Next, for four bars, the flute hovers around the melody in solo quaver figures; then the bassoon enters with wide leaps, well suited to the instrument, and in bars 28–32 both instruments, with their figuration, are added to the violin melody (see Ex. 9):

No. 6 opens with a march-like rhythm in the oboes, with syncopated notes in the strings. The trio is in D minor; it has two contrasting groups, of four bars each, in a polonaise rhythm,

supported in the second group by the dactylic accompanying
figure (see Ex. 10):

This wealth of musical and instrumental invention is also
characteristic of the twelve minuets, K.585 (1789), and the six
minuets, K.599 (1791). No. 10 of the first series is quite obviously the acme of the symphonic minuet. Real symphonic
greatness is achieved within the terse framework of the obliga-
tory groups of four bars (Ex. 11):

Once again the winds are richly endowed as soloists; in K.599,
No. 4 (trio), the oboe and bassoon are actually singled out for
concertante parts (Ex. 12):

The four minuets, K.601, and the two minuets, K.604, which
were also composed in the last year of Mozart's life, are of a like
character. The bird noises from the flutes, oboes, and bassoons
in the trio of K.601, No. 1, are charming; in the second trio (in

C) the hurdy-gurdy (which survived almost exclusively as a beggar's instrument) is introduced as – and with – a joke; it continuously alights upon an accented F sharp, the false (Lydian) fourth. It is difficult to say how many reminiscences of folk-songs and other quotations would have brought a smile to the face of the contemporary listener, but I believe the trio of K.60?, No. 1, includes a quotation of this kind. In any case, K.585, No. 12, offers a strain of real folk music: we actually hear the Alpine yodel (Ex. 13):

B. German Dances

In spite of the fact that elements from the *Ländler* or waltz influenced, to varying degrees, its melodic shape, the minuet remained the dance of a single couple who wished to display a highly stylized dance of courting. In 1785, however, couples also danced the minuet together, in country-dance fashion. The minuet was still the more formal dance of polite society. In the masked balls of the Redoutensaal, only the lower classes took part in the *Ländler* and waltzes, since the throng was too great for the upper classes to join in. The German Dance was also a dance for couples, but as each partner embraced the other, all were able to dance together simultaneously. Those German Dances by Mozart which have survived date from 1787 and after. It was only then that the old German Dance became, if not presentable at court, at any rate presentable at court balls. The six German Dances, K.509, were composed in Prague in 1787, in the happy mood which followed a successful performance of *Figaro* and a successful concert. On this occasion, Mozart, for the first time, wrote dances for a large orchestra, including, in addition to the strings, two flutes (and piccolo), oboes, clarinets, bassoons, horns, trumpets, and drums. He writes these first German Dances in quavers: the tempo of the old waltz had probably already become quicker, though not so quick as in the ballroom scene in *Don Giovanni* (MM. 120–144). German Dances in Prague, as early as 1748,[1] had quite a

[1] cf. Engel: op. cit., p. 34.

comfortable, waltz-like air about them. The six which comprise
K.509 are combined in a real cycle, since each dance with its
Alternativo, that is, in all, four : ‖ : repeated sections, is followed
by a bridge passage of four to eight bars, which prepares the
way tonally and, to some extent, thematically for the next
dance. No. 6 opens with a flourish of trumpets; the cycle's long
coda of seventy-five bars is based on the themes of the sixth
dance and its attractively gliding Alternativo, and builds up
two gigantic Mannheim crescendos out of short, repeated
figures. In No. 2, Mozart quotes the aria, 'Come un'agnello',
from Sarti's opera, *Fra i due litiganti il terzo gode*. But there is a
difference between this quotation of the aria, its use as a theme
for the variations for piano, K.460(454a), of 1784, and its emer-
gence in the dining scene of *Don Giovanni*; here, the quotation
(Ex. 14) includes those enticing, clicking acciaccature which remained popular features of the Viennese waltz to the days of
Lanner and Strauss:

The trio of K.536, No. 6, is perhaps a quotation from Susanna's
'Deh vieni non tardar' from *Figaro*, which it resembles. In the
German Dances the bass line always differs from the bass in the
minuets where the *basso seguente* of earlier times runs in crotchets,
whilst pedal-points and repetition of the same notes in two, four,
eight, and even thirty-two bars (K.567, No. 2, trio) are frequent.
Fanfare-like figures played in unison, both at the opening
(K.567, Nos. 2, 4, 6, and others) and in the second part (K.586,
No. 11) are characteristic; we find the clicking acciaccature
presented most attractively in K.567, No. 1, but in a positively
Johann Straussian manner in K.586, No. 9 (Ex. 15):

The woodwind chords and enticing acciaccature which are introduced alternately in the trio of K.571, No. 4, are charming,
while the trios in the minor – for instance, K.571, Nos. 2 (cf.

Ex. 1) and 6, K.567, No. 5, K.586, No. 5, and K.602, No. 4 –
are thoroughly reminiscent of Schubert. The subdivision of the
rhythm in K.586, No. 6, was also popular later, and recurs in
Schubert (Op. 77, No. 7). The trio of K.571, No. 3, comprises
woodwind chords alternating with violin and flautino passages,
an instrumental procedure which Beethoven used in the trio of
his first Symphony. The humorous character of some of the
German Dances comes out in such jokes as the 'Canary Bird' in
K.600 (a contemporary, F. Gassmann, also wrote a German
Dance called 'Gli uccillatori'), and the 'Sleigh Ride', the trio of
the German Dances, K.605, No. 3, with sleigh bells in A, F, E,
C, and G. The theme is like that of the second half of K.600,
No. 2. Mozart had already been introduced to the jokes in his
father's burlesque symphonies ('The Sleigh Ride' and 'The
Peasants' Wedding'.)

These German Dances, like the minuets, are full of delightful
melodic and instrumental ideas; they sometimes anticipate the
romantic Viennese waltz. The codas must also be mentioned.
That of K.571, like Haydn's 'Farewell' Symphony (No. 45), dies
away with quiet, forlorn chords, heard successively on the
violins, oboes, horns, and pizzicato bass: the joke is over!

C. Contredanses

The third group of dances embraces the contredanses for
orchestra, of which Mozart wrote thirty-nine. The contre- or
contra-danse, originally an English dance, and sharply contrasted to the stiff, aristocratic minuet, had conquered the Con-
tinental dance world over a hundred years previously. It is a
communal dance, properly called Country Dance, emanating
from the popular and rural culture described in John Playford's
The English Dancing-Master: or . . . Rules for . . . Country Dances, a
book which went through eighteen editions between 1651 and
1728. Kellom Tomlinson's *The Art of Dancing*, a splendid
production of 1735, confirmed the great success scored by the
new dance. Numerous printed and manuscript collections on
the Continent testified to the enthusiastic reception enjoyed
everywhere by the contredanse. It was danced longwise, or as a
chain dance, with numerous couples dancing simultaneously in
the style of party games. The country dance permits music
much varied in invention, with changing figuration and a wide

range of metre – 6/8, 2/4, 2/4 in triplets, 3/8, and dotted rhythms. The titles and names of the dances refer to persons, places, and historical events, or are quotations from folk-songs. How the actual dance determined the musical form is illustrated by a letter from Leopold Mozart, dated Rome, 14 April 1770: "Wolfgang", he writes, "is splendid and sends herewith a contredanse. He would like Herr Cirillus Hofmann to make up the steps for it; when the two violins play as leaders, only two persons should lead the dance; but whenever the orchestra comes in with all the instruments, the whole company should dance together. It would be by far the best arrangement if it were danced by five couples. The first couple should begin the first solo, the second dance the second and so on, as there are five solos and five tutti passages."[1] The dance in question is the contredanse K.123(73g) for two violins and bass, two oboes, and two horns. The two violins play eight bars and the tutti answers with eight bars on the same subject (*a–A*, *b–B*, *c–C*, *d–D*, *e–E*).

The four contredanses K.267(271c) written for the Salzburg Carnival in 1777, combine four dances, each of four 'turns', in four different keys (G, E flat, A, D) and three different metres (6/8, ¢, ¢, 2/4); various instrumental groups and tutti alternate in eight or four bars, in accordance with the grouping of the dancers. In the first dance the thematic structure of the four repeated sections ('turns') is of interest.

The first motive of the four-bar group[2] is resumed on another degree of the scale in the third and fourth groups, repeated bar by bar in groups five and six, and inverted bar by bar in groups seven and eight (see Ex. 16):

Ex.16
K.267 [271c] No.1

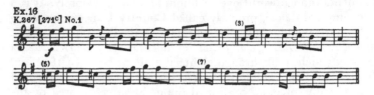

The six contredanses K.462(448b) are similar: they were obviously written in a genial mood. Charming and varied ideas

[1] Anderson: op. cit., Vol. I, pp. 188–9.

[2] P. Nettl: *Mozarts Prager Kontretänze*. Bericht über die musikwissenschaftliche Tagung der Internationalen Stiftung Mozarteum in Salzburg, 1931. Leipzig, 1932, p. 133.

are fashioned within the smallest possible form. Minuet and contredanse are combined in the two minuets with interpolated contredanses, K.463(448c), of 1784. The second 'Menuetto cantabile' is played in adagio tempo – as already mentioned, the minuet could contain a great variety of possible tempi. The nine contredanses, or quadrilles, K.510(K.Anh.293b), are not Mozart's. A contredanse comprising four parts and a final 'Marcia turca' (K.535) is entitled 'La Bataille'. The orchestra, of piccolo, clarinets, bassoon, trumpet, drum, violins, and bass, imitates battle-music in the second and third parts. The Turkish march introduces local colour in its motives, in the high upbeat, with appoggiatura, in the rhythm of the drum and the string basses struck with the bow ('col legno di battuta').

An advertisement by the Vienna copyist Lausch, in the *Wiener Zeitung* of 19 March 1788, calls the piece 'The Siege of Belgrade'. Joseph II declared war on the Turks on 9 February 1788, and a siege of Belgrade was planned which, however, did not take place until 1789. The victory of Field-Marshal-Lieutenant the Prince of Coburg, of 22 September 1789, was celebrated in a contredanse entitled 'The Victory of the Hero Coburg' (K.587). Perhaps the opening subject is a little folk-song. In bars 16ff. quite a dramatic effect is produced by a trumpet call and a tremolo in the minor, after the style of battle music. Two contredanses (K.603) from the last year of Mozart's life are exceptionally charming. The second dance, marked Andante, moves without pause into an eight-bar Allegro of a minuet character.

On 14 January 1787 Mozart reported from Prague: "At six o'clock I drove with Count Canal to the so-called Bretfeld ball. . . . I looked on . . . with the greatest pleasure while all these people flew about in sheer delight to the music of my *Figaro*, arranged for quadrilles and waltzes."[1] In the five contredanses (K.609), probably written in 1791, Mozart himself arranged 'Non più andrai' from *Figaro* for violins, bass, and flute. No. 5 is also entitled 'The Hurdy-gurdy Players'. The movement recurs, in a setting for two flutes and horns, under the title, not yet explained, of 'Les filles malicieuses'. 'The Hurdy-gurdy Players' was so called because in the fourth 'turn' the first violin plays a little phrase of eight

[1] Anderson: op. cit., Vol. III, p. 1344.

bars with a sustained open G (Ex. 17), which takes no notice
of the bass –

Ex.17
K.609, No.5

like beggars on the hurdy-gurdy. The passage (Ex. 17) resembles
the solo violin part in the rondos of the violin concertos, K.216
and 218. Mozart's father had also used the 'hurdy-gurdy' in his
burlesque symphony (also a well-known song: see below, K.32).
The contredanses are especially interesting to us, since Mozart
wrote innumerable genuine country-dance tunes as themes for
his variations and as subjects in his rondos and other movements,
particularly the finales of sonatas and symphonies.

II

A. Isolated Works

One of the earliest works for orchestra is a 'Quodlibet' (*Galimathias musicum*, (K.Anh.100a(32))) which the boy Mozart
composed in The Hague on his journey from England, with his
father and sister, for the installation of Prince William V of
Orange in March 1766. It is a series of eighteen movements, the
first of which is a D major Overture, in the Italian style, of the
utmost brevity, a miniature movement of thirteen bars. The
Overture may have been added to the Quodlibet, which is in D
minor, at a slightly later date; the piece closes in F major. In the
individual movements there are obvious quotations from folk-
songs. No. 10 makes use of the song 'On the Castration of a
Boar' ('Eahna achte muassens' sei[n]'). No. 5, the Pastorella,
employs a similar tune (Ex. 18), presumably a folksong; it is
almost identical with the melody of the trio in Leopold Mozart's
burlesque symphony, 'Die Bauernhochzeit' ('The Peasants'
Wedding').[1]

The only vocal movement, the choral No. 19, 'Eitelkeit!
Eitelkeit! Ewigs Verderben', does not really fit in. In the auto-

[1] *Denkmäler der Tonkunst in Bayern*, IX/2, p. 144.

graph it appears merely as a sketch, without words. The Allegretto, No. 7, quotes, according to Einstein, the beginning of a song, 'Gedult beschützet mich', from Valentin Rathgeber's *Augsburger Tafel-Confekt* (Part II, No. 11). Augsburg was not only the home of this type of burlesque in music, but also the home of Mozart's father, who commended the *genre* – exemplified in his own burlesque symphonies – to the attention of his son. Nos. 11 and 16 of his *Galimathias musicum* contain long, rising, and

falling chromatic passages which are humorously intended; No. 18 includes a fugue on the Dutch National Anthem, 'Willem van Nassau'. (Mozart had already arranged and written piano variations (K.25) on the anthem in the same year.) His father helped him with the fugue.

B. The Masonic Funeral Music, K.477(479a)

The external stimulus for the composition of this work, which is as significant a personal document as it is an artistic one, was the death of two members of a Freemasons' Lodge, 'Zur gekrönten Hoffnung in Orient in Wien', which Mozart himself had joined early in 1785. The two Masons were the Duke Georg August von Mecklenburg-Strelitz, Imperial and Royal Major-General, and the Hungarian-Transylvanian Court Chancellor, Count Franz Esterházy von Galantha; they died respectively on 6 and 7 November. Mozart wrote the work for the funeral which was to take place on 17 November. The depth of feeling in this work can hardly be attributed to any particular intimacy with the deceased brethren: it arises rather from an absorption in the whole problem of death, upon which Mozart often pondered deeply. As a work of art, the Funeral Music is especially interesting because it is one of the works with a *cantus firmus* (Ex. 19) which closely approaches the chorale fantasias in *Die Zauberflöte* ('Der welcher wandelt die Strasse') and the *Requiem* ('Te

decet'). Mozart wrote out the *cantus firmus* separately, at the end
of the autograph (Ex. 20):

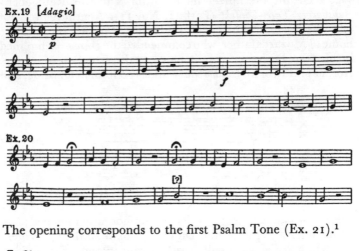

The opening corresponds to the first Psalm Tone (Ex. 21).[1]

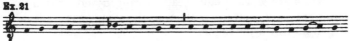

The rest represents a collation of several psalm melodies to
which was added the penitential Psalm 51, 'Miserere mei Deus',
sung at funerals. The liturgical melody is lent a march-like
rhythm. Mozart evidently brought to mind a real or visionary
funeral in which, after a sorrowful introduction, the coffin is
carried past, whilst the psalm tune is played as a march by a
curious and unique collection of winds: oboes, and clarinets together, three basset horns, bassoon (or, rather, double bassoon,
since what is prescribed is the 'Gran Fagotto'), and two horns.
After the conclusion of the liturgical melody, the themes of the
introduction gain in tragic intensity. The whole movement is
imbued with incomparable visionary and dramatic power,
whether it be regarded as the prelude to a series of Masonic rites
or merely as a funereal scene considered with the inward eye of
a dramatist. The introduction begins with repeated, sighing,

---

[1] The first part of the *cantus firmus* is also identical with the old Gregorian lamen-
tation chant ('Incipit Lamentatio Jeremiae') used by Haydn in the 1760s. Cf.
H. C. R. Landon: *The Symphonies of Joseph Haydn*, Vienna and London, 1955,
pp. 285ff., and especially n. 17 on p. 293. – EDS.

mournful chords in the woodwinds, to which, at the fifth and sixth repetitions, are added piercing chordal figures on the violins, chromatically extended. While the wind chords, now animated, continue, the violins, in an outburst of grief, thrice utter excited cries of lament above the tremolo and syncopations of the strings (Ex. 22):

Two deep chords in the winds announce the real funeral procession – the march tune is first accompanied by a quietly plaintive figure on the strings; in the second part, the atmosphere of sorrow is increased by the projection of the introduction's more agitated figures over quivering basses. After the end of the march tune (the *cantus firmus*), a calmer mood seems to set in with the undulating syncopations of the violins and the two sighs of the oboes: but mourning bursts out yet again. The second part of the introduction leads into the coda, with its tearful violin figures, which dies away pianissimo, in a chromatic ascent, after oboe sighs which seem to rise to heaven. This Funeral Music, but sixty-nine bars in length, is evidence of the passionate depth of Mozart's feeling and, at the same time, is one of the noblest examples of classical perfection. The use of the psalm from the Catholic funeral rites proves that Mozart, in the Masonic ritual, could make symbolic use of music from the Christian liturgy.

[Translated by Stanley Godman]

BOOK LIST

[Standard Mozart biographies have not been listed.]

H. Engel: 'Der Tanz in Mozarts Kompositionen', *Mozart-Jahrbuch*, Salzburg, 1953, pp. 29ff.

P. Nettl: 'Mozarts Prager Kontretänze', *Bericht über die musikwissenschaftliche Tagung der Internationalen Stiftung Mozarteum in Salzburg*, 1931. Leipzig, 1932.

JENS PETER LARSEN

THE SYMPHONIES

M OZART's career as a symphonist spanned the period from
1764 to 1788. In terms of years, it differed not so very much
from Haydn's, which began in about 1760 and ended in 1795.
But the curves of development of these two composers, who were
the first great classical symphonists, were markedly different.

Haydn was approaching his thirtieth year before he began
to write symphonies, and he was over sixty when he finished his
last. He found very swiftly a highly personal approach to the
problems of a rather new musical *genre* which, with his symphonies dating from about 1770 onward, he decisively influenced. And although his symphonic development passed
through various phases, a continuous line is clearly discernible
throughout that development.

Mozart began his activities as a symphonic composer when
he was only eight years of age, and they ended in his thirty-
second year. So it is hardly to be wondered at that his early
symphonies reveal a less defined personal approach than
Haydn's. More distinctive features emerge only in the works of
the period 1773–4, when he was still only seventeen to eighteen
years old; but just at that time he ceased to write symphonies
regularly. It appears that between 1774 and 1779 he turned to
symphonic composition only during the journey to Paris in
1777–8. Then, in the last twelve years of his life he wrote no
more than nine symphonies, amounting to one-fifth of his total
symphonic output; but among them are some of the finest
symphonies ever written.

The earliest Mozart symphonies date from his stay in London in 1764–5. About then a new concert series, the Bach–Abel
concerts, were started, and they played a leading part in
London musical life for many years. Mozart was always highly
receptive, and his earliest symphonies (K.16 and 19) were
obviously the result of the impression made on him by the
symphonic style of these two composers. It resulted in the
boy copying out in his own hand the whole of one of Abel's
symphonies which, at one time, was accepted as a Mozart work:

K.18(K.Anh.109[1]). But fundamentally he owed far more to
Johann Christian Bach, whom he always held in high esteem.

The symphonic style which Mozart learned from J. C. Bach
had acquired its character from Italian *opera buffa*. Originally
intended simply as a prelude to the opera, the symphony, in
about the middle of the eighteenth century, established itself as
a concert piece; but the spirit of *opera buffa* survived for a long
time in those symphonies which were Italianate in manner.
They were slight, attractive works—musical entertainments
which on no account were to be taken seriously. The special
quality of the better kind of *buffa* symphonies is its simple grace,
its 'sentimentality' in the eighteenth-century sense, expressed
with particular refinement in the slow movements. An outstanding example of this *Empfindsamkeit* is the middle movement
of J. C. Bach's *Lucio Silla* Symphony, which in our day has been
frequently revived in concert programmes (see Ex. 1).

Ex.1

Judged by the standards we have come to accept since
Beethoven and Brahms, the symphonies of this type are all very
short and simple. They consist of an easily flowing Allegro,
built out of sonority and motion, an expressive Andante, and a
very simple Presto in 3/8 or related tempo, either a stylized
minuet or a country dance.

Mozart's first symphony, K.16, is a *buffa* symphony of this
sort. One might ask whether, perhaps, Leopold Mozart gave
his son some help in this first attempt; but the question is of no

importance. A distinguishing and touching feature is undoubtedly the feeling it gives of something childlike and halting.
Melody, modulation, texture, form – everything is simple,
primitive. None the less, although, of course, it really consists
of nothing but clichés, the work makes an impression, even, one
might say, an impression of a personal quality. One can almost
sense the delight the young composer takes in sonorities, in
amusing himself with an orchestra, in achieving something
without stopping to think whether posterity was left anything
new and astonishing.

In the spring of 1765, while still in London, Mozart wrote the
D major Symphony, K.19, which is very clear evidence of
J. C. Bach's influence. Compared with the first symphony, the
D major represents an astonishing advance in capacity. One
would hardly judge that its composer was still a child. It is
much more 'grown up', and displays a mastery of melodic and
formal resources that can be taken as indicating a certain
'maturity'. At the same time it lacks entirely the unsophisti-
cated charm which is such a marked feature of K.16. Naturally,
this symphony, too, is crammed with stereotyped turns of
phrase drawn from the sphere of the *buffa* symphony: the unison
opening, the dynamic contrast within the main theme, the
'drum' bass (i.e., repeated notes), the delicate cantabile quality
of the middle movement, and so on. But it is hard to believe
that a nine-year-old boy could so surely create the illusion of
an adult composer.

Still more surprising in this respect is the B flat major Symphony, K.22, which was probably composed at The Hague, at
the end of 1765. The style is still decisively determined by the
buffa symphony, but both individual touches and the shape as
a whole point to other precursors besides. A genuine orchestral
crescendo in the Mannheim style is a characteristic feature of
the first movement. The loosening of the texture by resort to
short imitations is another. But the most striking feature is the
manner in which this first movement has been reorganized in
formal respects. Whereas in the two preceding symphonies a
not fully worked-out sonata form without complete recapitulation is met with, here we have a typical ritornello construction
with a fourfold statement of the ritornello (the main theme).
This form, which was derived from the baroque concerto, is
typical of a large number of pre- and early classical symphonies,

and especially of those written in places influenced not so much by *buffa* traditions as by survivals of the baroque 'chamber-music' traditions – for instance, Mannheim and Vienna. Concerto traditions may also be traced in the ternary slow movement. On the other hand, the finale is pure *buffa*. The beginning of this movement is striking for its direct reminiscence of an episode in *Figaro*. Of course, it does not follow that Mozart made use of this theme, so to speak, twenty years after writing the symphony. Obviously it is only one of many instances of certain characteristic phrases returning again and again in Mozart's works. Not consciously so, but rather because he hit quite spontaneously upon ideas which took a similar course. We shall come across further examples later on.

After the long foreign tour of 1764–6 Mozart rested for barely a year in Salzburg before setting off on another journey with his family. Wyzewa and St.-Foix have attempted to ascribe an F major Symphony, K.76(42a), to this interim period, whereas Einstein thought it had been composed in the autumn of 1767 at the earliest, after Mozart's arrival in Vienna. One or two special features distinguish the work. The finale appears without doubt to have borrowed its main theme from a well-known gavotte by Rameau, a fact which might suggest the influence of Viennese traditions. The Andante is definitely of a minuet character, though somewhat stylized. It is followed, however, by a genuine minuet with trio (a further pointer to Vienna), in which the minuet character stands out very strongly. For this reason one might agree with Einstein in thinking that this minuet may have been composed later than the other movements. St.-Foix regards this symphony as an important composition, but I am not quite able to agree with him.

During Mozart's residence in Vienna he composed at least three symphonies: K.43, 45, and 48; and perhaps two others: the G major, K45a, first published from the parts in the Monastery of Lambach by Wilhelm Fischer in the *Mozart-Jahrbuch* of 1923, and the unpublished B flat major Symphony (K.45b). In these works we can easily trace the influence of the Viennese symphonic tradition as it has come down to us in compositions by Wagenseil, Holzbauer, Hofmann, Gassmann, and others, or in Haydn's early symphonies, though, indeed, after 1760 Haydn, like Mozart, pursued his own line of development outside Vienna for many years. Perceptible evidence of Mozart's reorientation

is provided by the very fact that with a single exception (K.45a)
all these symphonies are in four movements, the third being a
minuet. While the *buffa* symphony long continued to cling to
the three-movement form, Vienna in the 'sixties was slowly
coming to regard four movements as normal for a symphony,
with a minuet as third movement. This stroke was first and foremost the after-effect of the specifically Austrian divertimento
tradition. A further characteristic of the Viennese symphonic
tradition, the broadly laid out first movement with a full
recapitulation, and a development as a kind of varied exposition, is a slight tribute to the close connection between the symphony and the traditions of the baroque concerto.

K.43, which is presumably the earliest of these symphonies,
is in four movements, but characteristically enough it has a
first movement which has not forgotten the *buffa* traditions. In
general, it is quite a charming little work. One listens to it not
as the precocious product of a wonder-child, but as an attractive early classical symphony which, needless to say, is intended only as pleasant entertainment and not as the communi-
cation of personal confessions. The first movement is far from
original, but reveals something of its author's gift for organizing
his material. The functions of the various sections within the
movement can clearly be discerned: the pronounced principal-
theme character of the first section; a short bridge passage; the
second subject, not a particularly striking melodic invention,
but in definite contrast (melodically, dynamically, and instru-
mentally) to the first; and then, as close to the exposition, an
episode once more conceived primarily in orchestral terms.
The continuation is in Italian style: a simple development of
the main theme with an incomplete recapitulation. The second,
very pretty movement is decidedly cantabile: the melody was
taken direct from a duet in Mozart's Latin school-opera,
Apollo et Hyacinthus (K. 38), which he composed in Salzburg
in 1767. The instrumentation (flutes; horns; muted first violin;
pizzicato second violins; first and second violas; pizzicato
'cellos and basses) must be regarded as rather subtle for a slow
movement of the time. The last two movements, a rather heavy
minuet and a finale *à la gigue*, point to divertimento traditions.

The D major symphony, K.45, which a few months later
Mozart utilized as the overture to *La finta semplice*, K.51(46a),
offers a less clear picture. In the first movement there is no

definite indication of the transition from the exposition to the development and from the development to the recapitulation, and the successive sections lack defined indications of their functions. The whole movement is built out of traditional orchestral figures. The Andante is very simple, and, like the minuet, possesses no special characteristic. The best part of the work is the finale, a stylized gigue with effectively contrasted dotted and triplet rhythms.

The two symphonies K.Anh.221(45a) and K.48 unmistakably reveal a closer approximation to the Viennese symphonic style. In many respects the G major Symphony (K.45a) harks back to the pre-Haydn symphony, and especially to Wagenseil. As often with the latter, the first movement is somewhat like the first movement of a baroque concerto; it is more on the lines of an orchestral tutti, with interpolated solo episodes, than an alternation of thematic sections and bridge passages. The Andante is more after the fashion of a divertimento, and might well be a faint reminiscence of Haydn's quartet movement well known by the title 'Serenade', composed some three or four years previously; typically, a brief solo for the horns is so written that it can be played also by the lower strings; the wind instruments, in fact, can be dispensed with. The strict style, which since the days of Fux and Caldara in Vienna had only been lurking beneath the surface, to come into prominence again at the beginning of the 'seventies, is indicated by a number of episodes both in this Andante and in the concluding Presto, a finale which also revives concerto-style episodes such as the characteristic opening (Ex. 2) of the development (or rather, middle section, since there is no real suggestion of development in this movement).

Of all these symphonies, the D major, K.48, which was composed in December 1768, shortly before the departure of the Mozart family for Salzburg, most closely approaches the Viennese traditions in the wider sense. In this instance there is a special affinity with the composer with whom Mozart later was to have an intimate relationship, Haydn. At this time the senior composer was living in provincial isolation as Prince Esterházy's *Kapellmeister*, and exploring new lines of symphonic development. Anyone acquainted with Haydn's early symphonies must be astonished at this early evidence of Mozart's peculiar capacity to assimilate, vitally and unequivocally,

another composer's style, and yet retain a personal, not simply an imitative, quality. The affinity with such works as Haydn's Symphonies Nos. 3 and 13 is quite obvious. And here, at last, in the first movement of K.48 the Viennese tradition has also exerted its influence *formally*. The exposition is followed by a development of approximately the same length (twenty-six as against thirty-three bars) and of similar melodic content, and a recapitulation of practically the same length as the exposition (thirty-four bars), but with the very characteristic difference that the episode which functions as a 'second subject' in the exposition, and plays a similar role in the development, drops out altogether in the recapitulation, since it represents only an episode, and not a genuine second subject. As in similar symphonies by Haydn, the orchestra is here reinforced by trumpets and drums. After the outspokenly tutti character of the first movement, the simple string Andante, which is also reminiscent of earlier Haydn models, introduces a fine contrast. The minuet brings back the tutti character of the first movement. The finale in 12/8, a stylized gigue, brings the symphony to a festive end. This symphony marks the first milestone in his development as a symphonist.

He remained at home in Salzburg scarcely a year. At the end of 1769 Leopold took him to Italy, and there they remained until the spring of 1771. It is not certain whether he composed any symphonies during his residence in Salzburg. On the other hand, from the time of the first journey to Italy we have quite a number of symphonies which afford us an insight into his progressive development as a symphonist. The symphonies concerned are K.81(73l), 95(73n), 97(73m), 84(73q) and 74. It is entirely characteristic of Mozart (one might even call it self-evident) that after his incursion into the realm of the Viennese symphony during his stay at Vienna, these 'Italian' symphonies again draw nearer to the *buffa* traditions. This applies to melody and texture, but also to orchestration and formal structure. It is highly characteristic that of these five symphonies four are in the customary symphonic key of D major; and it is just as characteristic that only two of them are in four movements with minuet. It cannot even be ruled out that in both these cases the minuet was composed later.

But the most essential aspect of these symphonies is that they were entirely a product of the *opera buffa* spirit. While living in Vienna Mozart had drawn closer and closer to the tradition of the concerto-symphony, to the earlier symphonic trend which had resulted from a fusion of the forms of the concerto and divitimento with the style of the Italian symphony. Now he was writing for an Italian public. So he turned his back on his adoption of Viennese traditions and once more wrote symphonies whose character was determined by the obligation that they should, above all, sound brilliant: the lay-out of the parts was a secondary question.

It is not easy to trace any course of development in these symphonies, if only because their chronological order has not been precisely determined. We shall content ourselves with indicating certain common traits. A homophonous, definitely chordal texture is fundamental almost throughout, and to a large extent rather stereotyped orchestral figures. Very typical is the repetition of short, unrelated phrases (*Redikte*). From the melodic aspect one could, perhaps, speak of a new creative idea in the second subject of the first movements of K.74 and 84, and in each of these symphonies the 3/8 cantabile middle movement indicates a growing intensity of melodic expression. The use of short wind solos is another premonition of the future. In formal respects, on the other hand, everything is rather traditional. Characteristic traits, pointing to the traditions of the *buffa* symphony, are the very short developments, and the linking of the first and second movements (K.74 and 95). Another noticeable feature is the rondo-like finale of K.74. Of these five symphonies, K.74 and 84, more than any of the others, deserve revival.

After this first journey to Italy, the two Mozarts remained in Salzburg only some five months before travelling to Italy again. During these months (from the end of March to the middle of August 1771) a further series of symphonies was written. We cannot establish precisely how many there were, but they certainly included K.75, 73(75a), and 110(75b). In these symphonies, too, we find little that points to the future. Yet, compared with the preceding Italian symphonies they offer a very different picture. Their character is again governed by Austrian traditions, but the effect as a whole is more intimate, more of a chamber-musical category. Are we to regard this as a reflection of the liaison with Salzburg? Or is there a connection with the move, pronounced at this very period, towards a revival of chamber music, especially of the string quartet, which found its most distinguished expression in the three Haydn quartet series, Opp. 9, 17, and 20? Or is there quite a different explanation?

Here again no one symphony stands out. One would perhaps single out the slow movement of K.73 as the piece most worthy of remark, for its fine cantabile, and even more for the short dialogue between first violins and first oboe. The rondo finales of K.73 and 110 are rather characteristic. The very brief developments in these two symphonies suggest the influence of the suite rather than the concerto. A tendency to favour imitation technique is frequently noticeable; it is particularly marked in the minuet of K.110. A special feature is to be noted in K.75, right at the beginning, where the melodic lead is transferred to the oboes. All in all, certain new influences are making themselves felt, among them, undoubtedly, Haydnesque influence, or perhaps even more precisely that of Joseph and Michael Haydn. During these years Mozart's symphonic development had not achieved stability.

The two symphonies K.96(111b) and 112, which are said to date back to the period of Mozart's second Italian journey, once more indicate that his symphonic development at this time had not reached any new creative phase. K.96 is one of the symphonies in which the orchestra is reinforced with trumpets and drums. It is based primarily upon the display of orchestral effects: in the first movement, tutti effects derived from broken-chord melody, in the Andante, detailed pianoforte effects. In K.112 the clearly laid out, Haydnesque first movement, with its happily contrasted second subject and closing material, is particularly distinctive, whereas the other three movements are quite traditional.

After his return from the second Italian tour Mozart's life entered a period which was associated with symphonic activity to a greater extent than ever before or after. Between the New Year and August 1772, the beginning of the third Italian tour, he wrote eight symphonies; between the homecoming in March 1773 and the journey to Vienna in August of that year he added a further five; and after the Vienna visit (July to September), in the period from November 1773 to May 1774, there were another four. All in all, about one-third of his total symphonic creation belongs to this comparatively brief period.

Comparing these symphonies with their predecessors, we see at once that now he was on the verge of a final resolution of the problem. After his repeated vacillations between the Austrian and Italian styles and forms, the Mozart symphony definitely turns towards the Viennese tradition. The Italian influence is on the wane. Even so, Mozart's development as a symphonist continues to work through a fusion of Austrian and Italian elements; but one can hardly fail to recognize that the Viennese influence is now decisive.

Even if we draw up a simple list of the keys of these symphonies, we note an obvious difference between them and the keys of the earlier works. In the main, it is characteristic of the symphonies dating from the first Italian tour that four of the five are in the customary key of D. In the eight down to August 1772 we find a far greater tonal variety: one in D, one in C, one in F, two in G, two in A, and one in E flat. And it is significant that only two of these works are in three movements; the other six are in four (with minuets). These elementary observations can be supplemented by noting the changes in thematic formation, general structure, etc.

There is a fine example of the fusion of Viennese symphonic traditions with distinctly Italian cantabile in the first symphony of this series, K.114, in A major. In it, there is a characteristic contrast with the Haydn symphony. For Haydn, a fundamental requirement of symphonic organization is the development of strong basic motives, and his thematic invention consists primarily of the statement of those characteristic motivic shapes which make development of this type possible. In Mozart's later works the dominant tendency is the statement of a whole series of fine cantabile themes: symphonic development results from their interplay and contrast. Where Haydn, the instrumental musician, aims at a fundamental unity as the basis of a sensitive variation form, Mozart, the dramatist, gives free rein to the invention of continually new and characteristic themes and motives. (Later on we shall see that in his last and greatest symphonies he achieved a fusion of these two tendencies.)

If we compare the opening themes from K.114 and 134 (the last of the eight symphonies), the contrast is at once obvious (see Exx. 3 and 4).

Ex. 4, from K.134, is a typically Haydnesque theme, whose main object is not a cantabile line, but the presentation of a characteristic motive which determines all the movement's development. Ex. 3, from K.114, is altogether different. Here the decisive factor is the cantabile, the finely unfolding, melodic line, the *theme* as a tranquil unity in itself. One or two other

characteristic touches must also be mentioned: the dynamic contrast within the theme, and its immediate development without break after its initial statement. This development has to follow immediately just because the theme is self-contained.

The A major Symphony, K.114, is certainly one of the most inspired of this period. One could point out many beauties in this work, such as the developmental transition, the second subject with its hint of quartet style, and the short, but delicately wrought development with elegant wind and string dialogue, all in the first movement; the mixture of cantabile and concertante in the Andante; the effective contrast between the

Ex.4

baroque minuet and the cantabile trio; the firm insistence upon the true finale character of the last movement.

The next symphony, K.124, in G major, adds no essentially new features: the influence of Vienna is even more marked. The most personal movement is the finale with its traces of quartet style. The three-movement C major Symphony, K.128, is typical. Inspired by influences from the style of the baroque concerto, the Allegro is dominated by an unbroken rhythmic impulse which effectively exploits the contrast between quaver motion and triplet rhythm. The Andante grazioso has again a quartet quality about it, while the finale, a stylized gigue, is also primarily rhythmic in character, like the first movement. The following symphony, K.129, in G major, is more traditional. The first movement returns to the *buffa* melodic line and the finale, likewise, is atavistically contrary in style to the fore-going finale movements. One might almost conjecture that there was some special reason for this momentary regression.

The F major Symphony, K.130, brings with it a further loosening of the symphonic development of these few months. The first movement crosses concerto and *buffa* elements to excellent effect. In the Andantino grazioso we find an example of the cantabile middle movement in 3/8 which Haydn also introduced in this same year, as a new contribution to symphonic writing. The dancing minuet leads to a distinctive trio with contrasting basic harmonies. The finale, on the other hand, is more distinguished for its length than for any outstanding beauties. The E flat Symphony, K.132, pulses with a lively spirit. It is only slightly *buffa* in style, but its mood is *buffa* throughout. In no sense a big symphony, K.132 is one of the most charming of this series. The first theme of the first movement is in fact a presage of the opening of the later piano concerto in the same key (K.482; 1785), and it employs the same effect, a dynamic contrast within the narrowest frame. The second movement was written twice; the second version is an Andante cantabile in 3/8. Further fundamental contrasts are to be found in the minuet, against whose light filigree the composer sets a trio of a kind we have encountered before. The tendency towards 'strict' harmony results in an almost grotesque effect, and one has to take this 'serious' harmonic sequence simply as a good joke. In any case, in the closing Allegro Mozart lets the mask fall; the movement is pure entertainment music, evoking the gaiety of the dance. It is in rondo form with a gavotte-like, quite primitive theme, ultimately of French origin, but probably derived from J. C. Bach or Vienna. Anyone who takes offence at this 'banal' finale should leave it alone. Those who are receptive to imperishable, artless humour will treasure it.

Of the last two symphonies of these creative months, the first, in D, K.133, has a first movement with an unusual structure (the first subject acts as a kind of closing ritornello) and harks back to certain more special predecessors, and perhaps to the influence of Mannheim, though the style does not point in that direction. The finale, like several others of this period, is evidence of the growing importance of this movement, of the balance now being achieved between first and last movements. The main theme of the last symphony in this series, K.134, in

A, has already been quoted (Ex. 4). Not only the theme, but the symphony as a whole reveals the unmistakable influence of Haydn. True, the first movement has a formal structure like that of K.133, but any Mannheim influence seems to be excluded on stylistic grounds. The finest movement in the symphony is the substantial Andante. If any affinity with Mannheim is to be looked for here, it is to be found in the movement's effective dynamic contrasts and climaxes.

The four symphonies, K.162, 181(162b), 182(166c), and 184(166a), which date from the spring of 1773, all betray the influence of the third Italian tour, from which Mozart had recently returned. All four are in three movements without a minuet. In the first movement, which by the way can assume a very varied shape, we do not find the customary two-part structure with repeats. The development is very short, or wholly missing. In idiom, too, the works have in part certain aspects in common, but they mix the Italian and domestic styles and thus do not offer especially clear stylistic features.

The first two are of the least interest. In K.162 certain concertante episodes are prominent, with contrasts partly sonorous, partly dynamic, as in the second subject both of the first and second movements. In K.181, the second subject of the first movement assumes even more definitely the character of a simple piano episode within the frame of a rather homogeneous tutti scheme. The first movement is in two-part sonata form without a development, and leads directly into the Andantino grazioso. This is, so to speak, an oboe aria, with framing ritornellos and solo passages for oboe with string accompaniment. The middle movement in turn leads without break into the finale, a lively and unpretentious rondo of a frankly divertimento character.

Compared with these two somewhat characterless symphonies, the other pair, K.182 and 184, expresses a much stronger personality. In K.182, Mozart's special predilection for building a coherent phrase of great inner tension from various motives of a markedly contrasting nature is evident from the very beginning. Here, too, characteristic intervening interludes are prominent, whereas the second subject is somewhat more traditionally inclined. A short episode in imitation serves as the transition, first to a very short, modulating passage, then to a kind of ritornello-like repetition of the main theme at the close. The second movement is a beautiful Andantino grazioso in simple rondo form, whose refrain, i.e., the main theme, seems to be reminiscent of J. C. Bach. The orchestration makes an essential contribution to the pleasing effect; muted violins with flutes doubling at the octave carry the main melody, accompanied by horns and violas above pizzicato basses; in the intervening episodes, the flutes are set against the strings, or join with the horns in an interlude for unaccompanied wind instruments. The finale is somewhat traditional, even archaic, a 3/8 Allegro which recalls Haydn's early symphonies.

In K.184, as in K.181, we have a three-movement symphony with the first movement leading into the second, and the second into the third. The first movement is again divided into tutti sections and piano episodes, but with no basic rhythmic differentiation, as a result of which the movement makes a quite uniform impression. The form, with its rondo tendencies, approximates to that of the baroque concerto-movement, and the second movement, too, has a taste of the baroque in the trio-sonata style of its beginning. A finely contrasted little episode for wind instruments leads to a rather brief, modulating passage, and later to the finale, an Allegro in 3/8 and the most interesting part of the symphony. Here we find an early example of a movement in which the pronounced 'finale' character is classical in its distinction. Two influences which were to prove decisive in Mozart's creative activities in the years to come, the concerto and the divertimento, seem to be at work. The movement's whole rhythmic impulse, the suggestively soloistic violin passages, and the alternation of forte and piano episodes point to the concerto—in the classical, not the baroque, sense. The tendency towards a thin texture and miniature imitation suggests the divertimento and more especially the sphere of the string quartet: in fact, the movement as a whole points strongly towards Mozart's mature style.

A sojourn in Vienna in the late summer of 1773 brought new inspiration, for without doubt Mozart came to know there some of the newer Haydn symphonies. In the years *c.* 1770–2 Haydn, with a series of powerfully expressive symphonies, had paved the way for a revitalization of the form. A new and similar reanimation is to be found in the symphonies which Mozart composed between November 1773 and May 1774, and especially in K.183 in G minor and K.201 (186a) in A major. One can hardly doubt that this intensification in expressiveness is to be attributed to the influence of Haydn's symphonies. Here we have one of the first marked results of the constantly renewed and reciprocal Haydn–Mozart influence, which was one of the most distinctive features of the Viennese classical period.

Together with these two symphonies, we must also consider K.199(162a), 200(173e), and 202(186b). K.199 has been allotted to the spring of 1773, and some writers have sought to link it with the two above-mentioned symphonies; but quite apart from the date inscribed on the work itself, April 1774, I do not think the attribution is satisfactorily substantiated. K.199 has, it is true, the same three-movement structure as the others; but it seems to me that the style suggests quite other connections. The first movement appears to be Haydnesque, both in form and content, yet it has more in common with the symphonies of the 1760s than with the climactic works of 1770–2. In this movement, the sections are very clearly distinguished. The themes and intervening interludes are well characterized, with, at times, a subtle variation of the episodes when repeated (cf. bars 36–43 with 44–51). The second movement, also very precisely organized, foreshadows Mozart's middle period, in contradistinction to the other movements, which are closer to the style of earlier precursors. Little touches such as the chromatic appoggiatura formations, or the frequently altered chords V^7 of V, may be noted. A refined detail is the exploitation of the octave leap as a link in the transition from the close of the exposition to the development. The finale, with its contrapuntal tendencies, suggests the string quartet, though certain of Haydn's early symphonies may be an influence.

The D major symphony, K.202, displays a mixture of old and new. The first movement shows traces both of the older concerto style as well as a future evolution; the latter is seen in the filigree motive-work. The middle movement is once again purely a string quartet movement of a somewhat archaic character. The minuet is definitely of a baroque colour, whereas the finale, which has a certain similarity with the finale of K.181, discloses influences from divertimento and quartet.

The Symphony in C major, K.200, is far more Mozartean, and the very opening theme, with its forward drive, at once raises the work above the level of its more traditional companions. We are now approaching the time when the theme is destined to play a far more decisive role in the total structure than was hitherto the case in the earlier symphonies of Haydn and Mozart; and the individual character of this theme is unmistakable. Its importance is further enhanced both by its use as the basis of an imitational section at the beginning of the development and by its repeat at the close of the movement, so reminiscent of the concerto. In this movement, moreover, the second subject's subtle interplay between strings and wind instruments is noteworthy. The second movement is a typical example of a fine cantabile melody with simple chordal accompaniment, con sordini. The minuet is rather Haydnesque, but the finale is Mozartean throughout. The whole movement is marked by a breathless, forward-striving evolution deriving from the effective contrast between the two basic motives of the main theme: the trill-motive and the ostinato-like quavers. The climax is reserved for the close, where, in a quite unexpected crescendo, Mozart irresistibly carries his listeners away.

The 'little' G minor Symphony, K.183, like all the Mozart symphonies written before about 1780, was formerly given scant regard, but it has been removed from its obscurity during the last few decades; and because of its key there has been a tendency to bring it into rather too close a relationship with the 'great' G minor Symphony (K.550). Some have wanted to see in K.183 a kind of 'self-confession', the expression of a personal mood, of a depression. I do not believe any such explanation is required: Mozart's choice of this key was hardly the result of a personal conflict, but due simply to his acquaintance with Haydn's series of symphonies in minor keys written about this time, and more particularly with the G minor Symphony, No. 39 (*c.* 1768–69). It is quite obvious that Mozart's concern with symphonic problems during those years must, in any case, have forced him to try his hand at a symphony in a minor key. But even if we cannot attribute any deeper psychological significance to the work, it remains one of the most interesting of this period.[1]

[1] That Mozart may have been influenced by Haydn's example, or felt obliged "to try his hand at a symphony in a minor key" does not, in our view, exclude the "deeper psychological significance" of the actual musical *result*, i.e., the composition itself. What is of significance, perhaps, is not how Mozart happened to select his key, but in what that selection culminated. The choice of key may have been casual or externally determined, but in neither case does it rule out the singularity of expression of the works concerned. In short, the attribution of 'psychological significance' to a work is not invalidated simply because there is a seeming lack of such significance about the initial stimulus. We must be wary, at the very least, of ascribing too much to influence or convention, a far too simple, though superficially

Its expressive character is at once apparent in the unison opening theme. As in Haydn's Symphony No. 39, the musical events derive fundamentally from the rhythm, and, as in many Haydn symphonies, the rhythmic tension dominates the movement until well beyond the middle of the exposition, which may therefore be divided into three parts: opening section (bars 1–29), evolving transition (bars 29–58), and closing part (bars 59–82). There is ample contrast, in both rhythmic and motivic detail; it is, however, quite typical of this symphony that the separate motives do not tend, as so often in Mozart, to emerge as charming 'individualities', but are subservient to the unfolding of the total rhythmic impulse. Consequently, despite all the contrasts, the impression left is preponderantly one of uniformity. Apart from the main subject itself, the most pregnant passages are the above-mentioned transitional section's opening in imitation and its subsequent projection of a motivic fragment which, in turn, is developmentally connected with motives of the first section. From the motivic standpoint, the development proper looks forward to the finale with a new imitational passage. A short coda is suggestive of the tradition inherited from the concerto: the device of using the opening subject again at the close.

The second movement opens with a very pretty theme, built out of a dialogue between bassoons and muted violins. In harsh contrast to this outspokenly cantabile melody there follows a motive, pure *buffa* in character, which covers only 2 × 2 bars, and which, apart from its repetition in the recapitulation, plays no further role whatever in the rest of the movement. It is difficult to decide whether Mozart attached any special significance to this motive; in the total structure it seems to operate as a foreign body. On the other hand, the minuet and trio emerge with stronger features and a character firmly maintained throughout. The minuet offers unison and chordal motives, forte and piano effects, one against the other, the whole being supported by a rhythmic foundation suggestive of the

---

convincing, method of accounting for a work's genesis, which neglects the fact that a powerful artistic compulsion will eventually find a suitable means of expression. Einstein remarks: "In [K.183] ... the choice of key alone transcends the boundaries of simply 'social' music, and even contradicts the nature of such music. What purpose of the day can this document of impetuous expression have served?" (*Mozart*, p. 223). – Eds.

baroque. The trio is a lovely interlude for unaccompanied wind instruments, with delicate refinement of detail, such as the small imitational passage in the middle and the three-part passage in parallel motion towards the end. The finale has an affinity with the first movement, and is even more homogeneous in character; but through its prominent dotted rhythm it does not escape the danger of slightly exaggerating this same homogeneity. There is still a considerable distance between this and the great minor-key works of the 1780s.

The A major Symphony, K.201(186a), is the crowning achievement of Mozart's early symphonies. Not that it tries to surpass the fundamentally expressive quality of the G minor; but in the A major, Mozart resorts to other means to master the more extroverted type of entertainment music which is the basic character of the older symphony. The prime feature of the A major is its fusion of symphonic and chamber-musical styles, a synthesis which was a central problem tackled by Haydn in his symphonies of the same period. It also played a part in Mozart's development, albeit a less significant one. But in K.201, and more especially in the first movement, its influence is unmistakable. At the heart of this movement is the form of the just emerging string quartet, together with chamber-musical forms from the baroque period, such as the suite and chamber sonata. Distinctively rhythmic impulses are felt, while in harmonic terms it reveals a maturity of conception which raises it above its predecessors. But the chamber-musical influence is noticeable, above all in the continuity of the texture, as is the individualized quality of the part-writing, which is evident from the very beginning.

The theme of the first movement (Ex. 5) immediately discloses an intensification of expression. Comparison with the theme already quoted from K.114 (Ex. 4) clearly reveals the particularly progressive features of Ex. 5. The earlier theme was outstanding for its cantabile quality and its fine melodic development; but this is only to be found in the melodic line itself. The melody of the upper part is at first set off against a subsidiary part and only later given an orchestral accompaniment; but even this takes the shape of a simple chordal structure without independent melodic part-writing. The first period of the theme in K.201 has a similar distribution of roles, the first violins having the melody, with string accompaniment; but

the effect, none the less, is very different. The emphatic contrast
between the rhythmic, pulsing theme in the upper part and the
gently gliding movement of the lower parts, together with the
far more subtle harmonic texture, which achieves a stronger
coherence within the period as such, give to the theme a much
more powerful individuality.

Ex.5   *Allegro moderato*

Str.

Ob.

Hn. A

    Its special impress, however, is not fully revealed in this first
period.   Only during its repetition and further continuation do
we realize that the melody in the upper part is so written that it
can be played against itself in close, rather free imitation between the upper and lower parts, with the result that the repetition has a distinctive, climactic quality. Another essential

feature of this imitational episode calls for comment. At the time the symphony was written, imitation still usually involved a return to baroque traditions, both texturally and thematically. But while the theme is laid out primarily for later imitation, stylistically it belongs wholly to the 'modern' symphonic manner. The synthesis of 'circumscribed' (*gebundenen*) and 'free' (*freien*) styles, which constituted one of the main problems of the growing Viennese classical style, found a happy solution in this early work.

The opening period is particularly impressive. There follows an attractive concertante development, consisting chiefly of tutti effects, with two cantabile episodes; a second subject, which perhaps recalls a lesser-known pioneer of the Viennese classical style, Vanhal; and an unassuming episode in imitation. In the development, the part-writing is again more strongly individual, and right at the close there is yet another imitative development of the main theme in a clearly shaped coda.

The slow movement is 'carried' by a broad melody in the upper part. The expression is intimate and subdued – quite literally so, with muted strings. Here, too, there is an unmistakable deepening of expression as compared with the earlier symphonies. The minuet is also chamber musical in its trend; it is derived from a quite elementary dotted motive, which is developed with truly Mozartean delicacy. The finale is hardly up to the level of the other movements; and although it certainly has its beauties, as a whole it is more traditional.

Having reached this early summit in his symphonic development, Mozart travelled a path similar to that of Haydn a few years earlier. A reaction set in, and in Mozart's case it was even more radical in effect than it had been in Haydn's. The latter's symphonies had changed in character, with a return to greater emphasis on their qualities as conventional entertainment music; but Mozart temporarily gave up writing symphonies altogether. Between the summer of 1774 and the spring of 1778 he apparently wrote not one symphony. As in Haydn's case, we may wonder whether an intrinsic or extrinsic reaction was at work. Had Mozart reached a stage at which, at least for the time being, he had nothing essentially new to say? Or was he simply a little tired of the symphony as such, after the spate of new symphonies written during the preceding three years? Or was it due to his Archbishop, who no longer wanted any symphonies? It is quite possible that Salzburg failed to understand the new kind of symphony represented by works like the G minor and the A major. In any case, there is a definite trend towards entertainment music also noticeable in Mozart's case.

Two other forms of orchestral composition replace the symphony in Mozart's writing during these years: the violin concerto and various types of divertimento. In 1775, he wrote five violin concertos, the major part of his compositions in this form. During his Salzburg years he wrote divertimenti and serenades at frequent intervals, some only for wind band, others for mixed ensemble. These and the large-scale serenades, also for strings and wind, fill the gap in Mozart's symphonic production. And here, as so often in the history of art, we find that a seemingly circuitous route can in fact be the quickest way to the goal. It can hardly be doubted that his preoccupation with the violin concertos, the divertimenti, and serenades, led to a broadening of the framework of Mozart's orchestral style which he would not have achieved had he continued solely along the path of symphonic writing.

Solemn splendour and energy in the first movements, a smiling grace in the slow movements, courtly elegance in the minuets, an irresistible rhythmic impetus in the finales – none of this is new in Mozart's work, but never before (and to some extent never again) had it been achieved with such maturity. The total impression left by these works is more one of external brilliance than is the case with the symphonies and chamber music, where the emphasis is placed rather on expressiveness and intimacy. But what festive music these pieces are! One can understand Einstein's verdict on certain of them: "[They] are among the purest, gayest, most satisfying and most perfect that ever assumed musical form; and there are people who would trade a whole act of *Tannhäuser* or *Lohengrin* for one of these works, a lost paradise of music." It is certainly not music for an atomic age. But let us hope that the present cultural trend will not reduce us to the level where this kind of music will find itself homeless.

The peak of this development is the so-called 'Haffner' Serenade, K.250(248b). This eight-movement work was the most stately orchestral piece that Mozart had so far composed. Up to this stage in Mozart's career there were, even in his finest symphonies, movements or parts of movements in which maturity was still not quite complete; but in the 'Haffner' Serenade we have a work at whose artistic perfection one can only wonder. We have passed a new boundary. From now on it would seem fruitless to speak of increasing mastery, of development, or advance: a sovereign in the kingdom of art had assumed the position which was being held in readiness for him.

After the peaceful – for Mozart, all too peaceful – Salzburg years, Mozart, in 1777–8, made his last, great journey to Mannheim and Paris, where, though he met with some rewarding experiences and received strong musical impressions, he did not get the position he had hoped for. In the very midst of his agitating experiences at Paris, in the summer of 1778, he wrote a symphony which strikingly demonstrates his artistic detachment. The 'Paris' Symphony, K.297(300a), reveals not the least trace of his difficult circumstances. How realistically he attacked his task is evident from one of his letters, in which he described the work he was putting into the symphony, and quite uninhibitedly reveals his attempt to achieve an element of surprise.

When we compare this symphony with its predecessors we see at once that we are confronted by something essentially new. In Paris, Mozart had the possibility of writing for a much larger orchestra than the Salzburg court ensemble, and he set to work to assimilate the new resources which were now available to him. The entire symphony is stamped by his delight in writing for a full orchestra. The sure handling of composition and symphonic mastery which were fully developed in the 'Haffner' Serenade is not wanting in the 'Paris' Symphony. If we had not had the concertos, the divertimenti, and the serenades of the Salzburg years before us, the existence of a symphony of this character and content would have seemed quite inexplicable. There is some justification for describing this symphony written for Paris as the first fully mature symphony in the Viennese classical style.[1]

Once more the first movement contains hints of the baroque concerto. It is not to be classified entirely as a ritornello symphony, and we must regard it rather as a work in a form between the concerto and the sonata symphony. There is a special concertante effect in the second theme with its dialogue between

---

[1] On the other hand, it could be said that K.297 is not really a Viennese classical symphony at all, but rather a conscious attempt to write an orchestral work in the grand Mannheim style: it is, therefore, more an imitation than a true assimilation, and in K.318 and K.338 the 'grand manner' is far more personally (and thus more convincingly) set forth. – Eds.

strings and wind. Mozart wrote the slow movement twice. Le
Gros, the director of the *Concert spirituel*, persuaded him to write
the new version, which is hardly up to the level of the outer
movements.[1] The first version, rightly defended by Mozart in a
letter to his father, is a fine example of a characteristically
Mozartean type; it also is an intermediary form, half an expanded song-form, half a free sonata structure (without development, but with repetition of the main theme group at the
close, in the manner of a ritornello). The melodic structure is
also to a large extent song-like, but of course in the manner of
an instrumental song. The character of the siciliano still pervades the movement, though strongly remodelled and stylized.
In this concerto-like symphony there is no minuet. The finale is
dominated throughout by rhythmic play, carried on a quaver
movement, to which are counterposed striking motives in longer
note-values; this contrast, moreover, is emphasized by effective
dynamic contrasts. A further contrast must be specially mentioned: the textural antithesis between the homophonous first-
subject group and the polyphonic second-subject group, which
foreshadows similar effects in later finales.

From January 1779 to the early summer of 1781, when he
finally secured his release from the Archbishop's service, Mozart
was again resident in Salzburg, continually yearning to escape
from its constraint. His productivity was restricted. During this
period he composed relatively little, and he hardly trod any new
ground. But certain first-rate compositions date from these
years. Of symphonies and like works, we must call attention to
an Overture-Symphony in G (K.318), a Symphony in B flat
(K.319), a large-scale Serenade in D (K.320), a counterpart to
the 'Haffner' Serenade, and probably written for a similar
purpose, and a Symphony in C (K.338).

We do not know what moved Mozart to take up the sym-
phony after so long a pause. Possibly the success of his 'Paris'
Symphony turned his mind back to the form. The G major
Overture-Symphony (K.318), his first attempt, is like the 'Paris'

---

[1] Hitherto, the earlier slow movement, i.e., the one printed in the *Collected
Edition* and generally known today, was believed to be the final version. See
Köchel-Einstein. Recent research, however, has shown that the revised movement
was the one published in parts in 1789 by the Parisian firm of Sieber; no modern
edition includes this revised Andante. See Hermann Beck: 'Zur Entwicklungsgeschichte von Mozarts Symphonie in D-dur, K.V.297', in *Mozart-Jahrbuch*, 1955.
– EDS.

in offering a wide orchestral range. But the Symphony in B flat
(K.319) composed a little later, is carved of very different tim-
ber. The traditions of the Austrian chamber symphony are
again revived, though in one characteristic they were not fulfilled: the minuet was not composed till three years later, on
the occasion of a Viennese performance. It is, however, in complete accord with the other movements, and properly speaking
only with its composition was the symphony complete.

The Viennese symphonic style can be traced, as it were, from
the very first note; indeed, the chamber-musical quality is
present in the actual orchestration. As in the symphonies of
1770, Mozart is content with an orchestra consisting of strings,
oboes, bassoons, and horns, whereas the G major Overture-
Symphony also mustered flutes, four horns, trumpets, and
drums.[1] Together with the large orchestra, expressly orchestral
effects are also discarded: the broad tonal effects, the crescendos
and diminuendos, and so on. What is lost in external brilliance
is, however, replaced by other qualities, notably by the true
chamber-musical homogeneity of the movements, a feature
characteristic of the entire symphony. One little speciality of
this work must be mentioned. In all three movements (of the
original version) Mozart shaped the middle part in identical,
rather unusual, fashion. Instead of placing a true development
between the exposition and the recapitulation, he has instead,
in each movement, a contrasting section – a more or less contrapuntal development of one or two new motives – with a
modulatory continuation in the recapitulation.

The first movement presents a beautiful example of the
strictly sustained chamber style. Like so many first movements
in 3/4, this one, too, is preponderantly rhythmic in quality; an
unbroken, pulsing dynamism, with a flowing quaver movement
as basic rhythm, sometimes alone, sometimes interplaying with
themes and motives of stronger substance. These themes and
motives return again and again, but when they are absent one
feels that they are only suspended, not completely dropped. The
contrapuntal development in the middle section is mainly built
up on two motives, a stressed, broken-chord motive and an
accompanying counter-motive which is exactly identical with
the well-known motive from the finale of the 'Jupiter' Symphony.
There are also contrapuntal details at several points in the

[1] The timpani part is added in the autograph in another hand. – EDS.

exposition, and, as in the earlier A major symphony, a happy blend of the contrapuntal and free symphonic styles.

The slow movement, a lovely cantabile Andante moderato, is also distinctively chamber-musical in style, dominated throughout by the string writing. We are brought closer to the sentimentality of the time, and the total effect is far from the worldly elegance of the 'Paris' Symphony. The minuet, composed later, is unmistakably Viennese. In the finale, where Mozart gives free rein to his humour, the main feature is again its rhythm; basically the movement is a stylized gigue. The principal subject may suggest Beethoven's Eighth Symphony, but the two other prominent themes, the naively clever second subject and the closing theme, first introduced by woodwind alone, are so stamped with the *buffo* spirit that one cannot but think of Rossini. Thereafter, the contrapuntal middle section is rather surprising in its effect; but quite soon it is spiced with motives rhythmically enhanced, until, in due course, with a unison passage we reach the recapitulation, which again returns us to the previous *buffo* effects. It is a charming, jolly finale, but a little out of keeping with the two (three) preceding movements.

At this point the D major Serenade, K.320, must be mentioned, as a counterpart to the 'Haffner' Serenade. Like the 'Haffner', this is a piece symphonic in character, laid out on a large scale. One can see at a glance why both works, in shortened form, were played as symphonies. K.320, a no less significant work, is very different in its basic mood to the 'Haffner'. The festive brilliance of K.250(248b) is, in K.320, toned down to a darker, almost austere note. It is as though behind this work one can sense the composer's realization that the world, after all, is not always festive and brilliant, but can show at times a very serious face. (For this reason, the title which is occasionally attached to this work, the 'Posthorn' Serenade, can give a very false impression; the term refers only to an episode of a subsidiary nature.)

In the late summer of 1780, Mozart wrote the last symphony he was to compose in Salzburg, K.338 in C major. This, too, is a large-scale orchestral work, not written in the Salzburg chamber style, especially in its flanking movements. Both formally and in its content, the first movement is distinctly concerto-like. Anyone measuring it by the 'sonata-form' concept of the customary treatises on that form would find it almost entirely inexplicable. But if we consider it as an intermediary form, between symphony and concerto, everything falls into place. Such touches as the suppression of the exposition's repetition, the rather free shaping of the 'development' (which, in reality, is a concerto episode), the uninhibited presentation of the exposition's material in the recapitulation, and, finally, the stressed repetition of the first subject (ritornello) right at the end, are in the manner of the concerto. This first subject, in unison, harks back especially to the concerto tradition, but a number of other motivic details points in the same direction. Besides, however, the concerto trend, a second influence is discernible, one that is also found in Mozart's later symphonies, namely, *opera buffa*. This influence is clear in two respects: in the melodic material as such, its unusually distinctive cantabile quality, often accompanied by a tendency to metrical 'smoothness' of themes and motives; and in the leaning towards motivic multiplicity, towards a construction which is based on a continual interchange of motives, and not on the fundamental uniformity of the motivic material *per se*.

The slow movement, a beautiful Andante di molto, is unusually thinly orchestrated; only bassoons are added to the string ensemble, and yet it is not in the least a string quartet movement. Nor does it belong to the lyrical type, such as the middle movement of the 'Paris' Symphony. This movement, too – it is full of melodious grace – makes us think of opera. In it, Susanna's and Zerlina's magic seem to be anticipated. Opera was Mozart's burning desire. In this movement, for a moment, he revealed his desire, which we see in all its clarity. In formal respects also the movement is unusual. It is strictly binary, to a degree exceptional at this period. It comprises, as it were, an abridged sonata form, i.e., exposition, exact recapitulation, but no development. A new episode, of only four bars, expedites the lead-back from the close of the exposition to the beginning of the recapitulation; and the same episode, extended to eight bars, serves as the recapitulation's epilogue.

The finale is again in concerto style, a large, stylized gigue. As so often in movements of this kind, the effect depends on the interplay between the sustained quaver movement and the ever-varied separate motives. Towards the close, there is a direct reminiscence of the concerto in the well-known six-four chord, plus a trill on the dominant – somewhat unexpected in this context.

The last ten years of Mozart's life, after his break with Arch-bishop Hieronymus in 1781, and his removal to Vienna, were not exactly rich in symphonies. The six great works dating from this period may be traced to various stimuli, and do not repre-sent any single main line in his development during these years. The first of them, the 'Haffner' Symphony, K.385, in D major, was written in great haste in 1782, as was the 'Haffner' Seren-ade in 1776, to celebrate a festive occasion of the Salzburg family. The second, the 'Linz' Symphony, in C major, K.425, was composed in equal haste in 1783, because Mozart wanted to give a concert during a brief stay at Linz, and had no suitable symphony available. The third, the 'Prague' (or the 'Sym-phony without minuet'), K.504, in D, was composed at Vienna towards the end of 1786, probably with an eye to the forth-coming journey to Prague, where the first performance of *Don Giovanni* was to be given, and where this symphony also had its first performance, in January 1787. We have no evi-dence that there was any special occasion for the composition of the last three symphonies, written in the summer of 1788, those in E flat, G minor, and C major (the 'Jupiter'), K.543, 550, and 551. It is perhaps a natural assumption that Mozart turned to the thought of composing symphonies again because of Haydn's success with his six 'Paris' symphonies written in 1785–6. Is it pure chance that the first volume of the six 'Paris' symphonies, which the Viennese publisher Artaria issued in December 1787, also contains three symphonies in C major, G minor, and E flat (Nos. 82–4)? Be that as it may, it is natural to assume that there was some connection between Haydn's success-ful 'Paris' symphonies and the three written by Mozart in 1788.

From the foregoing summary it is obvious that one can hardly speak of a symphonic tradition in Mozart's Viennese period. These six symphonies are more or less *pièces d'occasion*. But what occasional pieces! He wrote the 'Haffner' Symphony straight off, movement after movement, and sent it away at once; six months later, when he received a copy in Vienna, he wrote to his father on 15 February 1783: "My new Haffner Symphony has positively amazed me, for I had forgotten every single note of it. It must surely produce a good effect."

The 'Haffner' Symphony is midway between symphony and serenade. Originally it had an introductory march and a second minuet (between the first allegro and the slow middle movement), but Mozart struck both out for the Vienna performance, and thus the symphony became the normal four-movement work with which we are familiar today. But the serenade character, the festive, positive attitude to life remained. It is immediately apparent in the first subject of the first movement. The splendid gesture of the opening motive, whose characteristics are wide, melodic leaps and a strong rhythmic accent, represents much more than a striking announcement of the first movement; it is the movement's whole foundation. We have already referred to the influence of *opera buffa* on the symphony, an influence revealed *inter alia* in the tendency toward motivic multiplicity. But in this movement we have something quite different: an extraordinarily powerful motivic concentration. The opening motive dominates the course of the whole movement. It is first exploited in unison, and immediately after in imitation between the melody and the bass (rather like the theme of K.201, described above; cf. Ex. 5). Afterwards, it is combined with other motives, as in the episode of second-subject character which comes a little later; and then again in imitation as the driving force of a long modulation in the development section. These multifarious presentations of the principal motive are interspersed with typically orchestral transitions which have no specific thematic quality. The movement conveys an exclusively concertante impression; but it is highly concentrated, since it is carried by this dominating motive.

The slow movement is less outstanding; it is a light, flowing movement, characteristic motives playing one against another, in which the serenade influence is easily recognizable. The minuet, too, has the quality of festive, noble, serenade music; its trio, a little marvel of unproblematical music-making, is wholly enchanting. The finale, again a very striking piece, is one of the many examples of a brilliant fusion of sonata and rondo structures which we find in Mozart's finales. The basic form derives from the rondo, but the shape of the themes is more characteristic of sonata style. A fine detail deserves special mention. In bar 10, Mozart introduces as no more than a subsidiary motive in the bass a small, conventional trill and broken-chord figure. But out of it he produces, in due course, an essential motive, which in somewhat varied form comes to play a rather important role. It is worth observing how he accomplishes this transformation. Still one other point must be mentioned. The movement is usually played very fast – fast even for a presto. But in fact that was how Mozart wished it. In one of his letters to his father he wrote: "The first Allegro must be played with great fire, the last – as fast as possible." (One may naturally wonder whether he would have put the point so unreservedly had he been acquainted with the 'tempo virtuosity' of our day!)

Of all these later symphonies, the 'Linz', K.425, displays perhaps the least individuality; but even so it is a magnificent, fine-sounding work. It is difficult to avoid tracing Haydn's influence in it, though St.-Foix rightly says that at this stage of Mozart's development his own individuality is so marked that only to a very limited extent can one speak of outside influences.

For the first time in Mozart's symphonies we have a slow introduction. Here, as in the few other instances where he used the device, it is of great subtlety. The introduction achieves its aim completely: it quickens expectations, but does not satisfy them. Only, perhaps, one might conclude that in this case the note of pathos in the introduction presages something more profound than that which actually follows.

The first movement is distinguished less by the greatness of the conception than by the well-rounded, classic quality of its structure: first subject, transition, second subject, and final group are clearly differentiated. The form of the second subject is quite unusual. We do not have a cantabile second subject such as we so often find in Mozart. Instead, there is an episode, with stressed inner contrasts (bars 71ff.). The first half of the second subject is in E minor (the dominant's relative minor); it is played tutti and forte, in contrast to the subject's second half which moves from C to G major, the first two bars scored for wind alone, the third and fourth for strings, while all four bars are piano. The repetition varies the instrumentation and dynamics with truly Mozartean subtlety. Now the subject's first half is played piano, and the varied melody is given to oboes and bassoons with string accompaniment, whereas the somewhat altered second half appears in the forte and tutti version. The rather short development is built out of a couple of motives from the exposition, and then, in a freer section, seems to anticipate moments in the finale. The recapitulation is exact, with a short codal expansion at its close.

The slow movement, a stylized siciliano, is a splendid example of this andante form, which both Mozart and Haydn used so frequently. The clarity of the structure, the movement's thoroughly cantabile quality, its many beauties, melodic, textural, and modulatory, all contribute to the effect of a noble classicism. The minuet suggests Haydn, especially in the mosaic work characteristic of the entire movement, with its significant small motives. A fine detail is the use of the modified repetition of the opening motive as a closing motive. The trio is close to the *Ländler* in character.

Like the first movement, the finale is very clearly designed: first-subject group and transition (bar 28); second theme group (bar 58); final group (bar 116); and in conclusion yet another, small, epilogic group (bar 148), are all clearly contrasted one with another. However, this clear division is not achieved by strong differentiation between the themes or motives. The individual periods are distinguished, above all, by tonal development and dynamic planning. But threads of motivic and thematic relationships link one period with another in such abundance that the movement makes a powerful, homogeneous impression. Thus, we have common motives (e.g., bars 1, 28, 58, 148, etc.); melodic affinity (bars 32, 116); and similarity in textural contrast (first subject, transition). It was not only Haydn's influence that undoubtedly played a by no means inessential part in the even clearer 'finale character' of the movement, but also the baroque type of melodic development, significantly present, for instance, in the tutti unison episodes (bars 9, 28), the phrases in imitation, which amount almost to fugal writing (bars 73ff., 116ff.), and, by no means least, the large-scale sequential patterns of the development. The recapitulation is very exact. A slight expansion of the epilogic group suggests a small coda which, in the manner of the baroque concerto, brings the movement to a close with a final quotation of the opening theme.

The 'Prague' Symphony, K.504, is one of the select masterpieces of classical music. In the musical horizon of the general listener, it is hardly regarded as on the same level as the three great symphonies of 1788, though it in no way falls short of them. Which of these four works is ranked the highest must always remain a matter of personal preference. The 'Prague' Symphony was composed between *Figaro* and *Don Giovanni*, and one can see that it has spiritual affinities with both operas. The

whole work testifies to the happiest of inspiration: each movement has its own unmistakable stamp, corresponding to its
function within the general scheme of the work.

The opening consists of a magnificent adagio introduction.
We have already mentioned the real pathos in the introduction
to the 'Linz' Symphony; but it must be admitted that the introduction to the 'Prague' commands an even deeper language of
expression. One sees it not simply as an expressive introductory
threshold, but, like the overture to *Don Giovanni*, as a drama *in
nuce*, leading us into a world full of contrasts and tension, a world
in which there may, possibly, be moments of idyllic peace, but
which, in the last resort, is dominated by the everlasting struggle
between good and evil.

If the introduction, compared with its predecessor, contains
an enormous intensification of expression, we find an even
further intensification when we come to the first movement
itself. No one could suggest that there is any relaxation of tension
in the transition from the introduction to the subject of the
Allegro. It is less emphatically expressive in its character, but
the tension is latent at every point, even if it is less directly
perceived. In this movement, the synthesis of baroque traditions
and the symphonic style reaches a new peak. The many eulogies
which have been devoted to the brilliant blend of symphonic and
contrapuntal writing in the finale of the 'Jupiter' Symphony
could be applied with equal justification to the first movement
of the 'Prague'.

Whereas the first movement of the 'Haffner' Symphony represented a magnificent concentration on a single main motive,
this movement is no less consistently a continuous development
of a whole series of pervasive motives, of which the most important are the three opening ones (bars 37–40, 41–2, and 43–4,
wind), and that of the transition (bars 55–6). After the first
subject group and the subsequent transitional passage have
stated these motives, and after they have been submitted to a
preliminary development, they frequently reappear as the
movement proceeds. They are contrasted to the second subject,
which is the only symphonic, rounded-off theme (bars 96ff.);
it is strikingly prominent just because of its textual contrast to
the afore-mentioned developmental motives.

Like several of the first movements already discussed, the
form of this movement is not clarified by reference to the tradi-

tional concept of sonata form, but must be related to the ritornello structure characteristic of the concerto. And here the striking feature is the tendency for the movement to fall into an arrangement of two ritornello groups, the first subject and transitional groups, as they would be called in sonata-form terminology. If we designate these two groups as A and B, and the second subject group as C, we arrive at the following, very striking structure for the whole movement:

$$\overset{I}{A}\ B\ \overset{V}{A^1}\ C\ B^1 : \| : \overset{V\text{-}I}{A'}\quad \overset{VI}{B'}\quad \overset{I}{B}\ \overset{I\text{-}V}{a'}\quad \overset{I}{A^{(1)}}\ C\ B^1$$

The return to the varied first subject in the dominant, with corresponding displacement of the second subject to the movement's close, is often found in Haydn: in his case, too, it was an after-effect of the concerto tradition. But the reintroduction of group B after the second subject is most uncommon. While the contrapuntal working out of the two ritornello groups in the development is quite straightforward (irrespective of the quality of the working-out), the lead-back from development to recapitulation is again exceptional. After an initial modulation, and then sequential treatment of the transitional motives from bar to bar, the development (bar 177) slips unnoticed into a recapitulation of part of the exposition (bars 59ff.). After a few bars, however, it transpires (when the opening theme returns, bars 189ff.) that even now the development has not yet come to an end. At bar 208 the main motive finally appears in the exit key, and the listener is given the impression that now the true recapitulation is coming. What follows can, in fact, be regarded thus, but, as may be seen from the brief schematic diagram above, only the second part of the exposition ($A^{(1)}\ C\ B^1$) is repeated. The amalgamation of development and first subject which we have just described is exceptional only in relation to sonata form, for viewed as a descendant of concerto tradition, the movement is perfectly clear in design; there is complete unanimity between the motivic material, which throughout both initiates and requires development, and the almost improvisatory character of the form.

This magnificent, synthesizing structure is followed by a beautiful Andante, of the simplest form in respects both large and small. We find again a multiplicity of motives, but here they are not built into complex constructions, but, through a well-planned succession of themes, achieve an effective total development. As in the operas, e.g., the finale to the second act of *Figaro*, Mozart displays his incomparable power to conjure up ever new themes and motives, which have the greatest immediacy of expression and yet are of the profoundest musical subtlety. The many and varied nuances of expression, and their compelling fusion, are the chief impressions left by the movement.

The finale is as different again from the Andante as the Andante is from the first Allegro. Its two main features are a light, swift-flowing motion and a quite unencumbered grace. There is a direct relation with *Figaro* in the first subject, a motive which inevitably suggests the charming duettino between Susanna and Cherubino in the second act. This *Figaro* motive is used with extraordinary frequency, since in contrast to the regular structure of the Andante, the finale is pervaded by rondo-like touches. The ground plan is that of sonata form, but it is modified by the principal subject's – or ritornello's – appearance in almost every transition and linking passage. The result is a very clear rondo emphasis which accentuates a homogeneity already determined by the uniformity of the motivic material. A special feature of the movement are the chromatic exchanges between the strings and woodwind, presented in an almost choral fashion.

The three 'great' symphonies which Mozart wrote in the summer of 1788 differ very widely in character. We must regard their diversity of expression, above all else, as a reflection of Mozart's fertility; but there is little justification for considering them as a 'planned' trilogy.

We have already mentioned a temptation to find some connection between these three works and Haydn's 'Paris' symphonies. How close one chooses to make this connection must be left undetermined. But one thing is clear: the curve of development of the classical symphony reached a first summit in Haydn's and Mozart's symphonies of *c.* 1772–4, and then experienced a fluctuating rise and fall for some ten years; but from about 1785 onward, the curve rose to a sudden and violent climax, embracing Haydn's 'Paris' symphonies of 1785–6, Mozart's 'Prague' Symphony of 1786, his last three symphonies of 1788, Haydn's 'Tost' and 'd'Ogny' symphonies of 1787–8, and his twelve London symphonies of 1791–5, and concluding with Beethoven.

Of these three symphonies the first, in E flat (K.543), composed in June 1788, is closest to Haydn's style, e.g., in external lay-out and in many formal and textural details. (Needless to say, we are not thinking of banal 'imitation', but of assimilation on a high level.) Once more we have a slow introduction, and once more it is solemn, exalted music, which at once arouses the greatest of expectations. Certain of its characteristic features, such as the dotted rhythm, the swift, demisemiquaver scales, and the sustained, full-voiced chords, derive from the predecessor of the classical 'slow introduction', i.e., the first part of the late, baroque French Overture.

In the first movement itself we come first to a beautiful, singing theme of near chamber-musical quality. Mozart varies its repetition very judiciously by transferring the main tune to the basses. This chamber-musical effect is followed by a long tutti, and, apart from a second-subject group, which includes a charming dialogue between strings and woodwind, the rest of the exposition is largely dominated by a typically orchestral style. The development is built throughout on material from the exposition, and the recapitulation is exact.

In the slow movement, the outstanding chamber-musical tendency of the Allegro's first subject is brought to full fruition. The central feature of the rondo-like structure is a beautiful cantabile theme, with which are contrasted two episodes of very different character. The first is prominent in the minor group. It first appears in F minor, the relative minor of A flat; but its second appearance is in the very distant key of B minor. The second episode, one of the finest passages in the entire symphony, is a further development of a small motive which earlier in the movement is heard only in passing, but which now reveals unsuspected developmental and imitational potentialities.

The distinctively Mozartean trio of the minuet brings a favourite instrument, the clarinet, into the foreground.

In the finale, Mozart has clearly laid hold of a Haydn-type of last movement and fashioned a truly Mozartean movement from it. The homogeneity of the movement is this time closely connected with motivic unification. The opening motive, in the very first bar of the movement, provides the basis for a large part of the finale's further development. But this powerful unity is counterbalanced by continual variety of treatment; the basic motive passes from part to part, appears alone or linked to

other motives, and the movement's manifold variety is further
enhanced by varied instrumentation and varied modulations.
The entire symphony, alive with joy and love of beauty, is
proof of Mozart's spiritual versatility.

The *joie de vivre* of the E flat Symphony was followed by the
passion of the G minor, K.550, completed one month later.
Unlike the E flat work, the G minor, as well as the third and last
symphony, the C major, originally had the traditional oboes in
place of clarinets. On a later occasion Mozart introduced
clarinets into the G minor, at the same time altering the oboe
part. Trumpets and drums are absent from both versions.

Of the last three symphonies, the G minor is undoubtedly the
most original. In interpreting its essential quality, however, the
purely personal element is quite frequently given too great an
emphasis. It is interpreted as the expression of a 'private' mood,
and the attempt is made to bring it into relationship with
Mozart's personal situation, which by then was obviously desperate, despite the fact that the two other symphonies express
quite a different mood. But to argue thus is surely to do Mozart
an injustice, for in his fundamental outlook he remained 'classic',
seeking to master all the varieties of expression, but not identifying his musical expression with his personal, 'private' mood.[1]

In K.550, two features deserve special notice: the piano opening, very rare in any eighteenth-century symphony, and the
pronounced rhythmic impulse which is characteristic of the
first subject. A slow introduction followed by a piano opening

[1] See n.1 on p. 173. It would be mistaken, as Professor Larsen rightly emphasizes, to attempt to pin down the content of K.550 to a 'private' mood, in the sense
of seeking for a literal biographical parallel to the music. On the other hand, the
quite exceptional degree of tension generated by this symphony can only have
sprung from an inner tension of a most violent nature. The peculiarly disruptive
nature of this symphony's inspiration manifests itself in many a remarkable passage,
in the first eight bars of the finale's development, for example, whose explosive
unison gesture is symptomatic of the *pressure* of inspiration; the peculiar violence of
that inspiration, indeed, is responsible for the passage's primarily disintegrative
character – one so disintegrative, in fact, that Mozart was compelled to adopt a
new principle of organization. (See H. Jalowetz, 'On the Spontaneity of Schoenberg's Music', *Musical Quarterly*, October 1944; L. Dallapiccola, 'Notes on the
Statue Scene in *Don Giovanni*', *Music Survey*, III/2/1950; and especially H. Keller,
'Strict Serial Technique in Classical Music', *Tempo*, Autumn, 1955.) Schoenberg, in
his *Harmonielehre*, pointed to passages of surprising harmonic tension in the symphony's first movement. The phenomenal tension of K.550 far transcends a
'personal' mood, but it represents, nevertheless, a vital aspect of Mozart's artistic
personality. K.550 expresses it at its most extreme. – Eds.

to the first movement proper is frequent enough, but only rarely do we find a piano marking at the very beginning. An earlier example, in K.114, has been discussed above (see Ex. 4). The rhythmic intensity in K.550 is not entirely without precedent. The later A major symphony, K.201 (Ex. 5), is an obvious example.

But to the G minor there is a very special parallel of a different sort; we recall one of Mozart's most famous arias, Cherubino's 'Non so più' from *Figaro*. The opening theme's rhythmic impulse sets the entire movement in motion. The total effect of the movement derives from this irresistibly impetuous central feature. From the very beginning one is conscious of a strong, dual rhythmic scheme: the markedly personal themes are contrasted to the flowing accompaniments of the violas. Beginning as a subsidiary rhythmic accompaniment, this almost ostinato-like quaver movement grows more and more powerful as a primary driving force.

An interruption of the rhythmic flow occurs only with the arrival of the second-subject group. The theme takes shape as a dialogue between wind and strings, and their subtle interplay makes a substantial impression. But even as this group is passing to its close, the rhythmic activity returns, to remain the dominant factor to the end of the exposition. A discreet intimation of the first subject's leading motive rounds off the exposition on the one hand, but also prepares us for the development, where the main theme alone is prominent. The motivic material is highly concentrated, a concentration assisted by a marvellous variety of textural and modulatory devices. The lead-back to the recapitulation is a little marvel in itself: everything seems to point to a regular repetition of the opening, but by means of the slightly premature introduction of the melody Mozart effects such an imperceptible transition that the recapitulation is in progress before we are fully aware of it. It is in fact a little changed from the opening, but the impetuous flow is continued to the very end of the movement.

The second movement is of an intensity of expression which is itself rare enough in the classical symphony. One would have been justified in expecting some relaxation of the tension, but that is the last thing that could be said of this movement. Though the form is perfectly clear, the contrasts are so pronounced that at times it might even seem, like a slow introduction, deliberately to avoid a closed melodic structure; an appearance of constant tension is thus maintained, and the slackening of tension saved for the next movement. The development's pronounced climax emerges from a single motive taken from the exposition. Passages of magnificent harmonic tension occur throughout the movement (bars 29ff., 44ff., 56ff., 100ff., 115ff.), which is dominated by a force dramatic in its nature, but of an absolute and musical kind.

The minuet is unusually serious and strict in mood. Striking, too, is its almost archaic tendency toward linear polyphony; but even more striking is the three-bar grouping, which is frequently quoted. The trio is a complete contrast. For the first and last time in this symphony a note of idyllic peace sounds in the music.

The finale again is dominated by rhythm, perhaps even more so than the first movement. Two basic rhythms determine the shape: the crotchet figure of the introductory motive, and the quaver figure of the counter-motive which immediately follows. The entire finale is based both rhythmically and melodically on these two motives. The pace slackens only during a short second subject. Exposition and recapitulation are concerned chiefly with the second motive. On the other hand, the brilliant development is wholly shaped by the opening motive. In its combination of motivic homogeneity with textural variation and richness of modulatory colour, it is a perfect realization of the developmental concept in the classical symphony.

As the third member of this symphonic trilogy Mozart gave us K.551 in C, the so-called 'Jupiter' Symphony, or the 'Symphony with the closing fugue'. (Neither name, though both are old, has anything to do with Mozart.) Compared with the untraditional mood of the G minor, the C major may appear somewhat reactionary. Not that we need be seriously influenced by its having been called 'Symphony with the closing fugue', which title could have been given only at a time when the idea of a fugue was of something quite exotically remote. But irrespective of the coda, treated in imitation, which has given rise to this name, the C major Symphony is in many respects traditional.

Like so many other symphonies in this key, K.551 belongs to a tradition which runs from the old Intrada, through the Overture-suite, to the symphony, where we find the type in such works as Haydn's No. 48 ('Maria Theresa') or No. 82 ('L'Ours').

Therefore for the C major Symphony an autochthonous style is even more of a *sine qua non* than for the E flat Symphony. At the same time, however, the C major work is occupied far more than the E flat with the development of definite themes and motives, for, as we have seen, the E flat (and especially its first movement) is marked for long stretches by a rather uniform tutti style. The former structural method is stressed in the first movement of K.551, and even more so in the finale. The middle movements are distinguished from the outer two by their rather looser construction, and it is undoubtedly the outer movements that are chiefly responsible for the work's general impression.

The basic material in the development of the first movement consists primarily of the following themes and motives: the first subject with two contrasting motives (bars 1 and 3[2]); the tutti figure, with its contrasts between the dotted rhythm and the demisemiquaver motive (bar 9); the counter-motive to the main theme (bar 24); the second subject (bar 56); the secondary motive (bar 72); and the epilogue, which makes the impact of another second subject (bar 101). The structure built out of this thematic and motivic material is thoroughly organic. The first subject and the transition are linked together as follows: the first subject ends with a striking half-close which suggests a first half-period; the transition begins (bar 24) as a second half-period, but then glides into modulating sequences, in preparation for the dominant. The second subject is beautifully wrought, with two or three motives interchanged, among them the dotted motive from the first subject (bars 2–3), which was active in the transition. A little surprise brings this period to a close with a general rest, and there follows a contrast, in the minor, prior to a cadence. A brief transitional passage, built round a variant of the dotted motive, prepares the entry of the epilogue, which is effectively marked by a second general rest. The epilogue and a short cadence group round off the exposition.

The development first cleverly exploits the epilogue, and assigns a leading role to a hitherto hardly noticeable small motive (bar 108). The close of this part of the development is marked by a brief but effective modulation to F major, whence the first subject is introduced: but note, not in its function as first subject, but as a transitional theme (cf. bars 24ff.). So there is no 'false recapitulation' (to make use of this often abused term). The transitional theme is further developed; it leads to a sturdy tutti (with a characteristically linear bass part) while the 'Cinderella' motive drawn from the epilogue completes the circle with the lead-back to the exact recapitulation.

The slow movement, an Andante cantabile, is an incarnation of the simple aristocratic pathos of the mature Viennese classicism. Perhaps it is the very character of the slow movement which most plainly represents the newly achieved style, something that could be said equally of the other two symphonies. In this work, Mozart created a language which was not merely a further development of the melodic element in earlier symphonic movements, but a predecessor of the fundamentally new, or, let us say, 'modern', speech. The principal features of this expressive language are undoubtedly the rich harmonic texture, the basically harmonic character of the themes, and the fine transitions and modulations, for instance bars 23–7 (notice the linear effects), or bars 35–9. The subtle orchestral treatment also makes an essential contribution. As in the slow movement of the G minor Symphony, we can trace an affinity with the style of the slow introduction, for instance the free rhythmic and metrical development of bars 47–55 (development). Within the cyclic structure, this Andante occupies a position markedly different from that of the Andante in the G minor Symphony.

There is no unusual feature in the minuet and trio.[1]

The finale comprises the statement and working out of a series of motives, whose potentiality is only fulfilled as the movement proceeds. Among these the following must be specially mentioned: (1) the traditional contrapuntal theme (bars 1–4); (2) the first transitional motive (bars 19–22); (3) the second transitional motive (bars 56ff.); (4) the second subject motive (bars 74–7); and (5) its extension (bars 76–7). To make reference easier we designate these five motives as a, b, c, d, and d^1.

---

[1] It is perhaps worth noting that the second part of the trio, i.e., beginning with ‖:, clearly foreshadows the chorale theme of the finale. In fact, K.551 shows Mozart's conscious or unconscious preoccupation with thematic interrelationship between the movements. The second violin and viola figure in bars 9ff. of the first movement has a distinct connection with the semiquavers in bars 9ff. of the finale. Professor J. N. David, however, undoubtedly goes far when he suggests, in a recent book on the 'Jupiter' (see book list), that the entire symphony is based on one common chorale melody (never stated in its entirety). See also R. Steglich, 'Interpretationsprobleme der Jupiter-Sinfonie', *Mozart-Jahrbuch*, 1954. – Eds.

The movement is basically a sonata structure with enlarged coda. Various imitational episodes are interpolated into the structure, and they culminate in the final canonic apotheosis of the coda. The first subject seems to be complete at bar 19, and the first transitional motive begins in the same bar, apparently introducing a modulation, but in fact only leading into a half-close (bar 35). Here there is an analogy with the first movement, for the first subject returns, suggesting a second half-period, but really passing into a transition. This repetition of the first subject opens with motivic development, at first (bars 36–52) a five-part imitation of the main motive. The transition brings first a sequential treatment, in imitation, of a new motive (c, bars 56–62), then a stretto based on b (bars 64–70), which passes into a cadence on the dominant of the dominant at bar 73. The second subject begins innocently enough as a cantabile theme, but after two or three bars a small accompanying contrapuntal episode appears in the woodwind (bars 76–80 and 82–6), which already hints at a collective plan; motives d^1, c, and b are, in passing, brilliantly and effortlessly combined. The continuation consists of further imitational developments on motive c (bars 86–94); d, abbreviated (bars 94–8), and then in full (bars 98–110); and, after a predominantly homophonous extension, b (bars 135–7).

After an introductory quotation of the first subject, the development concentrates exclusively on motive b, enhanced by little woodwind quotations from the first subject. Once more the lead-back to the recapitulation is outstanding (bars 219–25). The recapitulation itself draws the first two periods (first subject and transition) somewhat together, and varies them with an interpolation of the first subject, sequentially treated, instead of using the first small imitational episode. The continuation keeps very close to the structure of the exposition. The climax follows only after a repetition of the second part (bars 357ff.). A short episode built on motive b emerges; a free imitation of motive a leads directly into the final synopsis. This famous coda is in fact a short, five-part canon on the motives d, a, c, d^1, c^1, and b, in that order (bars 373–400), which at last leads into an abridged repetition of the movement's opening section; the 'false transition' on this occasion leads directly into the closing cadence.

*　　　*　　　*

In Mozart's last three symphonies, we can observe the confluence of decisive lines of development: the C major Symphony in particular is nourished by the spirit of baroque forms such as the overture, the concerto, and the fugue; the E flat, on the other hand, inclines more strongly toward the fusion of chamber-musical, divertimento, and symphonic styles; while in the G minor, patent influences from the world of opera are also intermingled. These three works are not only a synthesis, but also the noble expression of a unique individuality.

[*Translated by H. C. Stevens*]

BOOK LIST

[Standard Mozart biographies have not been listed.]

F. Bayer: 'Über den Gebrauch der Instrumente in den Kirchen- und Instrumentalwerken von W. A. Mozart', *Festschrift, Beethoven-Zentenarfeier*, Vienna, 1927.

H. Beck: 'Zur Entwicklungsgeschichte von Mozarts Symphonie in D-dur, K.V.297', *Mozart-Jahrbuch*, 1955.

E. Blom: 'Mozart', in *The Symphony*, edited by R. Hill, London, 1949.

N. Broder: 'The wind-instruments in Mozart's symphonies', *Musical Quarterly*, XIX/1933, pp. 238–59.

E. Bücken: *Die Musik des Rokoko und der Klassik*, Potsdam, 1929.

—— 'Der galante Stil', *Zeitschrift für Musikwissenschaft*, VI, pp. 418ff.

L. Dallapiccola: 'Notes on the Statue Scene in Don Giovanni', *Music Survey*, III/2/1950, pp. 89–97.

W. Danckert: 'Mozarts Menuettypen', *Bericht der Mozarttagung Leipzig*, 1932.

J. N. David: *Die Jupiter-Symphonie. Eine Studie über die thematisch-melodischen Zusammenhänge*, Göttingen, 1953.

A. E. F. Dickinson: *A Study of Mozart's Last Three Symphonies*, in *The Musical Pilgrim* Series, London, 1927, ²/1940.

H. Engel: 'Über Mozarts Jugendsinfonien', *Mozart-Jahrbuch*, 1951. (See also Hausswald.)

W. Fischer: 'Zur Entwicklungsgeschichte des Wiener klassischen Stils', *Studien zur Musikwissenschaft*, III, 1915.

G. Hausswald: *Mozarts Serenaden*, Leipzig, 1951 (important review by H. Engel in *Musikforschung*, 1952).

A. Heuss: 'Die kleine Sekunde in Mozarts g-moll Symphonie', *Peters Jahrbuch*, 1934, No. 40, pp. 54–66.

H. Jalowetz: 'On the Spontaneity of Schoenberg's Music', *Musical Quarterly*, XXX/4/1944, pp. 385–408.

H. Keller: 'Strict Serial Technique in Classical Music', *Tempo*, Autumn, 1955.

T. Kroyer: Forewords to the Eulenburg scores of Mozart's Symphonies K.385 (No. 437), 425 (No. 502), 504 (No. 446), 543 (No. 415), 550 (No. 404), and 551 (No. 401), Leipzig-Cologne, 1931 et seq.

H. C. R. Landon: *The Symphonies of Joseph Haydn*, London, 1955.

R. Reti: *The Thematic Process in Music*, London, 1961.

G. de St.-Foix: *Les sinfonies de Mozart*, Paris, 1932; Eng. translation, London, 1947.

F. Schnapp: 'Neue Mozartfunde in Donaueschingen', *Neues Mozart-Jahrbuch*, II, 1942.

D. Schultz: *Mozarts Jugendsinfonien*, Leipzig, 1900.

S. Sechter: *Das Finale der Jupitersymphonie. Analyse* (herausgegeben von D. Eckstein), Vienna, 1923.

G. Sievers: 'Analyse des Finale aus Mozarts Jupiter-Symphonie', *Musikforschung*, VII/3 (1954), pp. 318–31.

R. Sondheimer: 'Die formale Entwicklung der vorklassischen Sinfonie', *Archiv für Musikwissenschaft*, IV, 1922.

—— *Die Theorie der Sinfonie im 18. Jahrhundert*, Leipzig, 1925.

—— 'Die Entwicklung des Orchesters in der vorklassischen Sinfonie', *Das Orchester*, 1927.

R. Steglich: 'Interpretationsprobleme der Jupiter-Sinfonie', *Mozart-Jahrbuch*, 1954.

C. Thieme: *Der Klangstil des Mozartorchesters* (thesis), Borna-Leipzig, 1936.

D. Tovey: *Essays in Musical Analysis*, Vol. I (Symphonies), London, 8/1948; Vol. VI (Supplementary Essays), London, 1939.

B. A. Wallner: 'Ein Beitrag zu Mozarts Londoner Sinfonien', *Zeitschrift für Musikwissenschaft*, XII.

ADDENDUM

H. C. R. Landon: 'Die Symphonien', *Mozart Aspekte*, Olten, 1956.

[*This book list is compiled by the Editors*]

FRIEDRICH BLUME

THE CONCERTOS :
(1) THEIR SOURCES

Many problems face the musicologist who considers the form in which Mozart's various concertos have survived. Grouping them by the type of instrument for which the solo part is written, we find that in each group there are works which raise no problem whatever, and others which involve some controversy. This does not mean that the 'major' works are straightforward and that problems arise only in regard to what one may term the 'by-products'. On the contrary, such outstanding works as the oboe Concerto, K.271k, the Concerto for wind instruments, K.Anh.9(297b), and the violin Concerto, K.268(365b), are among the most problematic. The problems that arise are partly concerned with the date of composition, partly with the composition itself, and at times even with the question of its authenticity; for even on this point there is not always unanimity among the experts. And the problems arise not only in regard to completed works, but even to the numerous fragments, sketches, and drafts. No one who plans to give a general picture of Mozart's concertos can leave these smaller works out of account. In many departments, such as the sinfonie concertanti, they help to complete the picture.

This chapter is devoted to a consideration of Mozart's collected concertos; they will be subjected to critical examination, and the present state of our knowledge will be reviewed. For this purpose the concertos will be divided into four main groups: (1) concertos for wind instruments; (2) sinfonie concertanti; (3) concertos for one or two violins; (4) concertos for one, two, or three pianos.

I. Concertos for Wind Instruments

1. *For Trumpet.* According to a letter written by Leopold Mozart on 12 November 1768, the twelve-year-old Mozart wrote a concerto for performance at the consecration of the *Waisenhaus* Church in Vienna on 7 December 1768. The *Wiener*

Diarium for 1768 reports this ceremony, at which the Imperial household was present, and mentions a Mass composed by Mozart, but says nothing of a concerto. So it is not certain whether the work was actually performed. The music of the Mass and the Offertorium, K.47a and 47b, has probably been lost; the trumpet Concerto, K.47c, is completely unknown.[1]

2. *For Bassoon.* A concerto in B flat for bassoon, K.191(186e), of which the autograph was dated 4 June 1774, has been preserved in its entirety. The autograph was formerly in the possession of A. André, but is now lost. The sources for our text of the concerto are the two editions of André's first printing, of 1801 and 1805; according to Victor Junk,[2] like all the printed music of that period they were "corrected in a slovenly fashion". So far as its essential structure is concerned, the version that has come down to us is probably correct, but the André text often appears to be defective. Another bassoon concerto, in F major, K.Anh.230(196d), was advertised in an old catalogue issued by Breitkopf & Härtel; but to date, this work has not come to light, so it is impossible to decide if it really originated from Mozart. Whether the three bassoon concertos which Mozart is said to have composed for the Freiherr Thaddäus von Dürnitz at Munich were actually written, and whether one of these is identical with the B flat Concerto, K.191(186e), or with the lost F major Concerto, K.Anh.230(196d), must remain open questions until new sources have been discovered. On the other hand, it is certain that the bassoon Concerto in B flat, K.Anh.230a, which Max Seiffert published with Litolff's of Brunswick from a manuscript in the Scheurleer Library at The Hague, has not the slightest connection with Mozart. In its thematic material, its harmony, rhythm, its treatment of the solo part and orchestra, even in its compositional structure, the

[1] Professor Karl Pfannhauser, Vienna, has cleared up the vexed question of the *Waisenhaus* music in his lecture, held at the Mozarteum on 16 August 1954, *Neue Forschungsergebnisse zu Mozarts Kirchenwerken von 1768*. The *Waisenhausmesse* is none other than the Mass in C major, K.139(114a); the Offertorium is K.117(66a). Professor Pfannhauser was kind enough to inform me personally that the trumpet Concerto was definitely performed; not only do we have the evidence of Leopold Mozart's letter of 12 November 1768 to L. Hagenauer, but Professor Pfannhauser has found documents showing that the work was played on several occasions in the succeeding years. At one point, the musical MSS. at the orphanage were transferred from one place to another and sorted out, and in the process Mozart's concerto was apparently destroyed. It is unlikely that a second copy exists. – Ed. [H. C. R. L.]

[2] Foreword to his edition of the concerto, Eulenburg, No. 784.

concerto is quite unlike Mozart. It is even more incredible that
Seiffert does not include it among the Dürnitz concertos of 1775,
but declares it to be "a creation of his maturer years", assigning
it to the period 1780–5, and so bringing it into close proximity
with the great master concertos. This is an excellent instance of
the way criticism based on sources can be overestimated, while
criticism based on style, is underestimated. If the editor had
taken the trouble to make even a superficial analysis of the work
from the aspect of style, he would have seen that it has nothing
in common with Mozart's style and technique. He has simply
relied on external evidence: on the title-page of the manuscript
is the inscription "dal Signore Mozart". But anyone who is acquainted with the vast number of manuscripts bearing the inscription 'Haydn' or 'Mozart' lying in South German and Austrian archives, which in reality have nothing whatever to do
with either composer, can hardly marvel enough at such credul-
ity. For the present it must be accepted that we now possess only
one bassoon concerto by Mozart.

3. *For Oboe.* It can now be taken as certain that the flute Concerto in D major, K.314(285d), is a refashioning of a previous
oboe Concerto in C major. In his 1937 edition of Köchel, Einstein
listed it on p. 346 as an oboe concerto, K.271k. The point
at issue is connected with the concerto which Mozart composed
at Salzburg in 1777 for the oboist Giuseppe Ferlendis (who had
entered the service of the Archbishop of Salzburg on 1 April
1777), and which he mentioned in his letters of 3 December
1777 and 14 February 1778, from Mannheim.[1] The period during which the concerto was written falls between the date of
Ferlendis's entry into the Archbishop's service and Mozart's
journey to Mannheim (22 September 1777). Leopold's first mention of it is in a letter dated 15 October 1777. Friedrich Ramm
played it repeatedly in Mannheim; Mozart himself again made
use of it in Vienna in 1783. B. Paumgartner[2] has supplied the
information that the original composition of the oboe concerto,
in C major, is contained in a bundle of parts at the Mozarteum,
but that the work for flute in D major, K.314(285d), is a genuine
'reworking' of the material, and not simply a transposition. We

---

[1] Printed as an oboe concerto in Hawkes' Pocket Scores, No. 173.

[2] 'Zu Mozarts Oboenkonzert C Dur', *Mozart-Jahrbuch*, 1950, pp. 24–40; F.
Schröder came to the same conclusion independently: 'Ist uns Mozarts Oboenkonzert für Ferlendis erhalten?', *Musikforschung*, V/1952, pp. 209–11.

know that Mozart was put to some embarrassment by his obligations to the Dutch dilettante flautist De Jean in Mannheim. He had promised to write three flute concertos for him, but supplied only one (K.313(285c)). As a way out of his difficulty he resorted to the expedient (which formerly we could only conjecture) of rewriting the Salzburg Ferlendis Concerto of 1777 as a flute concerto for De Jean in 1778.

A concerto for oboe, in F major, exists in printed parts in the Milan Conservatoire, the author's name being given as Ferlendis. G. de St.-Foix[1] attempted to claim this for Mozart and thought of it as Mozart's concerto for Ferlendis. But the printed parts clearly state Ferlendis as the composer, and number it as his Op. 13. The concerto itself has hardly any feature that would credibly justify its being ascribed to Mozart, and there is no external evidence to support St.-Foix's assumption. Einstein and Paumgartner are of one mind in declaring that "we must leave the authorship with Ferlendis". In addition to the oboe Concerto in C major, K.271k, which has come down to us complete, there is a fragment of an oboe concerto in F major, K.293(416f). In all probability, Mozart began it in the spring of 1783, when at Vienna, with Count Esterházy's oboist, whose name is not known, as the intended recipient. The autograph fragment which has survived offers the first sixty-one bars of the first movement, and it is highly probable that it is the draft of the concerto which, according to Mozart's letter to his father of 15 February 1783, he planned to compose for the oboist we have mentioned. He also wanted to transfer his 1777 concerto written for Ferlendis to the same player, and he asked Leopold to send it to him. Later he acknowledged its receipt. It would appear that he handed over only the old concerto to the Esterházy oboist, and did not go on with the new one, K.293(416f), which he had begun, but had not continued. It is also possible that the nine-bar sketch, K.416g, belongs to this fragment. In view of the magnificent opening tutti, one must consider it a serious loss that Mozart never finished this work.

4. *For Flute.* Mozart informed his father on 10 December 1777 that the flautist Wendling had forwarded to him in Mannheim a commission from the Dutchman, De Jean ("Our Indian") to write "three short, simple concertos and a couple of quartets for the flute". Of the works commissioned, two undoubtedly

[1] 'Mozart ou Ferlendis', *Rivista Musicale Italiana*, XXVII/1920, pp. 543 et seq.

were composed: the D major Quartet for flute, violin, viola, and
'cello, K.285, and the flute Concerto in G major, K.313(285c).
The concerto has survived in its entirety. But the autograph is
lost, and the only source we have is a copy in the library of the
Gesellschaft der Musikfreunde, Vienna, which almost certainly
dates from the 1790s, and the first printed edition, issued by
Breitkopf & Härtel in 1803. The version we have today can
certainly be accepted as essentially the same as the original, if
in the adagio movement we substitute two oboes for the two
flutes which are prescribed in the Mozart *Collected Edition*,
Series XII, No. 13.[1] In details certainly many of the variants
seem open to question. Einstein championed the view that the
Andante in C major for flute and the same orchestral accompaniment, K.315(285e), was composed by Mozart as a substitute for the D major Adagio of K.313(285c), "which might
have been too difficult for the amateur performer". It could be
that the Andante was intended as a replacement of the slow
movement of this concerto; but Einstein's argument is not very
convincing, since the outer movements are far more difficult
than the Adagio. If De Jean was able to play them, he could
hardly have found the Adagio so difficult. The Andante in C
major (in the original without tempo indication) has survived
intact, and was printed by André as early as 1800. For the
second of the three concertos commissioned by De Jean, Mozart
handed over the flute Concerto in D major, K.314(285d). We
have already discussed the fact that this is really a refashioning
of the oboe Concerto in C major, K.271k. Mozart changed the
oboe solo part so satisfactorily to meet the needs of the flute that
posterity has regarded it as essentially an original flute concerto. But De Jean, who was probably acquainted with the circumstances, certainly refused to pay Mozart the full amount of
his commission. The autograph of this concerto is also missing.
Our sources are a manuscript score and a manuscript set of parts
in the library of the Gesellschaft der Musikfreunde, Vienna,
and a first edition published by Falter at Munich *c.* 1810(?).
Consequently, the details of the variants to this concerto are also
quite unreliable. R. Gerber[2] declares the Viennese parts to be
"full of errors". He made many corrections to it, and above all

[1] R. Gerber proposed this adjustment in 1936, in his Eulenburg edition of the
score (No. 779), and, later, Einstein in his revision of Köchel.
[2] Foreword to his edition of the score, Eulenburg, No. 771.

attempted to restore the doubtful passage in the third movement, bars 152 et seq., which Rudorff inaccurately amended in the *Collected Edition*, Series XII, No. 14. But he, too, did not succeed in establishing the correct version of this passage; the first to achieve it was Paumgartner.[1] With these reservations, the two concertos, in G major and D major, can both be regarded as 'original' flute compositions by Mozart. The many doubts concerning the textual variants do not affect the fact that we possess two complete and distinguished flute concertos from Mozart's hand. The D major Rondo for flute and orchestra, K.Anh.184, on the other hand, is a transposition of the C major Rondo for violin and orchestra, K.373, which was written in Vienna in 1781 and was transcribed for the flute probably only after Mozart's death. The violin version derives from an autograph dated 2 April 1781. It can no longer be traced, but it was originally in the possession of J. André, who published the Rondo in 1800. We have only printed texts of the flute arrangement; which of these is the earliest cannot be stated with any certainty.

5. *For Horn.* The earliest example of this form of concerto is the Rondo in E flat for horn and orchestra, K.371, written in 1781. The autograph contains the solo part complete, but the orchestration is only partly realized. It is one of the many autographs in which Mozart fully realized the solo part as well as the tuttis and the orchestral bridge-passages between the rests in the solo part, but postponed the elaboration of the requisite accompaniment until a more convenient moment, and never took up the work again. Mozart always worked *ad hoc*; if there was no special occasion for which a work was required, the unfinished sections remained unfinished. A similar instance of this is the violin Concerto in E flat K.268(365b); and in some respects the piano Concerto in D major, K.537, is an analogous case.[2] The horn Rondo, K.371, is certainly only a fragment of a completely planned (or executed?) concerto. A number of small fragments, K.371(K.Anh.98b, 98, and 97), belongs to its first movement. It was very probably intended for

[1] op. cit., p. 39.

[2] cf. G. de St.-Foix in *Bulletin de la Société Union Musicologique*, II/1922, pp. 106–7, where he drew attention to an important passage, from one of Mozart's letters, which dealt with his method of working; see also my Foreword to the Eulenburg edition (No. 719) of the concerto, K.537, and *Acta musicologica*, IX/1938, pp. 147–9.

the Salzburg horn-player, Ignaz Leutgeb (Leitgeb), who was later in Vienna.

The Concerto in D major, K.412 (386b), has also survived only in fragmentary form, though the first and third movements exist in completely finished autographs (the first movement dated 1782, the third (formerly K.514), 1787). It is certain that these two movements did not originally belong together; that can be judged from the dissimilarity in the instrumental allocation. No case is known of Mozart writing out the movements of a single work at such a long interval of time. The collocation of the two movements of K.371 as the outer movements of a concerto has come about through custom. Einstein at one stage thought that the autograph fragment in E major, K.Anh.98a, might be the middle movement for this work. Although we have ninety-one completely worked-out bars in autograph form, Mozart, unfortunately, did not finish the task. Einstein, however, in his *Berichtigungen und Zusätze* (to his revision of Köchel), has rightly suggested that this fragment is not an Andante but the beginning (Allegro) of another horn concerto, and has nothing to do with the D major work. That the rondo of K.412 (386b), formerly K.514, was written for Leutgeb, whom, as is well known, Mozart readily made the butt of his good-natured banter, is indicated by many marginal indications in his own hand.

The three well-known horn concertos, all in E flat, K.417 (1783), K.447 (1783?), and K.495 (1786), have come down to us complete. The autograph of K.417, which was intended for Leutgeb, has partly survived.

The autograph of K.447 is at present owned by the heirs of Stefan Zweig, London. St.-Foix and, earlier, J. A. André doubted whether all of this concerto was composed in 1783 (chiefly because the middle movement bears the unusual inscription "di W. A. Mozart"). But it is difficult to assume that Mozart made it up from single movements composed in different years; that would be completely contrary to all his normal practice in composing concertos. We can take it as certain that K.447 was also intended for Leutgeb. K.495 has survived in incomplete autograph form, and it expressly bears the inscription "für den Leitgeb [*sic*]". So the situation at present is that we have only three complete horn concertos, these being the three known works in E flat, K.417, 447, and 495. To these must be added the two complete single movements of K.412(386b), and the movement K.371, the solo part of which has wholly survived, but not the orchestral score.

6. *For Clarinet.* The only concerto for clarinet is that in A major, K.622, which, although it has survived in a not wholly authentic version, is of masterly and unearthly beauty; it was composed after *La Clemenza di Tito* in the autumn of 1791. It was intended for Anton Stadler, for whom Mozart wrote many other solo pieces: the Trio, K.498, the clarinet and basset horn parts to his vocal trios, the clarinet Quintet, K.581, the solos in *Tito*, etc.[1] The work has survived in its entirety. Our sources are André's first edition, 1801, and a copy derived from Aloys Fuchs's collection, both of which are faulty.[2] The autograph is lost. The variants of the *Collected Edition*, Series XII, No. 20, were corrected by Gerber, as far as possible in the absence of an autograph copy. A draft of the first movement, consisting of one hundred and ninety-nine bars (K.584b), in G major and for basset horn (also composed for Stadler in 1789), has survived in autograph form; it proves to be essentially identical with the first movement of K.622. George Dazeley[3] has proved conclusively that the work passed through several stages. The sketch of the first movement for basset horn, K.584b, could well have been the first stage. But then the concerto, complete in all three movements, must have been rewritten for a clarinet in A with an extended compass and thus for some form of basset horn in A. In the course of this revision, Mozart worked over the orchestral movement, K.584b, and added bassoons (it was not, therefore, simply a matter of transposing and continuing K.584b). Only then, after this intermediate version, which to-day is not known, and which was also the last version to come from Mozart's own hand, was the concerto adapted for a clarinet in A of normal compass; it was certainly not done by Mozart, but by an unknown arranger, probably for André's printed text of 1801. In the course of this adaptation, the solo part was

[1] For information on Stadler, see M. K. Ward: 'Mozart's Clarinettist', *Monthly Musical Record*, 85/1955, pp. 8–14.

[2] R. Gerber, in his Foreword to his edition of the score, Eulenburg, No. 778.

[3] 'The Original Text of Mozart's Clarinet Concerto', *Music Review*, IX/1948, pp. 166–77. See also R. Tenschert: 'Fragment eines Klarinettenkonzertes von Mozart', *Zeitschrift für Musikwissenschaft*, XIII/1931, pp. 218–22; and W. Reich: 'Bemerkungen zu Mozarts Klarinettenkonzert', *Zeitschrift für Musikwissenschaft* XV/1933, pp. 276–8.

deformed and corrupted in a number of details. Today we have Mozart's last master concerto not in its original form, but in an adaptation by an unknown hand.

A critical review of the manner in which the concertos for wind instruments have come down to us is very instructive. It shows that Mozart wrote concertos for a definite instrument only at a definite time and always for a definite player or client. In so far as they were completed at all, the bassoon concertos were written for Dürnitz during the years 1774–5; and as Mozart never again had close relations with any other bassoon player, amateur or professional, he never composed another bassoon concerto. The oboe Concerto K.271k was commissioned by Ferlendis, and after 1777 Mozart did not write another until a new patron made his appearance at Vienna in 1783; as the sketch K.293(K.416f) was not completed, one can conclude that the client cancelled his commission. The flute concertos were composed in 1778 for the amateur De Jean; the Concerto for flute and harp happened to be composed in the same year for the Duc de Guines; at Paris Mozart probably lost contact with De Jean, and so the third of the three concertos he had commissioned was never written. So far as we can tell, the horn concertos were all written for Leutgeb; they were 'favours' (at the head of the autograph of K.417 is the note, "took pity . . . on that ass . . . of a Leitgeb, in Vienna, 27 May 1783"). In Mozart's biography no other horn soloist appears after Leutgeb,[1] and so we have no more horn concertos, while those which have come down to us were all written in the period 1781–6. Mozart began to occupy himself with writing for the solo clarinet only when he found a satisfactory soloist in Stadler, for whom he composed from 1789 to 1791. He wrote not one horn concerto 'on spec.', still less for publication, and not one of his wind concertos was published in his lifetime. Nor was it mood or inspiration that occasioned a composition, but demand, an opportunity to have a work performed, someone's need of friendly assistance, or a paid commission. Furthermore, it is instructive to observe that even as early as 1778 Mozart's skill came into play to modify works already in existence for other instruments, though the modification was effected so thoroughly

[1] I regard as arbitrary Einstein's assumption that the rondo of K.412(386b), formerly 514, was "apparently written for a different virtuoso", made in his *Mozart*, London, 1946, p. 285.

that one would not recognize the origin of the new solo part. Finally, it is instructive, too, that even in this sphere Mozart's unfinished sketches enable us to recognize his method of working: solo parts (sometimes, but not always, with bass), orchestral tuttis, and bridge-passages are the first to be written; then we get the more finished elaboration; while the notation of a full accompaniment was reserved for the last stage. This knowledge is of value to us when we come to study the sinfonie concertanti and the violin concertos.

II. SINFONIE CONCERTANTI

Sinfonie concertanti are a form of concerto in which several solo instruments play in various combinations in concert with the orchestra. In Mozart's time the *genre* was by no means as popular as had been the concerto grosso some fifty years earlier. But the form offered a composer an opportunity for striking, colourful effects, and must have been very attractive to a musician with so subtle a sense of sound as Mozart's. The form had but little to do with the old concerto grosso of Handel's and Geminiani's day. The strict division between ripieno and concertino had disappeared. The soloists no longer came forward as *corpus favoritorum* in contradistinction to the ripieno. What happened rather was that the new form of the three-movement orchestral symphony projected occasional solo sections from within itself, and thus produced a cross between the symphony and the solo concerto. It descended from Tartini through Nardini, Locatelli, and Christian Bach, through the Mannheim masters, such as J. Stamitz, Karl Stamitz, Eichner, Filtz, and others, down to Haydn (whose earliest 'symphonies' are in part sinfonie concertanti). Mozart's sinfonie concertanti were (as may be inferred from their composition within the space of one year) particularly stimulated by Rosetti, by the two younger Stamitzes, and by Ignaz Holzbauer and Cannabich in Mannheim. The Viennese divertimento and serenade, with their bias towards folk-tunes, fondness for wind instruments, and mixture of styles (one recalls the insertion of entire solo concertos or concerto movements for violin in Mozart's serenades), had their influence. As the very name 'sinfonia concertante' shows, the result was not uniform; it varied with each composer. The terminology, too, was not consistent: often one finds simply 'concerto' or 'sinfonia' when in reality a 'sinfonia concertante' is intended. In any case, Mozart's sinfonie concertanti are far more concertos than symphonies. The solo parts are extremely exacting; the way they blend with the orchestra, and their subtle tonal effect, indicate how much the form appealed to the composer.

All the works in this form were composed within the brief compass of the years 1778–9, during the Mannheim–Paris journey and the immediately following Salzburg period. So far as we know their ultimate destination, they were, like the wind concertos, all occasioned by commissions or through friendly obligations.

The series of sinfonie concertanti begins with that in E flat for four wind instruments and orchestra, K.Anh.9(297b), which was written in 1778. This is a composition which presents especial problems in regard to the manner of its survival. According to Mozart's letter from Paris of 5 April 1778, he had written a sinfonia concertante for his four friends, the Mannheim windplayers Wendling, Ramm, Stich (Punto), and Ritter – in other words, for flute, oboe, horn, and bassoon. These players wished to perform the work in the *Concert spirituel*. The conductor of the concert, Le Gros, had acquired the autograph manuscript. But by 1 May it transpired that the performance was not given (the reasons are unknown). From the dates of Mozart's letters we can determine that the sinfonia concertante was written between 5 and *c*. 20 April 1778. In a letter dated 3 October 1778, Mozart mentions that he intended to write down the work again later. It is doubtful whether he ever did; in accordance with his custom, he would have put his intentions into practice only if he had had four equally outstanding wind players at his disposal, or if he had found someone to commission the work. But there is no question of this latter. So long as the contrary cannot be proved, we must hold to the view that only one autograph of this sinfonia concertante was made, i.e., in the Paris 'original version' with flute and oboe. The inevitable deduction is that not only has the autograph remained untraced, but that the whole work has been lost to us. Köchel's first edition (1862), and the first three editions of Jahn's biography of Mozart (1856–91) made no mention of it. Only in the fourth edition (which appeared long after Jahn's death in Deiters's 1905 revision) did it emerge that Jahn had managed to obtain a copy; unfortunately, he does not mention his source. This copy, which, together with Jahn's literary remains, was deposited in the former Prussian State Library at Berlin, is the only one known to us. It is not written in Jahn's hand, and is very unreliable. The score of the *Collected Edition* (Series XXIV, No. 7a), which was prepared from it, represents an attempt at emendation; my edition[1] goes further and attempts a reconstruction. As the Jahn copy could have come to light only a little time before his death, i.e., between 1867 and 1869, a contemporary source must have been still in existence at that time,[2] but has since disappeared. The specific problem raised by this sinfonia concertante is this: from where did the version for oboe, clarinet, horn, and bassoon, as we have it today, come? All four instruments are treated quite idiomatically and entirely in Mozartean style. The oboe part shows no sign of being rewritten from what was originally a flute part, while the clarinet part is a perfect model of 'clarinet' writing; it fully exploits the low register, the favourite common-chord arpeggios, as well as the best register for cantabile playing. From the manner in which Mozart rewrote the oboe Concerto K.271k as the flute Concerto K.314(285d), we know that he was a virtuoso at reshaping a solo line for another instrument by sheer sleight of hand. (The instance of the basset horn movement, K.584b, and the clarinet concerto, K.622, cannot be cited here, as the latter version was not Mozart's.) All honour to Mozart's virtuosity: but the oboe and clarinet parts of the Sinfonia Concertante K.Anh.9(297b) could not have been realized from a previous flute or oboe part without a complete revision of the entire work. So we are confronted with the doubt whether K.Anh.9(297b) is the Paris composition of 1778 in any sense at all; and, if it is, by whom and when it was transformed into the present version. Several circumstances can be cited in favour of the accuracy of the date. The orchestral

---

[1] Eulenburg, No. 755.

[2] In my Eulenburg edition I was thinking of the autograph. Probably it was this fact that occasioned Einstein's remark: "The autograph was then, *c.* 1865, still available and may possibly turn up again." (Einstein's "1865" seems to be an arbitrary assumption, since the second edition of Jahn's book, published in 1867, which he himself edited, does not mention the sinfonia concertante.) Today I would be more inclined to think that some anonymous person in the 1860s made a copy from a text written out in Mozart's lifetime or a little later, and that this text already offered the oboe and clarinet version. The presumed single autograph, however, can have had only the original Paris distribution, i.e., with flute and oboe; and I think it very unlikely that an arranger in the middle of the nineteenth century could have re-instrumented this 'original version' in the specifically Mozartean style the work reveals today.

lay-out is closely akin to that of the Concerto for flute and harp, K.299(297c), of 1778, as well as to that of the Concerto for two pianos, in E flat, K.365(316a), of 1779; on the other hand, it does not achieve the chamber-musical lucidity of the Vienna concertos. The serenade character of the variation movement is closely akin to the 'Haffner' Serenade (K.250(248b)), of 1776, and the Salzburg Serenade, K.320, of 1779. The 'flourish' between the variations, which is used as a refrain, recalls the 'Serenata notturna', K.239, of 1776. What tells against the date 1778 is the presence of the clarinet, which Mozart used neither in Salzburg nor in Paris – not, in fact, before Vienna. But the work could not have come into existence in Vienna after February 1784, otherwise it would have figured in Mozart's list of works. It is an even more improbable hypothesis that the revision of the Paris 'original version' was undertaken by a strange hand; there is not one bar in all the sinfonia which does not bear witness to Mozart's authorship. The only remaining hypothesis – not a very probable one, to be sure – is that Mozart again took up the old composition in the last years of his life, when he was working in collaboration with Stadler, and did not enter it in his own list of works because it was a reworking of old material. But then the question immediately arises: who could the other wind players have been? And surely Mozart would have mentioned any performance of the work? So the date, the copy, and the manner of survival of this magnificent and musically joyous composition must remain obscure. We could solve the mystery only if the source from which Jahn's copyist made his version came to light, or else the autograph once owned by Le Gros. But though the origin of the work is still obscure, it would be entirely misguided to throw premature doubts on the authenticity of the version we have, since in every detail of the composition – if not in every detail of the variants – Mozart's hand is clearly recognizable.

The Paris period (1778) also saw the composition of the Concerto in C major for flute and harp, K.299(297c), which the Duc de Guines commissioned from Mozart, through Baron Grimm, for himself and his harpist daughter (and still had not paid for, four months after its delivery). We have the complete autograph; no problems at all arise from its survival.

The fully composed fragment of a concerto in D major for piano and violin, accompanied by a large orchestral ensemble,

K.Anh.56(315f), dated 1778, belongs to the period immediately following the sojourn in Paris. Mozart began it for an *Académie des Amateurs* which was to be founded in Mannheim, and he wrote the first one hundred and twenty bars of the first movement. The autograph has survived. Einstein remarks of its magnificent opening (which was printed in the *Collected Edition*, Series XXIV, No. 21a), "it must be counted among the greatest of losses to art that Mozart did not complete this work". One certainly agrees with him: if this sinfonia concertante had been completed in the style of the noble opening tutti, its unusual combination of instruments alone would have ensured it a place among the most frequently performed of Mozart's concertos. He must have intended the work for himself and the violinist Ignaz Fränzl, who was to direct the *Académie*. Nothing came of the performance because the Mannheim Orchestra was disbanded, and it is presumably for this reason that Mozart left the opening bars untouched. So once more, in this fragment, we have evidence of the connection between his outward circumstances and his activities as a composer.

On the other hand, nothing is known of the occasion for which the Sinfonia Concertante in E flat for violin and viola, K.364(320d), was composed. The autograph was formerly possessed by A. André, but has now disappeared; only a few bars of the first movement and the sketch for a cadenza, both in Mozart's hand, have survived. André's first edition, published in 1801, was probably based on the autograph; at present that edition is the sole source for the sinfonia. It is true that the date 1779 is not confirmed documentarily; but it must be regarded as very probable, especially since the original MS. of the double concerto has a scordatura of the viola (notation in D major: the viola is tuned a semitone higher) in common with that of the fragment of a triple concerto in A major, K.Anh.104(320e), the autograph of which, in the Salzburg Mozarteum, indicates that it belongs to the same period. Like K.Anh.56(315f), this fragment leaves us conscious of one of "the greatest of losses to art". The one hundred and thirty-four bars which have been written down, or sketched out, for the first movement of a sinfonia concertante for violin, viola, and 'cello (K.Anh.104(320e)) reveal that if Mozart had completed it, the result would have been nothing less than a companion piece to K.364(320d). The triple concerto was most likely planned in conjunction with the double concerto, and intended for the same players. Unfortunately, we do not know the names of the Salzburg violist and 'cellist whom Mozart could have had in mind during 1779–80; his own opinion of musical conditions in that town at this period was extremely unfavourable,[1] and we have no information to indicate that it was a paid commission. However, it is obvious that, for whatever reason, the series of sinfonie concertanti begun in Paris was continued in Salzburg. Einstein is of the opinion that the thirty-two bar fragment of the orchestral rondo in A major, 'La Chasse', K.Anh.103(320f), belongs to the unfinished triple concerto; and so he dates this fragment 1779, in opposition to Mena Blaschitz,[2] who accepts the date 1788. But the orchestration diverges somewhat from that of K.Anh.104(320e), a circumstance that in other instances Einstein always regards as an indication that they are not connected, e.g., the two horn movements K.412(386b).[3] Whatever the reason which moved Mozart to write the brief sketch, 'La Chasse', there is nothing to show any connection between it and this or any other triple concerto. And in that case Einstein's dating of 1779 is subject to considerable doubt.

Thus, of the five sinfonie concertanti which Mozart planned and began, he completed three; the fragments of the other two afford us an insight into a very important section of his 'workshop'. We have no knowledge of the circumstances that compelled him to leave the various sketches unfinished; only in the case of the double concerto K.Anh.56(315f) can we conjecture that his failure to complete it had some connection with the break-up of the Mannheim orchestra. From the proximity of the Concerto for violin and viola and the fragment of the triple concerto to the Concerto in E flat for two pianos, K.365(316a), we may deduce that in Salzburg, too, some interest was shown in the form: K.365(316a) was also written at Salzburg, in 1779. But evidently during his stay at Vienna Mozart had no further opportunity to use sinfonie concertanti.

III. CONCERTOS FOR ONE OR TWO VIOLINS

Mozart's first work for violini concertanti was the Concertone in C major, K.190(166b), written at Salzburg in 1773; we do

---

[1] cf. Abert: *Mozart*, Vol. I, pp. 757 et seq.
[2] *Die Salzburger Mozartfragmente*, Bonn, 1926. [Dissertation.]
[3] Einstein, op. cit., p. 284.

not know for what players. It is a hybrid work, 'between two styles', for, in addition to the two violins, the oboe and occasionally even the 'cello emerge as soloists, so that one could classify it as a sinfonia concertante. Not without justification, in a letter dated 11 December 1777, Leopold Mozart associates it with the 'Haffner' Serenade, K.250(248b) and the two 'Lodronische Nachtmusik' pieces, K.247 and K.287(271b). At a later period, Mozart himself appeared to attach less value to the work; but he played it to Wendling at Mannheim in 1777, and Wendling recommended a performance in Paris. As we have it today, the Concertone derives from an autograph formerly in the possession of the publisher, A. Cranz, who brought out the first (?) printed edition in 1870. The autograph is at present in the hands of a collector in Switzerland. The version in the *Collected Edition* (Series XII, No. 9) must be regarded as unreliable, and a new edition based on the autograph is therefore urgently needed.

April 1775 saw the beginning of the series of famous violin concertos; five of them were created in swift succession: the B flat, K.207; the D major, K.211; the G major, K.216; the D major, K.218; and the A major, K.219. The autographs of the first four are in the former Prussian State Library, Berlin; the autograph of the A major Concerto, K.219, is now in the Library of Congress, Washington. The close connection between these concertos, all five of which were composed during the few months from April to December 1775, for the Salzburg Court leader, Brunetti, is also literally documented by the fact that the first four have survived in a single bundle, which originally also included K.219. In 1776, Mozart replaced the finale of K.207 by a more weighty movement, K.269(261a); and for K.219 he composed (also in 1776) a new "Adagio for Brunetti, since the one was too studied for him", as Leopold Mozart wrote; this, too, was in E major, K.261. Both substitute movements have survived in autograph form in Berlin. In addition to these manuscripts, we can cite certain early printed texts as sources: André published K.211 in 1802, K.218, *c.* 1807, K.269(261a) and 261 as early as 1801 (at a time when no printed edition of the complete concertos in B flat, K.207, and A major, K.219, was available). K.218 (the 'Strassburger' Concerto, as the Mozarts called it, since the Musette theme in the Rondeau harks back to a folk-tune also employed by Dittersdorf) can be taken as a warning against hasty judgment. Since we have learnt[1] how closely in this concerto Mozart followed a D major violin concerto by Boccherini (Mozart could have met him through his connections with Baron de Bagge, to whom Boccherini had been introduced in 1767) we have to be even more circumspect than before in attempting to differentiate between the genuine and the false. For in this work, typically Mozartean writing is clothed in the garment of a strange model; one may not therefore regard agreement with, or dependency on, a strange model as justification for challenging the authenticity of a work otherwise fully guaranteed – provided, of course, that it reveals Mozart's hand. And, on the contrary, the recurrence of a theme from a genuine Mozart work in a doubtful piece is not to be accepted too readily as proof that the doubtful piece is authentic. The tests of construction and style are always more trustworthy than the simple fact that themes recur. The survival of these five violin concertos and the two substitute movements raises no special problems. R. Gerber,[2] who checked all the five concertos from the autograph manuscripts, found no cause for doubt.

The situation with regard to the two other violin concertos – those in D major, K.271a(271i), and in E flat, K.268(365b) – is very different. The autograph of the first was originally owned by F. Habeneck, of Paris. The violinist Eugène Sauzay made a copy from this text *c*. 1835 for his teacher and father-in-law, Baillot, and this copy still exists in Paris. That the original was an autograph is guaranteed by the form of dating which Sauzay reproduced as follows: "di Wolfgango Amadeo Mozart Salisburgo li 16 di Luglio 1777". Another copy, once in Aloys Fuchs's collection, is now in the former Prussian State Library at Berlin. Its variants are hardly reliable, but in essentials it correctly reproduces the work; A. Kopfermann based the first printed edition of the concerto on this source, giving a revised version. R. Gerber[3] also revised the concerto from the same source. The doubts raised as to its authenticity are quite unjusti-

[1] E. von Zschinsky-Troxler: 'Mozarts D-Dur-Violinkonzert und Boccherini', *Zeitschrift für Musikwissenschaft*, X/1928, pp. 415–22. See also H. Keller: 'Mozart and Boccherini', *Music Review*, VIII/4/1947, pp. 241ff.

[2] See his textually identical Forewords to Eulenburg editions Nos. 763, 764, 747, 748, and 717.

[3] Eulenburg edition, No. 766.

fied. They are based on the circumstance that in a few small sections of the slow movement the solo violin has double stoppings in tenths, and that in a number of places in the concerto it ascends to positions that are unusual in Mozart's violin concertos; but there are analogies in the concertante movements of certain divertimenti and serenades written about the same time. It is hard to understand why these peculiarities of violin technique should be the basis for throwing doubt on the authenticity of the entire concerto. Einstein[1] has quite rightly seen that these virtuoso embellishments could very possibly have been nineteenth-century additions. (It is perfectly easy to find ways of reducing the respective passages to simpler performance, but it must be observed that in Mozart's day the *res facta* was very often elaborated by the virtuoso's improvisation.) But one must question the validity of his opinion when he writes, "One must certainly think that the arranger went still farther, and consequently it is impossible to restore the original shape of the work as it existed in 1777." Very close analysis reveals that K.271a(271i) is characteristic of Mozart's technique; and not one passage allows of any room for doubt in regard to themes, harmony, rhythm, construction, and orchestration; the structure is, in fact, directly connected with that of K.218 and 219. For this concerto in particular, the assumption that Mozart wrote down only "a hasty sketch"[2] is completely invalid. On the other hand, Einstein's argument that the work is probably authentic because the finale has a motive which echoes the 'Gavotte Joyeuse' in *Les petits riens* (K.Anh.10(299b)) is unconvincing, in view of the fact that in structure and style the work fits perfectly into the series of Mozart's authentic violin concertos. A writer who is purist enough to be offended by the technical peculiarities of the solo violin part has, nevertheless, no right whatever to throw doubt on a Mozart composition otherwise fully certified and wholly mature.

The dispute over the authenticity of the violin Concerto in E flat, K.268(365b), has been inflamed by similar faulty argument, and has been waged with even greater heat. For this work we have no autograph. Our source is the printed edition issued by J. André as early as 1799; a second edition, 'arranged' by F. X. Gleichauf, was prepared from it *c.* 1835. Apparently

---

[1] In the third edition of Köchel, K.271a(271i).
[2] Einstein: op. cit., p. 281.

no copy of the first edition has been discovered; all the later editions are based on the second, 1835, edition. So we are unable to judge whether this fully agrees with the first edition, and, if it does, what is meant by the word 'arranged'.[1] But, since André issued his first edition in 1799, in the very same year that he acquired the complete Mozart musical remains, any falsification is *ipso facto* highly improbable. In his statement concerning revisions, made in the *Collected Edition* (Series XXIV, No. 19), E. Rudorff has appealed to defects in the orchestral writing in support of an out and out attack on the authenticity of the concerto as a whole; he expresses the view that it is "not impossible that here some Mozart material or other has been ineptly made use of by a strange hand". Einstein accepted this criticism, which applies only to certain parts of the orchestration, and even went farther; he followed Rudorff[2] in expressing the opinion that Mozart wrote only "a sketch of the first movement and perhaps a few opening bars of the Rondo", and then went so far as flatly to declare that the middle movement is "certainly a crude forgery".[3] C. B. Oldman[4] conjectured that the violinist J. Friedrich Eck (to whom, according to an unverified story, Mozart played the concerto) might have written it down from memory and completed it. This view is contrary to the fact, long attested by musical history, that a musician may go so far as to take over the themes, the technique, and the external form from another musician, but can never imitate the other composer's flow of invention or his structural homogeneity. To achieve that, Eck would have had to be a genius of Mozart's calibre; and even then, the concerto would certainly have been very different. G. de St.-Foix stated the issue very pertinently in an exemplary analysis of the concerto, as

---

[1] Since these lines were written, a copy of the first edition has emerged in London. I am greatly obliged to Dr. E. F. Schmid of Augsburg for drawing my attention to it, and to Mr. H. J. Laufer, the owner of the copy, for his permission to use it. A comparison shows that, minor divergences apart, the actual notes of the first edition correspond to André's later edition, and hence with the version of the *Collected Edition*. So far as phrasing and dynamics are concerned, however, there are numerous divergences. It seems to follow that a second editor had a hand in the second edition. The striking and un-Mozartean expression marks (e.g., 'Una corda G' in all three movements, or the '*pp* perdendosi' at the end of the first movement) are already to be found in the first edition.

[2] In his revision of Köchel, K.268(365b), and *Mozart*, p. 376.

[3] op. cit., p. 281.

[4] 'Mozart's Violin Concerto in E Flat', *Music and Letters*, XII/1931.

long ago as 1922.[1] The work is one of those in which Mozart did not care to go through all the stages of composition. He wrote down the solo part and the ritornelli in full (though not all, perhaps, in the case of the finale) and sketched in indications of the orchestral transitions; in these parts the concerto indubitably reveals all Mozart's characteristics. The remainder, i.e., the orchestral accompaniment, and a number of the orchestral bridge-passages and similar sections, he left incomplete; these parts are not up to standard. The second movement, in its entirety, remains highly controversial. Presumably André had the unfinished manuscript completed by someone else, in order to have a work suitable for publication (the faultiness of the score makes it doubtful whether it was André himself, or Süssmayer, as Wyzewa–St.-Foix and Abert suggested). This supplementary work was done clumsily and defectively; St.-Foix[2] has suggested a very plausible emendation to one passage in the first movement. The question whether the collaborator added virtuoso effects to certain passages in the solo line is not particularly important in so far as the question of authenticity is concerned. It is very likely that he did. But, to judge from the violin technique alone, there is absolutely nothing that would necessitate such a conclusion, since difficulties similar to those found in this concerto are to be found elsewhere in Mozart. (See above, K.271a(271i).) Stylistically, however, many passages in the violin part leave the impression that the arranger transferred to the solo line material that properly belongs to the orchestra.

Even at the time of the first André edition the authenticity of this concerto was challenged by an anonymous writer in the *Allgemeine Musikalische Zeitung*, 1799, pp. 93–4. Like all the later criticisms, this was directed against the orchestration and its violation of the elementary rules of composition. It is characteristic (as St.-Foix has put it) that "the commentators have done their utmost to specify the faults and the all too evident gaucheries in the orchestral accompaniment without perceiving the grandeur, the spirit, and the admirable flow of the part for

---

[1] 'Le dernier concerto pour violon de Mozart (K.268)', *Bulletin de la Société Union Musicologique*, II/1922, pp. 85–116. Unfortunately, I have been unable to see a second article by the same author on the same concerto, published in *Revue de Musicologie*, 1925.

[2] loc. cit., Appendix.

the solo violin, and without bothering to study the internal structure of the pieces and the specific features of their style". The judgment of an anonymous writer of 1799, of someone who had failed to comprehend the actual circumstances, has been passed down from generation to generation until the present day. Owing to the unsatisfactory position in regard to sources, one can hardly hope that the problem will be solved by resort to the method of textual criticism; in this case the method of comparative analysis of style comes into its own. Close analysis shows that the question of the authenticity of K.268(365b) can be unequivocally decided in a positive sense, so far as the solo part and most of the tuttis are concerned. It would be a grateful task to improve the defective orchestration. As St.-Foix says: "So much the worse for those who, faced with one of the noblest works of the master's maturity, have seen in it only the faults of harmony or the poverty of the writing, and for whom all the Mozartean . . . beauty of the concerto, all the flow of its inspiration . . . have remained a dead letter." Whether we are to accept 1784–5, which St.-Foix has championed, and for which he has adduced a number of very good reasons, or whether Einstein's date of 1780 is to be preferred, must remain undecided. Certainly the old Köchel date of 1776 is too early; in its texture the work dates after, not before, K.271a(271i). It is unlikely to have been written after February 1784, since it does not appear in Mozart's list of works. For this reason St.-Foix's opinion that it was written for Regina Strinasacchi (for whom Mozart also wrote the violin Sonata in B flat, K.454, in April 1784) is untenable. At present one must be content to place the Concerto within the period *c.* 1777–83.

The enigma of the so-called 'Adélaïde' Concerto in D major, K.Anh.294a, which Marius Casadesus first issued in 1933 in a piano transcription (B. Schott's), is still unsolved. The source is inaccessible. According to Casadesus' Foreword to his edition and information he has supplied in a letter,[1] it consists of an autograph manuscript in two staves, of which the upper stave carries the solo part (including 'tuttis', i.e., probably including the upper voices of the 'tuttis') and the lower carries the bass.

---

[1] I did my best to obtain permission to examine the source, which Einstein also never saw. I am sincerely grateful to M. Casadesus for all his readiness to help, and for the information he has sent me. Unfortunately, he too was not in a position to let me have a microfilm of the manuscript.

In other words, we have a short score. The upper stave is no-
tated in D, the lower in E; the new edition is in D major.[1] So
far there is nothing unusual about the manuscript, for it is well
known that Mozart often wrote down the first draft of a composition in the form of a short score.[2] The surprising feature is
the date, which, according to the Schott edition's Foreword, is
26 May 1766. It is taken from a dedication accompanying the
manuscript, and addressed to Madame Adélaïde de France, the
eldest daughter of Louis XV. All the misunderstandings appear to have arisen from this dedication. Einstein justly remarked that it was not usual to provide a manuscript with a
dedication to a high personage, but he then flatly concluded
that the whole thing was a fraud, whereas he should have followed up the obvious explanation: presumably the manuscript
short score and the attached dedication have come together only
by chance; in reality they have nothing to do with each other.
As long as the source remains inaccessible it is surely better to
work on such an hypothesis than reject the work altogether. By
separating the concerto from the quite unacceptable date of
1766, the hypothesis leaves us free at least to undertake a serious
examination of the musical circumstances. The date is unthinkable, and not only on biographical grounds; the earliest concertos of Mozart's own composition which have survived are the
Concertone K.190(166b) and the piano Concerto K.175, both
of which date from 1773. It is quite unlikely that Mozart wrote
any concerto before that year, and in any case a concerto written prior to 1768 would have found a place in Leopold's list. If
we accept the hypothesis, we are still faced with the question:
to what work does the dedication really belong? The dedication
is written in a manner similar to those of Opp. Nos. 1 and 2,
K.6 and K.8, published in Paris in 1764; but it is not verbally
identical with them, so it must have belonged to another work.
However, the question is no longer of interest. If, unencumbered
by the date, we turn to an analysis of the work, we can, of
course, consider only the solo part and the upper voices of the
tuttis, plus the bass, since in the new edition all else is the editor's
handiwork. Although such an analysis does not yield any entirely unequivocal result, it does indicate that Mozart's authorship is not to be dismissed without further ado, as Einstein

---

[1] M. Casadesus would have regarded an edition in E as more sound.

[2] cf., for instance, the sketches for the piano Concerto in B flat, K.450. See below.

believed. In particular, his remark,[1] "to put it mildly, a piece of mystification *à la Kreisler*", is going too far. The concerto, which, once it is separated from the 'dedication', should no longer be called after Adélaïde de France, is well worth discussing. True, it is not particularly original in its invention, but in that respect does K.207 or K.211 surpass it to any extent? And, in structure, is it not very closely akin to these two concertos? Naturally, one cannot assert that it is authentic Mozart until one has seen the source. But what if some day it is established that the short score is a genuine autograph? Certainly we would still not have a completely finished violin concerto, but we would have at least a work which considerably enriches our knowledge of Mozart's first steps in this form. It is not entirely excluded that here we have to do with the sketch of a concerto written between April and June or July 1775. The five violin concertos of that year tell us a great deal about Mozart's artistic development, and in the course of writing them he made extraordinarily rapid progress in composition, such as any other composer would have required decades to achieve. April and June 1775, with their K.207 and 211, were largely surpassed by the following September, with K.216; while there was a further leap forward with K.218, composed in October. It is quite possible that the 'Adélaïde' Concerto would have a place in the initial phase of this amazing process.

Before leaving the violin concertos we must mention the Rondo in C major, K.373, composed in Vienna in April 1781, for Brunetti, who was giving concerts there. This is the rondo which also exists in a flute version in D major, K.Anh.184 (see above, flute concertos). André's first edition, of 1800, was based on a dated autograph which today is no longer to be traced. An 'Andante für die Violin zu einem Konzert' in A major, K.470, of which Mozart recorded the first four bars in his list of works under the date 1 April 1785, has vanished. Einstein conjectures that it was a substitute middle movement for Viotti's sixteenth violin concerto in E minor, for whose outer movements Mozart also wrote trumpet and drum parts (K.470a) when he performed the work at a concert in the *Mehlgrube*. Another concerto, in F major, for 'cello, K.206a, dated March 1775, formerly existed in autograph form in the Malherbe collection. But it has completely disappeared; possibly it was only a fragment.

[1] op. cit., p. 278.

Our survey of Mozart's violin concertos yields the total of seven complete and authentic works, of which only one, K.268(365b), is incomplete, lacking as it does part of the orchestral accompaniment; the additions made to the last work by an arranger are controversial. In addition, we have a concerto surviving only in a short score and so far not authenticated. We have, moreover, two complete substitute movements and an independent rondo, which cannot be related to a definite concerto. Then there is the double Concerto K.190(166b), the Concertone. We have no knowledge of any fragments or sketches for violin concertos or of movements for such concertos. Only the Andante, K.470, has been completely lost. It appears, then, that for this group of concertos everything that Mozart planned was more or less completely carried through, and everything that was completed has survived. This is a very different result from that which obtains in regard to the wind concertos and the sinfonie concertanti. We find the same chronological characteristics in the case of the violin concertos as we noted in our discussion of the wind concertos and the sinfonie concertanti: their composition fell within a single period. So far as they can be dated exactly, they were all written, with the single exception of the Concertone, during the years 1775–7: the date of composition of K.268(365b) is the subject of dispute. Only K.373 and 470 were composed considerably later. This uniformity in compositional period is also to be deduced from the outward circumstances, and especially from the fact that they were written for the one player. The five concertos of 1775, the substitute movements, K.269(261a), K.261, and the Rondo, K.373, were all written for Brunetti; we can take it as practically certain that the Concerto, K.271a(271i), written in 1777, was also intended for him. Only one work, K.268(365b), leaves us uncertain as to who was the intended recipient. There is little room for the conjecture, often expressed in Mozart literature, that he wrote the violin concertos for his own use.

IV. Concertos for One, Two, and Three Pianos

The piano concertos form by far the most extensive group in the concerto class, for it includes twenty-three complete works. Yet, so far as their survival is concerned, they present the fewest problems. We need not consider the early arrangements of other composers' sonatas and sonata movements which the boy

Mozart worked up into what may be called 'little concertos' for playing on tour during the years 1765–7, i.e., K.107(21b), K.37, 39, 40, 41. As the result of research by Wyzewa and St.-Foix in 1908 we know that they contain no original material. A period of from six to eight years separates them from the first personal and complete piano Concerto, K.175; during that period there is no mention of Mozart writing concertos of any kind. Einstein has related certain fragments to this interim period – namely, the group K.43c. Mozart's object in writing them, and their inter-relationship, certainly needs more thorough study.[1] It is not even established that these sketches were intended for a piano concerto.

Mozart's first complete piano Concerto, K.175 in D major, was composed in Salzburg in 1773. He probably wrote it for his own use. The autograph is lost. He took it with him to Munich in 1774; he played it again at Mannheim in 1778, and at Vienna in 1782 and 1783. In 1782 he replaced the original finale by a new one, K.382 (formerly K.Anh.209); the autograph of this finale is in the Berlin Library. With this same finale the concerto was printed by Boyer at Paris in 1784, by Schott at Mainz in 1785–6, by Artaria at Vienna in 1800, and by André at Offenbach in 1802. The original finale remained unprinted; the new one was published in a piano arrangement by Artaria in 1787. Of all Mozart's concertos this was the one most frequently printed during his lifetime and in the years immediately following his death. The autograph manuscript was originally bound together with K.238; yet apparently Mozart never thought of the two concertos as belonging together. At least, he never mentioned the point.

On the other hand, the three concertos, in B flat, K.238 (January 1776), in C major, K.246 (April 1776), and E flat, K.271 (January 1777), form a coherent group. Mozart probably wrote K.238 for himself, K.246 for the Countess Lützow in Salzburg, and K.271 for the French pianist Mlle. Jeunehomme, who may have visited Salzburg at the end of 1776. Mozart himself played all three concertos at a private concert in Munich on 4 October 1777, and also used the first two in Mannheim. He wanted to sell all three to the Paris publisher and engraver J. G. Sieber, who published the six piano sonatas, K.279–284, for him. But the project fell through. André was the

---

[1] They are scattered about in various places, partly in Prague and Pressburg, and were not available to me.

first to publish the three concertos (in parts), in the years 1793, c. 1800, and 1792 respectively. K.238 was published by Hummel at Amsterdam in 1796 and by Breitkopf & Härtel in 1804; K.246 was issued by Amon at Heilbronn c. 1800; K.271 by Schott at Mainz in 1795, and c. 1793 by Amon. These two latter issues seem to contradict Einstein's opinion that Sieber declined the three concertos on account of the special difficulties of K.271. The number of issues clearly testifies that Mozart's early piano concertos were among the first of his works to be popularized and to enjoy considerable circulation; not one wind concerto, not one sinfonia concertante, not one violin concerto was printed in his lifetime. All three concertos have survived in autograph form; K.238 is in the Library of Congress, Washington; K.246 and K.271 are in the Berlin Library. The fact that we have the autographs and other sources leaves us with no problems as to their survival.

In the middle of these three concertos we have Mozart's one Concerto for three pianos, in F major, K.242 (February 1776); it was composed in Salzburg for the Countess Lodron and her two daughters. Despite the unusual lay-out, Mozart was able to get the work performed both at Salzburg and at Mannheim during 1777–8; he had the arrangement for two pianos sent him in 1781. The autograph is in the Berlin State Library. Authentic parts, in Leopold's hand, are now in the Memorial Library of Stanford University, Stanford, California; Wolfgang made corrections in these parts for the first violins, the basses, and the third piano. An arrangement for two pianos, in a copyist's hand with Mozart's own superscription, is attached to the original parts. In this form it was first published by André in 1802, one or two years after the Concerto for two pianos, K.365(316a). In the original version (three pianos) it appears to have had its first publication about 1865, also by the André firm. This concerto owed its composition to a special commission at Salzburg, but it appears that Mozart wrote the Concerto for two pianos in E flat, K.365(316a), for himself and his sister; this was at the beginning of 1779. It is close not only in time to the sinfonie concertanti K.Anh.56(315f) for piano and violin, 1778; to K.364(320d) for violin and viola, 1779; and to K.Anh.104(320a) for violin, viola, and 'cello, in 1779; in its invention, structure, and sound it is much more akin to these sinfonie concertanti than to the playful and *galant* Concerto for three pianos, K.242.

When Mozart obtained further performances of this magnificent work at Vienna in 1781 and 1782 he enriched the outer movements with clarinets, trumpets, and timpani. The autograph manuscript is in the possession of the former Prussian State Library at Berlin; André arranged its first publication in 1800. Its survival presents no special problems. Apparently Einstein was able to find a close connection between this and the piano Concerto, Op. III, No. 6, by Johann Samuel Schröter, which Mozart came to know in Paris in 1778.[1]

A further group of three works consists of the piano concertos in A major, K.414(386), composed in 1782; the F major, K.413(387a), of 1782–3; and the C major, K.415(387b), also dating from 1782–3. These were the first to be written in Vienna. All three autographs are in Berlin. The three concertos were composed during the first creative ecstasy of the Vienna years, shortly after *Die Entführung* and the 'Haffner' Symphony, K.385, and very close to the string Quartet in G major, K.387. The disparity in compositional features between this group and the earlier group of 1776–7, and even K.271, is enormous. The dating and numeration which Einstein adopted were based on Mozart's letters of 28 December 1782, 4 and 22 January 1783, and on an advertisement which Mozart inserted in the *Wiener Zeitung* for 15 January 1783. It follows that one concerto was ready at the end of 1782; the two others must have been added in January 1783. In his advertisement Mozart invited subscriptions for MS. copies of the three concertos. In April 1783 he offered them to Sieber in Paris for engraving, again without success; their first printing was by Artaria at Vienna in 1785. From Mozart's letter of 28 December 1782 Einstein concludes that K.414(386a) was the first of the three to be written. The present finale of this concerto appears to be a replacement, since the Rondo K.386 bears the date 19 October 1782, and might well have been the original finale, in which case we would have a similar situation to that of K.175, which also had an original finale which was not reproduced in the first printed edition. The instrumentation of K.386 is not completed throughout.[2] The autograph of the Rondo has been lost except for a few fragments, one of which is in the Sibley Musical Library, Rochester (U.S.A.). The close external relationship of these three con-

---

[1] op. cit., pp. 296 et seq.

[2] Einstein filled in the missing parts and published the work in Vienna, 1936.

certos finds its counterpart in their technical and compositional features; Mozart himself referred to this circumstance both in his newspaper advertisement and in his letter of 26 April 1783 to Sieber, saying that he had "three piano concertos ready, which can be performed with full orchestra, or with oboes and horns, or merely a quattro". How deliberately, moreover, he pursued a very definite middle course while composing them is indicated by his letter to his father of 28 December 1782: "These concertos are a happy medium between what is too easy and too difficult; they are very brilliant, pleasing to the ear, and natural, without being vapid. There are passages here and there from which connoisseurs alone can derive satisfaction; but these passages are written in such a way that the less learned cannot fail to be pleased though without knowing why." Here one clearly sees how conscious he was of his masterly craft. He was obviously aiming to come into the public eye by composing piano concertos. Whether the fragment of a first movement to a piano concerto in D major, K.Anh.55(387c), scored only for violins, bass, and horns, is really to be attributed to the same period, as Einstein thinks, can be left unsettled.

With this group, all the problems of dating come to an end. The entries in Mozart's own list of works, which he began in February 1784, happened to start with the piano concerto in E flat, K.449, composed on 9 February 1784.[1] The autograph is in Berlin. Although in point of time it is a close neighbour of the three following concertos, those in B flat, K.450, D major, K.451, and G major, K.453 (all four were composed between February and April 1784, and occupy the first, second, third, and fifth places in Mozart's list), K.449 does not belong to the group. "It does not belong at all to them", Mozart himself wrote on 26 May 1784. In its lay-out it is more akin to the preceding group of 1782–3; the wind instruments are not obbligati ("written more for a small than a large orchestra"); it can "be performed a quattro without wind instruments" (15 May 1784). Mozart wrote it, not for himself, but for the Viennese pianist Barbara Ployer, as he himself stated in the superscription to the score. It was not printed during his lifetime; André published it in 1792.

---

[1] It is doubtful whether the dates in Mozart's catalogue always indicate the actual date of completion of a score, or whether they sometimes denote only the date of the entry, which could possibly be some time after the completion of the score. (See K.450.)

The three concertos K.450, 451, and 453, on the contrary, are closely related, as Mozart himself declared (26 May 1784): they are concertos "which are bound to make the performer perspire". He composed K.450 for himself, and played it in public as early as March 1784.[1] We lack a first performance date for K.451. K.453 was also intended for Barbara Ployer, who played it on 10 June 1784. All three works have survived in autograph form. K.450 is in the Thuringian State Library at Weimar; the others are in Berlin. K.453 was printed by Bossler, at Speyer, in 1787; the two others were published only posthumously: K.450 by Artaria in 1798, and K.451 by Hummel in Amsterdam in 1792.[2] The manner in which K.450 has survived is of especial interest because of the sketches included in the autograph manuscript, which Mozart again rejected while working on the concerto.[3] They afford us a glimpse into Mozart's workshop. All three concertos also have internal affinities. They initiate the unique synthesis of the concerto and symphonic styles which Mozart created in the piano concerto; from now on he continually sought new ways of resolving this synthesis. They also mark the beginning of his classical master concertos, every single one of which has its own individual character. From now on the conventional formulae, flourishes, and figures, common to the time, drop more and more into the background and make way for inventions and ideas which are new for each occasion.[4] It is not by mere chance that they were composed at the same time as the six quartets dedicated to Haydn: they mark Mozart's arrival at mature mastery, and the arrival of Viennese music at its classical period.

[1] Einstein claimed that it was K.449 that was played at this concert on 17 March 1784, but Mozart would hardly have chosen such a chamber concerto for his public appearances. Einstein's objection to K.450 does not hold good because the date for K.450 which Mozart gives in his list of works – namely, 15 March 1784 – does not necessarily mean that the score was only completed on that date. The parts could very well have been written out between the completion of the score and the date of entry.

[2] As long ago as 1935 I vainly searched for an alleged issue of K.453 by Boyer, at Paris in 1785. (See my Foreword to the Eulenburg edition of the score, No. 760.) So far as I know, no copy of this issue has since come to light.

[3] cf. the Foreword to the Eulenburg score, No. 743. Einstein has repeated my statement, while misunderstanding it, in his edition of Köchel. Cf. also H. J. Moser in *Musikforschung*, IV/1951, and Einstein in the *Journal of the American Musicological Association*, I/1948.

[4] The violin Concerto K.268(365b) is far from being so distinctive, and for this reason I think St.-Foix's suggested date of composition is too late.

The group relationship which we have observed hitherto does not apply to Mozart's later piano concertos; and it is noteworthy that as they develop in individuality and grow more and more difficult there is a rapid decrease in the frequency of printing. The B flat Concerto, K.456, written in 1784 for a Paris concert given by the blind Maria Theresia Paradis, has survived in autograph form;[1] André published the first edition in 1792. The Concerto in F major, K.459 (1784), has also come down to us in autograph form; Mozart possibly composed it for his own use. If the opinion expressed by André in his first edition (1794), and by Rellstab in his catalogue (1795), is correct, Mozart played it as well as K.537 on 15 October 1790, at his concert celebrating the coronation of Emperor Leopold II at Frankfurt.[2]

Probably the Andante in C major, K.Anh.59(466a), a sketch for the middle movement of a concerto, belongs to K.459. Einstein, in the third edition of Köchel, incomprehensibly tried to claim it for the D minor Concerto K.466. In his *Berichtigungen und Zusätze* he suggests that the sketch belongs .to the F major work. The sketch includes trumpets and timpani, which instruments are not found in the autograph of K.459. But they are listed in Mozart's Catalogue[3] and may (as was often the case in the eighteenth century) have been added on separate sheets, or even composed after the score was completed. The small fragment K.Anh.65 may also belong to this C major movement.

From this point, all the concertos have survived in autograph form. The D minor, K.466, was composed in February 1785, and Mozart performed it at one of his own concerts during the same month. Similarly, he composed and played the C major Concerto K.467 in March 1785 (as one can see, in this *genre* also he always wrote *ad hoc*). A small sketch probably belonging to it, K.467a, has survived. The concertos in E flat, K.482, in A major, K.488, and in C minor, K.491, had a similar origin, for immediate performance at Mozart's own subscription concerts;

[1] Very recently a contemporary MS. score of K.456 has come to light. It may be a second autograph, whereupon we should be faced with an exceptional case among Mozart's concertos.

[2] O. E. Deutsch and C. B. Oldman: 'Mozart–Drucke', *Zeitschrift für Musikwissenschaft*, XIV/1931, p. 345.

[3] The allocation of parts in Mozart's list of works are not always correct; see, for instance, the statement "2 violas" for the concertos K.450, 451, 453, 466, 467, 482, 488, 491, and 503.

he composed them during the period December 1785 to March 1786, and played them in Lent, 1786. In place of the present F sharp minor Adagio to K.488 he originally seems to have planned a D major movement, K.Anh.58(488a); in place of the present finale there were originally two other sketches of themes, K.Anh.63(488b) and K.Anh.64(488c). In opposition to M. Blaschitz, Einstein has plausibly argued that all these fragments belong to K.488. K.482, 488, and 491 were written immediately prior to *Figaro*; immediately afterwards, Mozart also composed the Concerto in C major, K.503 (December 1786); presumably he played it during Lent, 1787. The last two concertos follow after a longer interval. The Concerto in D major, K.537 (February 1788), the second 'Coronation' concerto, which Mozart played at Dresden in April 1789 and in October 1790 for the Emperor's coronation in Frankfurt, is, by way of an exception, not entirely complete in the surviving autograph. It is probable that K.Anh.57(537a) is an earlier sketch for the first movement, as Einstein suggested. On the other hand, one can hardly agree with him when he brings the D minor fragment, K.Anh.61(537b), into relationship with the 'Coronation' Concerto; the orchestral arrangement diverges from it, and in addition a middle movement in D minor to a concerto in D major would, for Mozart, be very unusual.

Einstein in his revision of Köchel lists as K.537c (formerly K.Anh.62) a sketch to a piano concerto in E flat, which, it was suggested, "could have been the first thought of a twin piece [to K.537]". In Einstein's *Berichtigungen und Zusätze*, however, the sketch is attached, quite rightly, to the slow movement of the C minor Concerto, K.491. The orchestration, listed in Köchel with trombones, is incorrect: through erasures on the autograph the entry '2 Corni' was misread as '2 Posan'; but it is clear that Mozart meant horns, not trombones (Einstein, op. cit., p. 1,029). The full complement of woodwind in the sketch also points to K.491.

Of all the long succession of Mozart's great Viennese piano concertos, from K.456 to K.595, only one, the last, was printed in his lifetime; Artaria advertised it in the *Wiener Zeitung* in August 1791. But the six concertos K.467, 481, 488, 491, 503, and 595 were all published by André from the autograph manuscripts, in his edition *c.* 1801: "Six grands concertos, dédiés au Prince Louis Ferdinand de Prusse", an edition which must have had a wide circulation at the time. Beethoven was acquainted with it. All these concertos have been safely assured of survival in authentic texts by the existence of the autographs. That, of course, does not mean that the text of the *Collected Edition* is reliable – quite the contrary. Revisions of all these concertos have revealed with what astonishing frivolity and often complete irresponsibility Mozart texts were distorted in the nineteenth century. Comparisons with the autographs[1] have shown that there are often twenty, thirty, and more deviations from the original to every page of the score. They include slight, but often distorting errors of phrasing, dynamics, tempo indications, expression marks, and often wrong notes or values, misleading grace notes and ornaments, etc. Repeats are treated with great inconsistency. The figured-bass accompaniment for the piano which Mozart provided (as Beethoven did in his early piano concertos) is suppressed throughout. One may state without exaggeration that the *Collected Edition* of Mozart's works and the practical editions based on it offer no more than the skeleton of his compositions. It would be wholly misleading to consider that there are no problems associated with the survival of his most famous concertos. While the versions we have are accurate in their fundamental structure, their text has been greatly corrupted in details.

How scrupulously accurate as a rule Mozart was in his autograph manuscripts can be demonstrated again and again, in the case of each concerto. There is an excellent instance in K.488, where Mozart himself went wrong once or twice in notating the A-clarinet, but expressly corrected the errors on an attached sheet. Certain obscurities remain only in the manuscript of K.491, which was obviously written in great haste and under internal strain. It is in fact a noteworthy exception when once, as in K.503, the true version of a motive happens to remain uncertain.[2]

The autograph of K.537 is a remarkable exception. It allows us to reconstruct Mozart's method of working exactly; the first step is to write down the solo instrument's line, the first violins, and the bass; the second is the realization of the orchestral

---

[1] cf. my Forewords to the following Eulenburg editions: Nos. 743, 760, 761, 721, 739, 737, 736, 740, 774, 719, and 775; also the studies by H. F. Redlich in *Music Review*, VII/1946 and IX/1948, and his Foreword to Eulenburg edition No. 796.

[2] See my Foreword to Eulenburg edition No. 774.

score; the third is the addition of trumpets and timpani. In this autograph, however, the notes for the left hand of the solo part are missing for long stretches.[1] But in André's printed edition, 1794, these sections had already been filled in by an unknown hand, and they have been accepted by all the later editions. Of all Mozart's piano concertos, in this single case the solo part is not entirely of his own composition.

The following comparative table is very instructive:

Köchel No.	Survival of Autograph	Editions published in Mozart's lifetime
175	No	Two
238	Yes	None
242	Yes	None
246	Yes	None
271	Yes	None
365(316a)	Yes	None
413(387a)	Yes	Two (or three?)
414(386a)	Yes	Two
415(387b)	Yes	One
449	Yes	None
450	Yes	None
451	Yes	One (or two?)
453	Yes	One
456	Yes	None
459	Yes	None
466	Yes	None
467	Yes	None
482	Yes	None
488	Yes	None
491	Yes	None
503	Yes	None
537	Yes	None
595	Yes	One

The table reveals with terrifying clarity by what slender threads has hung the survival of most of the concertos. Of the twenty-three, only seven were published in Mozart's lifetime; the others were all published from his manuscript remains. Of the autograph manuscripts, only two (K.450 and 466) mani-

[1] For an exact indication of the passages referred to see my Foreword to Eulenburg edition No. 719.

festly were not included among the material that André bought from Constanze Nissen in 1799. So we must regard it as one of the greatest pieces of luck in all musical history that the manuscripts of the keyboard concertos which Mozart left fell into the hands of a family who preserved them, acting as faithful trustees of this precious heritage. Who knows how many of Mozart's greatest works would have disappeared and been completely lost to posterity but for the intervention of the André family?[1] Bearing in mind that in so far as the woodwind concertos, the sinfonie concertanti, and the violin concertos were concerned, nothing whatever was published in the composer's lifetime, one sees at once that, except for a few printed pieces, all Mozart's compositions in concerto form could easily have disappeared, if it had not been for this great good fortune. The frivolity with which later publishers have treated this heritage is all the more irresponsible.

If we compare this state of things with that relating to Beethoven's works, or even Haydn's after the 1770s, the striking difference in the contemporary reaction to and estimate of the three masters will be obvious. From the 'Dressler' Variations and the 'Kurfürsten' sonatas of the twelve-year-old Beethoven onwards, almost every work he wrote was printed in his lifetime, the majority of them being published in several or many editions. From the middle of the 1770s onwards the publishers of all countries fought for Haydn's compositions, and today nobody can say exactly how many printed editions were issued during his lifetime. But Mozart's greatest masterpieces remained in manuscript, the concertos as well as the last symphonies, the great operas, and the string quintets. Their fame began to spread only the moment he was dead, a fame, however, which continued right down to the generation of the young romantics, before they became common property. Then, truly, they became the illuminating torch of the romantic age.

[1] The numerous manuscript copies of Mozart's concertos, scattered all over the world, have not been mentioned in this chapter. Their value and the role they have played in the survival of Mozart's concertos are uncertain, and have not yet been investigated. In particular, the question of what contemporary copies exist and on what sources they are based must be subject to further scrutiny.

[*Translated by H. C. Stevens*]

H. C. ROBBINS LANDON

THE CONCERTOS:
(2) THEIR MUSICAL ORIGIN AND
DEVELOPMENT

THE musical atmosphere in which Mozart grew up was perhaps ideal. His father, Leopold, was a composer of far more talent and ability than have hitherto been recognized: we picture him as a rather fussy, humourless pedant who wrote an important violin treatise and occasionally a symphony or two. But Leopold was a good composer, if not a great one; and his music has an innate sense of form, an intuitive feeling for orchestral values and – here and there – the earthy sense of humour we find in some of his letters. He also displays in many of his orchestral works the same love of experimentation that we usually associate with Joseph Haydn. Leopold's symphonies and divertimentos are full of bizarre and delightful instrumental effects: a Symphony in G major (MS. in the Monastery of Lambach) has a part for a solo posthorn; another, the *Sinfonia La caccia* (*Denkmäler der Tonkunst in Bayern*, new edition by the Universal Edition) uses four horns and guns; while yet another hunting piece, the *Sinfonia* in D entitled 'Jagd Parthia' (MS. in Lambach) is scored for two horns and strings, to which is added a 'Cucolo obl:', i.e., a cuckoo obbligato.

In the charming 'Toy' Symphony, hitherto attributed to Joseph Haydn, but which E. F. Schmid[1] has now rightfully ascribed to L. Mozart, we see not only Leopold's sense of humour at its best, but also his deep and abiding affection for the folksongs of his native South German and Austrian countryside. When in Italy, young Wolfgang wrote to his sister (Bologna, 6 October 1770): "I wish I could soon hear the Berchtesgaden [Mozart uses the nickname 'Pertelzkammer'!] symphonies, and perhaps play the little trumpet or fife in one."[2] We can easily

[1] See E. F. Schmid: 'Leopold Mozart und die Kindersinfonie', *Mozart-Jahrbuch*, 1951.

[2] Austrian 'Toy' symphonies were often called 'Sinfonia Berchtesgadensis' or 'Berchtoldsgadensis', after the town of Berchtesgaden, where children's instruments were manufactured.

234

imagine Wolfgang's homesickness when he thought of his
father's setting of the Austro-Bavarian folk-song, 'Mörkts auf ihr
Herrn, i waiss was Neus' (dialect for 'Now listen, you men, and
I'll tell you something new'), which is one of the movements
in the 'Haydn' *Sinfonia Berchtoldsgadensis* (Ex. 1):

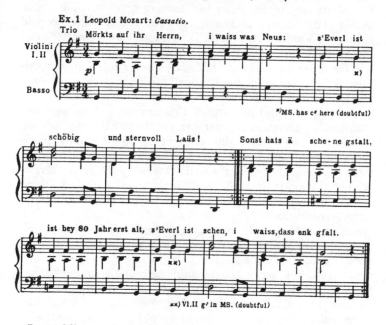

Ex. 1 Leopold Mozart: *Cassatio.*

Leopold's music is an interesting fusion of German and
Austrian elements (it will be recalled that he was a native of
Augsburg): it is not so baroque, nor so stiff, as the Viennese pre-
classical style, and something of the easy grace of neighbouring
Italy may be found in the melodic content and the general texture. But orchestrally Leopold's music is clearly a product of
South Germany, which was dominated by the new technique of
the Mannheim Court Orchestra, led by the Bohemian, Johann
Stamitz. This is not to say that the elder Mozart can be considered an exponent of the Mannheim school – far from it. But
the geographical position of Salzburg was such that Viennese,
Italian, and South German elements could meet and effect
a modest internationality of style. Salzburg, though a provincial court, was certainly more receptive to 'foreign' tastes

than many a larger and more pompous Austrian or German town.

Apart from Leopold Mozart's own music, the young Wolfgang was soon busily studying that of the Viennese and South German schools; his own early copy-books and the archives of the Monastery of St. Peter in Salzburg give us a fair cross-section of the composers then in vogue: the two Haydns, Leopold Hofmann, Vanhal, Wagenseil, Dittersdorf, with a smattering of the North Germans (C. P. E. Bach) and the Mannheimers – this was the music that served as Mozart's first models in composition. A brief survey of the concerto form about the year 1760 may therefore be welcome.

The concerto and its parallel, the concerto grosso, were unquestionably the most popular forms of the late baroque period, i.e., the first half of the eighteenth century. In the years 1740–60 the symphony gradually became the favourite instrumental form (the recently begun thematic catalogue of European symphonies from *c*. 1740 to 1800[1] will include an estimated 15,000 works); but the concerto continued to have a widespread popularity, second, indeed, only to that of the symphony. We find countless works for flute, violin, and harpsichord (or pianoforte), and a goodly number for less popular instruments, such as the oboe, clarinet, bassoon, horn, 'cello, or trumpet. Double and triple concertos became fashionable, especially in the Mannheim school (e.g., Karł Stamitz, 1746–1801, son of the famous Johann: see below), and these works were often called *sinfonie concertanti*. In this way, elements of the old concerto grosso, with its characteristic contrasts of solo and tutti, were gradually absorbed into the concerto, making the hybrid *sinfonia concertante*, and even into the symphony itself (cf. Haydn's Symphonies Nos. 6–8, 31, 36, 72, etc.).[2]

The pre-classical concerto was a fully developed form by the year 1760, four years after Mozart's birth; and we can study its development in numerous works by Mozart's immediate precursors, such as C. P. E. Bach (1714–88), J. C. Bach (1735–82), Carl Ditters von Dittersdorf (1739–99), Gluck (1714–87), Joseph Haydn (1732–1809), Johann Michael Haydn (1737–1806), Leopold Hofmann (*c*. 1730–93), J. J. Quantz (1697–1773), J. S. Schröter (1750–88), J. B. Vanhal (1739–1813),

[1] By Professor Jan La Rue and the author.
[2] cf. *The Concertos* (*1*), p. 209.

G. C. Wagenseil (1715–77), and scores of lesser-known composers. It is, however, precisely this critical transitional period, i.e., the link between the baroque and classical periods, which is very little known today; and the few rays of light cast by the important *Denkmäler* and *Monumenta* publications leave whole schools unexamined, while the selection of a particular composer, such as the Wagenseil works in the *Denkmäler der Tonkunst in Österreich*, often gives a distorted or one-sided picture of his activity. The publication of a whole volume by M. G. Monn (1717–50) lends to this thoroughly minor figure a currency and an importance which he certainly does not deserve, whereas much more characteristic and significant composers, such as Leopold Hofmann, Carlos d'Ordoñez (1734–86), Florian Gassmann (only his operatic compositions have received attention in the Austrian *Denkmäler* edition), and in particular the brilliant and versatile Vanhal, are but names to the average music historian. Study of the history of music has been to a great extent hampered by the method usually chosen: we are taught the development of this art through the greatest figures it has produced; we view its course through a galaxy of brilliant names; and thus we proceed from Palestrina to Bach and Handel, touch lightly on Gluck *en route* to Haydn and Mozart, and arrive, as it were, at the pinnacle of music, i.e., Beethoven. It can hardly be expected that, in these circumstances, the student can, for example, fully grasp the profound change of style which occurred between the baroque period and that style commonly known as the 'Viennese classical'. The chronological proximity of Bach and Handel to Haydn – who wrote his first concertos, mass, string trios, clavier sonatas, and symphonies before Handel's death in 1759 – has led us to overlook the origins of the sweeping change in style which was, to all intents and purposes, established before Haydn began composing.

This fallacious historical approach is, however, limited to the study of music; for it would never occur to a student of pictorial art to make a study of the Italian Renaissance exclusively through Giotto, Masaccio, Michelangelo, Leonardo, and Raphael. And yet this ridiculous limitation is exactly of the kind imposed on musical history. Recently, it is true, a renewed interest in music of the baroque era has led us to re-visit the by-paths of the seventeenth and early eighteenth centuries: not only have great figures of historical importance, such as Schütz and

Monteverdi, been re-examined and re-evaluated, but composers of such originality and beauty as Marc Anton Charpentier, hitherto completely unknown to the general public, have been rediscovered.

But although our modern age has accomplished much in clearing away the mists of ignorance surrounding the development of music in the Middle Ages, the Renaissance, and the baroque, there remains a vast field of activity which has scarcely been touched: the origin and development of the Viennese classical style. Various scholars have attempted to show the bridges between the baroque era and the mature style of Haydn and Mozart: but neither the Viennese scholars' champion, M. G. Monn, nor the Mannheim school, rediscovered by Riemann and offered to the world as the missing pre-classical link, successfully clarifies this important transitional period – the one because he is, when all is said and done, a rather dull figure of minor importance whose compositions are firmly rooted in the scholastic Viennese baroque manner; whilst the Mannheim school, brilliantly founded by Johann Stamitz (1717–57), later became constricted by its self-imposed limitations and degenerated into a vogue, continuing its sheltered existence in a world from which it had gradually become completely isolated.

In the foregoing paragraph we have referred to the origins and *development* of the Viennese classical style. It seems to be firmly entrenched in our textbooks of music history that Haydn and Mozart, with a little assistance from Gluck, established the late eighteenth-century Viennese style. Actually, nothing could be farther from the truth: Viennese classical music was an amalgamation of many forces, and it remained for Haydn and Mozart to raise the existing style to a level of unique perfection. It is, as said above, symptomatic of our faulty musical education that we know very little indeed of Haydn's and Mozart's Austrian contemporaries. Yet these long (and unjustly) forgotten 'smaller masters' played a vital role in the establishment of a musical culture which, if only to judge from the greatest figures it produced, has exerted an influence on the history of music so profound and so lasting that its effect cannot yet be fully measured and appreciated.

The form of the pre-classical concerto was inherited from the baroque era and adapted to the newer style; and the path from J. S. Bach, whose E major violin Concerto clearly foreshadows the motivic technique of sonata form to, say, the Michael Haydn violin Concerto in B flat, written about forty years later (1760), is not so long as one might imagine. It took many years – indeed, until the late Mannheimers and Mozart – before the concerto entirely lost baroque traits of form, melody, and harmony. And the pre-classical concerto is still widely coloured by baroque thought – even Joseph Haydn's works.

The formal construction of the first movement is the most standardized, the least flexible in its basic contours. Expressed in the simplest formula, the average first movement may be outlined as follows:

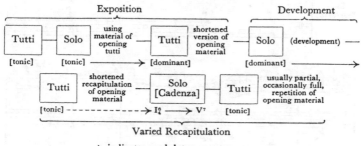

——→ indicates modulatory passage or passages.

As shown by this simplified graph, the material of the first solo is taken from that of the opening tutti: this is a characteristic of almost every pre-classical concerto, extending through all those of Haydn (including the late D major harpsichord Concerto, the 'cello Concerto in D of 1783, and the trumpet Concerto in E flat of 1796); it is important to remember this trait in view of Mozart's later use of the form. In the earlier concertos, i.e., those written before *c.* 1760, the fourth general section (solo in the dominant) is perhaps best described as a 'varied exposition'; there is often no real attempt at working with motives, or any development in the later sense of the word. Figurations, usually in broad sequences, fragments of the main subject in more remote keys, occasional alterations of solo instrument with short tuttis – this is the course of the average pre-classical 'middle section'. Even in Haydn's works it is not until the concertos of the 1780s and 1790s that there is any attempt to fuse the principles of the symphonic and quartet sonata-form with the concerto structure: Haydn's traditionalism and conservatism in

Ex. 2. Johann Michael Haydn: violin Concerto in B flat (completed 20 December 1760) – autograph in the Esterházy Archives, Budapest: first movement, Allegro moderato.

    (a) Conclusion of first tutti.   (b) From the development.

the concerto are the more curious and unexpected in view of his bold experimentation in other forms. The concertos of his brother, many of which were written in or about the year 1760, when he was at Gross-Wardein, are far more interesting, formally and in every other respect. As early as Michael's violin Concerto in B flat (1760) we find a definite – and successful – attempt to develop the material in the fourth section: even when the violin solo appears to be indulging in typical baroque figuration, it will be seen, on closer examination, that (a) the figurations are in fact closely related to material in the exposition and (b) the development is continued in the orchestra part. The parallel to Mozart's technique twenty-five years later is obvious. This example will also serve to illustrate the typical baroque characteristics of this pre-classical concerto language, in which newer rhythmic features (e.g., the figure of bars 2 and 3 in Ex. 2(a)) are superimposed on the elegant sequences so beloved of the older generation.

The slow movements often preserve the same basic structure as that of the first movement: e.g., Joseph Haydn's violin Concerto in A (c. 1765?), organ Concerto in C (1756?); Michael Haydn's violin Concerto in B flat, Double Concerto for viola and organ or harpsichord (1757–61?), flute Concerto in D (c. 1760–70?); several of Leopold Hofmann's harpsichord concertos (MSS. in Westdeutsche Bibliothek, Marburg); and numerous concertos for harpsichord by Wagenseil (MSS. in the Monasteries of Stams in Austria and Metten, Bavaria). But there is generally much more freedom in the second and third movements, formally, melodically, and harmonically. We find in the Adagio of Joseph Haydn's violin Concerto in G (c. 1760?) the following scheme:

Tutti (tonic) – Solo (tonic, same material) —→ dominant (still solo, but alternating with short tuttis – development) —→ cadenza – Concluding tutti.

In other words, there are only two full tuttis, at the beginning and at the end, though the tonal scheme approximates to that of the average first movement. The Adagio of Joseph Haydn's violin Concerto in C (c. 1761?), on the other hand, may be analysed as follows:

Introduction, tonic (solo and tutti).	Arioso, tonic and modulations, leading back to tonic (solo). Short tutti leads to cadenza.	Introduction, tonic (solo and tutti).
A	B	A

The Double Concerto by Michael Haydn, mentioned above, has a beautiful Adagio in which the various solo entrances differ from the usual in that there are two solo instruments, each of which is given its own thematic entrance (i.e., A–A′, etc.). An even more varied formal structure is found, for instance, in J. C. Bach's harpsichord Concerto, Op. VII, No. 5, in E flat (slow movement, marked Andante, in C minor):

> Tutti (tonic) – Solo, same material (tonic) —→ Short tutti, using previous material, relative major leading back to – Solo (same material, tonic), with development (or rather extension), leading to cadenza and final tutti (tonic).

This curious tendency to start the second solo again in the tonic is also found in Joseph Haydn's harpsichord Concerto in G (second movement, Adagio, C major), where one finds the following:

> Tutti (tonic) – Solo (tonic, same material) ending with orch. accompaniment on dominant – Solo (tonic, same material, but again extended), leading to cadenza – Tutti (tonic, shortened).

This A–A′–A″–A‴ form is not, of course, the usual practice; but we encounter it again in Leopold Hofmann and in at least one Dittersdorf violin concerto.

The final movements, as in contemporary symphonies and divertimenti, favour quick time, that is 2/4, 3/8 or barred C; but we also encounter many finales in 6/8, 3/4, and even 9/8 or 12/8. Michael Haydn likes a swift 3/4, e.g., violin Concerto in B flat (1760), or 2/4, e.g., Double Concerto, whereas Joseph's early concerto finales are usually in 3/8. Some of J. C. Bach's concertos close with a 'Tempo di Minuetto' – again a favourite finale for symphonies and chamber works of the pre-classical period. The close relationship between other instrumental forms is also seen in the finale of Joseph Haydn's organ Concerto in C (1756?), where there are actually :||||: as in a quartet, symphony, or divertimento. The form, too, is closely allied to that of the average quartet or symphonic finale:

> Tutti (tonic) – Solo (tonic, same material) —→ Solo and tutti (dominant: new material) :||: Solo (dominant, first

subject) —→ Tutti (tonic, first subject) leading into solo (extension) —→ Bridge tutti leading back to first subject in solo —→ Solo and tutti (the 'new' material at the end of the exposition, now in the tonic).

Excluding the double announcements obliged by concerto form, the structure, with its primitive 'second subject', its rudimentary sonata form-cum-ABA, and the shortened *fausse reprise* at the beginning of the 'development',[1] is typical of Haydn's early symphony and quartet finales. An interesting step forward, structurally and musically, is made by Michael Haydn's flute Concerto in D. Instead of relying on a quick time to produce a 'final' character, Michael has retained the 4/4 metre also used – in a much slower (*Allegro moderato*) tempo – for the opening movement. Michael has used more flexible rhythmic figures and a humorous, light opening theme to differentiate his concluding Allegro assai from the opening movement (Ex. 3). (This same attempt to lighten the melodic content of the finale may be traced in Joseph Haydn's symphonies of the late 1760s and 1770s.) A further innovation is the thematic material given to the flute at its first entrance (Ex. 3(c)): for the first time in any of the concertos hitherto examined, new thematic material is given to the solo instrument at its first solo entry. Michael has, however, kept the structural thread intact by giving the opening material to the accompaniment.

Mozart knew and respected the works of the 'Salzburg' Haydn, and it is entirely possible, even probable, that he heard this very flute Concerto, of which MS. parts are preserved in the Monastery of St. Peter in Salzburg. But the young Mozart's style received an even more powerful impetus from another part of Europe altogether.

We have mentioned one work by J. C. Bach in the course o our analysis. The Mozarts arrived in London in April 1764, and remained there over a year, during which time Wolfgang wrote his first symphonies. The 'English' Bach, gracious, elegant, man-of-the-world, and a highly successful composer, made a strong impression on the young Mozart, musically the strongest of his formative years; and his early symphonies and chamber music written in London and for some time afterwards show

[1] cf. Landon: *The Symphonies of Joseph Haydn*, London, 1955, pp. 197, 206 (*fausse reprise*), and 215.

how deep was the impression that J. C. Bach made. Nor was this influence limited to these childhood years, for traces of Bach's style remained with Mozart throughout his life. The strong opening themes, often dotted, the kind of phrase which is so aptly termed *Redikt* in German (small, symmetrical figures, usually with some characteristic rhythmic or melodic tag), the repeated

Ex. 3 (a) 1st movt./1 Satz: *Allegro moderato*

(b) Finale: *Allegro assai*

(c) *Ibid*.

Ex. 3. Johann Michael Haydn: Concerto for flute and orchestra in D (*c.* 1760–70?)
– MS. parts in the Monastery of Lambach.

(a) First movement: Allegro moderato.   (b) Finale: Allegro assai.   (c) Ibid.

pedal-point quavers in the bass line – all these are stylistic details that became absorbed and assimilated into Mozart's style.
It is no accident that a symphony by Bach's colleague and com-
patriot, C. F. Abel, was long thought to be the work of the
young Mozart (K.18, now K.Anh.109[1]): an authentic symphony (K.132) is built along very similar lines (Ex. 4):

Ex. 4 (a) C.F. Abel, *Sinfonia*, Op. VII, No. 6

(b) Mozart, *Sinfonia*, K. 132

Or one may find the typical opening of a J. C. Bach symphony
in this or that work by Mozart (Ex. 5). If we compare the 'new'
rococo style of J. C. Bach, or Abel, with the rather stiff and old-
fashioned Viennese pre-classical style, it is clear that the new
manner must have momentarily erased everything else from

young Wolfgang's mind: his London sketch-books are filled
with Bachian themes, and his compositions are full of the new

rococo spirit. Johann Christian's symmetrical second subjects,
with the characteristic *a–a′* construction, are models even for
late-period Mozartean thought (Ex. 6).

(second subject repeated by
oboes, horns and viola)

(Just before he left London, or just afterwards, Mozart arranged three of J. C. Bach's sonatas as concertos – K.107(21b).
The concertos K.37, 39, 40, and 41 are now known to be arrangements of sonatas by Raupach, Honauer, Schobert, Eckard, and C. P. E. Bach. Wolfgang chose typical *galant* pieces,
and his modest orchestration – perhaps with Leopold's helping
hand – is deft.)

The three Italian journeys provided the young Mozart with
first-hand experience of Italian opera. The interim Viennese
trips must have introduced him to the new works by Haydn
and Vanhal, but the impressions gained in Italy were at first

stronger: typical Bachian themes are now coloured by the imaginative world of the *opera buffa*. During the early 1770s, however, the influence of Joseph and Michael Haydn again returns: the new string quartet style of Joseph Haydn's Opp. 9, 17, and 20 can be easily traced in the Italian quartets of 1772–3 and, even more, in the Viennese quartets of 1773 (K.168ff.); Michael's orchestral style is clearly felt in the divertimenti and serenades, and the Salzburg church music style practised by Adlgasser, Eberlin, and Michael Haydn himself is strongly reflected in Mozart's church music of this period. The Concertone for solo oboe, two violins, 'cello, and orchestra (K.190(166b)), composed in Salzburg in May 1773, is typical of Mozart's lighter divertimento-serenade technique; and the gentle chromaticism in the theme of the Andante grazioso, which might at first glance be considered wholly Mozartean, is actually a reflection of that found in numerous works by Michael Haydn. The Concertone is a pleasant, gracious work, but only a foolish critic would attempt to find in it many of the elements that constitute Mozart's mature language.

After returning to Salzburg from the unsuccessful Viennese journey of 1773, Mozart wrote his first piano Concerto, K.175 (the earlier works were, as we have seen, arrangements). This is one of the earliest of Mozart's compositions in which there is real originality of thought, and K.175, in the brilliant key of D – with trumpets and drums – is certainly the equal of any pre- or early classical concerto known to us. It is an historic moment: the first of a *genre* in which the composer was to reign supreme, and if K.175 is not a great work, it contains real flashes of genius. The contrapuntal finale, for example, is on a far grander scale than the concerto finales of his precursors; only Vanhal, in his piano Concerto in C (MS. in the Monastery of Schlägl), reaches anything like the brilliance of form and orchestration found in K.175, and Vanhal's concerto is probably later than the year 1773. Mozart's finale, incidentally, seems to have been too severe for his audiences, for when in Vienna, he replaced it with the witty Rondo in D, K.382, which was an immense success and had to be repeated. The sudden flash of inspiration is not limited to K.175, for Mozart wrote two highly original symphonies during this period (end of 1773): K.183 in G minor and the enchanting K.201 in A.

We may pass over the unimportant bassoon Concerto,

K.191(186e), which by no means fulfils the promise of K.175 –
quite the contrary: its charming conventionalities return rather
to the style of the Concertone. In fact, Mozart seems to have
turned his back deliberately on the contrapuntal severity of
K.175, for the ensuing violin concertos (K.207, 211, 216, 218,

Ex. 7. Concerto in D, K.175, Finale

etc. (compare the beginning of Ernst
Eichner's Symphony in G, Op.
VI, No. 4).

219) present an *embarras de richesse*: melody is piled upon melody,
and new ideas succeed each other in blissful insouciance of
each other and of any strict formal pattern. What immediately
captivates the listener is the matchless elegance of conception
and execution, the suavity of orchestration – which even at this
comparatively early stage has that natural brilliance which is
so characteristic of mature Mozart – and the luxurious delight
in pure melody. The form, on the other hand, is perhaps best
described by 'uneconomical'; Mozart cares not the least that,
for instance, the first subject of the opening movement of K.218
never has a chance to appear in the recapitulation. His lovely
themes are seldom discussed.

A major change in Mozart's style begins in the year 1776: the
sudden advent of maturity. In my opinion, the 'Haffner' Serenade (K.250), written in the summer of 1776, is Mozart's first
great orchestral work – that is, the first in which technical ability
and musical genius are perfectly wedded. It still, of course, preserves its serenade character in the two movements for solo
violin (II and IV); but the flanking D major movements and
the minuets are purely symphonic in style. The increasing
orchestral quality of the serenades may be traced through the
magnificent 'Posthorn' Serenade (K.320) through the heroic

windband serenades of the early Viennese years to its final symphonic culmination in the 'Haffner' Symphony (K.385). Those who know the later Mozart will find in K.250 passage after passage in which the music of the Vienna period is presaged: the sudden veil drawn over the music by a harmonic change; the gliding poignancy of chromatic passing notes; the profoundly disturbing emotional quality that underlies so much of the apparently gay atmosphere — all these are marks of Mozart's mature and supremely individualistic style. Something of this broad, majestic style may also be found in the strange 'Credo' Mass (K.257), though a kind of chilling emotional impartiality makes it a less personal experience than the foregoing serenade.

One month after the composition of the mass (December 1776), Mozart wrote the piano Concerto in E flat, K.271, apparently for the French virtuoso, Mademoiselle Jeunehomme, who must have passed through Salzburg at this time. K.271 was preceded by three concertos of the year 1776 (K.238 in B flat, K.242 for three pianos in F, and K.246 in C for the Countess Lützow); in view of their relative unimportance – in a chapter of this length one is forced to be ruthless – we shall concentrate on the E flat major Concerto, with which any discussion of Mozart's great piano concertos must inevitably begin.

The new symphonic style of K.250 is, of course, reflected in the E flat Concerto; but the work is essentially chamber musical rather than orchestral in texture, and even the tuttis have a kind of happy intimacy about them. K.271 is in many ways characteristic of that burst of energy and inspiration which often seems to characterize the first mature works by a great composer. The easy freedom of form, in which a compact unity is produced by a seeming diversity of elements, is also found in the symphonies of Haydn's full maturity (1771–4). Mozart's concerto, like Haydn's Symphonies Nos. 42, 45, or 47, quietly bursts the form which was bequeathed to him by his precursors: for K.271 is indeed far removed from the form and content of the pre-classical concerto.

The most obvious innovation is the entrance of the solo instrument in the second bar; after a short dialogue between piano and orchestra, the real tutti, i.e., without piano, begins. This in itself startling procedure at once sets the stage, first, for the formal freedom which prevails throughout the concerto, and

secondly, for the work's chamber-musical atmosphere: by
breaking the pompous chordal subject, Mozart cleverly disperses
the formal quality inherent in most opening tuttis. He also veils
the division between the opening tutti and what would normally
have been the first solo by having the piano enter with a long
trill in the concluding bars of the tutti; and after four bars of
solo, Mozart promptly returns to a restatement of the very beginning. The listener, however, is in no way aware of any formal
disunity, and this is the secret of a master: to induce symmetry
through disparate elements.

Another important difference between Mozart's form and
that of the pre-classical concerto lies in the numerous themes

that are introduced in the tutti – something we have observed in
the violin concertos. But Mozart takes care that all these themes
– there are six distinctly recognizable in the tutti – shall be used
throughout the movement. Even typically orchestral tutti
figures, such as that of bars 14ff. (Eulenburg, p. 2), turn

into equally typical pianistic and virtuoso-sounding passages (bars 186ff., Eulenburg, p. 20). This constant division of material between solo and orchestra prevails throughout the movement: when Mozart reaches the second tutti (in the dominant), prepared by a full cadence, trill, and crescendo, we are led to think that the tutti, too, will be full scale; but nothing of the sort, for in the middle of the sixth bar (Eulenburg, p. 15) the piano seizes control again. And though the orchestration is modest (two oboes, two horns, strings), the use of the wind instruments in conjunction with the piano is typical of Mozart's orchestration in the 1780s. In the development section there is a beautiful passage lasting some twenty bars in which the oboes and piano are entirely unsupported (bars 160–80, Eulenburg, pp. 17–19). Even the horns have a chance to display their mellowest register: the melody of Ex. 8(a) (exposition) is given to horns and piano in the recapitulation (Ex. 8(b)). We shall point out one further formal detail in this opening movement. The very beginning divided the statement between orchestra and piano, as follows:

> tutti – pianoforte – tutti – pianoforte.

The recapitulation changes this procedure (Eulenburg, p. 21), i.e.:

> pianoforte – tutti – tutti – pianoforte,

and the music is then spun out and varied by the solo instrument.

Taking the first movement as a whole, we find that Mozart has retained only the bare outline of the typical pre-classical form, i.e., an A–B–A structure (exposition–development–recapitulation). Even the customary division – opening tutti, opening solo, second tutti in the dominant, second solo (development), third tutti (beginning of recapitulation), third solo leading to fourth tutti, cadenza (fourth solo), and final (fifth) tutti – is, as we have seen, merged and fused into one unified whole. It is typical that this delightful and inspired Allegro should close with the kind of dialogue between piano and orchestra with which it began; for the concluding tutti returns us to the second opening of the pianoforte (the long trill) in the exposition, and the spirited exchange continues right through the last bar.

The second movement, in C minor, is most remarkable, and like the first it, too, foreshadows the course of Mozart's late-period concertos; for this dark-hued Andantino has its spiritual roots in the opera. One critic not inaptly termed it an aria; but actually it uses elements of the Italian recitative as well (Ex. 9). The use of a mock recitative in a serious, non-operatic form

Ex. 9 *Ibid.*
Andantino

was not unusual in the eighteenth century, and there are instrumental recitatives in Michael Haydn's divertimenti and in Joseph Haydn's Symphony No. 7 ('Le Midi', 1761). But the fusion of opera and concerto in K.271 has perhaps a special significance for Mozart in view of the late piano concertos, such as K.467 or 503, in which are merged elements of the symphony and the opera. There occur other marks of Mozart's late-period style in this slow movement, too, such as the typical accompanimental figure in the left hand of the piano at bars 25ff. (Eulenburg, p. 38), and the intimate, shadowy pianistic figurations such as we will later encounter in the interpolated slow section of the finale of K.482. One charming detail: just before the end, Mozart reintroduces the recitative quoted as Ex. 9, but now given to the piano alone. The melodic line is slightly ornamented, and at the note marked with an arrow in Ex. 9 the piano plays an A flat (marked *fp*) instead of a C; and the final chords are not in unison, but in full harmony with triple notes in the violins. It is characteristic that the ornate and quasi-improvisatory melodic line often given to the piano is supported by the first theme in the orchestra (e.g., Eulenburg, p. 37): there is no longer any question of an accompaniment, but of two partners.

The finale, as Haas points out,[1] seems to race along in a Haydnesque vein; and the second theme (bars 43ff., Eulenburg, p. 55) is really closer to Haydn than to Mozart. The rondo form, which had recently achieved an enormous popularity throughout Europe, is marked by Mozart's gayest and most humorous brilliance. One of the subsidiary sections changes the time from barred C (presto) to a 'Menuetto cantabile' – of

[1] *Mozart*, p. 65.

course, in 3/4; but this minuet is only a minuet in name, for it is extended – formally, harmonically, and melodically – far beyond the usual dance form. The lead-back to the 'A' section, through a free cadenza, has the saucy elegance of a Haydn finale: surprises continue to the very end, e.g., the decrescendo in which the theme stammers to its final rousing cadence.

*   *   *

On his long journey through Germany to Paris and back, Mozart had a renewed opportunity to hear the famous orchestra at Mannheim. We know from his letters how impressed he was by the orchestra (*"sehr gut und starck"*), and we can imagine that *"es lässt sich eine schöne Musick machen"* with what was probably Europe's finest band. In 1777, the school itself, as seen through twentieth-century eyes, was perhaps on the wane (Johann Stamitz, its founder, had died twenty years before); but compared to the provincial Salzburg *Capelle*, Mannheim must have seemed to Mozart as exciting as was London to the old Haydn in 1791. What made the orchestra and its composers unique was not merely the famous crescendo and decrescendo, but the precision, the brilliant instrumental effects which were everyday practice for composer and orchestra, and the rich, sonorous scoring, particularly for woodwind. And if Cannabich, Holzbauer, and Karl Stamitz were not men of genius, they were men of great capability, with whom Mozart soon became – especially in Cannabich's case – quite friendly.

The effects of the Mannheim sojourn are noticeable, not so much in the friendly but rather perfunctory flute Concerto, K.313(285c), that Mozart wrote for the Dutch amateur, De Jean – K.314(285d) is now known to be a transcription[1] – but in the 'Paris' Symphony, K.297(300a), the *Sinfonia Concertante*, K.Anh.9(297b), and the large-scale overture to *Les petits riens*, K.Anh.10(299b) – all of which Mozart wrote in Paris. In fact we know that the symphony was specially fashioned "for these French cattle", i.e., with tongue-in-cheek, but one could regard it as a parody of the grand Mannheim style. The Mannheim sonority in woodwind scoring is clearly reflected in the *Sinfonia Concertante*,[2] written for four members of the Mannheim band who were in Paris at the time. The flute and harp Concerto in C major, K.299(297c), charming though it is, seems rather pale compared (*a*) with the spontaneous brilliance and beauty of the piano Concerto, K.271, and (*b*) with the rich orchestral effects of the three Parisian compositions listed above. Clearly Mozart's heart was not in the commission (the work was written for a highly unsympathetic French aristocrat, the Duc de Guines). What Mozart might have written in the way of a Mannheim-inspired concerto is seen by the forceful, magnificent fragment of a Double Concerto for piano and violin, K.Anh.56(315f).

The return to the hated provincial Salzburg in January 1779 marks the end of Mozart's youthful years; but it also marks the beginning of Mozart's final period of composition, i.e., that lasting from 1779 to 1791. Generally the inception of this period is placed in the earliest Viennese years, but, as I have said in another place,[1] this view seems quite untenable. Naturally the Viennese period can and should be subdivided, especially the first traces of what would have been an entirely new period (*Die Zauberflöte*, clarinet Concerto, 'Ave Verum', last piano Concerto, K.595, etc.). But if we take a broad view, and if we wish to define the point at which Mozart became a great – as opposed to a highly talented – composer, then I think we must begin with the works written in Salzburg during the years 1779 and 1780.

Mozart's concertos pursue the same kind of inner development found in his operas and string quartets (to a lesser extent in such forms as church music, and even symphonies): that is to say, the unbroken thread of development slowly unravels from work to work in the years of his maturity. In tracing this inner development, it is fascinating to observe Mozart's constant assimilation of external stylistic influences. It is characteristic of his quicksilver personality that he immediately and completely associates himself with any new style which happens to please him: when it is Mannheim, we are given a D major Symphony (K.297) which out-Mannheims Karl Stamitz or Holzbauer or Cannabich; when, in Vienna, it is J. S. Bach, Mozart rushes to compose fugue after fugue – many of which, significantly, are left unfinished. But after the initial spurt of association, Mozart then begins the far more important process of sifting, of accepting that which is congenial to his style and rejecting that which is foreign. The immediate Mannheim associations have been discussed above; the real fruit of his German experience, how-

[1] *The Symphonies of Joseph Haydn*, p. 377n.

ever, is seen in the magnificent row of works which Mozart wrote in 1779 and 1780: the 'Coronation' Mass, K.317 – by far the most splendid and integrated mass he had thus far written (Einstein is unquestionably correct in assuming that the organ Sonata, K.329(317a), belongs to K.317); the splendid, mature symphonies, K.318, 319, 338; the utterly symphonic 'Posthorn' Serenade, K.320; the opera *Idomeneo*, for which the composer retained an abiding affection throughout his life; the powerful, sombre 'Munich' Kyrie in D minor, K.341(368a); and the work which is specially significant for our present purposes, the *Sinfonia Concertante* in E flat for violin, viola, and orchestra, K.364(320d).[1] This work is far more representative of the new style than the merry, ebullient Concerto for two pianos in E flat, K.365(316a), and we shall therefore concentrate on the *Sinfonia Concertante*.

That K.364 is obviously a Mannheim-inspired work can be seen in a number of stylistic details. The very beginning, with the strong, dotted rhythm following a semibreve, is the kind of opening gambit we find in Karl Stamitz (Ex. 10), and towards

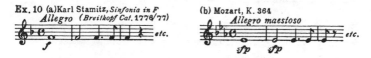

Ex. 10 (a) Karl Stamitz, *Sinfonia in F*
Allegro (*Breitkopf Cat.* 1776/77)

(b) Mozart, K. 364
Allegro maestoso

the end of the opening tutti there is a full-fledged crescendo over a pedal point (bass line, as usual, with repeated quavers), the melodic line rising two octaves to a shout of joy (Eulenburg, pp. 6f.). The lay-out of the orchestra, too, with two ripieno viola parts, points to an increased awareness of Mannheim orchestral sonorities. These are, however, details; for Mozart has now thoroughly digested these features so that the result is quite his own: typical Salzburgian alternations of string and wind instruments (taken from the serenade-cum-divertimento technique) are woven into the rich orchestral texture (Eulenburg, pp. 2f., 5, etc.). What strikes the listener even more than this fabulous sense of instrumental values, however, is the spiritual content of the ensuing C minor Andante. This slow movement is certainly the most personal of the three, with its throbbing, restless tuttis (produced by the Haydnesque use of 'broken melodic lines' in the accompanying viola parts, i.e., ♪♫)[2].

[1] See *The Concertos (1)*, p. 213.   [2] cf. Landon: op. cit., p. 333.

Into this beautiful and moving Andante Mozart also in-
duces broad contrapuntal exchanges between the two solo instruments (cf. especially Eulenburg, pp. 62f.), but naturally
and effortlessly, so that there is never a sense of intruding erudition – something that one does occasionally feel in Michael
Haydn's fugal finales and in Mozart's own church music.

One further detail will illustrate Mozart's spiritual growth.
We have mentioned the interjection of oboe and horn calls in
the opening Allegro, which, it was said, were derived from the
Salzburgian serenade technique. These little *Redikte*, with their
a–a', form, also serve to connect the first with the last movement
– unconsciously, perhaps, but Mozart's sense of unity is very
often implied rather than outspoken:

Ex. 11 K.364.

(a) Allegro maestoso (first movement).   (b) Presto (finale).

The underlying connection, however, is clear enough.

*   *   *

With his permanent residence in Vienna begins the series
of seventeen piano concertos in which Mozart soon reached
consummate mastery: he wrote three in the years 1782–3
(K.413, 414, 415), six in the year 1784 (K.449, 450, 451,
453, 456, 459), three in 1785 (K.466, 467, 482), three in
1786 (K.488, 491, 503), and the last two in 1788 (K.537) and
1791 (K.595).

It is not exceptional for an eighteenth-century composer to
write this great number of works in such a short space of time
(fifteen were written within five years, after which the continuity is broken); but, apart from Haydn's quartets, masses, and
symphonies, no late eighteenth-century composer displays the

steadily increasing awareness of the possibilities inherent in one single form that one finds in Mozart's Viennese piano concertos. A curious lack of serious musical criticism on the one hand and – especially in recent years – a blind adoration of everything he wrote, even in earlier years, on the other, have prevented a true appreciation of the unique qualities of Mozart's mature compositions. The layman is led to believe that all of Mozart is somehow divine and above any criticism, and with this unrealistic approach he cannot (or, if one will, dare not) differentiate between what is beautiful and what is sublime, between what is good Mozart and what is great Mozart. The pity of this uncritical attitude is that Mozart's real achievements – far greater than many of his most ardent admirers realize – are simply taken for granted. Nor is it a service to Mozart to establish his greatness by comparing him with J. C. Bach, Holzbauer, or Haydn. Composer A is never a genius because composer B is not, and Mozart's operas are not great operas because Haydn's are less great.

Mozart owes his unquestionable supremacy in the concerto to a number of reasons. In the first place his mature concertos, with a very few exceptions, are not primarily vehicles for the virtuoso, but a miraculous fusion of the symphonic and concerto forms, and are not, therefore, concertos in the pre-classical sense at all. Another reason, in part arising from the symphonic nature of the works, is the new kind of orchestration that Mozart developed, in which the orchestra is not a mere accompaniment, but a vitally important colouristic, formal, and melodic factor throughout. The main innovation is, of course, the use of the wind instruments; and how new this woodwind colouring must have seemed to the average eighteenth-century musician is clearly seen in Leopold's reaction. Wolfgang played "a wonderful concerto which he wrote for [Maria Theresia] Paradis . . ." – Jahn[1] thinks it was K.456 – and Leopold reports to Salzburg that he was so overcome by the "great pleasure of hearing the interplay of the instruments so clearly that tears came into my eyes for sheer delight". Mozart's freedom of form – in which only the bare outlines of the old concerto are preserved – is another important factor in these late works; but the freedom is not casual or experimental, as it was in the earlier period (e.g., K.271), and Mozart's rigorous self-discipline is nowhere more

[1] *Mozart*, III, p. 208.

admirable than in the formal construction of his late piano concertos. True freedom in any great work of music is almost always the result of arduous labour, and of all the Mozart myths none is more false than the suggestion that these works were dashed down without effort. The extant sketches to K.503 and those to the six quartets dedicated to Haydn show that Mozart's inspiration at its freest and most unfettered was produced by hours of iron-willed concentration. It goes without saying that these concertos are distinguished by extreme variety of emotional content: no one work is really like the other, and even the concertos in C major (Haydn's and Mozart's principal key of festivity and pomp), though all three (K.415, 467, 503) may at first appear similar in thought, are quite different from each other in all the important essentials. And, finally, these works are of vital importance as regards the treatment of the pianoforte; they establish the technique fitted for the new instrument, and with them the last traces of the older harpsichord writing disappear. We shall now take up these various features separately and attempt to illustrate the general points by specific references; and in order that the reader may follow these points throughout one movement, we shall analyse the opening Allegro of K.503, which may be considered the culmination and synthesis of Mozart's mature treatment of the concerto form.

In the course of tracing the various influences which played a major part in forming Mozart's mature style, two stand out at the beginning of his sojourn in Vienna. The first is the direct contact with the music of J. S. Bach and Handel which Mozart gained at the house of Gottfried van Swieten. The second, and essentially far more important, is his relationship, musical and personal, with Joseph Haydn. The two composers, though born nearly a quarter of a century apart, became close friends, but what is more important, they exerted a profound influence on each other's styles. Space prohibits a complete analysis of this mutual exchange of ideas, and for our purposes it must suffice to show the effect of Haydn's symphonic style on the form and content of Mozart's late concertos.

Haydn has often been called the father of the symphony. We now know that this is not true in the strict sense; but the more we study the work of the pre-classical symphonists, German and otherwise, the more it becomes clear that Haydn was, more than any other, responsible for the spiritual development of the sym-

phonic form. His symphonies of the years 1771–4 brought the
form to a new level of formal and emotional mastery; his en-
largement of the development section, his increasing sense of the
drama inherent in the beautiful symmetry of sonata form, his
steadfast principle of unity through small motivic fragments,
and his constant use of contrapuntal devices to ennoble the
forms bequeathed to him by his predecessors – all these factors
impressed the young Mozart profoundly. Mozart, like Haydn,
was far too individual a composer to attempt any slavish imitation of his older friend, and the finale of the piano Concerto in
D, K.451, must have convinced Mozart once and for all that
any imitation remains at best an imitation; for in this movement
there is too much Haydn, and not enough Mozart. But the assimilation followed rapidly and if, as we shall see in our analysis,
K.503 perhaps represents this fusion at its most brilliant, all the
concertos of 1785 and 1786 show the various ways in which
Mozart applied the new symphonic structure to that of the concerto, although the developmental tension is less in K.482 and
488 than in K.466, 467, 491, and 503. Thematic concentration
according to Haydn's principle is perhaps most apparent in
K.466, where the first motive is treated in various ways throughout the movement. The sullen, ominous opening becomes by
turns angry and dramatic (as in the first forte) or passionate and
almost hysterically gay (as in the F major tutti – Eulenburg, pp.
21f.), but it always returns, giving to the whole Allegro a sombre
unity. An even more monothematic stamp is impressed on the
first movement of K.467: here not only the principle but also
the execution are Haydnesque, and it is indeed a testimony to
Mozart's uncanny ability to assimilate the essence of a style that
this Allegro is wholly Mozartean in sound from beginning to
end. The march-like theme, announced piano and in unison, is
the bass of the first forte (a similar procedure is found in K.491):
no sooner does Mozart reach the next piano (Eulenburg, p. 4),
than the theme turns up in four-part fugato, which continues into
the next forte; and after an episodic exchange between woodwind and strings it reappears, again forte, as the tail-piece of the
tutti; whereupon the entrance of the pianoforte, after a few bars
of introduction, leads to a varied repetition of the main announcement. This continual return to one basic idea may be
traced throughout the movement. It is quite obvious, if one has
studied Mozart's creative output up to this point (1785), that

such a monothematic structure is the direct result of the composer's study of Haydn's methods. Indeed, the broad scale of the initial tutti in the earlier Viennese Concerto in C (K.415), with its sweeping imitations and rich, symphonic scoring, is clearly traceable to the C major pageantry of Haydn (which Mozart had already adopted in his Symphony in C, K.338). But whereas the grand manner is by and large limited to the tuttis of K.415, Mozart distributes the pageantry more evenly in K.467. It is typical of the C major concertos that the entrance of the pianoforte should be indirect; in his martial, brilliant C major style Mozart decentralizes the power of the tutti by slightly blurring its formal outlines, lest there be – as there was in K.415 – too much dynamic and colouristic difference between tutti and solo. And thus he takes Haydn's idea and reshapes it to suit his new purpose.

The orchestration of these concertos is a continual joy. It is a strange and quite inexplicable phenomenon that Mozart is seldom quoted in textbooks on orchestration; this, however, is simply due to the fact that his feeling for instrumental colour is so natural and so fundamentally artistic that it seldom intrudes on the senses. But this is, of course, the very mark of a great orchestrator: that one should never hear the scoring as scoring. Mozart is a far greater orchestrator than Beethoven, and it is quite typical of our dull textbook writers that they search through pages and pages of Beethoven to find, for example, stopped notes in the horn, when Mozart's mature music is full of altered horn harmonics (an astounding passage is in the first movement of the 'Prague' Symphony), which, however, are so natural in their context that they slide imperceptibly past the listener. Every one of the great concertos contains passage after passage of the most exquisite scoring. His treatment of the violas, often divided, is always fascinating. (In this respect his middle voices are richer and more varied than are Haydn's of the same period). But it is above all his treatment of the woodwind which calls for special attention. This, again, is another feature adopted from Haydn, who retained a particular affection for the woodwind throughout his life. Mozart's colouring is, however, entirely personal. If one compares the equally ravishing use of the woodwind in the slow movement from Haydn's 'Oxford' Symphony (No. 92), or in the Andante from Symphony No. 84, with bars 65–92 of the Andante in K.482 (Eulenburg, pp. 49–51) – to choose an example at random – the difference in sound is quite clear. Typically Mozartean is the broken arpeggio technique of the second clarinet; and, indeed, the use of the clarinet is in itself Mozartean; the deep affection that he had for this instrument and the basset horn, its deeper-voiced second cousin, is transferred to the oboe and the English horn in Haydn. What is absolutely unique in all these Mozart concertos is the combination of pianoforte and solo woodwind, which one finds in every work except K.449, the only one of the seventeen mature concertos in which the wind instruments are dispensable (Mozart said that the work "can be performed *a quattro*", without them). Examples are too frequent and too obvious to necessitate quotation.

One of the most interesting features of Mozart's instrumentation is the association of tonality and orchestration. The fact that clarinets first appear in the E flat Concerto, K.482, is no accident; there were C clarinets (Haydn used them throughout his late Notturni for the King of Naples), and Mozart could have used them in K.467. But they were reserved for this E flat work, and through their presence the entire orchestral colouring is different. The oboes are dropped, and K.482 has a mellow warmth, a lingering, sensuous loveliness, which we have not yet encountered (for a typical passage, see bars 12ff.). The soft orchestral sheen is partly the result of the key itself: the natural brilliance of the strings is much reduced in flat keys, and the wind instruments, trumpets, and drums included, are richer and more mellow in E flat than, for instance, in D or C major. For sheer beauty of sound no Mozart concerto approaches K.482. Clarinets are also retained in the next work, K.488 in A major, but they are now, of course, A clarinets rather than B flat. Mozart renounces the delight in pure orchestral sound, and the key of A major, combined with the scoring of K.482 without trumpets and drums, is now made to serve the most poetic and delicate of all the concertos written thus far. The woodwind (without the direct sound of the oboes) are now ethereal and occasionally even oblique in sound: there is a delicate fastidiousness, even in the tuttis, far removed from the luxurious delight of K.482. From K.488 to 503 is an equally profound metamorphosis, for K.503, with its solemn, towering grandeur, is neither sensuous, like K.482, nor poetic and chamber-musical, like K.488. The wind instruments in K.503 are again made to serve Mozart's new mood: oboes return, to replace clarinets; the trumpets and drums, now in their most majestic and martial key, contribute to the clear, glittering texture. The whole wind section has that peculiar impersonality so characteristic of its use in C major; but this is what Mozart wants, for the vast formal proportions must not be obscured by any orchestral distractions, and the orchestra must serve, first and foremost, to underline and support the basic structure.

Formally, the first movements follow the general outline of five tuttis and, counting the cadenza, four solos. Mozart solves the tremendous structural problem of combining the concerto and sonata (symphonic) form in a number of ways. He generally retains the tonic throughout the opening tutti (K.413 and 449 have subsidiary themes in the dominant, and in K.503 the tertian[1] modulations that occur later in the movement are presaged by the modulation C minor $\rightarrow$ E flat in the ritornello). Usually there is one large-scale opening theme and a cluster of secondary themes in this opening tutti, but we have also seen that K.467 is to all intents entirely monothematic. After 1784, it is rare that the soloist begins with the main subject, in pre-classical tradition, as, for instance, obtains in K.413, 449, 453, 459, 488, and 595 (K.413, 449, and 595 embellished). But it can happen that the material first given to the pianoforte is entirely episodic and improvisational in character, acting as a kind of prelude to the return announcement of the main theme (e.g., K.450, 467, and – with a particularly long procrastination – in 503). Mozart likes to place the opening subject of the tutti side by side with that of the soloist – a continual juxtaposition of ideas: occasionally the contrast is also enlivened by f and p, as in K.482; more often soloist and tutti join forces after the tutti has once intruded (K.466, 491), e.g.:

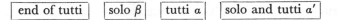

In the earlier works the fusion is less subtly accomplished: neither tutti nor solo of K.415 shares a common first or second subject; in K.451 the contrapuntal (canonic) material of the ritornello remains in the orchestra.

The second subject of the solo (not, as we have seen, neces-

---

[1] This word is an attempt to translate the important German word, *Terzverwandtschaft*, i.e., mediant or submediant relationships.

sarily the same as that of the tutti) is almost invariably in the dominant, but sometimes in the dominant minor (e.g., K.467, 482, 595), a feature which may derive from the pre-classical symphonic form, where the second subject was usually in that key (cf. Haydn's Symphonies Nos. 1, 2, 4, 10, etc.). The form of the double exposition, then, may be shown as follows:

Tutti: first subject (I), 2nd subject or subject group (I)

Solo: first subject (I) → 2nd subject or subjects (e.g., K.537) (V)

Tutti (usually with some fragment or fragments of initial tutti) (V)

The development is symphonic in nature and concerto-like in execution. It often happens that the development occurs in the orchestra, the soloist dancing about the principal idea in runs, arpeggios, broken figurations, and the like: K.491 is typical of this procedure. In K.466 the dualism between the tutti's first subject and that of the soloist is preserved, so that the development proceeds in a constant *a–b*, *a′–b′*, etc. The leads-back are, like all Mozart's leads-back, of special interest, and often of great poignancy. If the principal tutti theme is piano, the lead-back is gentle and the recapitulation often comes as a happy surprise. In K.467 the transition back to the reprise is of particular beauty, a long pedal on V supporting chromatic arabesques in the solo and sustained woodwind which seem to float down and alight on the tonic (Eulenburg, pp. 32f.). How graceful and expert is Mozart's orchestration here: the whole is held in piano, but the sound is full and the motion is constant, both in the strings with their ♪♫ and in the pianoforte's semi-quavers; the trumpets and drums also provide a subtle forward push by accenting half (trumpets) and whole bars (drums), so that the pedal point, in the horns and lower strings, will not be static. Suddenly everything drops away except the unison strings, again marked *p* – one of those dynamic marks, so frequently found in Haydn and Mozart, which are for the players and might foolishly be thought superfluous by a score-reader: the recapitulation is at hand. If the principal subject of the tutti is forte, the lead-back will be dramatic, so that the recapitulation arrives like a conqueror: K.503 is perhaps the finest example of this method.

The recapitulations are always varied, and usually shortened; here different solo and tutti themes will be combined, or the one omitted. The initial tutti will perhaps be split up into various sections and a certain amount of continued development may be found. Unlike Mozart's (and Haydn's) symphonies, the *fausse reprise* is banned from the concerto form; but if we cannot have that, we can have tonal surprises which even give the impression of a false *fausse reprise*, i.e., what appears to be a sham recapitulation is actually the real one. A famous example is the first movement of Haydn's Symphony No. 45; another is the Concerto, K.467, in which the grand tutti leads abruptly into F major, and to a new dialogue between soloist and orchestra (Eulenburg, pp. 35f.); not until the piano has finished a long run and has settled on the dominant seventh of C (bar 309) do we know that this is, after all, the real recapitulation.

The conclusions are often piano rather than forte (K.466, 467, 488, 491, 595), majestic in K.467, whimsical in K.488 and 595, and profoundly pessimistic in the two concertos in minor keys; in K.491 the pianoforte suddenly joins the orchestra in the final bars, to weave a series of shadowy arpeggios over the long tonic pedal point, while the orchestra continues its ghostly thematic allusions to the main theme.

In order that the reader may follow Mozart's new sonata-concerto form throughout the course of a movement, we have selected the Allegro maestoso of K.503 for a short analysis; musical examples have been reduced to the minimum, since it is assumed that our comments will be followed with the aid of an Eulenburg miniature score.

The immediate reaction to my choice of K.503 will probably be the assertion that this is the least popular of all the late piano concertos. Nevertheless, it seems to me that this Allegro represents the most perfect example of Mozart's fusion of the concerto with Haydn's principles of thematic and motivic work; and as such it is no accident that the developmental features of 1782–6 achieve their culmination and synthesis in this work, and also that it marks the end of the series (K.537 and 595 do not continue the present train of thought). In other words, I believe that in K.503 Mozart reached the ideal he had so long striven after. Its present lack of popularity is probably a reflection of its reception at the first performance in Vienna in December 1786 or early in 1787; for there is no indication that the Viennese, apart from a Haydn or a van Swieten, had any notion of Mozart's real stature. The intellectuality, the brilliance of form, and the complete negation of any deliberate virtuoso elements in K.503 left – and will always leave – the Philistines of the eighteenth, nineteenth, and twentieth centuries cold. There is, I think, a definite parallel between K.503 and *Così fan tutte*, the stage work in which Mozart most brilliantly and perfectly solved the structural, dramatic, and musical problems which had occupied so much of his best operatic efforts. Of course, *Figaro* and *Don Giovanni* will always put *Così* in the shade; but *Così* is nevertheless the synthesis, the summing-up of Mozart's approach to the Italian opera. And the one man who, of all the Viennese, really understood Mozart as an equal could be seen every morning in January 1790 walking arm-in-arm with Mozart to the rehearsals of *Così* – Joseph Haydn.

K.503 contains the essence of Mozart's approach to the sonata form: unity within diversity. Every great sonata movement he wrote – offhand, I cannot remember a single exception – contains this Mozartean postulate. Here the single unifying feature of the whole movement is, in typically Haydnesque fashion, a tiny motive which is at times treated purely rhythmically, at times melodically and rhythmically. The motive is first found in bars 18–19, where its resolution is upwards in the first violin, downwards in the second:

The germ of this figure turns out to be not only ♪♩♩, but also ♪♩, as we shall see in the course of the movement.

Now Mozart, like all great composers, has an impeccable sense for presenting his material at the right time; and the right time to announce this leading motive was not, in his eyes, at the beginning, *à la* Beethoven's Fifth, but after a splendid introduction, which sets the tone of the whole concerto. This opening section is also symmetrical, two forte chordal fanfares separated by a little *Redikt* in the bassoons and oboes (bars 7–8, etc.): the

introduction is therefore a kind of *a–b*, *a'–b'* entity in itself.
But because we are dealing with Mozart, the symmetry is not
mere repetition; and, like the twin towers of a Gothic façade,
if one looks very carefully one sees that the two sides, in this case
b and *b'*, are not quite identical, the position of the oboes and
bassoons being reversed. Tonally, too, all is not straightforward
C major, as it seldom is in great Mozart, and the little *Redikt* is
repeated in C minor, which leads us to Ex. 12. Before leaving
these opening bars, one should notice the dotted figure of the
timpani in 4 and 12. This ♩ ♫♩ ♩ figure is as Mozartean as his
chromaticism, and one encounters this rhythm in the brass and
drum parts – and often in all the instruments – of almost every
mature orchestral work (e.g., in Symphonies K.338, 385, 425,
and throughout the last four, but especially in K.551; cf. also
K.459, 467, 482, 537, etc.). Mozart uses this little figure as a
unifying factor in broad tuttis, a kind of reminder of his personality; and thus we find it at key places in K.503's Allegro,
e.g., bars 29–31 (Eulenburg, pp. 3f.), 43 (Eulenburg, p. 5), 74
and 80 (Eulenburg, pp. 8, 9), and so on. At the crucial tutti before the cadenza – almost always a point where earlier rhythms
are intensified – the motive is accelerated by adding repeated
quavers (bars 404ff.: Eulenburg, pp. 47f.), whereby it contributes to the forward urgency which comes to a rest (but not a
close) on the usual 6/4 chord.

The opening bars of K.503 are, taken as a whole, rather static,
as befits their introductory, mood-setting character; with the
advent of Ex. 12 we are whirled away in a constantly moving
rush of energy which prevails for some thirty bars. And whereas
the beginning was a straightforward chordal alternation of I and
V (or rather V⁷), the ensuing passage sweeps along in six or
seven parts and the harmonic texture changes from crotchet to
crotchet until the forte at bar 26. The definite tertian trend from
C minor to E flat lays the ground for the later mediant relationships. This whole second section is driven by the motive of Ex.
12; in the forte it is given to the bass line with running scales in
the violins as accompaniment, and after six bars we see that
Mozart has written in double counterpoint at the octave, for
the position of the violins and bass is reversed (Ex. 13).

The canonic disposition of this motive in Ex. 12 is preserved in
the extension of Ex. 13, and Mozart's contrapuntal fabric has
thickened still more: the rhythm of Ex. 12, altered to ♩ ♪♪♪♩♩ ,

is treated canonically between trumpets and horns (flute supporting the latter two octaves higher) and simultaneously with an octave skip between the violins and bass, while the middle

Ex.18

strings continue the development of Ex. 12. By this time we are thoroughly in the dominant, and remain there, pursued and driven by the leading motive, until a final cadence in G. Between the cadence and the second theme our leading rhythm appears in its altered form, ♪♫ ♩ ; and with this motive, thundered out in unison, we reach the second theme. But Mozart cannot escape the fascination and the power of this rhythm, and so we are hardly surprised to find that the second subject is ushered in by the three-quaver upbeat.

The second subject is in the tonic minor, and again, as in bars 17ff., we proceed from C minor to E flat; but here, the mediant is not merely suggested, as it was then, but firmly entered. The theme is then repeated by the whole wind choir and timpani in C major, giving it a kind of magic, diffused radiance. The three-quaver upbeat and its derivatives gradually come more and more into the foreground, terminating in the 'codetta', which interverts Ex. 12, and then rises in a short crescendo to a swift cadence. Now, we think, the pianoforte will enter, especially after three crotchets of silence. But Mozart is wiser and more subtle, and just as he has taken care to diffuse the strident power of C major by episodes in related major and minor keys, so now he blurs the sharp division between tutti and solo in a stroke of miraculous beauty (Ex. 14).

The second exposition does not begin until after the pianoforte has finished a little cadenza of its own. This interlude has a definite structural and colouristic purpose, i.e., to provide a

breathing spell before the opening tutti is again introduced.
Because of this episodic material, the opening again strikes
us with full force; Mozart, with his usual sense of proportion,
brings in the *forte* just once, in the tonic, leaving the corresponding answer *piano*, divided between soloist and orchestra (Eulenburg, p. 13). The previous static majesty of the *piano* interludes,

with their woodwind exchanges, is now rendered plastic by the
rippling downward semiquavers of the pianoforte; and throughout the repetition of the passage beginning with Ex. 12, the
right hand of the piano keeps up a constant run of these dancing
semiquavers.

The tertian modulations, pointed out above, were the logical
tonal progression from tonic minor to relative major. The
second subject now presents this mediant relationship in a new
guise: from a half-close on the dominant of C minor the pianoforte slides into E flat. The subsidiary themes of this second
exposition also provide an ideal illustration of unity within di-

versity. Diversity is achieved by the fact that the two themes of this second subject (bars 148ff. and 170ff., Eulenburg, pp. 17, 19) present new material; and the introduction of E flat is a clear attempt to provide tonal diversity. Unity is accomplished by the ever-present three-quaver upbeat, which appears in the middle of the E flat theme and at the end of the second, G major theme (cf. bars 187ff.). The concluding tutti of the exposition returns to Ex. 13, and the whole lasts only fifteen bars.

The development concentrates on the second theme of the tutti exposition, to which, however, is added the derivative of the three-quaver figure by way of a bridge. Further unity is produced by continual recourse to mediant modulations, which are pivoted by the three-quaver plus crotchet. Bars 228ff. modulate from G to E minor by the pivotal notes of b (III of G = V of E minor), and bars 250ff. from A minor to F major by the pivotal note of c (III of A minor = V of F): in the latter the transition is made by horns, trumpets, and drums, *piano*, to which the woodwind are added (Eulenburg, p. 28). The contrapuntal nature of the whole ritornello now directs the development, in which the first eight notes of the second subject are extracted and used canonically in the Haydn manner (one immediately thinks of the development in Symphony No. 104, written in 1795; but there are many examples in the earlier symphonies). The lead-back to the recapitulation, prepared harmonically and dramatically by a long dominant pedal (Eulenburg, pp. 33f.), is one of the most dramatic in all Mozart's piano concertos: the piano rushes down in broken octaves from its highest to its lowest register and the reprise crashes forth in all its brazen majesty.

With the score at hand, the reader will perhaps have learned something of the musical character of an opening concerto movement by Mozart. Our sketchy analysis is not, of course, in any way complete, and there is much that has been left for the reader to discover and explore for himself; but it is hoped that, through our brief introduction, he may – if he did not know K.503 – have sensed something of the grandeur, the matchless combination of contrapuntal, sonata, and concerto elements, and the exquisite structural proportions of one of Mozart's finest creations.

The slow movements, unlike the first, are not bound to any particular form, and we find A–B–As (with the usual alterations for concerto structure), two- and three-part 'reprise' forms, variations (e.g., K.482) and various kinds of rondos (e.g., K.466, 491) and da capos (e.g., K.488, 537, 595). The 'romance', usually a kind of rondo (K.466), is the vehicle for tender, reflective lyricism. The pianoforte writing varies from the richest part writing (e.g., the lush bass octaves at the beginning of K.414's Andante – cf. Ex. 17) to the simplest melodic lines, often with bare notes in the left hand (e.g., K.466, bars 40ff.; 491, bars 9ff.; 537, bars 44ff.). These passages of extreme melodic simplicity are really no more than sketched in the piano part, and it is obvious that Mozart filled in some of the bare harmonies with chords in the left hand, if, indeed, he did not ornament and embellish the melody itself. The execution of such 'sketches' presents an almost insuperable performance problem; a gifted pianist will know when such filling-in is necessary (so much depends on the circumstances), but any attempt to write down such improvisations usually ends in disaster.

The variety of fantasy found in these slow movements is astonishing. The deceptive simplicity of the romances in K.466 and 491 (strictly speaking, only the latter is so entitled) is balanced by the profoundly disturbing Andante in K.467: disturbing, too, because of the pulsating triplet quavers which are ever-present in the accompaniment, and also because of the dark, glowing chromaticism which creeps even into the first tutti. The liquid texture, with the subdued insistence of the full wind band (minus trumpets and drums), only makes the constant vacillation between major and minor more immediate (bars 10ff.; Eulenburg, p. 53). Seldom has Mozart presented a more complicated emotional pattern: yet the music seldom rises above the piano level, and the strong, conflicting currents are hidden far under the gently ebbing and flowing surface. It is the one movement in which the orchestra plays throughout; and, of course, there can be no cadenza, no interruption of this vast musical arch. Indeed, after the initial tutti the pianoforte is never silent for more than two bars, so closely woven is Mozart's orchestral fabric. This is the slow movement, above all others, that shows the symphonic – or, if one will, the purely musical – character of Mozart's late concertos: the soloist, while still a soloist, is not allowed one bar of virtuosity, nor a single note which does not contribute to the general form. Mozart's concertos are no longer mere concertos, but pure music, in which the soloist is but one of the many executants.

The rondo is the favourite form of the finales, and only a handful uses another form. K.413 derives from the J. C. Bach 'Tempo di Minuetto' finale. K.453 and 491 have variations in an allegretto tempo and, like Haydn's earlier slow variation finales (Symphonies Nos. 31 and 72), the tempo is accelerated at the end. K.453 is even marked 'Presto' and, as in Haydn's two symphonies, new melodic material of a strong folk-song character is introduced (Eulenburg, p. 79). Mozart, following Haydn, was struggling with the problem of how to raise the musical level of the finale to that of the first movement without destroying its basic 'final' character. K.449 is perhaps the first example of this struggle, and, as we might expect, it attempts to use the broad sonata structure of the first movement; contrapuntal extension is used on a wide scale, including a kind of stretto at the end (cf. also the conclusion of K.466). Following Haydn's example (Symphony No. 67), Mozart introduces an entire slow movement into the finale, as in K.415 and 482; in others we find clear traces of Haydn's brilliant invention, the sonata-rondo, in which A–B–A–C–A is superimposed on the sonata, the 'C' section becoming the development. In K.459 the merry little theme is balanced by a second thought (Eulenburg, p. 76) which is wholly fugal; and at bars 289ff. (Eulenburg, p. 95) the main theme and this second thought are combined in a brisk double fugue. Strong development sections are also found in K.466 and 488. The latter is one of the finest of the sonata-rondo movements; so closely does Mozart follow Haydn's pattern that the development section in K.488 is launched, as it nearly always is in Haydn's sonata rondos, by first returning to the tonic (Eulenburg, p. 71), by which the tonal concept of the rondo is preserved.

As in the slow movements, the pianoforte often begins the finales either alone (e.g., K.459, 466, 488, 537, 595) or with light orchestral support (e.g., K.450, 482). The melodies are often simple folk-tunes, which are, however, never *ordinaire*. The care that Mozart lavished on them is seen in the finale of K.503, originally a melody from the ballet music to *Idomeneo* (K.367);[1] the subtle adaptation of this simple theme for the purposes of K.503 is typical of Mozart's sense of presenting the right material in the right place. The 6/8 finale of K.482 has a definite relationship to the melodies of the horn Concertos in E flat, K.447

[1] For a penetrating analysis of the different techniques, see Hans Keller's comments in *Music Review*, XIV/2/1953, pp. 155–7.

and 495, also in the same metre; but K.482's treatment is far
more symphonic, and the light, dancing quality of the Allegro
is, as we have seen, set off by a slow middle section in the
subdominant (*Andantino cantabile*). Such a serious interruption
would be out of place in the friendly rondos that Mozart wrote
for the cheesemonger-hornist, Leutgeb.

Mozart's concertos are also of great historical importance in
the development of the piano. The gradual transition from

harpsichord to pianoforte is reflected on the contemporary title-
pages, where one almost invariably finds the note "*Pour le
Clavecin ou Forte-Piano*". This casual attitude was usually the
publisher's, not the composer's, and Haydn's sonatas, as early as
1771 (No. 20 in C minor), showed that he wrote with the piano

and not the clavicembalo in mind, although the latter is speci-
fied. It is, therefore, hardly surprising to find that Mozart calls
the instrument used for all his mature concertos a clavicembalo. But the technique is far removed from that of the harpsichord, with its percussive brilliance. What sounded piquant and
highly rhythmic on the cembalo (Ex. 15: Haydn's Concerto in
D, Artaria, 1784) did not sound attractive on the pianoforte,
and Mozart soon introduced his own special legato technique

(Ex. 16: Mozart's Concerto, K.482). The difference is especially noticeable in the treatment of the left hand; this particular disposition of the Alberti bass is highly Mozartean, and one finds it in almost every movement.

The long-sustained notes in Mozart's slow movements also reflect this new pianistic technique, and the Larghetto from K.595 or the Andante from K.414 are quite unthinkable on the harpsichord (Ex. 17); the octaves in the left hand, in themselves, are pianistic and not cembalistic, and the tender lyricism is clearly born of the beaten, not the plucked string:

The authentic cadenzas which are extant (and recently some new and in all probability genuine cadenzas have been discovered in contemporary MSS. in the Monastery of Melk) are the only places where Mozart indulges in any virtuosity *per se*; and even here musicianship triumphs over any technical display. The development of the new pianoforte technique is especially apparent here; for a typical case in point, the reader is referred to the cadenzas to K.453, reprinted in the Appendix to the Eulenburg score (pp. 97ff.). How utterly pianistic is the part writing; but the second cadenza to the slow movement (Eulenburg, p. 102) reveals a particular understanding of the new instrument's capabilities which it would be hard to find in any contemporary piano concerto (e.g., the writing in bar 2, the pearly runs in bar 6, and the octave writing in the right hand just before the closing trill).

The late piano concertos are too well known to require any general description of their various beauties. The extraordinary K.466 in D minor and 491 in C minor were the favourites of the romantic era, for obvious reasons: their passionate subjectivism and the wild *Sturm und Drang* that sinks to supreme depths of despair appealed strongly to the generation dazzled by Beethoven's gigantic art. The D minor "commands an historical key position", says Blume:[1]

"In the history of the species it indicates the moment in which the decisive turn to the 'modern' concerto takes place: under the influence of C. P. E. Bach's concertos and Haydn's symphonies, the piano concerto [is] . . . led into a path . . . which Beethoven then traverses and which, through the romantic epoch, leads directly to our times. In the history of musical sociology the D minor Concerto represents . . . the spontaneous will to [the] expression of artistic individuality . . . all conventionalities, already repressed [in the earlier works], disappear [to] make room for the 'language of the heart', as the aesthetics of the period termed it."

Although the two works in the minor key represent this fundamental change at its most dramatic, all Mozart's mature concertos may be said to express the "language of the heart"; but it has remained for our age to discover the beauties of K.453, 467, 482, 488, 503, or 595, in which the *Sprache des Herzens*, perhaps warmer and less burdened by ominous thoughts, is none the less intensely personal and moving.

The last two concertos stand apart from those of the years 1782–6, both chronologically and musically. K.537 is called the 'Coronation' Concerto, because it was supposedly played at Frankfurt in an 'Academy' which Mozart planned to coincide with the Coronation of Leopold II in October 1790. Mozart had not been invited officially, and the 'Academy' he gave on 15 October (see Fig. 2 opposite) did not achieve the success he had hoped. K.537 is in many ways a parallel to the 'popular' Haydn symphonies of the late 1770s and early 1780s: neither Haydn nor Mozart is at his best when trying to be deliberately successful. The superficialities of K.537 did much to convince the nineteenth century of Mozart's supposed shallowness, his courtly 'lackey' style, just as the enormously popular Haydn Symphonies *L'impériale* (No. 53), *La Roxelane* (No. 63), Nos. 76–81 (composed in the early 1780s), and the 'cello Concerto in D (1783) established the romantic conception of Haydn as a playful old fool. In K.537 everything glitters, everything shines: the heartbreaking realization that his public did not understand

[1] Introduction to the Eulenburg miniature score (No. 721, 1933).

Mit gnädigster Erlaubniß
Wird Heute Freytags den 15ten October 1790.

im grosen Stadt-Schauspielhause

Herr Kapellmeister Mozart
ein grosses

musikalisches Konzert

zu seinem Vortheil geben.

Erster Theil.

Eine neue grose Simphonie von Herrn Mozart.

Eine Arie, gesungen von Madame Schick.

Ein Concert auf dem Forte piano, gespielt von Herrn Kapellmeister Mozart von seiner eigenen Komposition.

Eine Arie, gesungen von Herrn Cecarelli.

Zweyter Theil.

Ein Concert von Herrn Kapellmeister Mozart von seiner eigenen Komposition.

Ein Duett, gesungen von Madame Schick und Herrn Cecarelli.

Eine Phantasie aus dem Stegreife von Herrn Mozart.

Eine Symphonie.

Die Person zahlt in den Logen und Parquet 2 fl. 45 kr.
Auf der Gallerie 24 kr.

Ilets sind bey Herrn Mozart, wohnhaft in der Kahlbechergasse Nro. 167. vom Donnerstag Nachmittags und Freytags Frühe bey Herrn Cassirer Scheidweiler und an der Caisse zu haben.

Der Anfang ist um Eilf Uhr Vormittags.

Fig. 2. The programme of Mozart's Benefit Concert, Frankfurt, 15 October 1790.

and appreciate the concertos of 1782–6 seems to have induced Mozart to purge the new work of any restless, disturbing elements. The slow movement begins with all the innocent beauty of those in K.466 and 491: but, unlike the earlier slow movements, there is no real contrast, and the middle section (bars 44ff.; Eulenburg, pp. 65ff.) is too close to the spirit of the first (cf. the tumultuous middle part of the 'Romance' in K.466).

But Mozart knew well how to fashion a popular concerto without any sacrifice of his artistic standards. There are four completed horn concertos of the Viennese period (K.412 in D, K.417, 447, and 495 in E flat), three definitely written for Leutgeb and one (K.447) possibly for another virtuoso.[1] Delightful as they all are, K.447 is the finest. It is scored for an orchestra of two clarinets, two bassoons and strings: the ripieno horns of the other E flat works are dropped, and the orchestral texture is richer and more symphonic. There is real nobility and grandeur in the forte which bursts into the lyric piano opening (any hornist immediately sees that the melody is fashioned for his instrument), and the second movement, again a 'Romance' in barred C, gives the soloist an opportunity to display his finest cantabile. The interesting feature of these concertos from the standpoint of the horn's development is the extraordinary freedom with which Mozart uses stopped notes. The eighteenth-century horn, as is well known, was a coiled instrument of brass tubing with a slight conical expansion on which all the open harmonic

K. 447
Ex.18 *Allegro*

The horn part has been transposed into its real sound in the above example. The note D flat happens to be an open harmonic on the E flat horn, but it must be 'lipped' up, as the hornist expresses it, to be in perfect tune. The G flats, Cs and E naturals must be stopped.

notes could be produced. About 1770 (or slightly earlier) it was discovered that the notes in between could be produced by inserting the hand into the bell of the horn, by which the tone could be lowered as much as a whole note. (Another technique, that of stopping and 'overblowing', was used to produce certain

[1] cf., however, *The Concertos (1)*, p. 206.

intermediate notes in the bass clef.) But even with a knowledge of this technique, Leutgeb's lips and fingers must have been pretty agile to cope with the D flat melody which suddenly appears in the development of K.447 (Ex. 18).

Mozart's model for these E flat works seems to have been a series of horn concertos by Anton Rosetti (Rossetti), a prolific composer of concertos for wind instruments, who was *Kapellmeister* at the Court of Prince Oettingen-Wallerstein in Southern Germany. Rosetti's form has the same general lay-out, with a 'Romance' in barred time as a slow movement and a finale in the favourite 'hunting' metre of 6/8: even the melodies are strikingly similar. It would be revealing to have a separate study of Rosetti's concertos for horn and their relationship to Mozart, for space prevents us from giving more than a brief reference. (The Rosetti MSS. are in the Oettingen-Wallerstein Castle at Harburg; additional MS. sources, some wrongly ascribed to Mozart (!), are in the Monastery at Melk.)

It is quite obvious that if he had lived, Mozart would have entered a new style about the year 1791. Some of his last compositions give us a hint of what this new period would have been, and some, indeed, actually cross the threshold into the style itself. *Die Zauberflöte*, the motet, 'Ave, verum corpus' (K.618), the little Adagio (K.356(617a)) and Quintet (K.617) for glass harmonica, and many parts of the Requiem belong to this new period. The main characteristics are, strangely enough, those that we usually associate with a *Spätstil* (e.g., Schütz, Haydn, Verdi): enormous but effortless technical ability, increasing preoccupation with harmonic problems (in Haydn and Beethoven this often takes the form of mediant and submediant relationships), a kind of remote, ethereal passivity, and an increasing abstraction of musical thought. In the reflective tranquillity of the E flat portions of *Die Zauberflöte*, in the quiet peace of the 'Ave verum', or in the hushed beauty of the Adagio for Marianne Kirchgessner's strange instrument, the glass harmonica, we meet a new, resigned Mozart, a Mozart who no longer really cared about worldly acclaim (even if it gladdened his heart to see *Die Zauberflöte* achieve real popular success). Biographically we think of the composer, labouring away at his standing desk "because it is easier to work than not to work"; of the unreal, frightening carriage ride with Constanze in the

Prater, through the fallen leaves of the last autumn he would know, and the quiet, unemotional way in which he suddenly began to speak of death; of the earlier farewell with Haydn, who left for England and immortality (they had spent the whole day together and Mozart wept bitterly at the end – "we shall never meet again"); and of the mad business of the grey-cloaked stranger, ordering the Requiem ("but it is for myself", thought Mozart). No one sensed better than Mozart that the end was drawing near.

On the threshold of this *Spätstil* stands Mozart's last piano Concerto, in B flat (K.595), completed shortly before his thirty-fifth birthday. He wrote the work for a concert given by the clarinettist Beer (Bähr) in Vienna on 4 March 1791, and we have no idea of its public reception. How different is K.595 from the full-blooded concertos of the earlier Viennese period, with their infinite promise of things to come. The chromaticism in K.595 is no longer restless, as it was in the slow movement of K.467, nor are there mysterious, hidden undertones of leashed passion. Nothing in the previous concertos prepares us for the calm, fatalistic simplicity of the Larghetto's beginning (pianoforte, unsupported). Like the slow movement of the E flat Symphony, we sense that this is a summing-up of what has been, the quiet harvest of those magnificent earlier years. The second tutti passage, at bars 32ff. (Eulenburg, pp. 43f.), is one of the most exquisite and poignant Mozart ever wrote. But even the aching chromaticism of the strings and bassoon over the horns' pedal point (32–4), or the urgent, thrusting G flat trills of the second violin part in bar 35, have a certain emotional repose about them, an inward self-sufficiency which no longer forces itself on the consciousness of the listener. The final return of the main theme, with its staggering orchestration in bare consecutive octaves (bars 103ff.), is still more introverted; denied the simplicity of its original harmonic background, and escorted on either side by flute and first violin, the melody floats, serene and unearthly, into the final tutti.

"With such an opus", says Blume,[1] "Mozart comes to an end of his work in the piano concerto. . . . All emotion, everything worldly and unessential have ebbed away. There is neither grief nor joy, neither irony nor despair, neither resignation nor con-

[1] Preface to the Eulenburg score (No. 775, n.d.).

solation. In the world of this 'noble simplicity and quiet greatness', emotions are vain."

There remains one single work, the clarinet Concerto in A major, K.622, Mozart's last instrumental music and, apart from the little *Freimaurer-Kantate* (K.623), the last piece he was able to complete. The original form, as a work for basset horn in G,[1] was begun late in 1789, but the completion did not take place until October 1791. Both the original plan and the execution were inspired by and written for Mozart's friend, Anton Stadler.

The clarinet Concerto is a typical product of the 'new' period which has been discussed above; no other work by Mozart is more imbued with that final, quiet resignation; but no other concerto has such a deep-seated satisfaction in pure orchestral sound. The liquid beauty of the clarinet writing is carefully supported by an orchestra of flutes, bassoons, horns, and strings, i.e., without the direct and more penetrating sound of oboes. The concerto is Mozart's farewell to the realms of pure music (there is little doubt that by October he must have guessed the extent of his illness); and how difficult this farewell must have been to someone who loved life as much as he did. There is always a moment when the desire to live is stronger than any philosophical resignation, and it will not, perhaps, be thought an exaggeration if one reads this extra-musical significance into a work written in Mozart's last weeks of creative activity; for of all Mozart's last music, this concerto is the most personal. In the Adagio, a tempo which always signifies the profoundest emotion in Mozart, there are times when an unbearable sadness seems to linger in the music, the more profound and tragic because it smilingly emerges from the serenity of a bright major key. As for the quick movements, I can find no better words than those of *A Winter's Tale*, used by A. Veinus in another connection: for in these two allegros the "heart dances, but not for joy".

[1] See *The Concertos (1)*, p. 207.

BOOK LIST

[Standard Mozart biographies have not been listed.]

Anon.: 'Mozarts Violinkonzert mit dem "Strassburger"', *Zeitschrift der Internationalen Musikgesellschaft*, IX/1908, pp. 225–6.

F. Bauer: *Das vorklassische deutsche Violinkonzert*. This book, occasionally quoted on Mozart's concertos was planned as a dissertation, but never completed.

M. Blaschitz: *Die Salzburger Mozartfragmente*, Diss., Bonn, 1926.

F. Blume: 'Die formgeschichtliche Stellung der Klavierkonzerte Mozarts', *Mozart-Jahrbuch*, II/Munich, 1924, pp. 83–107.

—— 'Zum Autograph von Mozarts Krönungskonzert', *Acta musicologica*, IX/1938, pp. 147–9.

—— Forewords to the editions of 13 piano concertos and the *Sinfonia Concertante*, K.Anh.9(297b), published by Eulenburg.

E. Closson: 'Sur un manuscrit de Mozart', *Acta musicologica*, VIII/1936, pp. 155–7.

G. Cuming: 'Mozart's Oboe Concerto for Ferlendis', *Music and Letters*, XXI/1940, pp. 18–22.

H. Daffner: *Die Entwicklung des Klavierkonzertes bis Mozart*, Diss., Munich, 1904; Leipzig, 1906.

G. Dazeley: 'The Original Text of Mozart's Clarinet Concerto', *Music Review*, IX/1948, pp. 166–72.

H. Dennerlein: *Der unbekannte Mozart*, Leipzig, 1951, ²/1954.

M. Dounias: *Die Violinkonzerte G. Tartinis*, Diss., Berlin, 1932; Wolfenbüttel-Berlin, 1932.

A. Einstein: 'On Certain Manuscripts . . .', *Journal of the American Musicological Society*, I/1948, pp. 13–16.

H. Engel: *Die Entwicklung des deutschen Klavierkonzertes von Mozart bis Liszt*, Diss., Munich, 1925; Leipzig, 1927.

R. Erlebach: 'Style in Pianoforte Concerto Writing', *Music and Letters*, XVII/1936.

R. Gerber: Forewords to the editions of various Mozart concertos published by Eulenburg.

C. M. Girdlestone: *Mozart's Piano Concertos*, London, 1948; French edition, Paris, 1939.

A. Heuss: 'Mozarts 7. Violinkonzert', *Zeitschrift der Internationalen Musikgesellschaft*, IX/1907, pp. 124–9.

R. Hill (ed.): *The Concerto*, London, 1952.

A. Hutchings: *A Companion to Mozart's Piano Concertos*, London, 1948, ²/1950.

V. Junk: Foreword to the edition of the bassoon concerto published by Eulenburg.

H. Keller: 'Mozart and Boccherini', *Music Review*, VIII/4/1947, pp. 241ff.

—— 'The *Idomeneo* Gavotte's Vicissitude', *Music Review*, XIV/2/1953, pp. 155ff.

A. H. King: 'Mozart's Piano Music', *Music Review*, V/1944, p. 161.

—— 'French and German Mozart Literature since 1939', *Monthly Musical Record*, 82/1952, pp. 37–9, 66–9.

—— 'Mozart's Lost and Fragmentary Compositions', ibid., pp. 235–8, 264–8.

—— 'A Census of Mozart's Musical Autographs in England', *Musical Quarterly*, XXXVIII/1952, pp. 566ff.

W. Merian: Foreword to the editions of the horn concertos published by Eulenburg.

H. J. Moser: 'Die Erstfassung des Mozartschen Klavierkonzerts, K.450', *Musikforschung*, IV/1951, pp. 202–4.

C. B. Oldman: 'Mozart and Modern Research', *Proceedings of the Royal Musical Association*, 1932.

—— 'Mozart's Violin Concerto in E Flat', *Music and Letters*, XII/1931, pp. 174–83.

B. Paumgartner: 'Zu Mozarts Oboenkonzert C Dur', *Mozart-Jahrbuch*, 1950, pp. 24–40.

G. Piccioli: *Il concerto per pianoforte e orchestra . . . da Mozart a Grieg*, Como, 1936, ²/1940.

H. F. Redlich: 'New Light on Mozart's Pianoforte Concertos', *Music Review*, VII/1946.

—— 'Mozart's C Minor Piano Concerto (K.491)', *Music Review*, IX/1948, pp. 87–96.

W. Reich: 'Bemerkungen zu Mozarts Klarinettenkonzert', *Zeitschrift für Musikwissenschaft*, XV/1933, pp. 276ff.

C. Reinecke: *Zur Wiederbelebung der Mozartschen Klavierkonzerte*, Leipzig, 1891.

H. Rietsch: 'Mozarts G-Dur-Konzert für Geige', *Zeitschrift für Musikwissenschaft*, X/1928, pp. 198–205.

G. de St.-Foix: 'Mozart ou Ferlendis', *Rivista Musicale Italiana*, XXVII/1920, pp. 543ff.

—— 'Le dernier concerto pour violon de Mozart (K.268)', *Bulletin de la Société Union Musicologique*, II/1922, pp. 85–116.

—— 'Mozart et les instruments à vent', ibid., V/1925, pp. 207–22.

F. Schröder: 'Ist uns Mozarts Oboenkonzert für Ferlendis erhalten?', *Musikforschung*, V/1952, pp. 209–11.

F. O. Souper: 'Mozart's Seventh Violin Concerto', *Monthly Musical Record*, 63/1933, pp. 49–50.

B. F. Swalin: *The Violin Concerto. A Study in German Romanticism*, Diss., Vienna, 1932; London, 1942.

R. Tenschert: 'Fragment eines Klarinettenkonzertes von Mozart', *Zeitschrift für Musikwissenschaft*, XIII/1931, pp. 218–22.

F. Torrefranca: *Le origini Italiane del romanticismo musicale*, Turin, 1930.

H. Truscott: 'Dussek and the Concerto', *Music Review*, XVI/1955, pp. 29–53.

H. Uldall: 'Beiträge zur Frühgeschichte des Klavierkonzerts', *Zeitschrift für Musikwissenschaft*, X/1928, pp. 139–52.

A. Veinus: *The Concerto*, New York, 1948.

F. Waldkirch: *Die konzertante Sinfonie der Mannheimer im 18. Jahrhundert*, Diss., Heidelberg, 1934; Ludwigshafen, 1931.

M. K. Ward: 'Mozart and the Clarinet', *Music and Letters*, XXVIII/1947, pp. 126–53.

—— 'Mozart and the Bassoon', ibid., XXX/1949, pp. 8–25.

—— 'Mozart and the Horn', ibid., XXXI/1950, pp. 318–32.

—— 'Mozart's Clarinettist', *Monthly Musical Record*, 85/1955, pp. 8–14.

J. A. Watson: 'Mozart and the Viola', *Music and Letters*, XXII/1941, pp. 41–53.

Th. Wyzewa and G. de St.-Foix: 'Les premiers concertos de Mozart', *Zeitschrift der Internationalen Musikgesellschaft*, X/1909, pp. 139ff.

E. von Zschinsky-Troxler: 'Mozarts D-Dur-Violinkonzert und Boccherini', *Zeitschrift für Musikwissenschaft*, X/1928, pp. 415–22.

GERALD ABRAHAM

THE OPERAS

Doubtless many people still regard Mozart as a 'pure' musician, as perhaps the greatest of all the creators of 'absolute' music. When one thinks of the piano concertos, the string quintets, the Concerto and the Quintet born out of the spirit of the clarinet, one hardly wants to argue with them. Nevertheless, his position as one of the greatest of opera composers rests on quite a different foundation; here his pure musicianship is only an added delight (to himself, as we shall see, only an ever-present help in time of trouble), his musical craftsmanship only the varnish over the paint. One can be technically crude in opera and still be successful, even great, while over-refined workmanship can be a positive handicap, as in the cases of Tchaikovsky's *Vakula* and Cornelius's *Barber*. What matters above all in the opera house is not the ability to write beautiful music, but the much rarer ability to create characters and dramatic situations in music, just as an ordinary dramatist creates them in words. Observe that they must be created *in* music, not taken ready-made from the librettist and *set* to music; the librettist can and must provide dramatic possibilities, or at least sketches for the characters, but he cannot create them in opera. Only the musician can do that. No composer can succeed as a musical dramatist simply by supplying a good libretto with appropriate music; he must himself have the gift of visualizing dramatic situations, of living in them, above all of thinking himself into the skins and skulls of his characters, no matter how diverse or how different from himself. Verdi, Wagner, Mussorgsky possessed this gift; Puccini had it in a more limited range; some opera composers, notably Tchaikovsky, have been able to identify themselves only with characters that are essentially or partially self-projections, and their success in the opera house has been correspondingly narrow. Mozart was most richly endowed with it.

This dramatic sense showed itself in Mozart at a very early age. When he was in London in the summer of 1765, the nine-

year-old boy's abilities were searchingly tested by Daines
Barrington.[1] Among other things –

"I said to the boy, that I should be glad to hear an extemporary *Love Song*, such as his friend Manzoli might choose in an
opera. The boy on this (who continued to sit at his harpsichord)
looked back with much archness, and immediately began five
or six lines of a jargon recitative proper to introduce a love song.

"He then played a symphony which might correspond with
an air composed to the single word, *Affetto*.

"It had a first and second part, which, together with the
symphonies, was of the length that opera songs generally last: if
this extemporary composition was not amazingly capital, yet it
was really above mediocrity, and showed most extraordinary
readiness of invention.

"Finding that he was in humour, and as it were inspired, I
then desired him to compose a *Song of Rage*, such as might be
proper for the opera stage.

"The boy again looked back with much archness, and began
five or six lines of a jargon recitative proper to precede a *Song of
Anger*. This lasted also about the same time with the *Song of Love*;
and in the middle of it he had worked himself up to such a
pitch, that he beat his harpsichord like a person possessed, rising
sometimes in his chair. The word he pitched upon for this
second extemporary composition was, *Perfido*."

His letters to his sister often show how his Italian travels in
years of boyhood quickened his observation of the dramatic element in general. He noticed how the Italians tend to dramatize
the little incidents of everyday life. Naturally, he was not for a
long time able to embody all this in his music; he lacked personal experience, deeper insight. The early operas, particularly
Bastien und Bastienne (K.50), contain some charming music, but
little else. But there are flashes of real characterization in *La
finta giardiniera* (K.196), composed in 1775 at the age of nineteen, and it is noteworthy that most of the flashes occur in the
ensembles; Mozart already seems to have seen his characters
more sharply when they were confronted with each other.

Mozart – at least the mature Mozart – did not take a ready-
made libretto and tamely set it, as Wagner supposed that he did.

[1] See his *Miscellanies*, London, 1781, p. 284.

Like Verdi, Puccini, and Richard Strauss, he was an active collaborator with the librettist. He was even, consciously, the senior partner; he remarks in a letter to his father written on 13 October 1781 while he was composing *Die Entführung* that "in an opera the poetry must be altogether the obedient daughter of the music".[1] Yet he hardly ever presses the librettist to give way in any passage for the sake of a purely musical point. As a practical dramatic composer he gradually acquired the faculty of visualizing characters and situations vividly for himself, more vividly even than the librettist; he could embody the character or situation for himself in music, and needed the words only to *carry* his music, so to speak, and define it beyond doubt for the audience. Mozart's aesthetic was indeed close to that of *Oper und Drama*, though Wagner failed to recognize the fact. Poetry must be "the obedient daughter" not because Mozart regarded the libretto as a mere peg on which to hang beautiful melodies, but because he was confident that he could convey so much of the drama in his music. Yet he does not cross every T and dot every I in his musical characterization as Wagner and later composers sometimes do, visualizing every detail of a character's action at certain points and conveying it almost pantomimically in the music – as with Beckmesser in the third act of *Die Meistersinger* – so that a really faithful actor is obliged to become almost a puppet whose movements are prescribed by the music. As we shall see, Mozart also occasionally makes pantomimic suggestions; but he always allows the actor plenty of freedom. The whole of the letter from which I have already quoted is most enlightening. Leopold Mozart has been critical of the libretto; Wolfgang replies admitting the justice of some of these criticisms, "still", he says,

"the poetry is perfectly in keeping with the character of stupid, surly, malicious Osmin. I am well aware that the verse is not of the best, but it fitted in and it agreed so well with the musical thoughts which already were buzzing in my head, that it could not fail to please me; and I would like to wager that when it is performed, no deficiencies will be found."

Later, after the remark about poetry being "the obedient daughter", he goes on:

[1] See E. Anderson: *Letters of Mozart*, London, 1938, Vol. III, p. 1150.

"Why do Italian operas please everywhere – in spite of their miserable libretti – even in Paris, where I myself witnessed their success? Just because there the music reigns supreme and when one listens to it all else is forgotten. Why, an opera is sure of success when the plot is well worked out, the words written solely for the music and not shoved in here and there to suit some miserable rhyme (which, God knows, never enhances the value of any theatrical performance, but rather detracts from it) – I mean, words or even entire verses which ruin the composer's whole idea. Verses are indeed the most indispensable element for music – but rhymes – solely for the sake of rhyming – the most detrimental. . . . The best thing of all is when a good composer, who understands the stage and is talented enough to make sound suggestions, meets an able poet, that true phoenix."

He ends, very characteristically: "Well, I think I have chattered enough nonsense to you." That should be a warning not to take all this too solemnly. Mozart was very different from Wagner, who always needed to clarify and rationalize his artistic instincts. Mozart could never have written a systematic explanation of his aesthetic of opera; he was an empiricist of genius, guided by the sure instinct of his genius, and chattering away about it all to his father. What it amounts to is perhaps this; a libretto has negative value. A bad one can sink the best music; the best of libretti cannot save poor music. But, given a tolerable libretto, a composer of the right sort can do all the rest.

What were the conditions that seem to have been essential to Mozart? Most obviously, perhaps, a real subject – however slight as in *Die Entführung* or artificial as in *Così* or muddled as in *Die Zauberflöte* – a dramatic action with a succession of crises and a final dénouement, which will shape the music. The subject, to attract Mozart, must be an entertaining one, one with plenty of sparkling life and gaiety. Even when there are elements that cause him to sound the profoundest depths of music, as in *Die Zauberflöte*, there are counterbalancing elements of the most light-hearted nonsense. *Don Giovanni* is not really a moral drama; the real terror of the hero's end is dispelled by the ironic humour of the final commentary. None of the operas that still hold the stage is a tragedy, none is even a 'serious opera'. Above all, the libretto must be full of characters, sketches for real live individuals who think and feel and behave like genuine persons.

Sketches are enough. Given the right sort of sketch, the composer will do the rest. Dramatic music can – indeed, as I have already said, to succeed it *must* – do more than merely dress up characters; it must embody them, no matter what the operatic convention in which the embodiment is framed. If the music is written by a genius such as Mozart, it can give them immortal souls as well. (Rossini could give Beaumarchais's characters musical flesh-and-blood; Mozart did more.) He nearly managed to breathe souls into the characters with which da Ponte provided him in *Così*, but *Così* is inferior to *Don Giovanni* just because the plot is so artificial, because the characters are less defined, more puppet-like than those the same librettist had given him in *Don Giovanni*. Mozart's power of dramatic creation was even able to save the 'reversed' characterization of *Die Zauberflöte*, in which the Queen of the Night, originally conceived by the librettist as a morally good character, became a wicked one, while Sarastro was transmuted from an evil to a good genius.[1]

Mozart's *obiter dicta* on the aesthetics of opera are sometimes quoted out of context, and are thus liable to misinterpretation. But we have a specially valuable series of comments dating from the latter part of 1780 and the beginning of 1781 when he was composing *Idomeneo* (K.366). It happened that Mozart was in Munich, his librettist Varesco in Salzburg. Leopold Mozart acted as go-between and Wolfgang's letters to his father contain a number of enlightening passages. He writes on 8 November 1780:

"I have just one request to make of the Abbate. Ilia's aria in Act II, Scene 2, should be altered slightly to suit what I require. "Se il padre perdei, in te lo ritrovo';[2] this verse could not be better. But now comes what has always seemed unnatural to me – I mean, in an aria – and that is, *a spoken aside*. In a dialogue

[1] See E. J. Dent: *Mozart's Operas*, London, 1913, ²/1947, pp. 218–19, and H. Abert: *W. A. Mozart*, Leipzig, 1923, Vol. II, pp. 258–9. Doubts of this generally accepted statement have been expressed by E. von Komorzynski: '*Die Zauberflöte*', *Neues Mozart-Jahrbuch*, Regensburg, I/1941, p. 154, and L. Conrad: *Mozarts Dramaturgie der Oper*, Würzburg, 1943, p. 358.

[2] Attention has been drawn to the almost exact resemblance the passage "la patria il riposo, tu padre mi sei" in this aria bears to "ich fühl' es, ich fühl' es, wie dies Götterbild mein Herz" in Tamino's 'Bildnis' aria. See A. Heuss: 'Mozarts *Idomeneo* als Quelle für *Don Giovanni* und *Die Zauberflöte*', *Zeitschrift für Musikwissenschaft*, XIII/1931, pp. 188–9.

all these things are quite natural, for a few words can be spoken aside hurriedly; but in an aria where the words have to be repeated, it has a bad effect, and even if this were not the case, I should prefer an uninterrupted aria. The beginning may stand, if it suits him, for the poem is charming and, as it is absolutely natural and flowing and therefore as I have not got to contend with difficulties arising from the words, I can go on composing quite easily; for we have agreed to introduce here an aria andantino with obbligatos for four wind-instruments, that is, a flute, oboe, horn, and bassoon. I beg you therefore to let me have the text as soon as possible."[1]

Reading that letter without reference to the actual music or the dramatic situation, one might suppose that this miniature quadruple concerto was being dragged in for a purely musical effect. Not at all. Ilia is a Trojan prisoner in love with a Greek prince; she is in a state of emotional confusion and, as Abert has pointed out,[2] the wind-quartet has the special function of conveying what she feels more deeply and less clearly, in contrast with what she actually expresses in song. Just so does Wagner's orchestra in *Die Meistersinger* tell us what Eva is feeling and thinking when she is only talking about her shoes. These are subtleties that no non-musical dramatist could achieve – or could achieve only through an actress of consummate genius.

On 13 November we find Mozart visualizing what happens in a shipwreck far more vividly than his wretched librettist had done. A king would not be left alone in a ship in extreme peril; if the librettist would like to have him alone *in the sea*, swimming for dear life, well and good. But if he is in a ship he must have companions whom he can dismiss later when he comes ashore. After the shipwreck Mozart would not have a proposed pantomime of Neptune stilling the waves; that could all be narrated; on the other hand, the stage-manager must see to it that there are fragments of wreckage on the stage, since Idamante mentions "fracassate navi" in his recitative in scene ten (22 December).[3] In the letter of 13 November, Mozart remarks that –

[1] Anderson: op. cit., Vol. II, p. 978.
[2] op. cit., Vol. I, p. 852. In checking various points in Abert I have been dismayed to find how many observations that I had supposed to be my own are based on his, all too well remembered from fascinated study of his great book twenty years or more ago.
[3] op. cit., Vol. II, p. 1030.

"The second duet is to be omitted altogether – and indeed with more profit than loss to the opera. For, when you read through the scene, you will see that it obviously becomes limp and cold by the addition of an aria or a duet, and very gênant for the other actors who must stand by doing nothing. . . ."[1]

Mozart often asks for cuts. He knows that music in itself slows up words; if a dramatic point has to be made and held for, say, five minutes, the librettist must supply much less dialogue than would be spoken in five minutes. He has a very sure sense of theatrical illusion, its possibilities and its limitations. An oracle has to speak in the last act of *Idomeneo*. "Tell me", he writes to his father (29 November) – [2]

"Don't you think that the speech of the subterranean voice is too long? Consider it carefully. Picture to yourself the theatre, and remember that the voice must be terrifying – must penetrate – that the audience must believe that it really exists. Well, how can this effect be produced if the speech is too long, for in this case the listeners will become more and more convinced that it means nothing. If the speech of the Ghost in *Hamlet* were not so long, it would be far more effective."

Even when Varesco had agreed to shorten the oracle's speech, Mozart found it "still far too long". "I have therefore shortened it", he told his father (18 January),[3]

"but Varesco need not know anything of this, because it will all be printed just as he wrote it."

As a matter of fact, the oracle's speech gave Mozart a great deal of trouble; it exists in at least three versions.[4]

Occasionally, on the other hand, Mozart wants more words from the librettist. He asks for Arbace's recitative in Act III to be lengthened "which owing to the *chiaro e oscuro* and his being a good actor will have a capital effect" (5 December).[5] The librettist had begun with despair and continued with despair; Mozart wanted "a slight glimmering of hope" to be inserted at

---

[1] Anderson: op. cit., Vol. II, p. 984.   [2] ibid., p. 1000.   [3] ibid., p. 1051.
[4] See *Collected Edition*, Series V, 13, No. 28, and Appendices VIII and IX.
[5] Anderson: op. cit., Vol. II, p. 1012.

one point, a little light to deepen the shade. Note too: "his being a good actor".

In fact, the singer in question (Panzacchi) had actually suggested the point to him. That also is highly characteristic. I think it is true to say that every part in every one of Mozart's major operas was composed with a specific singer in mind, a singer whose capabilities were well known to him. There, again, he shows himself a true man of the theatre. He not only wrote for particular singers; he readily accepted suggestions from them if, as here, they were good suggestions. Near the end of the opera he even scrapped a quartet for the sake of Raaff, the elderly singer of the title-role, who could be given an aria at that point instead; and when Raaff objected to singing such words as "vien mi a rinvigorir", with its "five *i*'s" (letter of 27 December),[1] Mozart sided with him in the ensuing argument with the librettist and Leopold. On the other hand, when Raaff criticized another quartet, 'Andrò, ramingo e solo' in Act III, because it gave him no scope to expand his voice – "Non c'è da spianar la voce" – ("As if in a quartet the words should not be spoken much more than sung," comments the composer), Mozart kindly but firmly refused to alter a single note (letter of 27 December).

To return to Mozart's struggle with the libretto: in the last scene of Act II there is a thunderstorm with great confusion on the stage, musically dominated by big choruses, and in the middle of all this Idomeneo was to sing an aria. It was Mozart, not the librettist, who realized that what Idomeneo has to say here must be said in recitative, not in melody; an aria would hold everything up. "Moreover there is the thunderstorm, which is not likely to subside during Herr Raaff's aria, is it?" (15 November).[2] A quick recitative was the right solution. So it went on; here a recitative had to be drastically cut; there a "quite simple march" had to be composed to make room for some stage action. From first to last, this series of letters shows Mozart as a practical man of the theatre.

Now *Idomeneo* (1781) is an *opera seria*. It is Mozart's finest work in this style and his last but one – the hastily written *La Clemenza di Tito* (K.621) of 1791. This great opera style of the eighteenth century with its somewhat generalized, superhuman types, however revitalized by Gluck, was unsuited to Mozart's livelier

---

[1] See Anderson: op. cit., p. 1035.   [2] Ibid., p. 985.

genius. Its spirit was infused here and there, however, into the five masterpieces which followed *Idomeneo*, strikingly ennobling them: the Queen's arias and the priests' music in *Die Zauberflöte*, the statue-music in *Don Giovanni*. But the five masterpieces belong to two different – contemporaries would have said 'lower' – categories: Italian *opera buffa* and German *Singspiel*:

Singspiele	Opere buffe
Die Entführung aus dem Serail (1782)	*Le nozze di Figaro* (1786)
	Don Giovanni (1787)
Die Zauberflöte (1791)	*Così fan tutte* (1790)

Whatever the *genre* to which Mozart's operas belong, he conceived them as unified musical compositions. That statement may seem rather obvious from one point of view, highly questionable from another. Are they not strings of arias, duets, larger ensembles, connected only by recitatives – not even connected by recitative in the *Singspiele*, where the dialogue is spoken? They are certainly not held together by recurrent themes as in Wagner; I am left sceptical by attempts to discover subtle embryonic *Leitmotive* in Mozart;[1] when Mozart harks back thematically – as when Figaro recalls 'Se vuol ballare' in Act II – he does so purely for dramatic effect, using 'thematic reminiscence' as every composer of the day occasionally did. The unifying element in every case is tonality; each opera ends in the key of the overture, however remote or complicated the key-system of the intervening numbers:

> *Idomeneo*: D major
> *Die Entführung*: C major
> *Figaro*: D major
> *Don Giovanni:* D minor and major
> *Così fan tutte:* C major
> *Die Zauberflöte:* E flat
> *La Clemenza di Tito:* C major

Mozart's overtures – always the last parts to be written, as with most composers – therefore literally set the key of each opera. They also 'set the key' in the metaphorical sense. They are not

---

[1] See, for instance, E. Graf: 'Das "Leitmotiv" des Cherubin', *Neues Mozart-Jahrbuch*, Regensburg, II/1942, pp. 201–10.

poetic, as Weber's and Beethoven's and Wagner's are: they do not attempt to epitomize a plot; they simply introduce. But they introduce with great skill, and there is always something in the overture – some allusion or hint – which links it unmistakably with the particular opera that is to follow. In two cases, *Die Entführung* and *Don Giovanni*, the overture runs without a break into the first number. We are so accustomed to hearing them played with concert-endings patched on – in the case of *Die Entführung*, not even by Mozart himself – that we forget how the end of the *Don Giovanni* overture modulates to lead into Leporello's 'Nott' e giorno' and how strikingly Belmonte's first aria in *Die Entführung* picks up in C major the C *minor* middle section of the overture. (The *Figaro* overture was also composed with a minor middle section, *andante con moto* in 6/8 time, before the recapitulation, but Mozart tore it out.[1]) Thanks to the convention of 'Turkish music' – triangle, bass-drum, and cymbals – the *Entführung* overture told a contemporary audience not only that it was going to hear a comedy, but that, as the title also promised, it was to be a comedy in an Oriental setting.

If *Figaro* has the perfect comedy overture, that to *Don Giovanni* more than hints at the serious undertones that rumble through *its* humour. Not only in the Andante; there is something feverish about the Allegro, and it is not surprising that nineteenth-century writers and musicians, from E. T. A. Hoffmann to Wagner – and Gounod – were moved by it to romantic exegesis. The *Così* overture is a little hard and heartless, like the opera itself, but it begins and ends with a delicious touch that no one understands until he has heard the opera. After the opening love-theme of the oboe, the lower strings drily interject, Ex. 1:

Ex.1 *Andante*

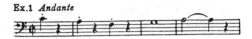

Near the end of the overture, after all the bustle and sparkle, the orchestra breaks off again to make the same comment. But the meaning becomes clear only when Alfonso sings it in the penultimate number of the opera: "All accuse the ladies, but I excuse them, if they change their loves a thousand times a day.

[1] Abert: op. cit., Vol. II, pp. 294–5. If the missing sixty-four-bar 'Fragment, vermutlich zu einer Oper' in D minor (K.Anh.101) ever turns up, we may be able to restore the original form of the *Figaro* overture for concert-hall use.

Some call it a vice, some a custom, but I see it as a necessity of the heart. The deceived lover has only himself to blame. So young and old, plain ones and beauties, *they're all the same.*" And the two unfortunate young men repeat it with him: "Così fan tutte."

The overture to *Die Zauberflöte*, like everything else in the opera, is in a class by itself. That it should be totally unlike any other *Singspiel* overture or any other Mozart overture is quite appropriate, for *Die Zauberflöte* is unlike any other *Singspiel* or Mozart opera. The three opening chords must have startled a *Singspiel* audience if for no other reason than their trombone sounds, weighted with associations of church and solemnity in general; here they have obvious bearing on the temple scenes. Even the number of the chords is significant. The number 3 plays an important, certainly not accidental, part in *Die Zauberflöte*: three ladies, three boys, three slaves, three temples, and so on. It is usually assumed that these 3's have a Masonic significance – for, as most people know, *Die Zauberflöte* is full of Masonic symbolism – though Leopold Conrad[1] has pointed out that the figure 3 frequently appears in German folklore and that the librettist Schikaneder might just as easily have got these symbolic 3's from the various stories of Wieland's *Dschinnistan*[2] which provided him with so many other elements in his plot. All the same, it is perverse to take those three opening chords for anything but Masonic knocks. But what is one to make of the Allegro of the overture? The first theme is unmistakably a comedy theme, but its fugal treatment is unexpected; like the opera itself, it is comedy immeasurably deepened. It was, of course, written later than the opera and is perhaps a purely symphonic continuation of the opera's characteristic mood. Perhaps one might consider it as Mozart's 'Thoughts on Completing *Die Zauberflöte*'.

Solo music in Mozartean opera, as in most opera between Monteverdi and Wagner, falls into two sharply distinguished categories: recitative (either *secco*, with continuo accompaniment only, or *accompagnato* by the orchestra) and song (whether styled aria, cavatina, canzone, or what you will). In Mozart's recitatives the *secco* variety predominates: true Italianate *buffo* recitative carrying cut-and-thrust dialogue almost as quickly as

[1] op. cit., pp. 364–5.
[2] Not *Lulu* only, as is generally assumed; see Komorzynski: op. cit., pp. 150–3.

normal speech. Accompanied recitative is very much rarer; it belongs essentially to *opera seria* and, as we have seen, *opera seria* was not a field in which Mozart was at his happiest. When he gives it us – apart from passages of accompanied recitative in finales and so on – we feel ourselves plunged at once into a more serious atmosphere; in fact, it is commonly a means of transition from a highly comic level to a serious one.

Let us see for a moment how Mozart's practice looks by comparison with earlier eighteenth-century opera. With Handel *secco* recitative managed all the ordinary business of advancing the action; the arias stopped the action and showed the actors expressing a characteristic emotion – one emotion at a time, but the succession of characteristic emotional reactions added up to a character. When Handel wanted emotional *action*, neither prosaic action nor static emotion, he wrote *recitativo accompagnato* (the mad scene in *Orlando*, Bajazet's death in *Tamerlano*, and other dramatic peaks). The so-called reforms of Gluck tended to dispense almost altogether with *recitativo secco* and to assimilate aria with accompanied recitative, giving to each some quality of the other. But practically all Gluck's operas, like practically all Handel's, are 'serious'. Gluck's reforms therefore meant comparatively little to Mozart, who preferred to develop character by setting one personality against another and to place emotional action in ensembles. For Mozart's dialogue any type of music weightier than *secco* recitative would have been too slow. (Compare the pace of Mozartean comedy with that of *Die Meistersinger* or *Der Rosenkavalier*.) His *secco* recitative is the lightest possible stylization of speech over the simplest harmonic background. But it is never, or hardly ever, perfunctory. Characterization begins even here; consider some of the marvellous handling of dialogue in *Figaro* – Susanna's pertness, Cherubino's charming, impudent philandering; Mozart has not merely set words to music; in composing them he has lived each character, and he knows how they would speak, what inflections their voices would have, and it is there in his music – not all there, but all that an accomplished actress could ask for as her material.

While Mozart seldom uses *recitativo accompagnato* for its own sake as a flexible music–dramatic medium, as so many composers before and after him have done, he employs it with wonderful skill for special purposes. Most of his memorable accompanied recitatives are given to tragic heroines or heroines taking themselves tragically. These noble, deeply-feeling women who get caught up in these comic worlds of lascivious aristocrats, rascally servants, and lively maids are rather a problem dramatically. (If they were not provided with such magnificent music, they would be a little like Dickens's heroines; as it is, they are like Ariadne among the masks in Strauss's opera.) Constanze in *Die Entführung* is a case in point; she does not really belong to its farcical world. After a comic scene between Osmin and Blonde, which ends with the pert English maid threatening to scratch his eyes out and his threatening her with "fifty on the soles of her feet", how is one to bring on an altogether serious heroine lamenting what she regards as an altogether serious fate? First Blonde is given a few lines of speech in a different, but far from tragic, vein. But we still have to be got back on to the plane of music – always a difficulty after spoken dialogue – and the orchestra alone does this. Then, after five adagio bars, Constanze's voice enters in recitative with steadily mounting intensity until her emotion wells out into an aria at the word "Traurigkeit". G minor is always a passionate key with Mozart and 'Traurigkeit ward mir zum Lose' is one of his most deeply felt dramatic arias.

Unhappily, Mozart followed that fine piece of characterization with another aria for her in another mood: heroic and defiant. From the purely musical point of view it is magnificent; dramatically it is the worst error of judgment in the whole of Mozart's operas. Constanze has just been telling her captor that she would rather die than be his; Selim replies, "No, not death but every kind of torture" ("Martern aller Arten"). This is the cue for her aria of defiance, echoing his last words; if ever there were a case for a voice entering at once, without instrumental prelude (as with Susanna's 'Sull' aria' in *Figaro*, Act III, Scene x), it is here. Instead, Mozart gives us sixty bars of orchestral ritornello, with concertante parts for flute, oboe, violin, and 'cello soli, before Constanze brings out her repartee, "Martern aller Arten mögen meiner warten; ich verlache Qual und Pein". Worse: none of the music is quite in character with Constanze. Worse still, a great deal of it is not characteristic or dramatic at all, but a brilliant piece of pure concert music. Mozart confessed that he made concessions in an earlier aria of Constanze's 'Ach, ich liebe' for the sake of Katharina Cavalieri's coloratura ("I have sacrificed Constanze's aria a little to the flexible throat of

Mlle Cavalieri").[1] 'Martern aller Arten' – an interpolation replacing an earlier duet – is one big sacrifice on the same altar.

To return to Mozart's accompanied recitatives: it is typical of their association with tragic heroines that Donna Anna in *Don Giovanni* is given no fewer than three – and Donna Elvira one. Donna Anna's first, 'Ma qual mai s'offre', a wonderful example of Mozart's dramatic power, occurs almost at the beginning of the opera. Don Giovanni has tried to seduce her; her father has rushed out after the seducer and has already been killed by him; Anna reappears with Don Ottavio to help her father – too late. After a few bars of *secco* recitative, the orchestra announces that she has found the body and there follows a great scene (for once) in the manner of Gluckian *opera seria*. The dramatic truth of the voice-part – of both voice-parts, for Ottavio intervenes (rather ineffectually, as throughout the opera) – following the quick succession of Anna's emotions (shock of horror, anguish at the loss, her fainting) is as realistic as anything in Mussorgsky. We should notice how the orchestra heightens and deepens everything: the shock of the A flat appoggiatura, the poignant woodwind discords higher at each repetition, the swooning violin figure as Anna swoons. It is worth while to follow this scene a little farther, since it shows so clearly how Mozart develops character. When Anna begins to come to herself, she thinks first of the murderer; she is practically raving, and Ottavio has difficulty in bringing her to her senses.

There are some wonderful details here: the gradually calming effect of a violin figure; the hard edge on Ottavio's voice (intensified by the harmony) at "Lascia, o cara, la rimembranza amara" – he is trying to master his own feelings; the wonderful tenderness of a dropping seventh on oboe and bassoon, punctuating his words, and which presently he actually sings ("hai sposo . . . e padre"). But the orchestra tells us that Anna is thinking of vengeance, not consolation (the basses play a descending-scale theme prominent in the overture), and she makes him swear revenge. Finally, all these fine details are swept away in an outburst of passionate emotion in which both are united: not merely, as Abert points out,[2] an outburst of revengeful feeling but rather of half-terrified excitement.

---

[1] Mozart to his father, 26 September 1781. Cf. Anderson: op. cit., Vol. III, p. 1143.
[2] op. cit., Vol. II, p. 485.

This great scene is not one of the excerpts from *Don Giovanni* familiar on concert platform and radio. Singers naturally tend to pick out the melodious things, the lovely tunes, with the result that a people like ourselves who are not a nation of opera-goers get a false impression of Mozart's operatic music. Even the 'melodious' pieces can give a wrong impression if heard out of their dramatic context. Professor Dent has spoken of Donna Anna's last aria, 'Non mi dir', rather disparagingly,[1] and it is admittedly more purely melodious, more Italian in style, than most of *Don Giovanni*; yet, rather undramatic though it seems to be, it adds some final touches to the musical portrait of a far from simple character. And what goes before it, "Crudele? Ah no, mio bene", illustrates once more Mozart's use of accompanied recitative to make the transition from *secco* dialogue to aria, from prose to poetry. First, in *secco* dialogue, Ottavio rather tactlessly presses Anna to forget her sorrow and marry him at once, and she, of course, refuses; he calls her "cruel". "Cruel? Ah no, my dear", she replies, and as she goes on to explain her feelings and the emotional temperature rises, the orchestra enters and actually sets the stage for her aria by twice beginning its melody. Then the woodwind take over the melody from the violins – flute, clarinet, and bassoon in three octaves, a typical Mozartean lay-out – and Anna herself sings it, telling us what it means, this tender but dignified, un-sentimental melody: "Don't tell me I'm cruel to you." She assures Ottavio very gently, very firmly, that she loves him truly, but that she cannot think of marriage until all this storm is past. (We cannot pause to consider whether she is telling the truth when she says she loves him; Donna Anna's 'real' feelings have been the subject of almost as much critical discussion as Hamlet's.) A note of anguish is sounded when she begs him not to torment her with reproaches. At the end comes what later would have been called a cabaletta: a livelier coda in which Anna looks to a brighter future and even breaks into a coloratura passage which at first strikes one as oddly out of character and has often attracted adverse criticism. But, properly sung, it is expressive coloratura – not merely a display cadenza – and the accompanying harmonies are a reminder that the shadows have in fact not yet lifted.

The aria, the solo set-piece, being concerned with emotion

[1] op. cit., p. 171.

rather than action, necessarily tends to be rather static. Whereas baroque opera had to build up its characters almost entirely from the emotional revelations of their arias, Mozart had other means at his disposal; so Don Giovanni himself has only two set arias, full-length solo pieces (in addition to the charming little serenade in Act II), in the whole work – one in each act. One is his great drinking-song, 'Fin ch' han dal vino'; the other, 'Metà di voi quà vadano', is so unmelodious, so unlike an aria in the conventional sense, that I do not remember ever hearing it sung separately, away from the stage. That is natural; it makes no sense as pure music; but it is one of Mozart's most masterly pieces of musical dramatization. Giovanni sings it when Masetto and the peasants come to avenge themselves on him; he is disguised in Leporello's clothes and, pretending to be his servant, supervises the trap to catch himself. Da Ponte did not provide words to stir the imagination: merely directions for setting the ambush and a description of the victim's dress. (It will be Leporello wearing it, of course.) But Mozart saw it all with his inward eye, and has wonderfully conveyed not the scene but the character. Giovanni naturally sings in the *buffo* character of Leporello, yet he reveals – and the orchestra tells us more clearly – that the servant's clothes conceal a master, and a masterful master at that. The whole thing is deliciously ironical: a piece of brilliant acting in music, which also displays the actor's enjoyment of his own brilliance.

The real Leporello also has only two arias, of which one – the 'catalogue' aria – is extremely familiar, while the other, 'Ah pietà, signori miei', in which he pleads for mercy from the avengers and then gives them the slip, is known only to those who know the whole opera. But even before his 'catalogue' aria, Leporello has had a short solo in which his musical characterization begins. Indeed, he is the first person seen on the stage when the curtain goes up. It was a well-established convention of *opera buffa* to open with a soliloquy by a comic servant, and it is a measure of Mozart's genius to see what he has done with it – apart from the fact that, before this first number is over, we have touched real tragedy. Leporello is much more than a comic servant; it is as wrong to make him a mere buffoon as to make Beckmesser one; he shares so many of his master's characteristics that (as Abert points out) he is almost the Don's vulgar counterpart. Nor is he completely a coward until confronted with the statue; he is rather an avoider of trouble. In 'Nott' e giorno', after only eight bars of grousing at his lot, he already begins to show the Don Giovanni side of himself. The libretto only says, "I want to be a gentleman and serve no longer", but for a moment the music lights him up, so to speak, from inside; notice the horns in thirds, underlining the voice-part, and the swagger of the little violin interjections. A lesser composer would have swept all this along in a lively *buffo* outburst; Mozart shows us Leporello really uplifted for a moment by this vision of himself as he would like to be, even visualizes him making some little swaggering gesture. In the second part of the 'catalogue' aria Leporello again begins to project himself into his master's skin; up to now he has only been telling Elvira *about* Giovanni, but at this point, as he describes his master's way with each type of woman, he imagines himself in his place. The music is much slower, a sort of minuet, and full of little picturesque touches – half of them in the orchestra – as Leporello describes the Don's technique with different types: with brunettes he praises constancy (heroic tutti flourish), with blondes sweetness (chromatic thirds). The Don loves equally "tall, majestic women" (sustained high D) and little ones (to a patter of semiquavers).

There is a curious touch when Leporello breaks off for a moment, after the return of the minuet theme, to mutter in recitative, "But his predominant passion is for young beginners"; the music suddenly modulates from D to B flat, the minuet is interrupted for a moment and a sinister staccato passage is heard on the bassoon. What does it mean? It has been suggested that Leporello has a sudden realization of his master's wickedness, but that is out of character; clearly Mozart visualized some piece of acting here, some stage-business that explained the point. Before the aria is finished, Leporello's temporary self-projection has collapsed before his innate coarseness.

Leporello's musical characterization is, of course, developed consistently, but he gets only one more chance to hold the centre of the stage and reveal his character in an aria. Here he is in quite a different position. He has been cornered and captured by the avengers, who crowd upon him, each pouring out a different accusation. His 'Ah pietà, signori miei', begging for mercy, is a striking demonstration that an opera aria need not be static; this one must be acted throughout. The central theme is Leporello's cringing; it is perhaps meant to be suggested by a little motive first heard on the strings directly after the opening bars, a slithering sort of figure which almost pantomimically suggests an apologetically wriggling body; it becomes more prominent towards the end and finally accompanies his exit as he edges his way towards a door in the wall and suddenly darts through it. But a dozen different shades pass over that main colouring. Of course, he is not really guilty; it is all his master's fault – "He's the master and he forced me." And then he addresses each of his captors in turn, adopting a different tone with each: confidential to Donna Elvira, hoity-toity to Zerlina, apologetic and embarrassed with Don Ottavio.

One most clearly recognizes Leporello's individuality – the fact that he is far from being a mere type of comic servant – by comparing him with one or two fairly similar characters in other operas. Of the other comic bass servants, one thinks at once of Osmin in *Die Entführung*, of Figaro, and of Papageno. Osmin, of course, is very obviously different; he is not much more than a compound of frustrated lust and cruelty. But Figaro? You have to think for only a few moments to realize that Figaro, too, is very different. Figaro is not only a more respectable character socially; he has more solid qualities. Although a bit of a rascal, he is not almost wholly one. Just as Leporello distortedly reflects Don Giovanni, Figaro reflects Almaviva; and Count Almaviva, though no angel, is not a villain. Don Giovanni is wicked – splendidly, flamboyantly wicked; the Count is never worse than very naughty. The whole opera is about the Count's 're-education' and how his wife and servants succeed in teaching him to behave; no power on earth, not even the supernatural power implicit in the statue, can make the Don behave; he goes to Hell rather than conform, without a word of repentance. This difference is reflected in their servants. Figaro is altogether more civilized than Leporello. He may be a comic figure, but he thinks more and feels more; he is more intelligent – there are streaks of pessimism in his make-up – and he can really suffer. Of his three big solos, two are obviously on a different plane from Leporello's music. There is his cavatina, 'Se vuol ballare', with its dignity and serious irony, and there is 'Non più andrai', the most popular tune in the whole opera, in which Figaro tells Cherubino that his philandering days at the castle are over. Figaro is in high spirits, rejoicing at Cherubino's departure, mocking, but without malice – very unlike the malicious coarseness of Leporello's mockery of Elvira in the 'catalogue' aria. But the point may be made more surely by considering Figaro's 'Aprite un po' quegl' occhi' in the last act, which belongs to the more normal type of *buffa* aria, and is therefore nearer to what might be sung by Leporello.

This aria presented the librettist with a problem, for it takes the place of the monologue in Beaumarchais where Figaro has a long diatribe against the social and political conditions of the day, the speech which more than anything else makes the play one of the documents of the French Revolution and which caused Louis XVI to ban its performance. Apart from political considerations, a paraphrase of Figaro's monologue would have been totally unsuited to music, but something seemed necessary in its place. Da Ponte's not very brilliant solution was to provide words for a *buffa* aria of a conventional type inveighing against the fickleness of women and the blindness of men. Figaro believes, quite wrongly, that his Susanna is being unfaithful to him. He has been established all through the opera as a real and sympathetic character; now, at the climax of his misery, he is to sing a conventional comic aria. How does Mozart deal with the problem? In two bars of *secco* recitative Figaro comments that all is ready – for the dénouement in the garden. Then in an *accompanied* recitative he gives vent to his sorrow: "O Susanna, Susanna, what pain you cause me, with that ingenuous face, those innocent eyes." There is nothing comic in that; he is a real man, really suffering. In this case the serious *recitativo accompagnato* does not lead to a serious aria; that would have been wildly out of character. Instead, it leads, surprisingly, to a comic one: but to a comic one transfigured because of it. Thanks to the altogether serious cry from the heart that has preceded it, Mozart is able to give this *buffa* aria the most subtly bitter and ironical flavour. Not that Figaro puts himself forward as *pagliacco*, the broken-hearted clown; he is much too sophisticated. He knows that, in the comic convention, a deceived bridegroom is ridiculous; so, despite his anger at womankind, he contemplates himself with grim humour and a wry face, all of which is wonderfully conveyed in the music; there is not a hint of such subtleties in the libretto. It is all in the voice-part, though sometimes the orchestra joins in to twit him like Susanna herself.

If Figaro is Leporello's superior, morally and intellectually, and a more solidly conceived figure, Papageno stands on the other side of Leporello. I will not say he is Leporello's inferior, but he is simpler. He is a rascal, too: sensual, a liar, a coward. But he is a much simpler rascal, almost an innocent rascal: a likeable peasant scamp without subtleties. So he appears in his two strophic songs, 'Der Vogelfänger' in Act I and 'Ein Mädchen oder Weibchen' in Act II, tunes so popular in cut that some people find it hard to believe that Mozart composed them; all sorts of ancestors have been found for them in German folk-music and contemporary opera, and there is even a persistent legend – which may after all be true[1] – that they were given him by Schikaneder, who was not only the librettist of *Die Zauberflöte*, but the original Papageno. It may be objected that there is not much characterization in these two songs, but they are perfectly in *his* character, such as it is, which has been shown more fully elsewhere in the opera. The same may be said of practically all the arias in *Die Zauberflöte*; they are very strongly typical. 'O Isis und Osiris' is the very voice of priesthood; 'Der Hölle Rache' is Revenge personified; the 'portrait' aria could be sung by any romantic young hero. For the characters themselves are types; they lack the comic vitality and human complication of the characters of *Don Giovanni* and *Figaro*. What makes *Die Zauberflöte* unique among Mozart's operas and among the world's operas is what we may call the overtones of its characters and the mysterious, fantastic musical world in which they live and breathe. It is a world in which Papageno and Sarastro can exist side by side without incongruity because we perceive through their music that each character has some deeper significance than the one superficially apparent. Papageno seems to be a simple bird-catcher, a sly, naive, and untruthful but amusing peasant, thinking of little but food and drink. But he not only catches birds; he wears a bird-like dress, and so we sense that he is, if not a bird himself, bird-like in essence – perhaps a symbol of nature.

The type-characters of *Die Zauberflöte* are exceptional; the persons who populate the greater part of the Mozartean world are as complicated as those of the everyday world – only twenty times more entertaining – and to comprehend fully Mozart's methods and powers as a dramatist in music we need to trace the development of one such flesh-and-blood-and-spirit character right through an opera. I have already remarked that

[1] See Komorzynski: op. cit., p. 168.

Mozart preferred to unfold and reveal character in the musical action and contrast of ensembles rather than in the relatively, admittedly not invariably, static music of the solo aria. The part of Susanna in *Figaro* is an outstanding example of this. She has two arias it is true: 'Venite, inginocchiatevi' in Act II, 'Deh vieni non tardar' in Act IV. The first, which she sings when they are dressing up Cherubino as a girl, is charming;[1] the second, sung just before the last finale, when all the threads of the tangle are to be finally unravelled or cut, is very much more than charming; it is one of the loveliest things in the whole score. But she – not her mistress – is the principal female character; the part was sung in the original production by Nancy Storace, who was the prima donna at Vienna, not the *seconda*.[2] She is on the stage with Figaro when the curtain goes up on Act I; she has the last aria in the opera; more significantly, she sings in every one of the ensembles. Even more than Figaro himself, she is at the heart of all the crazy goings on. Since she stands in a peculiar relation to every other important character, she constantly appears with one or another. There are six duets in *Figaro*: Susanna is one of the partners in each. There are two trios and a sextet: Susanna is in all three, and naturally she is to the fore in each finale.

The opera actually begins with two duets for her and Figaro, both allegro. Yet they are so contrasted that one gets no sense of monotony. The first, which brings up the curtain, is dramatically static – simply a picture of a situation – but not musically static. It may not tell us much about the two characters, yet it does establish their different temperaments. They are in the room that is to be their bedroom when they are married; Figaro is measuring it to see whether the bed will fit nicely – the orchestra almost pantomimically suggests his pacing to and fro; Susanna is trying on a hat in front of a mirror. She naturally wants Figaro to admire it, and she gets more and more impatient as he goes on with his reckoning, ignoring her. At last he has to give up and do the admiring; her melody triumphs, his disappears. It is clear that they are going to enjoy perfect happiness – so

---

[1] In the Vienna revival of 1789 it was replaced, rather oddly, by the arietta 'Un moto di gioja' (K.579).

[2] On the suggestion that the part of the Countess was originally written for her, and on the consequent interchange of parts in certain passages, see S. Strasser: 'Susanna und die Gräfin', *Zeitschrift für Musikwissenschaft*, X/1928, pp. 208–16, and S. Anheisser: 'Die unbekannte Urfassung von Mozarts *Figaro*', ibid., XV/1933, pp. 301–17.

long as Susanna gets her way. But the shadow of trouble appears in the little recitative dialogue that follows. Susanna shows that she does not care for the room they have been given, fine though it is; Figaro cannot think why, or why she will not tell him the reason. She retorts, "Because I'm Susanna and you're a fool." The second duet, 'Se a caso madama la notte', which follows, reveals what is worrying her and completely changes the mood. The drama begins to move. At first Figaro, still in high spirits, points out the advantages of the room, next to their master and mistress; if in the night either should ring, in a step or two they can be with them. But then the key darkens to G minor and Susanna says, "Supposing one morning the Count rings, and sends you three miles away; then in a step or two he could be at my door. . . ." Figaro is at once in a cold horror of jealousy. But she turns on him again: "Now, no suspicions or accusations! Be quiet if you want to hear any more." She already has the poor wretch completely at her mercy; she has no intention of being unfaithful to him, but she is determined to get full value out of the situation. At the end, the orchestra dies away in a mutter which suggests that more will come of all this.

The next duet in *Figaro*, 'Via resti servita', shows Susanna in action against Marcellina, the lady of mature years who wants Figaro for herself. The rivals begin in an atmosphere of excessive politeness; the violin figure at the beginning is another of the quasi-pantomimic figures; it suggests the act of curtsying. But Marcellina gets angrier and angrier; Susanna mocks her in coloratura triplets; and finally the orchestra bows her out. In speaking of the significance of such figures, are we attributing to Mozart subtleties that were not in his mind – at any rate, in his conscious mind – at all? I do not think so. Let us remember the letter to his father about 'O wie ängstlich' in *Die Entführung* (26 September 1781)[1] in which he speaks of the hero's "throbbing heart" expressed "by the two violins playing in octaves":

"This is the favourite aria of all those who have heard it, and it is mine also. I wrote it expressly to suit Adamberger's voice. You feel the trembling – the faltering – you see how his throbbing breast begins to swell; this I have expressed by a crescendo. You hear the whispering and the sighing – which I have indicated by the first violins with mutes and a flute playing in unison."

Whatever the significance of the violin figure, it is this that uni-
fies the duet as a musical composition. If we think of Mozart as
a man who passively accepted conventional musical forms in a
way that Beethoven, for instance, did not, we do him grave injustice; the subtle handling of form in the piano concertos alone
should be sufficient to blow such an idea to the winds. In the
operas one could hardly make that mistake at all if one paused
to consider the music in cold blood; but in the theatre one is so
swept along by the music and the action that hardly anyone
notices that the first duet in the opera ends with quite different
material from that with which it begins. It opens with Figaro's
'measuring' music and ends with the music of Susanna's new
hat, sung by both of them; in the middle the two are blended so
skilfully that no one notices the transition; all the same, Susanna's music has completely triumphed over Figaro's and ex-
tinguished it. Even in a number of Mozart's arias the musical
form is dynamic and dramatic. It is the same in 'Se a caso
madama': there is not only a dramatic change, when the emotional weathercock veers right round; the musical material
changes too. Only the orchestra for half a dozen bars at the very
end reminds us – ironically – of the beginning of the number.
(How often one has to speak of Mozart's irony! We hardly need
the testimony of his letters to tell us that irony was a highly important element in his make-up.) That surely is evidence of
supreme mastery of musical drama: to be able to compose such
striking emotional and thematic contrasts within a small frame,
leaving a total impression of unity free of even a momentary
suggestion of formal cramp.

So far we have seen Susanna pitted against only one other
character at a time; let us see how she manages with two. There
is a delicious scene of action in Act I, the first part of which is
played in *secco* recitative; indeed, hardly anyone but Mozart
would at that period have thought of setting any part of it as an
ensemble. The situation is farcical. There has been a scene between Susanna and Cherubino, which is interrupted by the approach of the Count; Cherubino hides. The Count begins to
make love to Susanna, but is interrupted by Basilio, the music-
master, and has to hide in turn. Basilio then begins a confidential
conversation with Susanna about the Count's pursuit of her and
Cherubino's affair with the Countess, all of which is agonizing
for Susanna, who cannot tell him that both the Count and

Cherubino are actually in the room. At last the Count can bear
it no longer; when he hears that *his* wife may be unfaithful to
him, he bursts out of hiding, and now, where (as Abert points
out[1]) most composers of the period would have given the Count
a 'rage' aria and then finished the scene with more *secco* recitative, Mozart composes a very typical Mozartean trio of action.
The Count has his outburst of rage; he orders Basilio to turn out
this vile seducer. Basilio begins to make excuses for his own behaviour; he is, of course, a much misunderstood character. (He
has his own unmistakable theme fairly consistently throughout
the trio.) But it is Susanna who dominates the scene. She is
genuinely scared – notice the D flats in her agitated quavers,
which pull the music into F minor – but her main concern is to
get the two men out of her room as quickly as possible. She tries
to distract their attention by pretending to faint; they rush to her
rescue and carry her tenderly to the sofa – where Cherubino is
concealed under a heap of clothes. That brings her round very
quickly: "Dove sono? Cosa veggio?" The men soothe her. Then
Basilio maliciously brings the conversation back to Cherubino.
"Of course," he says, "what I said was only my suspicion", and
Susanna tells the Count, "It's all slander. Don't believe this
humbug." But the Count says Cherubino must go. "Poverino",
indeed! Only yesterday (and the interpolated narration is told
in a patch of recitative) he caught him in another girl's room,
the gardener's daughter's, caught him concealed just like *this* –
and he throws the heap of clothes off the sofa. Observe how
Mozart handles the discovery. Instead of a commonplace
orchestral outburst, he gives us a single, long-held piano F on
oboe, horns, and violas (with only the quietest orchestral movement underneath); it is like the holding of a long breath. The
Count is dumbfounded, Basilio delighted, and Susanna over-
whelmed by the disaster. Cherubino is completely silent. Then
the Count recovers, turns on Susanna ("Ah, most innocent
young lady!") and the trio ends with all three expressing their
different feelings. The three-part writing is interrupted only
once by Basilio reminding the Count – ironically again – "What
I said about the page was only my suspicion."

It would take too long to follow Susanna all through the
opera, but we must at least see how she behaves alone, first, with
her master, then with her mistress. The first duet in Act III,

[1] op. cit., Vol. II, p. 306.

'Crudel! perchè', shows the Count making love to her, and the
first part, in A minor, is serious enough to show that he is, at
least temporarily, in earnest. Now, Susanna and the Countess
have already plotted the assignation and exchange of clothes,
so she has to give him some encouragement; besides, it is quite
clear that, however faithful to Figaro, she enjoys the attentions
of her master – provided things do not go too far. So all through
the duet she plays with the Count, half encouraging him and
promising at least to meet him in the garden in the evening. The
Count's A major love-making is marked by Mozart's favourite
device for putting over a penetrating cantabile melody: flute,
violins, and voice (instead of the more usual bassoon) spread
over three octaves (Ex. 2). The essentially instrumental nature
of the Count's melody is emphasized in the following bars.

Ex.2

We see Susanna with her mistress in the famous 'letter' duet; here she is simply the demure lady's maid. The Countess is dictating a letter to her husband, the letter which Susanna has to write giving him details of the promised rendezvous in the garden, which is to be kept not by Susanna, but by her mistress in Susanna's clothes. Susanna quietly echoes the Countess's verbal phrases, but Mozart avoids the obvious and commonplace device of making her echo the musical phrase. Nothing could be simpler than the orchestral accompaniment. The scoring is for strings, with solo oboe and bassoon. First and second violins are in unison throughout, and from beginning to end play nothing but an incessant quaver-figure of the utmost simplicity, accompanied by the lower strings in octaves playing either detached quavers or (occasionally) legato dotted crotchets on the two beats of the bar: two-part writing for strings on an absolutely unchanging pattern of the most childish nature. The effect is twofold: the extreme naivety emphasizes – irony again! – the plotting of the two minxes, and the very repetitiveness of the basic figuration builds up a curious tension, as in parallel passages in the symphonies of Sibelius. This is something which is going to have consequences, which is going to explode. As for the solo oboe and bassoon, they also keep strictly together, nearly always in octaves, sometimes in tenths. In the earlier part of the duet, as Abert (I think) was the first to point out,[1] they play only when Susanna is writing; they are always silent while the Countess is dictating, until near the end when the two women re-read the letter together.

Taken by themselves, these two duets, 'Crudel! perchè' and the 'letter' duet, suggest a Susanna who is hardly more than an ordinary soubrette. But in the opera they are not to be taken by themselves; they are further strokes in the musical portrait which has gradually been built up of the one and only Susanna. The final touch is provided by her aria, 'Deh vieni, non tardar', a very lovely piece often heard for its own beautiful sake in the concert hall. But it, too, loses much by being taken from its dramatic context.

After Figaro has sung his outburst against women, 'Aprite un po' quegl' occhi', he hides in the dusk of the garden. Other characters cross the stage and, after some twenty bars of *secco* recitative, Susanna – left alone in sight – sings the piece which is the

[1] op. cit., Vol. II, p. 345.

musical, not the dramatic, counterpart to his. First comes an accompanied recitative, fulfilling the usual function of transition from the prosaic level of *secco* to the level not this time of tragedy, but of pure poetry. It is quick and joyous: "At last the moment has come when I can, without a qualm, throw myself into my beloved's arms." It seems simple enough, but it is really very subtle. Susanna is singing *at* and *for* Figaro, whom she knows is hiding; but he does not know that she has him in mind and she does not intend him to know. He thinks she means the Count, and it is utterly characteristic of Susanna that she should sing to her real love and, at the same time, pay him out for his jealousy by tormenting him while doing so; that she should rejoice simultaneously in her deep and true love and in being mistress of the situation. This burst of exuberance dies down at once and then comes her aria, 'Deh vieni, non tardar'. Again the music is extraordinarily simple, with a pizzicato accompaniment and three woodwind soloists – the usual favourites, flute, oboe, and bassoon. But it is the purest poetry. Susanna is happy in her love, for she knows everything will soon be put right; she is moved by the stillness and beauty of the night; and she pours out her natural feelings. We have been allowed plenty of musical glimpses of her better self already; we know quite well she is not merely a pert, heartless soubrette; but here for the first time – it is the crown of the opera, before the final hurly-burly – all her real sweetness is disclosed. There is no flummery, no exaggeration, nothing outside the part; Mozart never for a moment forgets himself and allows her to become the Countess,[1] it is all very simple. Yet we know from the composition sketches that, whereas Mozart could do the most difficult-seeming things apparently without effort, this very 'simple' piece cost him infinite pains; the end, in particular, was rewritten again and again before he could get it right.[2]

If Mozart preferred ensemble to solo for the development of dramatic character, it is clear that his favourite forms of ensemble were duet and trio: the combinations which offer him

---

[1] Anheisser had no difficulty in demolishing Strasser's theory (see n.2, p. 303) that 'Deh vieni' was originally written for the Countess.

[2] See 'Revisionsbericht' to the *Collected Edition*, p. 87. Einstein prints the opening of the original version, 'Non tardar, amato bene', in his edition of Köchel, p. 622. For the 1789 revival in Vienna, when Susanna was sung by Adriana Ferrarese del Bene, Mozart substituted the vastly inferior show-piece, 'Al desio, di chi t'adora' (K.577). See also *The Concert Arias*, p. 347.

one character to strike against another or two others. When more characters are introduced, problems begin to arise. I say 'more characters' advisedly; the handling of four or five or six voices would present no difficulties to a Mozart. The problem is not musical, but dramatic: how to preserve the dramatic individuality of more than three voices and not merely to compose a number of beautifully woven parts. In the whole of *Figaro* there is, apart from the finales, only one ensemble larger than a trio: the sextet. *Don Giovanni* has only one quartet and one sextet – and the sextet is handled like a finale. There is just one quartet in *Die Entführung*. *Die Zauberflöte* has two quintets, one in each act, both for the same set of characters: Tamino, Papageno, and the three ladies.

That in itself is worth considering. For the three ladies are three vocal parts, but not three characters. It is true that the third lady is sometimes differentiated from her two companions musically – their parts may move in parallel while hers supplies the 'bass' to the trio – but, generally speaking, they are dramatically unanimous and either imitate each other or sing in three-part harmony. Since they amount to only one character, their quintets with Tamino and Papageno are, from the dramatic point of view, essentially trios. We see this at once in the scene of the giving of the magic flute – which is, incidentally, a first-class example of the muddle produced by the change of plot. The golden flute is a present from the wicked Queen, yet the three ladies seem to be good spirits, genuinely protecting Tamino. The changed libretto has to make believe that this is all pretence, but even the libretto does not make this clear enough, and the music unmistakably supports the original version; when the first lady gives Tamino the flute, she sings "O Prinz, nimm dies Geschenk von mir" to music that almost literally, though in quick tempo, anticipates 'O Isis und Osiris'; and when, near the end of the number, just as the three are leaving and the men ask, "How are we to find this castle of Sarastro's?", the tempo changes to andante, oboes are replaced by clarinets in the orchestra, and the ladies reply that "three boys, young, fair and wise" will appear and act as their guides, in music of utterly guileless loveliness. It is entirely characteristic of *Die Zauberflöte* that a number which begins with the farce of Papageno's locked lips should end with that solemnly beautiful music without any sense of incongruity.

Again, in this quintet the style is as different from that of
Mozart's Italian operas as Papageno's songs are from *buffo* arias.
Perhaps Mozart comes nearest in *Die Zauberflöte* to the style of
his Italian operas in his ensembles of action such as the first part
of the very next number – described in the score as a trio, though
really consisting of two very short duets; the first between Pamina and Monostatos, the second between Monostatos and
Papageno. In the Italianate half of the number, Pamina is
brought in by slaves, chained and left at the mercy of the lecher-
ous Moor – only to be saved in the most ridiculous way by
Papageno, of all people, to music that is purely in the style of
Die Zauberflöte and not in the least like that of the Italian come-
dies. (It will be remembered that Papageno and Monostatos
take each other for the Devil, back away, and bolt in opposite
directions.) In the smallest space we are taken from a serious –
or at least melodramatic – situation to a farcical one; within
seventy bars Monostatos is transmuted from Caliban to Golli-
wog.

In most complete contrast to this pseudo-trio of action is the
trio of the boys in Act II, 'Seid uns zum zweiten Mal will-
kommen', as static as a piece of ritual. Like the three ladies, even
more than the three ladies, the boys sing as one: in harmony, but
without dramatic differentiation. Musically, again like those of
the ladies, the two higher voices tend to run in parallel while the
lowest is pseudo-bass. In this trio, indeed generally throughout
the opera, they always sing together in simple three-part harmony. But what harmony! They are good spirits, spirits of
light – though promised in the first place by the three ladies who
are the agents of the evil Queen of darkness. Here in the second
act they come flying in to restore to Tamino and Papageno the
flute and bells of which they were deprived, and welcome them
a second time to Sarastro's realm; there is no real action to
carry forward, no character to unfold. So Mozart paints three
angelic beings, spirits of air and light, in what is perhaps the
most *delicately* beautiful piece of scoring he ever conceived –
scoring that must have given Berlioz an unforgettable lesson.
The wonderfully spaced out chords of the three voices, so transparent in the bright key of A major, are supported only by
strings (most of the time without double-basses), flutes, and
bassoons. The instruments hardly do anything but double the
voices and surround them with the most delicate, feathery little

demisemiquaver motives, In the introduction the three-octave lay-out is carried out in thirds (Ex. 3):

This is Mozart's customary solution when he has to deal with undramatic characters or situations in opera: to write the most sensuously beautiful music of which he is capable. No one comes away from a performance of *Die Zauberflöte* worried by the muddled dramatic motivation or the violent contrasts of musical style, of buffoonery and solemnity, or by the lack of roundness in the character-drawing of even the most normal human beings in the opera, Tamino and Pamina. One is no more troubled than one is by the incoherence of a dream. When *Die Zauberflöte* has been experienced in the theatre, the final, total impression is of a de Quinceyian dream in which the ultimate secret of the universe has been revealed – only it has unfortunately been forgotten in waking. What is really remembered vividly is the sonority of it all – something like the verbal sonorities that were all Coleridge could remember of his dream of Kubla Khan: the different planes of sonority, the cold, piercing plane of the Queen of the Night, the golden, transparent plane of the boys and the ladies, the profound and solemn tone-world of Sarastro and his priests, the gross and comic plane of Monostatos and Papageno, and in the middle – the standard of human normality – the figures of Tamino and Pamina. The hero and heroine may not be sharply drawn characters, like most of those in the Italian operas, but their music at least establishes them as human types, distinct from the magical or the superhuman, priestly beings in the opera.

If Mozart's difficulties in *Die Zauberflöte* arose from the number of characters outside the sphere of common human experience, in *Così fan tutte* the year before they had arisen from characters meant to be normal, but insufficiently individualized and rather conventional in their actions. The contrast with the other Italian operas is here one of quality, not of kind. But the characters and situations in *Die Zauberflöte* are so unlike those in Mozart's Italian operas and in his earlier *Singspiel*, *Die Entführung*, that he had to compose an entirely different kind – or kinds – of music for them. Instead of lively action, he often had to visualize something much more like ritual. He could perhaps think himself into the skins of Tamino and Pamina and Papageno, or even into those of noble or evil types such as Sarastro and the Queen in so far as they exist as real characters, but he could hardly have thought himself into the skins of the three boys or the three ladies or the men in armour; he could only paint them from outside, as beautifully as he knew how. He had adopted the same solution in *Don Giovanni* with the one character who did not – indeed, could not – stimulate his musical imagination: the wooden Don Ottavio, who is given the two loveliest arias in the whole work, 'Dalla sua pace' and 'Il mio tesoro'. He adopted it wholesale for the puppets of *Così fan tutte*.

Why, it may be asked, did Mozart accept such an artificial libretto as *Così*? One can understand his undertaking the challenge of *Die Zauberflöte*, with its Masonic symbolism which meant so much to him. But why waste loving labour on *Così*? The answer is that on this occasion Mozart had no choice. Just as Shakespeare is said to have written *The Merry Wives* because Elizabeth I wanted to see Falstaff in love, *Così fan tutte* was written because the Emperor Joseph II admired *Don Giovanni* and *Figaro*, particularly *Figaro*, and wanted another *opera buffa* by the same pair of collaborators; he is said even to have given da Ponte the subject, an anecdote based on a real happening. Mozart could not decline such a commission; for one thing, he was too hard up; so he did the best he could – and did it in a great hurry.

For want of dramatic stimulus, then, he lavished purely musical beauty – with the result that, although *Così* is not one of his finest operas, it is one of his loveliest scores. (There is a profound difference in dramatic value between a beautiful aria sung by a character who has already been built up into a solid, living personality, when the beauty acquires a special meaning – as with Susanna's 'Deh vieni' – and a beautiful aria sung by a character who does nothing but sing lovely tunes.) Although Mozart's irony has full play – indeed, its fullest play – in *Così*, it often seems here to place him right outside his characters. Consider Fiordiligi's great aria, 'Come scoglio', in which she protests that her constancy is like a mighty rock: a companion-piece in certain respects to Constanze's 'Martern aller Arten' in *Die Entführung*. It is not killed, as that aria is, by an endless orchestral ritornello, but it is even more out of character. In fact, its whole point lies in its wild incongruity. Mozart laughs, and invites us to laugh, *at* Fiordiligi singing an heroic aria about constancy. We do laugh, but at something much less subtle than the comedy of the self-revealing characters of *Don Giovanni* and *Figaro*. Fiordiligi might have deceived herself about her own nature, but she would never have deceived herself all that much.

Besides smothering his puppets in beautiful music, Mozart has another resource in *Così*: he multiplies ensembles. There are more in *Così*, which begins with a succession of three trios, than in any other of his operas, none of which has more than one or two ensembles larger than a trio (other than the finales). *Così*, however, has four: a quartet, two quintets, and a sextet. Why? Mainly, I suggest, because the characters are not real enough to present Mozart with the problem of preserving their individuality in a larger ensemble. The artificial symmetry of the plot helps. The two heroines are more distinct characters than the three ladies in *Die Zauberflöte*, but they can just as easily be fused in an ensemble. So can the two heroes. Thus it is easy for Mozart here, as in *Die Zauberflöte*, to cast five musical parts as, at most, three dramatic parts: the two girls against or with their two lovers, with the cynical old Alfonso taking an independent part. That is what happens in the second of the two quintets in Act I, the farewell quintet: the girls sob – and their lovers nearly sob too – and their voices unite in their "addio's", while Alfonso repeats (aside), "I don't know how to keep from laughing". In the later part of the earlier quintet, 'Sento, o Dio', there is a dual distribution: Ferrando, the more romantic of the two heroes, sides with the girls while Guglielmo joins Alfonso.

But the things one carries away from a performance of *Così* are not these rather conventionally comic and dramatic ensembles, but the exquisite pieces of purely musical composition where Mozart forgets the action and the characters – or gives them up as hopeless; for example, the trio which the girls and Alfonso sing in Act I as they watch the ship sail away. The girls forget to be sad; Alfonso forgets to be cynical; they unite their voices in three-part harmony, sometimes doubled by clarinets and bassoons, while the muted violins murmur incessantly throughout. In sheer sensuous beauty of sound this nearly matches the trio of the boys in *Die Zauberflöte*.

I have left to the last discussion of Mozart's finales, not from any punning sense of fitness, but because they are the most important and most complicated form of operatic ensemble he employed. They also have a peculiar historical importance, pointing to the way opera was to take in the nineteenth century. The finale, as Mozart gives it to us in his last and greatest operas – a continuous composition built up from a number of varied forms and types and combinations, but unified by a carefully planned key-scheme – this kind of finale was by no means the only way of ending an act of an eighteenth-century opera. A Handel act may end simply with an aria; indeed, Act I of *Figaro* ends with an aria, 'Non più andrai'. (Hence its long final ritornello with trumpets and drums which are not entirely motivated by the military context.) Or an act may end with a chorus, though *coro* in old operas often means only 'all the characters' rather than 'chorus' as we understand the word. In French opera an act probably – and if the last act almost certainly – would end with a dance or series of dances. *Opera buffa* had a different convention; an act often ended with a long number beginning with a solo or duet, but with one character after another appearing on the stage, thus building up a climax of sound-volume as well as of dramatic excitement. (Sometimes this is inverted – one character leaving after another – with comic effect.) Mozart's *opera buffa* finales are sometimes essentially elaborations of this device.

They are basically elaborations of it, but in reality much more. The finale of the second act of *Figaro* begins with the Count and Countess alone; later Susanna appears; then Figaro; then the gardener (who goes out again, however); and finally a group of three other characters emerges, Marcellina, Basilio, and Bartolo. (Beaumarchais ended his act with a further scene in which Susanna and the Countess discuss the rendezvous in the garden; da Ponte wisely cut it.) With each addition to the characters on the stage, there is a change in the fortunes of the drama, often with changes of key, tempo, and so on. All this musical and dramatic action takes a great deal of time, and the finale comprises more than eighty pages of full score. As the whole of Act II runs to only some hundred and thirty pages, roughly two-thirds of the entire act consists of 'finale'. It is an extreme case; the finale of Act III is much shorter. But the finale of Act IV takes up more than half the act, and in *Die Zauberflöte* nearly half the entire opera consists of the finales to the two acts. That in itself marks a striking difference from the ordinary *Singspiel*; Mozart himself had ended the three acts of *Die Entführung* with a trio, a quartet, and a vaudeville rounded off by a 'Turkish' chorus. The 'number opera' had begun to disappear long before Wagner's time; indeed, both Spohr and Weber had written completely through-composed operas – *Der Berggeist* and *Euryanthe* – without breaks or *secco* recitative, before Wagner had even begun to compose. Naturally, there are still plenty of vestiges of the set-number in them, but so there are in Wagner even after *Tannhäuser* and *Lohengrin*. But perhaps the first big step towards through-composed opera was taken by Mozart in this enormous development of the act-finale, in allowing it to swallow up more and more of the musical and dramatic space that would formerly have been given to separate numbers.

For the study of the Mozartean finale there is no better example than the second act of *Figaro*. It is a classical example of the perfect mating of music with a protracted dramatic action. The action moves almost continuously and, crisis succeeding crisis, in a steady crescendo of excitement which corresponds to the ever-increasing number of persons on the stage and, consequently, of solo voices at the composer's disposal. Each fresh situation produces a fresh grouping of the characters, and each situation lasts just long enough – the musico-dramatic pace and timing are wonderful throughout – for the composer to give it due musical space. Yet with all this dramatic bustle and diversity of moods, the whole finale is a musical entity, as convincing a unity as any Mozart symphony or concerto. The general musical plan is as follows:

(a)	Allegro: 4/4	E flat	Count and Countess.
(b)	Molto andante: 3/8	B flat	The same, plus Susanna.
(c)	Allegro: 4/4	B flat, with a wide range of modulation	The same.
(d)	Allegro: 3/8	G major	The same, plus Figaro.
(e)	Andante: 2/4	C major	The same.
(f)	Allegro molto: 4/4	F major	The same, plus gardener.
(g)	Andante: 6/8	B flat	The gardener leaves halfway through.
(h)	Allegro assai: 4/4	E flat	Count, Countess, Susanna, Figaro, Marcellina, Basilio, and Bartolo.

The symmetry – the last three sections corresponding roughly to the first three – and the alternations of tempo and metre are obvious. The key-scheme is equally clear: the firm establishment of E flat and its dominant, the unexpected leap to G major (the dominant to the fourth power), and the return to the tonic by keys each a fifth lower than its predecessor.

The corresponding dramatic action is this: (a) the enraged Count is trying to force the door from his wife's room into the locked ante-chamber where he believes Cherubino is concealed; at last the Countess gives him the key, and out walks – Susanna; (b) Susanna, grave and demure, wants to know what all the fuss is about; the Count is confounded, his wife happily mystified; (c) the initiative passes to the Countess, backed up by Susanna, but the Count is forgiven at last, and the three voices have just begun to unite in a trio of reconciliation when (d) in bursts Figaro. The abrupt change of key-centre here is motivated by an

abrupt change in the action. The fuss about Cherubino is over –
or seems to be over; all that Figaro wants to say is that his wedding preparations are complete and that he has come to fetch
Susanna. But the Count stops him; there is just one little point
he wants cleared up. So Figaro is wound into the main tangle
and the key-scheme begins to wind back through the cycle of
fifths that will end in E flat again. In (*e*) the Count confronts
Figaro with the anonymous letter he has written himself and
presses him hard while the women try to rescue him; for a
moment everything seems to be cleared up, and for a moment all
four voices join happily, when (*f*) in comes the indignant gardener with his broken flower-pot and his story of a man who
jumped out of the window. This produces a typical tripartite
grouping: the Count trying to get the gardener's story, the gardener – simple, honest soul – trying to tell it, and the other three
trying to discredit him by saying he is drunk. The climax of tension is reached when (*g*) the gardener hands Figaro, who has
claimed to be the jumper, the papers dropped by Cherubino; and
it is typical of Mozart that, as in the 'letter' duet, but here much
more powerfully, he conveys a sense of great tension by the extreme deliberation of the tempo and the extreme simplicity of
the orchestral figure that persists all through this section. Even
the Count's further discomfiture when the women get Figaro
out of this further difficulty is too brief to bring real relaxation.
This long-sustained 'dominant preparation' is released in the
tonic tutti (*h*), with the musical entrance of trumpets and drums
and the dramatic entrance of three of Figaro's antagonists: a shattering blow. Mozart now has seven solo voices to handle simultaneously, but in accordance with his usual practice he con-
trives to have only three dramatic parts. The three newcomers,
though more differentiated than the three ladies in *Die Zauberflöte*, generally keep together here. The Countess, Susanna, and
Figaro form the opposing group, denouncing the others as
rogues or lunatics. The Count has revived wonderfully, and
there is a superb moment when he calls out, "Silence! Silence! I
am here to judge"; for a time he provides the third dramatic
part. But, of course, he quickly sides with the enemy, both
dramatically and musically, and the act ends with the two
groups trying to shout each other down.

Mozart's finales contain many things unparalleled in the rest
of the operas, indeed sometimes unparalleled anywhere in

Mozart's music. Where, except in the finale of the second act of *Die Zauberflöte*, does one find Mozart working on a Protestant chorale? One expects the last finale of *Die Zauberflöte* to be something quite *sui generis*, and indeed it is, characteristically covering the whole range from profoundest solemnity to wild buffoonery. One of the funniest things in the whole opera is the Papageno–Papagena duet in G major, in this context a particularly bright key. The main key of the finale is naturally E flat, the tonic of the opera; but the first E flat section is followed and the last is preceded by sections in C minor (the music before Tamino's ordeal, and the Queen's last desperate attempt to defeat the powers of virtue). In the middle are several sections in C major and G major, so that G major occupies an especially 'bright' position suitable for comedy. But the passage of greatest solemnity is that which precedes Tamino's ordeal by fire and water, the first C minor stretch. Tamino is led in by two men in black armour and, after a terrific call to attention on strings and trombones, the staccato strings lay out a closely woven pattern of imitative counterpoint against which the melody of the chorale 'Ach Gott, vom Himmel sieh' darein' is sung by the two men and played by woodwind and trombones in four octaves. (The words are not that of the chorale but an assurance to Tamino that whoever treads this dangerous path with courage will be purified by fire and water, air and earth.) It is perhaps not merely a coincidence that C minor is also the key of the Masonic Funeral Music (K.477), another composition on a *cantus firmus* (obviously liturgical or ritual in nature)[1] and another of Mozart's most profoundly solemn works.

The second act finale of *Don Giovanni*, the supper scene and the arrival of the statue – again to trombone sounds, the most terrible trombone chords in all music – is the most famous of all Mozart's finales and a subject for endless commentary. Yet in a very different way that to the first act is sometimes quite as remarkable. The setting is the grand entertainment at Don Giovanni's house: dancing for the lower orders and a masked ball for any aristocrats who may care to come – such as the three avengers, Donna Anna, Elvira, and Don Ottavio. The use of dance music – here the famous minuet – as a background to operatic conversation was not unprecedented; Galuppi had employed a minuet in the same way in *La partenza ed il ritorno dei*

[1] See pp. 153f. and n.1 on p. 154, *The Smaller Orchestral Works*.

marinari (1765), and so had Piccinni in his *I viaggiatori*;[1] there
have been a number of instances since. But at a later point in
this finale Mozart outdoes everything his predecessors had attempted and brings off a *tour de force* which no one since has
tried to rival. The stage-band – strings, oboes, and horns – is
playing the minuet once more, again as a background to conversation. (Donna Anna can hardly bear the situation, and
again there is irony in the contrast between the cheerful music
and the suppressed passion of the avengers.) But presently
through the minuet we hear a second band in another room
tuning up, and soon it begins to play a contredanse in 2/4 time
against the 3/4 of the minuet; it has hardly begun before a third
band is heard tuning and then striking up a German Dance in
3/8, all three dances continuing simultaneously, a passage which
must be quoted (Ex. 4), since it is not always made clear in vocal
scores of the opera:

[1] Abert: op. cit., Vol. II, p. 512, where, however, the Galuppi date is misprinted.

There is dramatic point in all this as well; when the German Dance begins, Leporello forces the unwilling Masetto to dance it with him and prevents his going to the rescue of Zerlina, who has been dancing the contredanse with Don Giovanni and is now shuffled out of the room by her pursuer. As for the musical *tour de force*, even Mozart could hardly have kept it up much longer without destroying the natural ease of the three dance tunes, and it is almost a relief to the listener when Zerlina shrieks for help and the main orchestra breaks in with its sforzando dominant seventh in E flat.

All in all, the finales show Mozart the musical dramatist at the height of his powers. Far from being merely effective climaxes or dénouements, they are superb musical organisms, though organisms vitalized by drama. Mozart is never less the 'pure' musician than here; he is never concerned to send the audience away with one last memorable tune ringing in their ears. In any case, as we have seen, the memorable tune was for Mozart little more than a means *faute de mieux* so far as opera was concerned.

BOOK LIST

S. Anheisser: 'Die unbekannte Urfassung von Mozarts Figaro', *Zeitschrift für Musikwissenschaft*, XV/1933.

C. Benn: *Mozart on the Stage*, London, 1946.

E. K. Blümml: 'Ausdeutungen der *Zauberflöte*', *Mozart-Jahrbuch*, Munich, I/1923, pp. 109–46.

H. Cohen: *Die dramatische Idee in Mozarts Operntexten*, Berlin, 1915.

L. Conrad: *Mozarts Dramaturgie der Oper*, Würzburg, 1943.

E. J. Dent: *Mozart's Operas: a Critical Study*, London, 1913, 2/1947.

A. Einstein: 'Concerning Some Recitatives in *Don Giovanni*', *Music and Letters*, London, XIX/1938, pp. 417–25.

—— 'Eine unbekannte Arie der Marcelline', *Zeitschrift für Musikwissenschaft*, Leipzig, XIII/1931, pp. 200–5.

T. Georgiades: 'Aus der Musiksprache des Mozart-Theaters', *Mozart-Jahrbuch 1950*, Salzburg, 1951, pp. 76–98.

E. Graf: 'Das "Leitmotiv" des Cherubin', *Neues Mozart-Jahrbuch*, Regensburg, II/1942.

A. Heuss: 'Mozarts *Idomeneo* als Quelle für *Don Giovanni* und *Die Zauberflöte*', *Zeitschrift für Musikwissenschaft*, XIII/1931.

E. von Komorzynski: 'Die Zauberflöte', *Neues Mozart-Jahrbuch*, Regensburg, I/1941.

E. Lert: *Mozart auf dem Theater*, Berlin, 1918.

S. Levarie: *Mozart's 'Le Nozze di Figaro': a critical analysis*, Chicago, 1952.

A. Lorenz: 'Das Finale in Mozarts Meisteropern', *Die Musik*, Berlin, XIX/1927.

H. J. Moser: 'Dramaturgische Bemerkungen zu Mozarts *Don Giovanni*', *Mozart-Jahrbuch*, Munich, I/1923, pp. 95–108.

M. Pirker: *Die Zauberflöte*, Vienna, 1920.

W. Preibisch: 'Quellenstudien zu Mozarts *Entführung aus dem Serail*', *Sammelbände der internationalen Musikgesellschaft*, Leipzig, X/1909, pp. 430–76.

E. Schenk: 'Zur Tonsymbolik in Mozarts *Figaro*', *Neues Mozart-Jahrbuch*, Regensburg, I/1941, pp. 114–34.

A. Schnerich: 'Wie sahen die ersten Vorstellungen von Mozarts *Don Juan* aus?', *Zeitschrift der internationalen Musikgesellschaft*, Leipzig, XII/1911, pp. 101–8.

G. Schünemann: 'Zwei neue Szenen im *Don Giovanni*', *Neues Mozart-Jahrbuch*, Regensburg, I/1941, pp. 135–46.

S. Strasser: 'Susanna und die Gräfin', *Zeitschrift für Musikwissenschaft*, X/1928.

R. Tenschert: 'Die Ouvertüren Mozarts', *Mozart-Jahrbuch*, Munich, II/1924.

J. Tiersot: *Don Juan*, Paris, 1927.

H. W. von Waltershausen: '*Die Zauberflöte*': *Eine opern-dramaturgische Studie*, Munich, 1920.

E. Wellesz: '*Don Giovanni* and the *dramma giocoso*', *Music Review*, Cambridge, IV/1943, pp. 121–6.

T. W. Werner: 'Zur Kenntnis der Mozartschen Opernarie', *Neues Mozart-Jahrbuch*, Regensburg, II/1942, pp. 181–200.

ADDENDA

B. Brophy: *Mozart the Dramatist*, London, 1964.

J. Kerman: *Opera as Drama*, London, 1956.

D. Mitchell: 'The Truth about *Così*', *Tribute to Benjamin Britten on his Fiftieth Birthday*, London, 1963.

THE CONCERT ARIAS

ALTHOUGH there has been a Mozart renaissance in the last twenty years, the substantial *œuvre* of his concert arias continues to be neglected. There are, I think, two reasons for this neglect. First, the listener, in our days of urgent but suppressed extra-version, finds it relatively easy to identify himself with an instrumentalist on the concert platform or a singer on the opera stage, but relatively difficult to feel at one with a singer on a concert platform who aspires to the full status of prima donna, complete with orchestra, while not allowing her personality to be 'submerged' in a dramatic role. Secondly, the singer, being part and parcel of her age, reflects the attitude of the public. She is either ashamed to show off, and takes refuge in an academic style (most probably being unaware of both facts), or she treats a concert aria as an opera aria and drama-tizes its concertante style out of existence. At best, the concert singer will vaguely regret the absence of her accompanist at the piano, while the opera singer will be restrained by the lack of a stage, movement, and action. As the form of the concert aria was created, though not invented, by Mozart, and completed its history, though it did not die, with him, Mozart is the one com-poser to suffer from our present public and private indisposition. The solution of the conflict, of course, would be for the public and artist to realize the principles of stylization as applied by the classics to dramatic situations. In opera, the singer finds at hand the aid of coaches, conductors, and a sustained public interest. What still remains of her stylistic difficulties is dissolved there in the melting-pot of 'ensemble' and 'production'. In the concert aria, a singer stands and falls by her capacity to interpret the classical principles of stylization, and, at least unconsciously, many do not want to undergo such a test, particularly those 'with a career'. Let our soprano become the good musical gram-marian she should always be, and learn all about the things she does not know: the various kinds of accent (e.g., breath, lips, diaphragm) and their application in phrasing and cross-phrasing; the crescendo ⟨ and ⟩ ; the slide, late or early, on or after the syllable; the whole palette of conscious tone-colour and its relation to key; creative intonation, etc. If she is at all made of the right stuff such study will not inhibit but liberate her imagination, and we may, at long last, be blessed with an artist who is once more capable of rendering a vocal concerto.

A discussion of the form of Mozart's concert arias must begin with the recitative. In his mature concert arias the accompaniments of the initial recitatives are, by and large, richer even than those of his mature operatic arias. While actual arioso passages are surprisingly few, the harmonic and rhythmic structure of the orchestral passages reaches a high level of musico-dramatic tension almost from the outset. While in opera, relaxation must be provided between the numbers by the use of *recitativo secco* or the more customary forms of *recitativo accompagnato*, in a concert piece both the dramatic situation and the character of the hero or heroine must be 'put over' without delay. It could even be argued that the idea of the concert aria, in so far as it gives rise to a true formal concept and not to mere display, must founder on too radical a contradiction between the drama's demands for naturalism and the music's demands for stylization. In its successive aspect – the separation of recitative(s) and aria(s) – as well as in its simultaneous aspect – the stratification of musical functions in voice and orchestra – this contradiction is the life-giving absurdity at the root of every great operatic aria. The musico-logical problem becomes acute in the concert aria, and it needed a Mozart to solve it – in fact, if we except Beethoven's 'Ah perfido!' and Haydn's 'Arianna a Naxos',[1] which, however, is nearer to the cantata form, no one else has solved it.

Thus it is vitally important to compensate for the lack of a libretto's time-table of dramatic situations by the use of composing methods which will seem to augment a certain quantity of motivic material, and to extend an amount of actual time which, for conventional and technical (instrumental, vocal) reasons, cannot be enlarged in reality. The means which are most apt to help in this situation are alternate contraction and dilation of the metre, and a far-ranging, yet pertinent model of

---

[1] Haydn's 'Arianna' is in fact a cantata. His 'Scena di Berenice' (1795), however, is a real concert aria, one of the thirty-odd he wrote; 'Berenice', in our opinion a far greater work than 'Arianna', solves the problems of the concert aria (or, if one will, concert scene) better than any other Haydn work. – EDS.

cadential progressions. The development of these two features
can be followed from the recitatives of Mozart's earliest concert
arias to those of his two greatest, K.505 and 528. It is not so
smooth a development as that of comparable single stylistic
features in the quartets and symphonies, for the concert arias are
closely adapted to the capacities of the singers for whom they
were written. Furthermore, their public use varied between the
lizenze, the 'encores' sung by the prima donna at the end of an
opera, those that were inserted to take the place of certain arias
in operas not by Mozart, and the true concert arias or concertos
for voice and orchestra. Thus, when Mozart wrote his first pieces
for Aloysia Weber, whom, at the time, he hoped not only to
marry but to educate to musical greatness, he laid the founda-
tions of his proper concert-aria style (e.g., K.316(300b)). Later,
when it became apparent that Aloysia owed her success with the
public to a certain cold brilliance, fluent coloratura, and matter-
of-fact musicianship, Mozart supplied her with arias that
matched her musical and personal character (K.294, 316, 416,
419). An exception is K.418, but even this does not come up to
the standard of Mozart's two masterpieces in this *genre*, K.505 and
528, written for Nancy Storace and Josepha Duschek respectively. After this peak, Mozart returned, whether by necessity,
inclination, or obligation we do not know, to the style of Aloysia
Weber, though on the higher level of his last years (cf. K.538).
The later works in this form are unfortunately again insertions in
other composers' operas, written for Louise Villeneuve (K.578,
582, and 583.) We say unfortunately, because the new concertante
style, here on the threshold of emerging, could only be hinted
at in the circumstances, while Mozart found no opportunity to
write independent scenas in the remaining two years of his life.

But we must return to the problem of recitative in the true
concert aria. From the earliest beginnings, Mozart felt that the
need for integration in this section was paramount, and went a
long way towards achieving it. The recitatives of 'Ah, lo previdi' (K.272) have the following cadential schemes:

First Recitative: A minor – D minor – G minor – F minor – –
First Aria: C minor.
Second Recitative: A flat – E flat – modulations, reaching D
minor – B flat – C minor – B flat – – Second Aria (Cavatina): B flat.

While the second recitative, in which the tempo frequently changes from Andante to Allegro and back, is modulatory, corresponding to the heroine's conflict of emotions, the first recitative provides a good example of the way in which, in many works, the key of a first aria is approached: starting from a remote key, Mozart descends into the flat minors, taking care to omit the main key (C minor), but counterweighting it by a paragraph in F minor, on the other side of C minor. This is particularly appropriate in an aria that begins, not on the tonic, or even on a triad, but, in Beethovenian fashion, on the diminished seventh, with a ringing A flat topmost in the soprano. When the tonic, C minor, is reached in the third bar, in the form of an elegiac orchestral ritornello, we feel that the tonal peregrinations of the recitative have not been in vain.

In other arias, the plan is very different. Let us take for an example K.294, 'Alcandro, lo confesso':

Recitative (Andantino): B flat – C minor – – Aria (Andante sostenuto): E flat.

Metastasio's text, from *Olimpiade*, expresses King Clisthenes' astonishment at finding his son again, whom he believed dead; Mozart seems to have changed the meaning to express a woman's wonderment at being reunited with her lost lover. If the first lines of the recitative, "Alcandro, lo confesso, stupisco di me stesso" ("Alcandro, I confess it, My wonder, how repress it?"), are compared with the beginning of the aria, "Non so d'onde viene quel tenero affetto" ("I know not from whither has come my affection"), they will be seen to stand in the dramatic relationship of question and answer, i.e., of a progression from the dominant to the tonic. In this case, Mozart had to do no more than to separate these prime harmonic functions by a paragraph in the relative minor of the key of the aria at the moment when the heroine first confesses that she is disturbed by her emotions. He does not retrace this key, but with singular dramatic insight joins the aria's first tonic chord to the last dominant of C minor.

Of all the recitatives in the earlier arias, the finest is perhaps the majestic address of Alceste to her people in K.316(300b), 'Popoli di Tessaglia!'. The text, from Gluck's *Alceste*, describes the queen voicing her own and her people's grief at the death of her husband. Mozart, in a letter (30 July 1778) to Aloysia, considers this the best scena he had ever composed. But Einstein,[1] while stressing the excellence of the formal plan and the delicate orchestral treatment, with its solo oboe, bassoon, horns, and strings, goes on to submit: ". . . the deeper Mozart gets into the work, the more he thinks of the success of his beloved, with her astonishing staccato tones, and the less he thinks of the dramatic situation, and of the queen who is also wife and mother", and "[Mozart] did not finish [the work] until 8 January 1779, in Munich, a few weeks after the break with his beloved; perhaps he intended it as a sort of 'double bar', symbolizing the end of his relationship with her".

As far as the recitative is concerned, Mozart certainly has the dramatic situation in hand. In the following scheme (Ex. 1) of its cadential plan, the modulations are printed in full size, cadential movement and transitions *within* one key in small type. The figured bass is, of course, my own, and used only as a means of abbreviation.

The tonic key (C minor) is established in the first eight-bar phrase, which begins with a five-bar orchestral prelude stating the recitative's main motive – an elegiac changing note of a minor second, used sequentially, and followed by a descending scale motive over a chromatic accompaniment. In the last three bars, the voice enters with Wagnerian effect on a heavy augmented triad. The change to A flat coincides with the mention in the text of the late King's children. With the turn to the 'relative' F minor, their nearest living relation returns to her own grief. The brief A minor section is reached rather casually via a German sixth; to be sure, the entry of the ritornello in this key (bar 18) seems to have no programmatic purport, but it becomes the starting-point for one of Mozart's most amazing modulations. First, he merely seems to anticipate his late Vienna style by following a minor key with the dominant of its submediant (bar 20), but then this chord is revealed as only the pivot in a chromatic modulation which plunges us into the royal purple of D flat, to the pronouncement, "In this misfortune shall I first mourn the kingdom . . .?" After such romantic excess, a return to C minor is necessary. Bars 24–30, which reintroduce the chromatic 'grief motive' of the beginning, are, tonally and formally, the centre of this recitative, whose either end supports an arch of modulations. The following, very gradual, descent

[1] This and further references are to A. Einstein: *Mozart*, London, 1946.

through the flat minor keys of the circle of fifths (bars 32–41) is harmonically as stable as the corresponding first part of the first arch of modulations (bars 9–17), yet programmatically ("I come to join you in your prayers and libations") somewhat more epical. As might be expected, there appears at its end another bold stroke of harmony. By the sound of it, it is again a secondary seventh (bar 42) which seems to effect a daring enough modulation to the supertonic (F minor) of E flat. But it is spelled as a chromatic pivot chord (a German sixth) leading to E minor. Now even this, though an enormously wide step, would still have been intelligible in 1778. What falls right outside the scope

of the eighteenth century is the fact that the E minor resolution
is, in the end, suppressed, and the dominant of that key substituted (bar 43). E minor smoothly gives way to G, and we
find ourselves in the dominant of the tonic C minor. The whole
astounding process from bar 40 to the end relates formally,
on the one hand, to the audacity of bars 18–22; on the other, it
is the exact musical counterpart to the Queen's final sentence:
"Surely the anger of Heav'n will be placated when such a
kingdom, afflicted, unites in vows of true devotion, displaying a
spectacle of grief and anguish." In the Italian, the last clause
occurs, earlier on, as "con questo spettacolo funesto", with our
singular chord progression (bars 42 and 43) spanning the word
"funesto".

Let us now turn to the recitative of one of Mozart's greatest
concert arias, K.505, 'Ch'io mi scordi di te'. To this work, about
which more will be said later, there exists a companion piece,

K.490, 'Non più, tutto ascoltai', of March 1786: a "Scena con Rondo with violin solo for Bar[on] Pulini and Count Hatzfeld" composed for *Idomeneo* (Mozart's Catalogue of works). K.490, whose text is the same as that of K.505, and whose violin obbligato foreshadows K.505's piano obbligato, was composed to replace the original beginning of Act II in a private performance of the opera. While K.505 comes from the heart, K.490 is an occasional composition.[1] Its recitative is as lengthy and as boring as Mozart could be in 1786. It is true that, in order to explain the dramatic situation, Mozart had to set more of the text, while in K.505 he begins with the words "Ch'io mi scordi di te". But even from here on, K.490 is vastly inferior to K.505. Compare in both works the ends of the recitatives and – an important juncture – the beginnings of the arias (see Exx. 2 and 3).

---

[1] cf. F. Spiro: 'Die Entstehung einer Mozartschen Konzertarie', *Vierteljahrsschrift für Musikwissenschaft*, IV/1888.

While Ex. 2 is better than what precedes it, Ex. 3 is the final, concentrated, and meaningfully simplified version of the same idea. The words, so touching in the context, of "Come tentarlo" have a certain staginess in the vocal part of K.490, while the orchestra expresses no more than uneasiness. In K.505, however, the voice rises twice to an indignant question mark while the orchestra adumbrates the stealthiness of temptation. The modulation to the aria's B flat major in K.490 occurs within a bar at the end of the recitative – that in K.505, from G minor to E flat, is built into the first four bars of the aria, and sheds the steady light of the heroine's avowed constancy over the ensuing espressivo tune.

The point is that in the recitatives of the concert arias Mozart *had* to concentrate. This brings us to the other means we mentioned above of 'making a little go far', of extending actual into artistic time; namely, the alternate contraction and dilation of the metre. In 'A questo seno deh vieni' (K.374) of 1781, a concert rondo written for the Salzburg castrato Ceccarelli, Mozart contrived to create the impression of spaciousness in the very brief recitative by placing a più moderato phrase between two con moto phrases that are carried by a playful violin motive. In 'Ma, che vi fece, o stelle' (K.368) of 1781, Mozart does not change the speed of the recitative, but he twice introduces a little *p–f* string figure in semiquavers in a setting that otherwise consists only of crotchets and quavers. In the (Andantino) recitative of K.505, Mozart uses the rhythm of the thrice-stated orchestral ritornello to denote the rising agitation of the heroine (the Idamante of K.490 has here become a woman's role). In the following four bars the orchestra is almost silent, but breaks in with elemental force in the three identical statements (B flat, G minor, E flat) of the Allegro assai. It is true that the dramatic situation obliged Mozart to set the words "Venga la morte! intrepida l'attendo . . ." to a faster speed; but he does it with an abruptness (absence of modulatory links) and symphonic coherence (full sequences) that remind one of Beethoven's attempts to write 'against the voice' in the service of dramatic truth. Woe betide the soprano who would slacken the pace of Ex. 4:

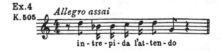

Ex.4
K.505   *Allegro assai*

in - tre - pi - da l'at - ten - do

It is as if the sudden presto passage at the fifth bar of the Count's great aria in *Figaro* had grown here to symphonic stature. In K.505 no more reference is made to the initial dotted rhythm, but after some sustained chords, an entirely new quaver rhythm (Andante) rises on the "Come tentarlo" phrase. In K.505, as well as in K.528 (which is yet to be discussed), the *recitativo accompagnato* has been set on its journey to the twentieth century, across the gulf of the nineteenth.

Having dealt with the special characteristics of the recitatives in Mozart's true concert arias, the question now arises as to the form of the aria(s) proper. Although a number of these is longer than Mozart's operatic arias, and a greater proportion has two sections, I cannot detect any basic difference between the form of the concert and operatic aria. At the point where the aria is reached, the emotional situation of a scena is determined, or ought to be determined, in a good eighteenth-century aria, and there arises no inner necessity for the concert aria to differ from an operatic aria in essentials of form. To be sure, this does not apply to the arias of K.272, 505, and 528, which are exceptions to the rule; but exceptions not by virtue of a different model of form dictated by the ambience of the concert platform, but by virtue of the singularity of their musical invention. Yet in all these arias, external, or at least a-formal, features can be traced which distinguish them from their operatic kin. In the absence of a scenario, lyrical phrases are allowed to luxuriate; the orchestra is more likely to behave as in a piano concerto – that is, surrounding the singer in the proximity of a concert platform, instead of propping him up from the orchestra pit; concertante elements abound in solo and accompaniment; the arias are more definitely written to suit the peculiarities of a certain singer, and, having three or more sections of varying speed, give a completely rounded picture of his or her character. Lastly, even in those arias which were expressly written as insertions in current operas, Mozart, in his customary 'I'll-show-you' mood, tries to go one better than the Anfossis, Cimarosas, and Martins, in spite of his avowals that he only meant to help out this or that opera singer (cf. Einstein's note about the row over Mozart's arias in Anfossi's *Il curioso indiscreto*, op. cit., p. 368). While this ambition made enemies for Mozart, it helped to maintain the quality of the 'inserted' arias.

In actual form, the arias are modelled on the current patterns of the late eighteenth century, with the proviso, of course, that they are written by Mozart. Apart from the matter of melodic inspiration, this means that the actual form the aria takes is more closely dependent on the motivic material, and this, in turn, on the dramatic situation, than with other composers. Let us set down a brief list of Mozart's principal concert arias, indicating the time and occasion of their composition and the ground plan of their form. Counting several fragments, but not lost works, and, of course, omitting songs, duets, etc., there are fifty-six secular concert, or occasional, arias extant. Most of them are for soprano, some for tenor or bass. Their Köchel numbers are:

K.21(19c), 23, 36(33i), 70(61c), 71, 74b, 77(73e), 78(73b), 79(73d), 82(73⁰), 83(73p), 88(73c), 119(382h), 146(317b), 178(125i), 209, 210, 217, 255, 256, 272, 294, 295, 316(300b), K.Anh.3(315b), 368, 369, 374, 383, 416, 418, 419, 420, 431(425b), 432(421a), 433(416c), 435(416b), 440(383h), 486a(295a), 490, 505, 512, 513, 528, 538, 539, 541, 577, 578, 579, 580, 582, 583, 584, 612, K.Anh.245(621a).[1]

In the space available, I cannot mention more than a round two dozen of these, and their choice is dictated more by my personal liking for them than by their historical position. I consider the arias K.505 and K.528 to be the summit of Mozart's achievement in this form, and have left their more extensive analysis to the end of this chapter.

K.217. 'Voi avete un cor fedele'
SOP., STR., 2 OB., 2 HN.

Text after Carlo Goldoni.
Comp. 26 October 1775, Salzburg. Insertion in Galuppi's Le nozze. There, Dorina teases two suitors; in Mozart's slightly varied version only one.

FORM

A – B – A' – B' – A'' – C

(A) is an Andantino grazioso in G major which is abbreviated and varied in (A'), and still further in (A''). (B) is an Allegro in

---

[1] The aria K.584a ('Donne vaghe') is now known to be from *La serva padrona* by Paisiello (Einstein's revision of Köchel, p. 1035). – EDS.

D major; (B') stands in G major – like the second subject in a sonata recapitulation – and has different colorature. (C) has the figuration, though not the harmony, of a coda.

K.272. 'Ah, lo previdi!'/'Ah!, t'invola agl' occhi miei'
SOP., STR., 2 OB., 2 HN.

Text from Paisiello's opera, Andromeda.
Comp. August 1777, Salzburg, for Josepha Duschek, wife of the pianist and composer Franz Duschek of Prague (cf. K.528). The lover of Andromeda has been mortally wounded by Perseus. She wishes to die, in order to await her dying lover by the River Lethe. This is a very inspired piece of which Mozart was justly proud. He exhorted Aloysia, who learnt it after Duschek, to "watch the expression marks – to think carefully of the meaning and the force of the words – to put yourself in all seriousness in Andromeda's position! – and to imagine that you really are that very person".

FORM

Recitative (Allegro risoluto): see analysis, pp. 326f. – – Aria (Allegro): A (C minor) – Transition 1 – B (E flat) – Codetta – Ritornello – A' – Transition 2 – B' (C minor) – Coda – – Second Recitative: Allegro – Andante – Allegro – Adagio – Allegro – Adagio – – Cavatina (Andantino): C – D – C' – E – D' – C" – Coda (Allegro).

The first aria is a sonata form with the short ritornello instead of a development. (B) and (B'), both lengthy sections, whose tune is repeated, behave tonally and formally like a second subject. At the 'recapitulation', (A') completes (A) by prefacing its diminished seventh with two bars of tonic. The Cavatina, in which the emotional tempest has subsided, returns to a more customary aria form, namely the compound rondo, where (C) is omitted after the central episode.

K.294. 'Alcandro, lo confesso'/'Non so d'onde viene'
SOP., STR., 2 CL., 2 FAG., 2 HN.

Text from Metastasio's Olimpiade.
Comp. 24 February 1778, Mannheim. Written for Aloysia Weber,

whom "it suits like a dress" (Mozart). This had great success with the Mannheim public and the composer Christian Cannabich.

FORM

Recitative, cf. p. 327. Aria: Part I (Andante sostenuto): A (E flat, orchestra) – A' (solo) – B (B flat, repeated) – – Part II (Allegro agitato; through-composed) – – Part III (Tempo primo): Transition (E flat) – B' (repeated, sequential and modulatory) – A" – Coda.

(A), leading to (A'), is as weighty as in a small concerto. (B), particularly in the form of (B'), where it is raised to a higher level, is a telling pictorial translation of its text, ". . . quel gel, che le vene scorrendo mi va . . . ". Mozart probably omitted the principal theme at the start of Part III because he did not want to come too near to the old da capo form. His solution, at this point, is not, however, very happy: Tempo I returns too suddenly, and the listener (and singer) find their feet only at (B'), eight bars later.

K.486a(295a). 'Basta, vincesti'/'Ah non lasciarmi, no'
SOP., STR., 2 FL., 2 FAG., 2 HN.

Text from Metastasio's Didone abbandonata.
Comp. 27 February 1778, Mannheim, for Dorothea Wendling, wife of the flautist in the court orchestra, former mistress of the Elector of Baden; as Einstein remarks, the text (the forsaken Dido) has been sought out by the singer herself, and is not inappropriate. He goes on: ". . . Mozart keeps in mind the conventions of the aria form and the abilities, obviously no longer remarkable, of the singer; but here again it is impossible for him to stick to the conventional scheme. He does not compose a special seconda parte, but rather sets the entire eight-line text to a steadily flowing melodic stream and inserts before the repetition, which is greatly intensified, a short free recitative instead. . . . The aria monumentale has become the scena."

FORM

Recitative – – Aria: Part I (Andantino espressivo): A (E flat) – B (B flat minor) – – Part II: Recitative (Allegretto) – – Part III: A' – Coda.

Part II is merely a contrasting 4-bar phrase. The best features of this work are the beginning of Part I, where E flat is reached from D major in a mere three bars, and (B), which, by degrees, works up to the harmonic *finesse* of its conclusion (Ex. 5):

K.316(300b). 'Popoli di Tessaglia!'/'Io non chiedo, eterni dei'
SOP., STR., OB., FAG., 2 HN.

Text by Calzabigi, from Gluck's Alceste.
Comp. June 1778, Paris – completed 8 January 1779, Munich, for Aloysia Weber.

FORM

For analysis of Recitative, see pp. 327ff. Aria I (Andante sostenuto e cantabile, C major): A (orchestra) – A' (solo) – B (modulatory) – C (C major) – – Aria II: (Allegro assai, C major): D – E (C minor → A flat → C minor) – E' (C minor → C major) – Coda.

In (A'), (A) is actually shortened from twenty-one to fourteen bars. In (B), Aloysia's coloratura get under way, while (C) begins as a tonal, but not melodic, counterstatement to (A') and

proceeds to a kind of fioritura (Ex. 6) which must have taxed
even Aloysia's accuracy:

Ex. 6 ARIA
Andante sostenuto e cantabile
K. 316

[qualche] rag - - - - - - [-gio di pietà]

(D) is no more than a transition of 12 bars to (E); but for its
key and modulations one could take the start of (E) for the
main theme of Aria II. But Mozart amply confirms C major as
the tonic in the later part of (E') which merges into a long,
utterly brilliant coda, in which the voice reaches g'''.

K.368. 'Ma, che vi fece, o stelle'/'Sperai vicino il lido'
SOP., STR., 2 FL., 2 FAG., 2 HN.

Text from Metastasio's Demofoonte.
Comp. January 1781, Munich, perhaps for Elisabeth Wendling,
daughter of Dorothea Wendling, the Elettra in Idomeneo.

FORM

Recitative, see p. 332. Aria: Part I (Andantino, F major):
A (orchestra) – A' (solo) – – Part II (Allegro, F major): B
(through-composed, turning towards dominant) – C (starting in dominant) – – Recitative (4 bars) – – Part III (Andantino, F major): A'' – – Part IV (Allegro, F major): B' –
Coda.

(C) has the function of a central development, which is made
possible by its incidence with the poem's dramatic climax: the
heroine compares the turmoil of her betrayed heart to a tempestuous sea journey. To the words "urto in un altro scoglio, del
primo assai peggior" (". . . hurtled from one rock to a worse
one"), she is buffeted, within thirteen bars, from E flat to A
major (Ex. 7).

(B') begins, strangely, not with (B)'s first motive, but with its
thirteenth bar; the section is magically transmuted into a coda
by the entry of the subdominant seventh, at the peak of the vocal
line (f''' – e flat''') but in the middle of a phrase (cf. the be-

Ex.7
K.368

ginning of the coda in K.505). Einstein comments on this work: "[It] is as full of *bravura* as the one for Aloysia [K.316(300b)], though written for a fuller and more heroic voice; but every note . . . is full of genuine passion, and the freedom of the form is carried to such lengths that nothing is left of the *aria monumentale*."

K.369. 'Misera, dove son!'/'Ah! non son' io che parlo'
SOP., STR., 2 FL., 2 HN.

Text from Metastasio's Ezio.
Comp. 8 March 1781, Munich, as a courtesy piece for Countess
Baumgarten, née Lerchenfeld, favourite of Prince Carl Theodor.
The last concert aria before Mozart moved to Vienna. The subject,
many times set to music, was well known in the eighteenth century.
Fulvia, grieving for her lost husband, implores the gods to smite her
with a thunderbolt.

FORM

Recitative (E flat) – – Aria: Part I (Andante sostenuto, E
flat): A – B – C – C' – – Part II (Allegro, E flat): D – E –
E' – Coda (quasi D').

The lengthy recitative is carried by a figure of distress in
descending thirds, to the rhythm ♩ ♫♫♩. (A) and (B) are so
short that they comprise both theme and section, but (C) is a
modulating paragraph whose beginning is resumed by (C').
Similarly, (D) is a single clause, but (E) modulates at length, re-
verting to its tune with (E'), which, in its turn, becomes a coda.
The coda's second phrase points to (D). The similarity between
the structures of the two parts of the aria makes it doubly certain
that Mozart was intent here on finding a new form: its essence
would seem to be symmetry *within* a melodic and harmonic
group, but asymmetry *without* it, i.e., between the aria's con-
stituents.

K.416. 'Mia speranza adorata!'/'Ah, non sai, qual pena'
SOP., STR., 2 OB., 2 FAG., 2 HN.

Text from Anfossi's opera, Zemira (Abate Gaetano Sertor).
Comp. 8 January 1783, Vienna, for Aloysia Weber. A song of fare-
well sung at the final moment of parting.

FORM

Recitative (Andante – Adagio – Allegretto – Andante –
Allegro assai – Adagio) – – Rondo (Andante sostenuto, B
flat): A – B (modulating) – A' (B flat) – C (leading to Più
andante and Allegro assai) – A'' (B flat, shortened) – C'
(shortened, leading to extended coda).

As can be seen, this lively recitative does indeed 'stretch time'. (B) is the first, quiet rondo episode; (C), which begins in a hushed E flat, develops into the lively central episode. (A″) and (C′) are both curtailed (rather than compressed) to make room for the brilliant coda. We have, again, a singular experiment with form, an adaptation of the compound rondo for the purposes of the concertante style. In the interest of progressively increasing the tension, the return of the first episode is suppressed, and the central episode is 'published' in two editions: the first under the supervision of the rondo theme, the second in its own right.

K.418. 'Vorrei, spiegarvi, oh Dio'/'Ah conte, partite'
SOP., STR., 2 OB., 2 FAG., 2 HN.

Insertion in Anfossi's Il curioso indiscreto (*author unknown*). *Comp. 20 June 1783, Vienna, for Aloysia Weber (Lange). Clorinda, denying her own devotion for her lover, urges him to seek happiness with Emilia, her rival for his affections.*

FORM

No Recitative. Aria: Part I (Adagio, A major): A (orchestra) – A′ (solo) – B (leading to dominant) – C (modulatory) – A″ – B′ – – Part II (Allegro, A major): D – E – D′ – Coda (Più allegro).

(A) is a forbear of Fernando's 'Un' aura amorosa' from *Così*. In Ex. 8 (from *Così*), the melody of Ex. 9 (K.418) is enriched, the rhythm simplified, the harmony the same:

Ex.8 COSÌ FAN TUTTE

Ex. 8 refers, of course, to the form the theme takes on its second appearance.

The theme of (A) enters in harmonic disguise at the start of (A″). This is a symphonic device made possible by the grand structure of the Adagio, which is, in fact, a kind of sonata movement with (B) and (B′) in place of a second subject. The following ternary Allegro is more conventional.

K.419. 'No, no, che non sei capace'
SOP., STR., 2 OB., 2 HN., 2 TRPT., TIMP.

Insertion in Anfossi's Il curioso indiscreto.
A bravura aria, comp. June 1783, Vienna, for Aloysia Weber (Lange). A third aria (K.420, 'Per pietà, non ricercate') was written by Mozart for the same opera, for the tenor Adamberger. Although Einstein prefers it to the two soprano arias, I cannot find much merit in it and therefore omit it. K.419 consists of a single, brilliant Allegro movement, without recitative. It had to be repeated at its first performance.

FORM

Part I (Allegro, C major): A – B (G major) – C (D minor →
C major) – – Part II (Allegro assai, C major): D – E (leading to coda).

The lines of demarcation in the above scheme are determined by the few, simple changes of key and figuration in this
aria. (B) begins with the quaver colorature of the second part's
latter half; the coda is an Italian closing formula. The chromaticism of (E)'s colorature is an at least semi-conscious ironiza-
tion of the composer's wonted chromatic profundity.

K.432(421a). 'Così dunque tradisci'/'Aspri rimorsi atroci'
BASS, STR., 2 FL., 2 OB., 2 FAG., 2 HN.

Text from Metastasio's Temistocle.
Comp. 1783, Vienna, probably for Ludwig Fischer, the first Osmin.

A very great work. The recitative (Allegro – Andante) contains, among other audacities, the Verdian cadence (Ex. 10):

The Aria (Allegro), too, foreshadows Verdi in his early thun-
derings, rather than Beethoven – cf. the continuous 𝄾𝄾 𝄾𝄾
movement of the strings, the 'strokes of lightning' in flute and
bassoon, the general rests before a tutti entry on a *sf*. The form
of the aria is A – B – A – C. (A) is in the tonic (F minor), (B)
in the dominant *minor* (a rare event, but highly dramatic); (C) is
more intense than (B) and leads, after a pause on a diminished
seventh, to a terse coda, ending *piano*. This work is a mature offshoot of the equally tragic K.272. But while, in the latter, the
dark, minor-mode progressions are penetrated by counterpoint

only in the orchestral ritornelli, in K.432 the voice is included in the horizontal aspect of the lay-out (Ex. 11):

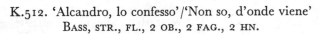

K.512. 'Alcandro, lo confesso'/'Non so, d'onde viene'
BASS, STR., FL., 2 OB., 2 FAG., 2 HN.

Text from Metastasio's Olimpiade.
Comp. 18 March 1787, Vienna, for Fischer.
The same text as K.294's, but here the original situation is restored: King Clisthenes (Bass) recognizes his lost son.

FORM

Recitative (Allegro molto, C major, ending on dominant of supertonic) – – Aria: Part I (Andante, F major): A – B (dominant) – – Part II (Allegretto, C major, modulatory, through-composed): C – – Part III (Tempo primo, F major): A' – B' (in tonic) – Coda.

Again, sections (B) and (B') of a large aria function as sonata second subjects. (C) is rather like a development in view of its key structure and its pronounced motivic allegiance to, though not dependence on, the main part's material. Einstein speaks of the grand style, and sharp contrasts of rhythm, harmony, and tempo of this aria. We can add to this the excellence of the orchestration. Notice how, in Ex. 12 from Part II, the superb

Ex.12
K.512

Allegretto

Nel se - no a de-star - mi sì fie - ri con-tra-sti

nel se - no

spacing of the instruments gives just the right colour to the fleet part-writing and harmonic disquiet of this passage, at the words, "My heart is stirred by these fierce contrasts". Scoring like this occurs in the late concert arias as frequently as in the last piano concertos and in *Così*.

K.513. 'Mentre ti lascio, o figlia'
BASS, STR., FL., 2 CL., 2 FAG., 2 HN.

Text from Paisiello's opera, La disfatta di Dario.
Comp. 23 March 1787, Vienna, for Mozart's friend Gottfried von Jacquin. A father's farewell to his daughter. The concertante character of the orchestra, especially the woodwind, is again very pronounced.

FORM

Part I (Larghetto, E flat): A (orchestra) – A' (solo) – B (modulatory) – A'' (leading to coda) – – Part II (Allegro, E flat): C – C' – D – C'' – D' – E (Coda, Più allegro).

Both parts are through-composed, and the above scheme is based on the implications of tonal and motivic relationship rather than on actual returns, however varied, of definite sections. Thus, the triplet figure for clarinets and horns in (A) makes, in the dominant, an unexpected appearance in the vocal line of (A''). (C') is a rather rondo-like, short reference to (C). In (C''), the same triplet figure, a kind of *Leitmotiv*, appears even more unexpectedly, now in tempo Allegro.

K.538. 'Ah se in ciel, benigne stelle'
SOP., STR., 2 OB., 2 FAG., 2 HN.

Text from Metastasio's L'eroe cinese.
Comp. 4 March 1788, Vienna, for Aloysia Lange; the last piece Mozart wrote for his sister-in-law. A lovelorn girl invokes the stars either to let her die or to bless her affection.

This is a vocal concerto in the form of one, undivided Allegro movement in F major. The form is seen to be basically ternary (A – B – A'), if one goes by the tonal indications:

after a middle part that leaves, and returns to, the dominant, E flat reappears, although not the original theme. Later, however, part of (A) returns in (A') in its original shape. Although, in an aria of this size, one could expect an approximation to a second subject within the (A) part, there is no *tonal* indication of one; only a welter of secondary ideas. Most of these are established, according to the manner, though not the structure, of a piano concerto, in the long orchestral prelude. This comparative formlessness matches the quality of the work's invention: the ideas are effective, often surprising in some detail, but not of sustained excellence.

K.541. Arietta: 'Un bacio di mano'
BASS, STR., FL., 2 OB., 2 FAG., 2 HN.

Text by da Ponte (?).
Insertion in Anfossi's Le Gelosie fortunate, *for the bass Francesco Albertarelli, who sang Don Giovanni in the opera's first Vienna performance.*
Comp. May 1788, Vienna. A witty Frenchman is giving ironic advice to a somewhat stupid lover – a Così *situation.*

FORM
Introduction (quasi recitative) – Aria (Allegretto, F major): A – B – A'.

(A') is (A) with a small coda attached. (A) anticipates exactly the closing theme of the exposition in the first movement of the 'Jupiter' Symphony, "and thereby shows how many *buffo* elements still haunt that most royal of all symphonies. But the aria is also a masterpiece of wit, vitality, brevity, showing a profound knowledge of the theatre" (Einstein).

K.577. 'Al desio, di chi t'adora'
SOP., STR., 2 BASSET HN., 2 HN., 2 FAG.

Comp. July 1789 for Adriana Ferrarese del Bene as the Countess, to replace Susanna's 'Deh vieni' in a performance of Figaro *in August 1789. Text by da Ponte (?).*

This dull aria is only mentioned here as a *Figaro* curiosity.

K.578. 'Alma grande e nobil core'
SOP., STR., 2 OB., 2 FAG., 2 HN.

Text by Giuseppe Palomba.
Comp. August 1789, Vienna, for Louise Villeneuve, the first Dora-
bella, as insertion in I due Baroni *by Cimarosa.*
The buffo *indignation of Madame Laura at the misdemeanours of*
her unworthy admirer. Einstein thinks that Mozart secretly pokes
fun at her in the orchestra part; probably he refers to the obvious
fussiness of some passages, including the 'catty' main theme.

FORM

No Recitative. Aria (Allegro, B flat): A (orchestra) – A'
(solo) – B – A'' – C – A''' – D (Allegro assai, a through-
composed stretta).

(D) is through-composed, not in the style of great, indivisible
paragraphs, but in the Italian style of comical repetition of some
'threadbare' motive (cf. Osmin's "Erst gehangen . . ."). As the
form, excluding the Allegro assai, is a full-grown rondo, the en-
hancing of (A)'s returns gains importance. The theme of (A'),

Ex. 13, acquires the veiled contrapuntal gravity of the piano
Concerto in C, K.467, when it appears (Ex. 14) in the form of
(A'').

K.580. 'Schon lacht der holde Frühling'
SOP., STR., 2 CL., 2 FAG., 2 HN.

Comp. 17 September 1789, Vienna, as insertion in the German
version of Paisiello's Der Barbier von Seviglia, *for Josefa Hofer,*
née Weber, an elder sister of Aloysia who was to be the first Queen

Ex.14
K.578

Al-ma gran-de, al-ma gran-de e no-bil co-re

of the Night. Apparently the production was abandoned, for Mozart left the MS. unfinished. In the orchestral introduction the violins and the bass are written in, and, farther on, the vocal part and bass line are complete, with an occasional sketch of the violins. But any singer who would like to perform this spirited piece will find it available in modern arrangements.

FORM

Part I (Allegro, B flat): A (orchestra) – A' (solo) – B (F major, modulatory) – – Part II (Andante, G minor): C – D (modulatory) – – Part III: A'' – B' (beginning in E flat) – Coda.

(B) again has the function of a second subject. (B') starts, without modulation, on the subdominant (E flat) instead of the expected tonic. While the main part of the aria is in the Italianate style, the middle part shows some awareness of the German text. Key and tune place this section in the neighbourhood of 'Zum Leiden bin ich auserkoren' from *Die Zauberflöte*, though it is not so serious; the love-plaint of the shepherdess for her 'shepherd' Lindor compels Mozart's tune in the direction of the North German Anacreontics.

K.582. 'Chi sà, chi sà, qual sia'
SOP., STR., 2 CL., 2 FAG., 2 HN.

Text by da Ponte.
*Comp. October 1789, Vienna, as insertion in Vicente Martin's Il
Burbero di buon cuore, for Villeneuve. The faithful Madame
Lucilla ponders on the causes of her lover's bad humour.*

FORM

No Recitative. Aria (Andante, C major): A – B – A' – C.

In this simple rondo, (A') is an exact replica of (A). The tune
of (C) is a new departure over a flowing semiquaver accompaniment. The simplicity of form and lay-out suits the sentimental
situation whose fun is in the eye of the beholder. This simplicity
also seems to tell us that, for the moment at least, Mozart prefers Villeneuve's charm to the aggressive technique of the Italian
prima donna war-horses.

K.583. 'Vado, ma dove? – oh Dei!'
SOP., STR., 2 CL., 2 FAG., 2 HN.

Text by da Ponte.
*Comp. October 1789, Vienna, as insertion in Martin's Il Burbero
di buon cuore, for Villeneuve. Madame Lucilla is full of be-
wilderment at the course her love seems to be taking.*

FORM

No Recitative. Aria: Part I (Allegro, E flat): A – – Part II
(Andante sostenuto, E flat): B – C.

Part I is pleasant, though conventional. Part II is an exquis-
itely simple and refined Tempo di Minuetto which will bore
many by its apparent primitivity, but will please the Mozart
friend of long standing. Section (C), beginning in the dominant,
is slightly more figurated than (B): the undulating triplets of
(A)'s accompaniment now invade the tune.

K.584. 'Rivolgete a lui lo sguardo'
BASS, STR., 2 OB., 2 FAG. 2 TRPT., TIMP.

Text by da Ponte.
Comp. December 1789, Vienna, for Benucci; intended for Così,

found too large in scale, and was replaced by No. 15 of Così, *Guglielmo's "Non siate ritrosi".*

A typical *buffa* aria, full of conventional formulae in its first (Allegro) and last (Allegro molto) parts. The middle part, or second, modulatory section of the Allegro, contains some felicitous harmony and phrasing. On the whole, "Non siate ritrosi" is a better piece.

K.612. 'Per questa bella mano'
BASS, D.B. OBBLIGATO, STR., FL., 2 OB., 2 FAG., 2 HN.

Author unknown.
Comp. 8 March 1791, Vienna, for Franz Gerl, the first Sarastro, and the double-bass virtuoso, Pichelberger.

FORM
Aria: Part I (Andante, D major): A (orchestra) – A' (solo) – B – A" – C – – Part II (Allegro, D major): D – E (including a small Adagio, ending on dominant) – E' – Coda.

The motivic material of the two parts is related, while the time changes effectively from the 6/8 of the Andante to the 4/4 of the Allegro. (E') is a modified, partial repeat of (E) in which singer and double-bass change places. The text, a conventional declaration of love, is treated in a straightforward manner. Mozart obviously did not here consider the double-bass a comical instrument, but a rather endearing one. Its fioriture are very agile, but not ridiculous, and the two soloists, particularly in the gentle Andante, give one the impression of two serenading swains whose corpulence has never yet handicapped them.

K.505. Scena and Rondo: 'Ch'io mi scordi di te'/'Non temer, amato bene'
SOP., PFTE. OBBLIGATO, STR., 2 CL., 2 FAG., 2 HN.

Text from Idomeneo, *Act II, Sc. 1 (Abate Giambattista Varesco).*
Comp. 27 December 1786, Vienna, "for Mselle Storace and myself" (entry in Mozart's Catalogue of works). Anna Selina ('Nancy') Storace was born in London, in 1761, of an Irish mother and an

Italian father, who was a double-bass player at Drury Lane. She studied singing in Italy, obtaining her first engagements there, and, in 1783, became a member of the Italian Opera in Vienna. She was the first Susanna, and Mozart was on the friendliest terms with her and her brother, Stephen Storace, who was one of his more gifted composition pupils. Before she left for London, early in 1787, Mozart wrote this scena as a farewell. "We have the impression that Mozart wanted to preserve the memory of this voice, no brilliant soprano and not suited to display of virtuosity, but full of warmth and tenderness; and that he wanted to leave with her in the piano part a souvenir of the taste and the depth of his playing, and of the depth of his feeling for her. . . . Few works of art combine such personal expression with such mastery – the intimacy of a letter with the highest grandeur of form" (Einstein).

FORM

See pp. 330ff. for an analysis of the Recitative. Rondo: Part I (Andante, E flat): A (Part 1, orchestra and piano – Part 2: soprano) – B (Part 1: modulatory – Part 2: in dominant) – A′ (E flat) – Transition – – Part II (Allegretto, E flat): C (Part 1: orchestra and piano – Part 2: soprano) – D (first episode $\longrightarrow$ dominant) – C′ (E flat) – E (central episode. Part 1: C minor – Part 2: A flat $\longrightarrow$ modulatory – Part 3: lead-back) – C″ (E flat) – F (third episode, E flat) – Coda.

It is puzzling why Mozart should have written "Rondo" over the Andante and not over the ensuing Allegretto. He either loosely refers to the ternary form of the Andante as a kind of germinal rondo, or he sees it as an introduction to the rondo proper. The third possibility would be that he felt a mysterious sort of basic thematic shape (*Urthema*) to underlie the themes of (A) and (C). They are, of course, nicely attuned, but (C) is no variation of (A), at least not in the usual meaning of the term.

The piano versions of (A) and (C) equal, in length, their vocal versions; the difference in figuration is very illuminating. When the piano does not have a theme, it has flowing concertante counterpoints – never the Alberti-bass type of accompaniment, which is left to the strings. The heroine's outbreak, to the words "Stelle barbare, stelle spietate" (bar 92 – bars are counted throughout from the beginning), provides the occasion for an unusual transition to the fast section of an aria: out of the blue, as it were, the piano develops a spiky, spiteful brilliance and leads up to the dramatic question (Ex. 15) with which the heroine closes this section:

Altogether, Mozart knew very well that at this level of inspiration and formal coherence he could afford the most startling changes of rhythm and lay-out without endangering the

intelligibility of his music. When the "cruel stars" are cursed again, namely in (E), the central, developmental episode of the Allegretto (bars 137–83), the crotchets of the last E flat phrase explode, in one breathtaking bar (Ex. 16), into semiquavers.

At the third mention of the stars, towards the end of (E)'s second part (bar 175), the same feat is achieved by entirely different means. Mozart depicts the 'sighs' of "Tu sospiri?" by crotchet appoggiature in the piano, while the bass changes from bar to bar. Two bars later, we are back in semiquaver motion, with the bass changing four times a bar (Ex. 17):

Ex. 17
K. 505
bars
170–175

Allegretto

Tu so-spi-ri?   o duol fu-ne-sto! che i-
-stan - - te è quo-sto! Stel-le bar-bare,

But the greatest of these rhythmic feats occurs with the last appearance of the "Alma bella" words in the middle of the coda (bar 222). Here, the reverse happens. Instead of an expected intensification of the rhythm after the free semiquaver colorature of voice and piano, Mozart settles on an ambling, serenely confident half-bar rhythm in the bass, while the piano's semiquavers are reduced to the status of an ornament, which yet holds the promise of a final cadential incandescence (Ex. 18).

The second part of (E) contains, just before the above-mentioned 'sighs', a famous harmonic digression (quoted in Einstein, p. 371) which becomes even more exciting than it is locally if one tries to hear it formally as a prolonged preparation of E flat's

Ex.18
K.505
bars
218-223

dominant, and therefore of section (C''), which is not to begin until twenty-five bars later, after the 'real' lead-back to the rondo theme with its dominant pedal (bars 178–83) has occurred. (F), replacing the second occurrence of the first episode, (D), is an unprecedented architectural master-stroke (bars 192–214). (D)'s tendency to the dominant is redundant here; time is short, the form has begun to quiver like an arrow in descent. Mozart, therefore, invents a new theme that just *points* to the subdominant (it does not reach that region). When, at last, the step to IV is taken, and the coda begins in earnest, we should expect a firm consolidation. But Mozart does not do what Beethoven would have done. The subdominant seventh floats in at the middle of a phrase (bar 214), and gives way, almost immediately, to that casual confirmation of the tonic we have seen in Ex. 18.

We do not know what were the actual relations of Mozart and the pretty Nancy, but this work is the most mature love-letter ever written in music. The author of the notorious 'Bäsle' letters has grown up. On the rope that stretches between dalliance and death, Mozart's heart dances.

> K.528. Scena: 'Bella mia fiamma'/'Resta, o cara'
> SOP., STR., FL., 2 OB., 2 FAG., 2 HN.

Text by da Ponte (?).
Comp. 3 November 1787, Prague, for Josepha Duschek (cf. K.272).
The work was written at the Duscheks' country place near Prague,
where the Mozarts were staying, five days after the première of Don
Giovanni. *According to Mozart's son, Josepha locked his father*
into a garden-house and did not release him until he had finished the
promised aria. He, in turn, surrendered the score on the condition
that she sang it by sight, knowing that the frequent tritone pro-
gressions (cf. Ex. 20) would be difficult for a singer of his era.
The protagonist of this aria is, in reality, a man. A hero, going to
his sacrificial death, takes leave of his beloved and of a friend to
whose care he entrusts her. Einstein thinks that "the names of
Cerere and Alfeo which occur at the end of the recitative, point to a
scene in Hades". We do not fully understand the situation, but it is
certain that, in Einstein's words, "Mozart used extreme means to
represent an extreme situation. . . . This is no piece for the public,
but rather what artists call a 'studio piece'."

FORM

Recitative (Andante, E minor – D minor – F major – B flat – C minor) – – Aria: Part I (Andante, C major): A – B (Part 1: G major – Part 2: modulatory) – A' – B' (Part 1: modulatory – Part 2: modulatory) – Coda – – Part II (Allegro, C major): C (Introduction) – D (theme, quasi rondo) – E (episode, through-composed) – D' – E' (→ G major) – D'' – E'' – Coda.

The first section of the recitative (bars 1–6) is an introduction whose elegiac figure, placed in the strings in canonic entries, is not to appear again. The piece 'begins' with the first (E minor) statement (bar 7) of a syncopated appoggiatura motive which, in its direct (a) and inverted (b) form, is the basic melodic figure of this section. Ex. 19 shows this figure before and after the indescribably beautiful modulation to F major on the words, "Yield all to fate!":

In the Andante, the voice enters with the theme of (A) after two orchestral bars. (A), in which theme and section coincide, is a 7+8 bar period, constructed thus:

Antecedent: 2 bars' orchestra – 2 bars' voice – 1 bar orchestral interjection – 2 bars' voice, continuing its interrupted 4-bar phrase.
Consequent: 8 bars' voice with normal accompaniment.

The consequent enters with a sudden, heart rending C minor, to the words "acerba morte", gives way to F major, and finally reaches C major. The first part of (B) is a gentle phrase of melting, Schubertian thirds, complete with a Schubertian turn to the minor (the G minor of bar 52). The second part of (B) brings those difficult chromaticisms, first on the epical afflatus of its first phrase (bars 59–63; cf. its bass with the ostinato in 'Dido's Lament' by Purcell – similar means for a similar situation), and

then in the ensuing phrase (Ex. 20) of sliding, modulating
dominant sevenths (bars 64–8).

The resumption of the words "Resta, o cara" belongs musically still to (B); (A) is therefore curtailed, and not resumed be-

fore the "acerba morte" phrase (bar 77). The first part of (B') is tonally unsettled by the influence of the preceding chromaticisms. Its tune is almost the same, but the bass wanders into transitional groups of four roots (bars 85–90). The second part of (B') equals that of (B). The coda (starting at bar 102) begins with a transposition to C major of that startling G major resolution in bar 70 (cf. Ex. 20). When, after a restatement of the 'sliding sevenths' (bars 105–8), this happens again, we have finally renounced the tortuous chromaticism and brooding polyphony of the Andante, and find ourselves in the C major of the Allegro.

Its first phrase (C) is one of those *a tempo* introductions to a proper theme which Mozart manages so well in his operas. Yet here its meaning is not dramatic but transcendental, to the words "Ah dov' è il tempio? dov' è l'ara?" ("Where is the temple? where the altar?"). The two short plagal cadences which follow the first rise of the Allegro (bars 123–5) stress the religious connotation of the IV–I progression (cf. Schubert's 'Junge Nonne', at the words "das Glöcklein vom Turm"). Nor is the C major of the 'rondo theme' at all C-majorish – the A flat of its consequent (bar 140) removes this bright key into the region of religious fulfilment. I call this Allegro a rondo because its theme (D) occurs three times in conjunction with three episodes. But, with the exception of the distinct tune of the G major passage in the central episode (E') (bars 175–80), these episodes are not self-contained formally or tonally; they grow out of (D) – cf. the beginning of (E) in bar 141 – and take the form of the latter part of (C) before they unfold into the theme (cf. the juncture of (E) and (D'), bars 160–5). It may be less pedantic to consider this 'rondo' an undivided, through-composed piece with a refrain, "questa vita così amara più soffribile non è", recurring to the tune of (D).

In the extended coda (bars 203 to end) the chromatic basses of the Andante are resumed in tempo Allegro and, partly, in ascending order (bars 211–16).

This work is a bridge between the metaphysical element in *Don Giovanni* and the yearning, unearthly element in the music of the romantic lyricists. Mozart has gone here to the limits of expression that are imposed on the classical artist by his overriding commitment to universality. Beyond, lie the private worlds of Schubert and Schumann, of Brahms and Wagner.

BOOK LIST

A. Einstein: 'Aria and Song', in *Mozart*, London, 1946, pp.
  355–80.
F. Spiro: 'Die Entstehung einer Mozartschen Konzertarie',
  Vierteljahrsschrift für Musikwissenschaft, IV/1888.

KARL GEIRINGER

THE CHURCH MUSIC

Mozart wrote church music from his early youth to the end of his life. As a boy of ten he composed a brief Kyrie (K.33) in Paris, and in his last illness he constantly worked on the Requiem (K.626), which he had no longer the strength to complete. During this quarter of a century he wrote more than sixty works, among them fifteen complete masses, the torso of the C minor Mass, the Requiem, four substantial litanies, two vespers, and numerous smaller pieces.

To bring order into this vast output, we shall subdivide it into four groups arranged chronologically, whereby significant events in Mozart's career, such as the visits to Italy and his move from Salzburg to Vienna, will help to determine the boundaries.

To Mozart's early youth, up to his first visit to Italy in December 1769, belong three masses and various smaller works, all of which are firmly rooted in Austrian traditions. We know through recent research of Karl Pfannhauser[1] that Mozart copied pieces by the Austrian court conductor Karl Georg Reutter (1708–82). The Psalm 'De Profundis' (K.93), hitherto considered a masterpiece of the young Mozart, and the fragment 'Memento Domine David', K.Anh.22(93a), are in fact excerpts from sacred compositions by Reutter which the lad put down in his eagerness to become familiar with them. Reutter was naturally not the only composer whose church music Mozart studied. He was thoroughly acquainted with the works of the famous Johann Adolf Hasse (1699–1783), who was then dazzling Viennese music-lovers with his technical brilliance, and by the Italian smoothness and tender beauty of his melodies. Young Mozart was, moreover, familiar with the sacred works of the leading Salzburg composers, such as Ernst Eberlin (1702–62), Anton C. Adlgasser (1728–77), J. F. Lolli (d. 1778), his own father, Leopold (1719–87), and Joseph Haydn's younger brother, Michael (1737–1806). Many earlier works, too, were still in the repertory of the leading churches, and the boy had ample opportunity to hear the great master works of the past,

[1] 'Mozart hat kopiert' in *Acta Mozartiana*, 1. Jg., 1954, Heft 2–3.

such as music by the Venetian, Antonio Caldara (1670–1736), and the two Austrian Kapellmeisters, Johann Stadlmayr (1560–1648), and Heinrich Biber (1640–1704).

The church music which the young Mozart studied was nurtured by various Italian sources. Its solid texture and the tendency to juxtapose groups of solo voices and vocal tuttis point to Venetian and Roman models, while the arias, with their brilliant coloratura display and the use of operatic effects, show a Neapolitan influence. In addition to these features imported from the south, however, Austria contributed her own traditional melodies, often derived from folk-songs, as well as a modest contrapuntal erudition.

The boy of twelve and thirteen gradually assimilated these various influences. His two first masses, K.49(47d), in G major, written in Vienna in October or November 1768, and K.65(61a) in D minor, completed on 14 January 1769 at Salzburg, belong to the category of the 'missa brevis' (short mass), which aims at a very concise structure and, in particular, telescopes the text of the 'Gloria' and 'Credo'. Mozart prescribes a very small orchestra of two violins, bass, and organ, to which one viola is added in K.49, and, according to traditional usage in Austrian sacred music, the instruments are only entrusted with short preludes and interludes, their chief function being to reinforce the vocal parts. Frequently the first violin doubles the alto in the upper octave, the second violin plays the part of the soprano, and the viola, if used at all, that of the tenor. In the first mass a certain youthful awkwardness is apparent in the patchwork character of the 'Credo', where the tempo fluctuates five times between allegro and adagio within thirteen bars. In the following mass the instruments show somewhat greater independence from the vocal parts, although Mozart, according to Salzburg tradition, discarded the viola part. The composer bestowed greater care on this work, and it is significant that for the 'Benedictus' he made three different versions before he decided on the definite one. This composition, in the minor key, displays a severe austerity which is rarely encountered in Austrian masses of the time. It is interesting to observe how the young composer tries to counteract the incohesion apparent in the first mass. At the beginning of the 'Benedictus' the violins quote a motive from the preceding 'Sanctus', while at the end of the movement the instruments anticipate the accompanying figure to be used in the 'Agnus Dei'. Thus, all three movements forming the second half of the mass are closely knit together.

The Offertorium, 'Veni sancte spiritus' (K.47, Vienna, 1768) employs a much richer orchestra in which oboes, horns, trumpets, and timpani are added to the basic group of strings and organ. It is a brilliant piece which reaches its climax in an extensive 'Halleluja' with alternating solo and tutti passages.

The following mass, in C major (K.66, known as the 'Dominicus' Mass and written in October 1769 in Salzburg) seems to pursue somewhat similar aims. This is not a 'missa brevis', but a substantial 'missa solemnis', in which trumpets and timpani are added to the string orchestra and organ.[1] The spiritual godfather of this mass, in which both the solo voices and the instruments display great virtuosity, is clearly Adolf Hasse. When, in the 'Quoniam' of the 'Gloria', the soprano sings rollicking coloraature (Ex. 1),

Ex. 1

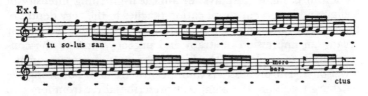

tu so-lus san - - - - - - - - - - - - - - ctus

we have the impression of an operatic performance rather than a church service. Thus, within the span of twelve months, young Mozart passed from a rather conservative style to an idiom reflecting the latest fashion in contemporary music.

To a second group of sacred compositions belong those works which Mozart wrote between 13 December 1769, when he travelled for the first time to Italy, and 13 March 1773, the day he returned from his third visit across the Alps. Between these journeys he stayed at Salzburg, and during these interim months he wrote a number of church compositions, including a mass, two litanies, two 'Regina Coeli', and an offertorium. In Italy itself he composed only an antiphon and a motet.

These works naturally display many features of the Neapolitan style. It is noteworthy, however, that we find in them definite traces of the 'Storm and Stress' movement which was

---

[1] A MS. in the Monastery of St. Peter, Salzburg, dated 1776, includes additional parts for two oboes, two horns, and two trumpets, partly written by Wolfgang, partly by Leopold Mozart.

sweeping Europe around the year 1770. Joseph Haydn, Florian Gassmann, Christian Bach, and many other composers wrote at that time works of strong subjectivism, stressing life's sombre aspects. Mozart's nature also inclined towards emphasis on darker hues, and in the works of this phase the gay and brilliant Neapolitan language is intermingled with a more personal, passionate idiom.

An interesting example is offered by his Missa Solemnis in C minor (K.139(114a)), which was probably composed at the turn of 1771-2.[1] The composition starts with an extensive 'Kyrie' consisting of a slow introduction followed by a faster section in da capo form. In the da capo section the words 'Kyrie eleison' and 'Christe eleison' alternate in a rather careless manner, showing that Mozart was more interested in creating a well-rounded musical form than in doing full justice to the liturgical requirements. On the other hand, the introductory slow section in C minor displays an almost frightening intensity of feeling and its fervent supplication reaches to the very depths of mankind's need for mercy. Similarly, the 'Qui tollis' in F minor creates an impression of strain and urgency through the constant clash of triplets in the higher voices and quavers in the lower ones. The orchestra is munificently treated. Following the Salzburg tradition, the composer prescribes three trombones, to which he added divided violas, two oboes, four trumpets, and timpani. His sensitive use of this large sound body is evident in sections like the 'Crucifixus', where muted trumpets combined with trombones produce an awesome picture of suffering.

In the *Litaniae de B.M.V.* ('Litaniae Lauretanae', K.109(74e), May 1771) and the 'Litaniae de venerabili' (K.125, March 1772), Mozart achieves the greatest poignancy of expression. There are deeply moving moments in both: the 'Miserere' in B flat minor of K.109 and the 'Viaticum', also in

[1] W. Kurthen, in 'Studien zu W. A. Mozarts Kirchenmusikalischen Jugendwerken' (*Z.f.M.W.*, III, p. 209), claims that this work was the mass destined for the consecration of the Vienna 'Waisenhauskirche' on 7 December 1768, of which Leopold Mozart reports. The present author feels inclined to adopt the view of Köchel's *Verzeichnis* (third edition by Alfred Einstein, Ann Arbor, 1947) and to ascribe the work to 1771-2, since it is too mature to be considered as the very first mass Mozart wrote. The opinion which Einstein voiced in his *Mozart* (London, 1946, p. 323), adopting Kurthen's theory, does not seem convincing. [See, however, Pfannhauser's article in *Mozart-Jahrbuch*, 1954, and *The Concertos (1)*, p. 201 and n.1. – EDS.]

B flat minor, of K.125, in which the outcry of the soprano is accompanied by a sombre lament in the lower voices (Ex. 2):

Ex.2

The two 'Regina Coeli' (K.108(74d), composed in May 1771, and K.127, composed in May 1772), which display a certain playful gaiety, also contain wholly serious sections. In particular, the soprano solo, 'Ora pro nobis', in A minor (from K.108), with a strongly expressive violin part, is a piece of deeply moving beauty.

In Milan, Mozart wrote the motet 'Exsultate jubilate', K.165(158a), for the castrato Venanzio Rauzzini, who had sung in his opera, *Lucio Silla*. The first performance took place on 17 January 1773. This is a brilliant cantata for soprano solo and orchestra consisting of two arias connected by a recitative and concluded by the famous 'Alleluja'. Joseph Haydn may have had the last section of this work in mind when he wrote his immortal anthem, 'Gott erhalte Franz den Kaiser'.

In 1772, Hieronymus, Count Colloredo had become Archbishop of Salzburg. When young Mozart returned from his third visit to Italy, he had, in his official capacity as *Konzertmeister* to the archiepiscopal court, to adjust his music to the demands of his patron. The Prince insisted, for example, on brief compositions for the masses which he celebrated. The sacred works Mozart wrote for the new ruler were not only shorter, but also simpler in character. The excrescences of the Neapolitan idiom were more and more restrained, which was certainly beneficial for Mozart's style; as a matter of fact, his own artistic development pointed in the same direction, and outward and inner reasons thus combined to produce a change in the composer's idiom. Out of the glorious cantilena of Italian music, the passionate expressiveness of 'Storm and Stress', and the solid craftsmanship of Salzburg church music he developed for his sacred compositions a language that was noble and yet light, technically competent and yet free of ponderousness. Contrapuntal features were henceforth integrated with ease into homophonic parts; in this choral style of rare perfection the fugatos and imitations soon became natural components of the music and no longer created the impression of learned display. After the three visits to Italy, he felt somewhat alienated from the musical idiom of his own homeland, and thus, in the spring of 1773, he once again began to study the works of his precursors and contemporaries. He copied out music frequently performed in Salzburg, and we have a manuscript in his handwriting which includes sixteen different works by Ernst Eberlin and three by Michael Haydn. The Kyrie (K.221(93b)) and Lacrimosa (K.Anh.21(93c)), which were until recently believed to be authentic Mozart, but which Pfannhauser recognized as copies of music by Eberlin, probably date from this period.

The sacred works written by Mozart up to the end of his service to the Archbishop include eleven masses, two litanies, two vespers, one 'Dixit et Magnificat', a 'Regina Coeli', the graduale, 'Sancta Maria', and three offertories.

The first of the masses (C major, K.167), written in June 1773, reveals Mozart's aim to break with the past and to write a work entirely satisfactory to the Archbishop. He simplifies the vocal equipment by dispensing with soloists, thus renouncing an important feature of his former sacred works, and he strictly observes the liturgical precept, usually neglected by him, whereby the first words of the 'Gloria' and 'Credo' were intoned only by the priest.

The following, strongly condensed Missa brevis in F major (K.192(186f), June 1774) uses only a small orchestra of two violins and bass, and places the emphasis on the voices, in which a solo quartet makes its reappearance. The tender, graceful, flexible melodic lines of this work have won it a place of its very own, and it is one of the few youthful sacred works of Mozart which are still performed. The composer is anxious to achieve unity in his 'Credo', and he repeats the liturgical melody (Ex. 3)

Ex.3

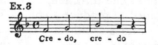

Cre - do,   cre - do

throughout the movement (a tune, incidentally, later employed in the finale of his 'Jupiter' Symphony). The 'Agnus', in D minor, has a grave beauty which is especially moving.

The same small orchestra is employed in the ensuing Missa brevis in D major, K.194(186h), written in August 1774.

Here Mozart seems to be influenced by the *Missa Sti. Nicolai* which Joseph Haydn had written two years before. Both in the expressive 'Et incarnatus,' using a minor key, and in the tender, singing 'Benedictus' for solo quartet, the youth follows the model of the older master, whose works he had eagerly studied for many years.

The Mass in C major, K.262(246a), composed in April or May 1776, is an unusually extensive work, and therefore known as 'Missa longa'. In this work the composer impresses us with his polyphonic skill, and it is perhaps more than mere coincidence that he wrote a letter in the same year to Padre Martini, the great Italian master of contrapuntal art, expressing his desire to discuss various problems with the scholar.

In 1776 three other masses were also written, all of them in C major. The Mass K.257, composed in November 1776, is known as the 'Credo' Mass, since the word 'credo' is emphatically uttered again and again throughout the 'Credo' section with an intensity and fervour anticipating Beethoven; moreover, the 'Credo' motive of the F major Mass (see Ex. 3) heads the 'Sanctus'. The 'Incarnatus' of this work seems to portray a pastoral scene, a device Mozart liked to employ in his sacred music, following Italian models. On the whole, however, the melodic life of the work seems to grow out of Austrian soil.

The 'Organ Solo' Mass (K.259) was written in December 1776. It demonstrates once more the influence that Joseph Haydn exercised on the young composer. As in the older master's *Missa Sti. Joanni de Deo*, written a year or two earlier, Mozart employed in the 'Benedictus' of his work an 'organo obbligato' part of expressive beauty.

The masses, K.258 and 275(272b), written in December 1776 and in the summer of 1777 respectively, aim at following the liturgical text as closely as possible. No specific form is used in the vocal sections; the composer attempts faithfully to reproduce the meaning of the words, while musical unity is provided through the employment of identical accompanying motives in the orchestra. In both masses the individual movements are *durchkomponiert*, to use a German term for which there is no proper English translation, in a manner subsequently used by Schubert in his songs. The texture in these masses is lucid and imbued with contrapuntal inspiration, thus approaching that "mixture of neatness and poetical grace"[1] which is characteristic of the mature Mozart's style.

There is also some resemblance between the last two masses which Mozart wrote in Salzburg: K.317, finished on 23 March 1779, known as the 'Coronation' Mass, because it was destined for a festive service commemorating the coronation of a miraculous image of the Virgin in the Church of Maria-Plain above Salzburg, and K.337, composed in March 1780. Not only are they both in C major, which key Mozart predominantly used in his sacred works of the period; they also have an almost identical orchestration employing, according to Salzburg tradition, trombones to reinforce alto, tenor, and bass voices of the chorus and a string orchestra without violas. To this basic body the composer adds oboes, bassoons, horns, trumpets, and timpani in K.317 and oboes, bassoons, trumpets, and timpani in K.337. Strangely enough, both introduce ideas in the 'Agnus Dei' soprano solos (e.g., 'Porgi amor') which Mozart later entrusted in slightly changed versions to the Countess in his opera, *Figaro*. The music in these masses reflects the graceful, luminous charm and serenity of Austrian architecture in the late baroque era. The 'Coronation' Mass is beautifully rounded off by the reappearance of a theme from the 'Kyrie eleison' in the 'Dona nobis pacem'. The work reaches its most stirring moment in the 'Et incarnatus' in F minor, when ethereal passages in the muted violins (Ex. 4)

Ex.4   con sord.

symbolize the mystery of the Incarnation. The 'Benedictus' of K.337 displays an almost archaic polyphony, a strange contrast to the 'Agnus Dei' in the key of E flat major in which the solo soprano is surrounded by a delightful concertante trio of oboe, bassoon, and organ.

The remaining church compositions written in Salzburg between 1773 and 1780 contain also many works both delightful and significant. In January or February 1775, during a visit to Munich, Mozart hastily wrote the Offertorium 'Misericordias

[1] cf. T. de Wyzewa and G. de St.-Foix: *W. A. Mozart*, Paris, 1912–46, Vol. II, p. 153.

Domini', K.222(205a), for the Elector, who had expressed a desire to test the composer's contrapuntal knowledge. Mozart attempted to show his skill to the best advantage, and the work abounds in artful imitations. He felt so pleased with the piece that he also sent it to his venerated friend, Padre Martini, who highly praised it. The main theme of the offertorium is based on Eberlin's 'Benedicite Domine' which Mozart had copied in 1773. Apparently the young composer wanted to prove that he could handle the idea of a well-known master with equal or even greater success.

More personal is the 'Litaniae de venerabili altaris sacramento' (K.243), composed at Salzburg in March 1776. Here we find gems of pure beauty, such as the tenor aria, 'Panis vivus', which seems to anticipate the 'Tuba Mirum' in the Requiem; the grandiose, sombre chorus, 'Tremendum'; the tender 'Dulcissimum convivium', where the triplets of the accompanying orchestra are somewhat reminiscent of the finale in Haydn's 'Farewell' Symphony (No. 45); and the magnificent 'Viaticum', in which an arrangement of the hymn 'Pange lingua' is presented by the soprano in the manner of a *cantus firmus*. In June of the same year Mozart wrote his Offertorium 'Venite populi', K.260(248a), where, for once, two mixed choruses oppose each other in seventeenth-century tradition. The baroque character of this piece is also evident in the designation of the violin parts as 'ad libitum'.

Mozart's two vespers ('de Dominica', K.321 of 1779, and 'de Confessore', K.339 of 1780) use the same psalm text and also show a decided resemblance in their musical character. The composer here adopts a concise and rather severe style, using themes which bear a certain resemblance to melodies of the Gregorian chant. A dramatic effect is produced in K.339, where, after a strictly contrapuntal 'Laudate Pueri', the 'Laudate Dominum' offers a sweet and warm soprano cantilena which competes with the melody of the first violin and is supported by a solo bassoon. When, in the second half of this piece, the chorus takes over, a climax of glowing beauty and warmth is achieved.

An intimate character pervades the *Graduale ad festum B.M.V.*, 'Sancta Maria' (K.273), written on 9 September 1777, shortly before Mozart's departure to Mannheim and Paris, and probably intended as a prayer for heavenly intercession in this important venture. It is as simple as it is deeply felt, using neither solo voices nor wind instruments, and quite free of the ornate trimmings to be found in some of Mozart's earlier church works. Although no contrapuntal forms such as the fugue or canon are employed, the texture of the work is of perfect transparency and each voice is entrusted with melodic lines of exquisite grace and beauty.

After Mozart had left the service of the Salzburg Archbishop, the compulsion to write sacred compositions no longer existed, and in the decade between 1781 and 1791 he seldom turned to church music. Only four sacred works are extant, and of these two remain incomplete, while one is extremely short. Yet these four pieces are among the master's greatest achievements.

The Kyrie in D minor, K.341(368a), was composed in Munich between January and March 1781, and though technically speaking Mozart was still in the Salzburg Prince's service, the work was clearly meant to prove to the Munich court (which had just heard his opera, *Idomeneo*) his capabilities in the field of church music; it is therefore in no way subject to the conditions prevailing in Salzburg, and we are justified in considering it as one of the sacred compositions of the period which started when Mozart gained his freedom.

Even the choice of key shows Mozart's independence. The endless sequence of works in C major which was probably due to the Archbishop's taste – almost two-thirds of his masses are in C major! – gave way to D minor, the key he was also to use in his last work, the Requiem. A mood of sombre sadness is

Ex.5

tinged with a passion which is but rarely brightened by flashes of hope. Mozart uses a large orchestra which greatly contributes to the poignancy of expression; for the first time in his church music he includes parts for clarinets and four horns; no solo voices are employed. The composer gradually reaches a stirring climax in the middle, after which the music slowly subsides, thus achieving a beautifully balanced construction. The chromatic descending *ff* chords in the violins which precede the entrance of the 'Christe eleison' proper seem to forecast the stirring effect to be heard before the first entrance of the chorus in the Requiem (Ex. 5).

The Mass in C minor, K.427(417a), written in the years 1782–3, in many ways occupies a unique position among Mozart's church works. For once he did not compose a mass with a specific practical purpose in mind. We learn from a letter to his father in 1783 that he had made a vow to write the mass if he brought Constanze as his wife to Salzburg, and to have it performed there with her as a soloist. In its whole conception, the mass is much more extensive than any similar work the composer had written. The 'Gloria' alone comprises no less than seven independent pieces. Moreover, Mozart is not satisfied with the four-part chorus used in all his other masses; he now requires a five-part chorus on several occasions, and even an eight-part chorus, supported by a full orchestra.

In its monumental grandeur and its decided leaning towards baroque polyphony, the work clearly reveals the tremendous influence of Bach and Handel, whose works he was then studying. Yet the C minor Mass is anything but a mere copy of the past style. In all its parts it is imbued with the peculiar sweetness and nostalgic tenderness which form so important a component of Mozart's own language; and within his sacred works the C minor Mass marks a peak of artistic achievement which Mozart was to exceed only in his very last work.

Unfortunately, the mass was not destined to be completed. Mozart finished the 'Kyrie', the extensive 'Gloria', the 'Sanctus', and the 'Benedictus'. The 'Agnus' was, however, never written, while of the 'Credo' only fragments have survived.[1] The finished sections were taken to Salzburg and performed at St. Peter's in August 1783; Constanze sang one of the two soprano solo parts. Mozart may have felt then that the work was conceived on too large a scale, and that it might prove difficult to have so large a mass used in a church service. Therefore he did not complete the composition, but, as he thought highly of the finished parts, he used most of them in 1785 for an oratorio

---

[1] In 1901 Alois Schmitt attempted to complete the mass by using parts from other sacred works by Mozart. There is good reason to doubt the validity of his method. In particular, it is regrettable that he used for the 'Crucifixus' a 'Lacrimosa' (K.Anh.21) which is in fact not by Mozart at all, but a fragment from a requiem by Eberlin. Cf. Pfannhauser, loc. cit.

entitled *Davidde penitente* (K.469) which he had been asked to write for a concert given for the benefit of the musicians' pension fund.

Among the few pieces which were not included in the oratorio is the 'Et incarnatus est', which had not been completed in the mass. Thus the composer clearly indicated that he was not satisfied with his draft for this movement, and actually the bravura aria of this section is a strangely incongruous piece which Mozart may have sketched to please Constanze; later he abandoned it, probably because he felt that it did not fit into the total conception of his exquisite work.

The four completed movements, 'Kyrie', 'Gloria', 'Sanctus', and 'Benedictus', belong to the greatest products of Austrian church music. The five-part 'Gratias' in A minor, for instance, is a deeply moving chorus of majesty and solemnity. A climax is reached in the stirring 'Qui tollis' in G minor, employing two four-part choruses which appear to Abert as "an immense procession of pentitents, crowding in heavy despair round the Cross and finally disappearing in the distance."[1] In the 'Sanctus' the orchestra assumes an important part and a vision of dazzling splendour overwhelms us.

Between the C minor Mass and the Requiem a small work of outstanding beauty was completed: the motet 'Ave, verum corpus' (K.618), of which the autograph is dated 17 June 1791. Mozart wrote it for Anton Stoll, a village teacher and choirmaster at Baden, near Vienna, where Constanze was taking the cure. In consideration of the little church's limited resources, he used only strings and organ as accompaniment. The piece comprises but forty-six bars; and rarely has so much fervour and classical beauty been poured into so tiny a vessel. Although in its whole conception it reminds us of the Graduale 'Sancta Maria' of 1777, the 'Ave verum' shows great progress in artistic economy.

Mozart's ultimate work, the Requiem (K.626), presents us with a puzzle that in all likelihood will never be completely solved. In July 1791 the composer was commissioned by a wealthy nobleman, Count Walsegg, to write a requiem. He agreed, and received a substantial advance towards the honorarium. Work on the operas, *La Clemenza di Tito* and *Die Zauber-*

[1] cf. Hermann Abert: *W. A. Mozart. Neubearbeitete Ausgabe von Otto Jahn's Mozart*, Leipzig, 1923–4, Vol. II, p. 149.

flöte, at first took up most of his time and the Requiem progressed
only very slowly. In the autumn he concentrated on the new
composition, but increasing weakness made it impossible for
him to complete it. When he died on 5 December 1791, only
the first movement, 'Requiem' and 'Kyrie', was completely
finished; the second to the ninth movements ('Dies Irae' to
'Hostias') were written down in Mozart's usual draft: the vocal
parts and the most significant sections of the instrumental accompaniment were inserted into the score, while the final
orchestration was left for a later period.

The widow, afraid that she might have to return the advance
on the honorarium, first asked the court conductor Joseph
Eybler and, when he refused, Mozart's pupil, Franz Süssmayer,
to complete the score. The latter undertook the task and, as his
handwriting strongly resembled that of his teacher, Constanze
was able to pretend that the score had been finished by her
husband.

In the nineteenth century, however, the deception was discovered, and attempts were made to determine the exact
extent of Süssmayer's participation. Undoubtedly Mozart had
managed to put down every little detail that mattered in a
kind of shorthand, so that a faithful student, familiar with
the style, could well supply the rest, and it may be said that
Süssmayer conscientiously and faithfully followed his master's
intentions.

However, Mozart's draft of the 'Lacrimosa' (No. 7) breaks off
after eight measures, and no sketches at all for the last three
movements have been unearthed. Must we assume that the
second half of No. 7 as well as Nos. 10–12 were conceived by
Süssmayer? It seems hardly possible to accept this contention.
We know that in the last stages of his illness Mozart constantly
discussed and sang the Requiem to his wife and to Süssmayer.
The pupil may have taken notes or Mozart may have noted
details on scraps of paper which have not survived. Apart from
a certain clumsiness in some of the orchestral sections, and a
number of small details which point to Süssmayer, all the movements of the score appear to have the characteristic Mozartean
touch. If Süssmayer's claim is true that it was his idea to conclude the work with the fugue from the 'Kyrie', he merely followed examples from Mozart's earlier masses (cf. K.220, 317).
Süssmayer deserves posterity's everlasting gratitude for having

rescued one of Mozart's most sublime contributions; but he should not be considered as the composer of large sections in the Requiem.

The choice of instruments for the work is most unusual. Mozart avoids the horns and all the light and gay woodwind. Neither flutes nor oboes are used in this score, and the clarinets are replaced by their darker-hued relative, the basset horn, which seems to have fascinated Mozart near the end of his life. The strings are frequently used in the lower registers, and the tonal palette is completed by bassoons, trumpets, trombones, and timpani. The result is a disembodied, dark timbre, perfectly expressing the solemnity and mystery of death. But despite its sombre majesty the work is imbued with an affirmative and soothing spirit. The inner peace and serenity which were granted to Mozart illuminate the whole Requiem, and the sadness it evokes is gentle rather than violent.

The first section, 'Requiem' and 'Kyrie', again testifies to the deep impression which the music of the past, in particular the art of Bach and Handel, had made on the composer. The Requiem theme is a traditional one which other composers – for instance, Handel – and, incidentally, Mozart himself (in his 'Misericordias', K.222) had used before; the soprano solo 'Te decet hymnus' employs an ancient Gregorian chant; and the two subjects of the double fugue are reminiscent of melodies in Handel's *Messiah* and C. P. E. Bach's 'Magnificat' respectively.[1] Out of such elements Mozart builds a concise structure of awe-inspiring power, in which the grandiose double fugue at the end seems to symbolize life's turmoil and the unending struggle to which mankind is subjected. (It is interesting to note that critics of the early nineteenth century assailed this rather unorthodox fugue as "barbaric muddle" and "wild gurglings",[2] to which verdicts Beethoven vehemently objected.) The 'Dies irae' conjures up the vision of the Last Judgment with fearful, truly apocalyptic grandeur, but the following, gentle 'Tuba mirum', given to the four vocal soloists and a solo trombone, strikes a note of reassurance. A message of this kind is presented with even more emphasis in the 'Recordare', a rondo-like move-

---

[1] Robert Haas (*Mozart*, pp. 155f.) has shown that the main theme of the 'Introitus' is based on F. L. Gassmann's Requiem. – EDS.

[2] cf. H. G. Nägeli: *Vorlesungen über Musik*, 1826; and G. Weber; *Cäcilia*, III, p. 216.

ment allotted to the four soloists which, after the overpowering 'Rex tremendae majestatis', offers heavenly relief. The 'Confutatis' may be counted among Mozart's most inspired and profound contributions. Tenors and basses accompanied by the full orchestra utter the desperate laments of the lost souls, whereupon angelic voices of high-pitched singers, merely supported by unison strings, pray for admittance among the chosen. Finally, the full chorus implores the Lord for help in the hour of passing, an entreaty uttered in "harmonies lofty beyond all earthly notions".[1]

The rest of the score, too, abounds in pieces of utter beauty and bold inspiration. Despite minor weaknesses, the Requiem on the whole impresses us as a homogeneous work which, in any case, belongs to the great treasures of our artistic heritage. It is a composition as transcendental as it is human, and out of tremor and guilt it leads us gently towards peace and salvation.

In Vienna it has been a long-established tradition to perform Mozart's Requiem in the Imperial Chapel every year on All Saints' Day. The various political changes in the twentieth century had no influence on this custom, which has provided thousands of Viennese with spiritual elevation. Similarly, many other sacred works by Mozart have maintained their place in Austrian liturgical use since the eighteenth century. The people who worship in the gay, colourful, ornate churches of the baroque era consider Mozart's sweet tunefulness and his graceful, light idiom as entirely fitting, and if he, at times, allows a certain coloratura display, one does not consider this to be out of place. It is significant that in southern Germany, Austria, and Italy the famous 'Motu Proprio' issued by Pope Pius X in 1903 has been given a far broader interpretation than in the Catholic West. In Mozart's native country no objections are raised against occasional lengthiness or the use of a full orchestra including 'noisy' instruments, such as trumpets and timpani, while certain liberties in the treatment of the sacred text are overlooked or quietly remedied. Even small churches use in their services the sacred music of Mozart, Haydn, Schubert, and Bruckner: works that are all rooted in the same basic attitude, through which all the resources of music are used to glorify the

[1] cf. B. Paumgartner: *Mozart*, 3rd edn., Zürich, 1945, p. 475.

Lord. In letting this exquisite music participate in worship, the Church in these countries has enriched the life of countless devout Christians.

BOOK LIST

[Standard Mozart biographies have not been listed.]

W. Kurthen: 'Studien zu W. A. Mozarts Kirchenmusikalischen Jugendwerken', *Zeitschrift für Musikwissenschaft*, III.

K. Pfannhauser: 'Mozart hat kopiert', *Acta Mozartiana*, I/1954, Heft 2–3.

KEY TO THE KÖCHEL NUMBERS
OF MOZART'S WORKS
MENTIONED IN THIS BOOK

This list is based, by permission, on the catalogue prepared by the late
Dr. Alfred Einstein, and printed in his *Mozart* (Cassell, 1946)

K.1, Minuet and Trio for piano in G.
K.2, Minuet for piano in F.
K.3, Allegro for piano in B flat.
K.4, Minuet for piano in F.
K.5, Minuet for piano in F.
K.6, Sonata for piano and violin in C, 221
K.7, Sonata for piano and violin in D.
K.8, Sonata for piano and violin in B flat, 221
K.9, Sonata for piano and violin in G.
K.9a, Allegro for piano in C.
K.9b, Andante for piano in B flat, 38
K.10, Sonata for piano, violin, and violoncello in B flat.
K.11, Sonata for piano, violin, and violoncello in G.
K.12, Sonata for piano, violin, and violoncello in A.
K.13, Sonata for piano, violin, and violoncello in F.
K.14, Sonata for piano, violin, and violoncello in C.
K.15, Sonata for piano, violin, and violoncello in B flat.
K.16, Symphony in E flat, 156, 157, 158
K.17, Symphony in B flat (dubious).
K.18, Symphony in E flat (by C. Fr. Abel: *see* K.Anh.109[1]).
K.19, Symphony in D, 156, 158
K.19d, Piano Sonata for four hands in C, 53, 76
K.20, Motet, 'God is our Refuge'.
K.21, Aria for tenor, 'Va, dal furor portata', 334
K.22, Symphony in B flat, 158, 361
K.23, Aria for soprano, 'Conservati fedele', 334
K.24, Variations for piano in G, 50
K.25, Variations for piano in D, 50, 153
K.26, Sonata for piano and violin in E flat.
K.27, Sonata for piano and violin in G.
K.28, Sonata for piano and violin in C.
K.29, Sonata for piano and violin in D.
K.30, Sonata for piano and violin in F.
K.31, Sonata for piano and violin in B flat.
K.32, *Galimathias musicum*, 50n., 152, 153

K.33, Kyrie in F, 361
K.34, Offertory, 'Scande coeli limina'.
K.35, *Die Schuldigkeit des ersten Gebotes*, sacred *Singspiel*.
K.36, Recitative and Aria for tenor, 'Or che il dover', 334
K.37, Concerto for piano (arrangement) in F, 224, 246
K.38, *Apollo et Hyacinthus*, Latin comedy, 160
K.39, Concerto for piano (arrangement) in B flat, 224, 246
K.40, Concerto for piano (arrangement) in D, 224, 246
K.41, Concerto for piano (arrangement) in G, 224, 246
K.42, *Grabmusik*.
K.43, Symphony in F, 159, 160
K.43c, Concerto for piano in G (sketches), 224
K.44, Antiphon, 'Cibavit eos'.
K.45, Symphony in D, 159, 160
K.46, Quintet (spurious).
K.47, Offertory, 'Veni Sancte Spiritus', 363
K.47a, Missa (Solemnis), 201
K.47b, Offertory, 201
K.47c, Concerto for trumpet, 201
K.48, Symphony in D, 159, 161
K.49, Missa brevis in G, 362
K.50, *Bastien und Bastienne*, Singspiel, 19, 284
K.51, *La finta semplice*, opera buffa, 160
K.52, Song, 'Daphne, deine Rosenwangen'.
K.53, Song, 'Freude, Königin der Weisen'.
K.54, Variations for piano in F. (= 547a).
K.55, Sonata for piano and violin (dubious) in F.
K.56, Sonata for piano and violin (dubious) in C.
K.57, Sonata for piano and violin (dubious) in F.
K.58, Sonata for piano and violin (dubious) in E flat.
K.59, Sonata for piano and violin (dubious) in C minor.
K.60, Sonata for piano and violin (dubious) in E minor.

K.240, Divertimento in B flat.
K.241, Sonata da Chiesa in G.
K.242, Concerto for three pianos, 225, 232, 249
K.243, Litaniae de venerabili altaris sacramento, 369
K.244, Sonata da Chiesa in F.
K.245, Sonata da Chiesa in D.
K.246, Concerto for piano (Lützow) in C, 224, 225, 232, 249
K.247, Divertimento in F, 215
K.248, March in F.
K.249, March in D (Haffner).
K.250, Serenade in D (Haffner), 178, 179, 180, 182, 184, 212, 215, 248, 249
K.251, Divertimento in D.
K.252, Divertimento in E flat.
K.253, Divertimento in F, 69
K.254, Divertimento (Trio for piano, violin, violoncello) in B flat.
K.255, Recitative and Aria for alto, 'Ombra felice', 334
K.256, Aria for tenor, 'Clarice cara', 334
K.257, Missa (Credo Mass) in C, 249, 367
K.258, Missa brevis (Spaur Mass) in C, 367
K.259, Missa brevis ('Orgel-Solo') in C, 367
K.260, Offertorium, 'Venite populi'; 369
K.261, Adagio in E for the violin Concerto (K.219), 215, 223
K.262, Missa (longa) in C, 367
K.263, Sonata da Chiesa in C.
K.264, Variations for piano, 'Lison dormait', 50
K.265, Variations for piano, 'Ah, vous dirai-je', 50, 51
K.266, Trio (Nachtmusik) for two violins and bass in B flat.
K.267, Four Contredanses, 150
K.268, Concerto for violin in E flat, 200, 205, 216, 217, 219n., 220, 223
K.269, Rondo concertante for violin and orchestra in B flat, 215, 223
K.270, Divertimento in B flat.
K.271, Concerto for piano (Jeunehomme) in E flat, 224, 225, 232, 249, 250, 252, 254
K.271a, Concerto for violin in D (disputed), 216, 217, 219, 220, 223, 257
K.271k, Concerto for oboe in C (Ferlendis concerto), 200, 202, 203, 204, 208, 211
K.272, Recitative and Aria for soprano, 'Ah, lo previdi', 326, 333, 334, 335, 343

K.273, Gradual, 'Sancta Maria', 369
K.274, Sonata da Chiesa in G.
K.275, Missa brevis in B flat, 367
K.276, Regina Coeli.
K.277, Offertory, 'Alma Dei creatoris', in F.
K.278, Sonata da Chiesa in C.
K.279, Sonata for piano in C, 19, 40, 224
K.280, Sonata for piano in F, 19, 40, 41, 224
K.281, Sonata for piano in B flat, 19, 40, 224
K.282, Sonata for piano in E flat, 19, 35, 40, 41, 224
K.283, Sonata for piano in G, 19, 35, 40, 224
K.284, Sonata for piano in D, 40, 41, 42n., 224
K.285, Quartet for flute, violin, viola, and violoncello in D, 135, 204
K.285a, Quartet for flute, violin, viola, and violoncello in G.
K.286, Notturno for four orchestras in D, 69
K.287, Divertimento in B flat, 78n., 89n., 215
K.288, Divertimento in F (fragment), 228n.
K.289, Divertimento in E flat, 69
K.290, March in D.
K.291, Fugue (M. Haydn).
K.292, Sonata for bassoon and violoncello.
K.293, Concerto for oboe in F (fragment), 203, 208
K.294, Recitative and Aria for soprano, 'Alcandro, lo confesso', 326, 327, 334, 335-6, 344
K.295, Recitative and Aria for tenor, 'Se al labbro mio', 334
K.296, Sonata for piano and violin in C.
K.297, Symphony (Paris) in D, 179, 180, 182, 183, 252, 254
K.298, Quartet for flute, violin, viola, and violoncello in A.
K.299, Concerto in C for flute and harp, 212, 253
K.300, Gavotte for orchestra in B flat.
K.301, Sonata for piano and violin in G.
K.302, Sonata for piano and violin in E flat.
K.303, Sonata for piano and violin in C.
K.304, Sonata for piano and violin in E minor, 44
K.305, Sonata for piano and violin in A.
K.306, Sonata for piano and violin in D.

K.381, Piano Sonata for four hands in D, 19, 54

K.382, Rondo for piano and orchestra in D, 224, 247

K.383, Aria for soprano, 'Nehmt meinen Dank', 334

K.384, *Die Entführung aus dem Serail*, *Singspiel*, 13, 226, 283ff.

K.384b, March (fragment), 68

K.385, Symphony (Haffner) in D, 66, 184f., 188, 226, 249, 266

K.386, Rondo for piano and orchestra in A, 226

K.386a, = 414.

K.387, Quartet for strings in G, 27, 103ff., 121, 127, 133, 226

K.387a, = 413.

K.387b, = 415.

K.388, Serenade for winds in C minor, 66, 67, 69, 70, 71, 73, 74, 76, 77, 79, 82, 83, 84, 86, 88, 89

K.389, Duet, 'Welch ängstliches Beben' (*Die Entführung*).

K.390, Song, 'Ich würd' auf meinem Pfad'.

K.391, Song, 'Sei du mein Trost'.

K.392, Song, 'Verdankt sei es dem Glanz'.

K.393, Solfeggi for soprano.

K.394, Fantasia and Fugue for piano in C, 59, 60

K.395, Capriccio for piano in C.

K.396, Adagio for piano (and violin) in C minor, 61

K.397, Fantasia for piano in D minor (D), 60

K.398, Variations for piano, 'Salve tu, Domine', 50, 51

K.399, Suite for piano in C, 61, 64

K.400, First movement of a Sonata for piano in B flat, 46

K.401, Fugue for piano in G minor.

K.402, Sonata for piano and violin in A (A minor).

K.403, Sonata for piano and violin in C.

K.404, Andante and Allegretto for piano and violin in C.

K.404a, Four Preludes to Fugues by J. S. Bach for string trio.

K.405, Five Fugues by Bach arranged for string quartet.

K.406, Quintet for strings (K.388) in C minor, 66, 69, 81, 132f.

K.407, Quintet for horn and strings in E flat.

K.408, Three marches for orchestra.

K.409, Minuet to a Symphony in C.

K.410, Adagio for two basset horns and bassoon.

K.411, Adagio for two clarinets and three basset horns.

K.412, Concerto for horn in D (fragment), 206, 207, 208, 214, 276

K.413, Concerto for piano in F, 226, 232, 256, 262, 271

K.414, Concerto for piano in A, 226, 232, 256, 270, 273

K.415, Concerto for piano in C, 226, 232, 256, 258, 260, 262, 271

K.416, Scena and Rondo for soprano, 'Mia speranza adorata', 326, 334, 340-1

K.417, Concerto for horn in E flat, 208, 276

K.418, Aria for soprano, 'Vorrei spiegarvi', 206, 326, 334, 341-2

K.419, Aria for soprano, 'No, no, che non sei capace', 326, 334, 342-3

K.420, Aria for tenor, 'Per pietà, non ricercate', 334, 343

K.421, Quartet for strings in D minor, 76, 81, 116

K.422, *L'oca del Cairo*, opera buffa (fragment).

K.423, Duo for violin and viola in G, 135

K.424, Duo for violin and viola in B flat, 135

K.425, Symphony (Linz) in C, 121, 184, 186, 188, 266

K.426, Fugue for two pianos in C minor, 57, 58, 84, 130

K.427, Missa in C minor, 371

K.428, Quartet for strings in E flat, 122

K.429, Cantata, 'Dir, Seele des Weltalls'.

K.430, *Lo sposo deluso*, opera buffa (fragment).

K.431, Recitative and Aria for tenor, 'Misero! o sogno!', 334

K.432, Recitative and Aria for bass, 'Così dunque tradisci', 334, 343-4

K.433, Arietta for bass, 'Männer suchen stets', 334

K.434, Terzetto, 'Il regno delle Amazoni' (fragment).

K.435, Aria for tenor, 'Müsst' ich auch', 334

K.436, Notturno for two sopranos and bass, 'Ecco quel fiero'.

K.437, Notturno for two sopranos and bass, 'Mi lagnerò'.

K.438, Notturno for three voices, 'Se lontan'.

K.439, Notturno for two sopranos and bass, 'Due pupille'.

K.440, Aria for soprano, 'In te spero', 334

K.441, Terzetto, 'Liebes Mandl, wo is's Bandl?'.

K.442, Trio for piano, violin, and violoncello in D minor.

K.443, Fugue.

KÖCHEL APPENDIX (ANHANG)

K.Anh.1(297a), Eight numbers to a Miserere by Ignaz Holzbauer (lost).

K.Anh.3(315b), Scena for Tenducci, 334

K.Anh.8(311a), Overture in B flat.

K.Anh.9(297b), Sinfonia Concertante, 210, 211, 253

K.Anh.10(299b), Ballet music to *Les petits riens*, 217, 253

K.Anh.21(93c), Lacrimosa [now known to be the work of Ernst Eberlin], 367, 371n.

K.Anh.22(93a), 'Memento Domine David' (Psalm 131) [now known to be the work of Karl Georg Reutter], 361

K.Anh.25(386d), Recitative, 'O Calpe!'.

K.Anh.42(375b), Sonata for two pianos in B flat, 66

K.Anh.44(426a), Allegro in C minor (unfinished), 57

K.Anh.55(387c), Concerto for piano in D (first movement, fragment), 227

K.Anh.56(315f), Concerto for piano and violin in D (fragment), 213, 214, 225, 254

K.Anh.57(537a), Sketch for piano Concerto in D, 'Coronation', 230

K.Anh.58(488a), Sketch for D major Adagio to K.488?, 230

K.Anh.59(466a), Sketch for slow movement to K.459?, 229

K.Anh.61(537b), Sketch for D minor Adagio to a piano Concerto (537??) 230

K.Anh.62(537c), Sketch for slow movement of piano Concerto in C minor K.491?, 230

K.Anh.63(488b), Rondo for a piano Concerto (488?) in A (fragment), 230

K.Anh.64(488c), Rondo for a piano Concerto (488?) in A (fragment), 230

K.Anh.65, Additional sketch to K.Ann.59 above?, 229

K.Anh.66(562e), String Trio in G (fragment).

K.Anh.80(514a), Quintet for strings (fragment).

K.Anh.97(371), Fragment of a horn Concerto, 205

K.Anh.98(371), Fragment of a horn Concerto, 205

K.Anh.98a, Fragment of a horn Concerto in E major, 206

K.Anh.98b(371), Fragment of a horn Concerto, 205

K.Anh.100a. *See* K.32

K.Anh.101, Fragment in D minor, probably of an opera (*Figaro* Overture?), 292n.

K.Anh.103(320b), Rondo in A, 'La Chasse', 214

K.Anh.104(320e), Sinfonia Concertante for violin, viola, and violoncello (fragment), 213, 214, 225

K.Anh.109^1 (formerly K.18), Symphony in E flat (by C. Fr. Abel), 157, 245

K.Anh.135, = 547a, 48

K.Anh.136(498a), Sonata movement and Minuet for piano in B flat.

K.Anh.138a, = 547a, 48

K.Anh.145a, Arrangement of K.616, 57, 61

K.Anh.171(285b), Quartet for flute, violin, viola, and violoncello, 76, 77

K.Anh.182 (arrangement of K.361), 'Pièces d'harmonie' for two oboes, two clarinets, two bassoons, and two horns, 68

K.Anh.184 (arrangement of K.373), Rondo for flute and orchestra in D, 205, 222

K.Anh.208. *See* K.24.

K.Anh.214(45b), Symphony in B flat, 159

K.Anh.216(74g), Symphony in B flat.

K.Anh.221(45a), Symphony in G, 159, 160, 161

K.Anh.226(196e), Divertimento in E flat.

K.Anh.227(196b), Divertimento in B flat, 69

K.Anh.230(196d), Concerto for bassoon in F, 201

K.Anh.230a, Concerto for bassoon in B flat (very dubious), 201

K.Anh.245(621a), Aria for bass, 'Io ti lascio', 334

K.Anh.293b. *See* K.510.

K.Anh.294a, 'Adélaïde' Concerto in D major, 220, 222

K.Anh.294d, *Musikalisches Würfelspiel*, 140

INDEX TO MUSIC EXAMPLES

387

GENERAL INDEX